The Pride of Place
* *
*

The Pride of Place

Local Memories &
Political Culture in
Nineteenth-Century
France

* * *
* *
*

STÉPHANE GERSON

CORNELL UNIVERSITY PRESS

Ithaca & London

Portions of this book have appeared in revised form in *The Journal of Modern History* 72, no. 3 (September 2000), © 2000 by The University of Chicago; *Romantisme, revue du XIXe siècle* 110 (4th quarter 2000); and *French Historical Studies* 26, no. 3 (summer 2003), © by Duke University Press. Permission to use this material is gratefully acknowledged.

First published 2003 by Cornell University Press
First printing, Cornell Paperbacks, 2003

Printed in the United States of America

Library of Congress Cataloging-in-Publication Data

Gerson, Stéphane.
   The pride of place : local memories and political culture in nineteenth-century France / Stéphane Gerson.
      p. cm.
   Includes bibliographical references and index.
   ISBN 0-8014-4134-X (cloth) — ISBN 0-8014-8873-7 (paperback)
   1. France—Cultural policy.   2. Regionalism—France—History—19th century.
3. Politics and culture—France—History—19th century.   4. Decentralization in government—France—19th century.   5. National characteristics, French.   6. Elite (Social sciences)—France.   I. Title.

DC33.7.G426 2003
306.2'0944'09034—dc21

                                                                          2003043883

"Image d'Epinal. Espace rassurant."

GEORGES PEREC,
Espèces d'espace (1985)

Contents

Acknowledgments

ALL BOOKS ARE local and this one is no exception. One cannot grow up in Brussels and remain indifferent to the question of local and national identities. French-speaking Belgians furthermore live in a culture that is saturated with artistic, journalistic, and political representations of France. Willingly or not, they become observers of France. And to observe France in the late 1970s and 1980s—on the French nightly news, if nowhere else—was to hear a great deal about decentralization. While this concept rarely captures the imagination of fifteen-year-olds, it has somehow resurfaced in my research agenda. For providing me with this distinctive outlook (and much else), my parents have my gratitude.

Financial support for this project has come from the Division of Social Sciences at the University of Chicago, the French Ministry of Foreign Affairs, the Andrew W. Mellon Foundation, and the Faculty of Arts and Sciences at New York University. I thank all of these institutions. At the University of Chicago, where this book began a decade ago, I could not have asked for a more receptive and exacting dissertation committee. Jan Goldstein and Colin Lucas took an interest in this inquiry when it was but an inchoate seminar paper. Mentors both, they have asked the necessary questions, provided a sounding board, and when necessary, offered reassurance. I am truly grateful for their wisdom and generosity. My running dialogue with Bill Hanks helped me refine my analysis and broaden my conceptual vision. Robert Morrissey proposed clarifications and developments that greatly aided the revision process.

The late François Furet offered support in Chicago and at the Centre de recherches politiques Raymond Aron, in Paris. In France, Alain Corbin welcomed me in his seminar at the Sorbonne and suggested fruitful lines of inquiry. Martine François kindly shared her knowledge of the Comité des travaux historiques et scientifiques. Anne-Marie Thiesse and Daniel Nordman cast a new light on some of my findings and pushed me to dig deeper. Numerous archivists and librarians went out of their way to assist me. I am especially thankful to Michel Vangheluwe, who patiently oriented me through the rich collections of the Archives Départementales du Nord.

At New York University, I have had the good fortune of joining an incomparable community of scholars of modern France. My French department colleagues invited a historian into their midst and made him feel at home. Ed Berenson has offered precious guidance and good cheer at the Institute of French Studies. Other colleagues have contributed to this project with valuable comments and suggestions: Charles Affron, Claudie Bernard, Herrick Chapman, Nancy Regalado, Susan Carol Rogers, Emmanuelle Saada, and Jerry Seigel. Many friends and colleagues have done the same beyond N.Y.U.: Avner Ben-Amos, the late Bill Cohen, Paul Cohen, Arnaud Coulombel, Ruth Crocker, Paul Edison, Laurence Gobin, Jean Goulemot, Kate Hamerton, Carol Harrison, Gerhard Haupt, Patrick Hutton, Jacqueline Lalouette, Gene Lebovics, Jo B. Margadant, Kent Minturn, Lara Moore, Nia Perry, Michèle Riot-Sarcey, Andy Shanken, John Shovlin, Judy Stone, and Torbjörn Wandel. Thanks to them all. I am immensely grateful to Caroline Ford, Sudhir Hazareesingh, Jennifer Milligan, and an anonymous referee for their careful readings of the entire manuscript. I alone, of course, am responsible for any remaining flaws in this book.

Neil Goldthorpe's humanity, eloquence, and passion for history continue to inspire me, as they have two generations of students. I am grateful to John G. Ackerman, director of Cornell University Press, for his interest in this project. Thanks, finally, to Dona and Stan Gerson for their welcome in Chicago, to the Gogel family for their Parisian hospitality, to Gay Block for making possible a year of writing in Santa Fe, and to Loupi for putting things in perspective. My deepest debt, however, is to Alison—we both know how deep. I could not have completed this project without her loving support and indulgence. To her and to our sons, Julian and Owen, I dedicate this book.

S.G.

Abbreviations

ACF	*Annales du Comité flamand de France* (Dunkirk)
AD	Archives Départementales
ADN	Archives Départementales du Nord (Lille)
AHN	*Archives historiques et littéraires du Nord de la France et du Midi de la Belgique* (Valenciennes)
AIP	*Annuaire de l'Institut des provinces et des congrès scientifiques*
AMD	Archives Municipales de Douai
AMDu	Archives Municipales de Dunkerque
AMM	Archives Municipales de Montargis
AMV	Archives Municipales de Valenciennes
AN	Archives Nationales (Paris)
ASD	Archives of the Société dunkerquoise pour l'encouragement des sciences, des lettres et des arts
BCF	*Bulletin du Comité flamand de France* (Dunkirk)
BCN	*Bulletin de la Commission historique du département du Nord* (Lille)
BMA	Bibliothèque Municipale d'Abbeville
BML	Bibliothèque Municipale de Lille
BNF	Bibliothèque Nationale de France (Paris)
BTH	Bureau des Travaux Historiques
BUGN	*Bulletin de l'Union géographique du Nord de la France* (Douai)
CHAM	Comité Historique des Arts et Monuments
Charmes	Xavier Charmes, *Le comité des travaux historiques et scientifiques (histoire et documents)*. 3 vols. Paris: Imprimerie nationale, 1886. Vol. 2.
CS	*Congrès scientifique de France* (proceedings of the annual congress, published in the city in which it was held)
CTH	Comité des Travaux Historiques
Delloye	Médiathèque Municipale de Cambrai, fonds E. Delloye
MAP	Médiathèque de l'Architecture et du Patrimoine (Paris)

MEC	*Mémoires de la Société d'émulation de Cambrai*
MMC	Médiathèque Municipale de Cambrai
MSD	*Mémoires de la Société d'agriculture, des sciences et des arts centrale du département du Nord séant à Douai*
MSDu	*Mémoires de la Société dunkerquoise pour l'encouragement des sciences, des lettres et des arts*
MSL	*Mémoires de la Société des sciences, de l'agriculture et des arts de Lille*
MSV	*Mémoires de la Société d'agriculture, sciences et arts de l'arrondissement de Valenciennes*
Min. Int.	Ministry of the Interior
Min. Pub. Instr.	Ministry of Public Instruction
RAN	*Revue agricole, industrielle et littéraire du Nord* (Valenciennes)
RDM	*Revue des deux mondes* (Paris)
RN	*Revue du Nord (de la France)* [Lille]
RSS	*Revue des sociétés savantes des départements* (Paris)

The Pride of Place

* *
*

Local Memories and Modernity

FRANCE MUST NOT be a collection of small nations," declared the Abbé Sieyès early in the French Revolution. "She is a unique whole." Echoed Camille Desmoulins, another revolutionary: "We are no longer from Aix or Arras. We are all French, we are all brothers."[1] Since the French Revolution at the latest, France has grappled with the local—with its numerous idioms, its entrenched popular customs, and the various political claims emanating from the provinces. The country's deep-seated fixation with the state and national unity has long devalued the local as particularistic and retrograde. The nation-state alone ostensibly innovated and it alone therefore carried historical significance. In France as elsewhere, sociological theories of modernization have furthermore dismissed the local as an obstacle to bureaucratic integration or expanding markets. Twentieth-century historians have thus undertaken massive regional theses, but typically to apprehend broad phenomena—social change, for instance—rather than discrete locales of innovation.[2] A shift, if any, occurred in the 1960s and 1970s, when anticapitalist and antistatist currents converged on the local as antidote to an all-controlling, uniform, technocratic society. To distant national institutions, these primarily leftist currents opposed local initiative and responsibility over singular, resourceful territories. The local became the physical location of a "new life" and civic action.[3] It also embodied a flexible "place of residence and activity," whose modes of association and social

1. Abbé Sieyès, quoted in Jean-Denis Bredin, *Sieyès: la clé de la révolution française* (Paris, 1988), 542; and Camille Desmoulins, quoted in Pierre Birnbaum, *La France imaginée: déclin des rêves unitaires?* (Paris, 1998), 64.

2. Albert Mabileau, "Variations sur le local," in idem, ed., *A la recherche du 'local'* (Paris, 1993), 22–23; and Pierre Bidart, "Présentation," in idem, ed., *Régions, nations, états: composition et recomposition de l'espace national* (Paris, 1991), 7. See also Paul Leuilliot, "Défense et illustration de l'histoire locale," preface to Guy Thuillier, *Aspects de l'économie nivernaise au XIXe siècle* (Paris, 1966), vii–xix.

3. By 1982, laws on decentralization created new administrative "regions" and delegated authority to local elected councils. See Lucien Sfez, ed., *L'objet local* (Paris, 1977), 10–12; Pierre Grémion, "Crispation et déclin du jacobinisme," in Henri Mendras, ed., *La sagesse et le désordre: France 1980* (Paris, 1980), 350; and Robert Lafont, *Autonomie: de la région à l'autogestion* (Paris, 1976), 18 and 187. On this rural turn and Third-Worldism, see Claude Karnoouh, "The Lost Paradise of Regionalism: The Crisis of Post-Modernity in France," *Telos* 67 (spring 1986): 13–16.

action grew appealing in a period of recession and limited geographic mobility.[4] Some scholars likewise turned to the local as an analytical category, capable of illuminating modern France's diverse social and political configurations.[5]

Yet many in France still dismissed the local as folklore or militant delusion.[6] Only in the past twenty years has the local become widely seen as the embodiment of civil society—an ideal, democratic space of social mediation, "experimentation," solidarity, and cultural affirmation in a changing world. Commentators speak of a vast "return to the local," rooted in new multicultural aspirations, fears of global uniformity, anxieties about immigration, the inroads of neoliberalism, and mounting discontent with centralization and traditional forms of politics.[7] Fueled in part by a growing curiosity for the fragmentary and the particular, scholarly studies of the local likewise abound.[8] Their subjects range from France's enduring diversity to its dynamic associations, from the construction of territorial organization and identities to the enthusiasm for the local past.[9] The local has clearly emerged as a key reference in discussions of citizenship and identity in modern France.

Or should we say *re*emerged? This book argues that, beginning in the early nineteenth century, the local and modernity were interlaced rather than inimical in France. I make this claim by analyzing, between the 1820s and 1880s, what contemporaries called the cult of local memories (*le culte*

For British parallels, see Raphael Samuel, *Theatres of Memory*, 2 vols. (London, 1994–98), 1:145–51.

4. Michel de Certeau (with Luce Giard), "L'ordinaire de la communication," in his *La prise de parole et autres écrits politiques* (Paris, 1994), 184–89.

5. Christian Bromberger, "Ethnologie, patrimoine, identités: y a-t-il une spécificité française?" in Daniel Fabre, ed., *L'Europe entre cultures et nations* (Paris, 1996), 15–16; and Jean-Paul Billaud, "Le grand angle et la loupe," *Autrement* 47, 'Le local dans tous ses états' (February 1983): 16–22.

6. Martin de la Soudière, "De l'esprit de clocher à l'esprit de terroir," *Ruralia* 8 (2001): 159–68.

7. Alain Duhamel, "La peur des régions," *Libération*, 27 January 2002; and Mabileau, "Variations," 21. On local political participation, see Loïc Blondiaux, "Démocratie locale et participation citoyenne: la promesse et le piège," *Mouvements* 18 (November–December 2001): 44–51; and Catherine Neveu, ed., *Espace public et engagement politique: enjeux et logiques de la citoyenneté locale* (Paris, 1999).

8. Sarah Blowen, Marion Demossier, and Jeanine Picard, Introduction to idem, eds., *Recollections of France: Memories, Identities, and Heritage in Contemporary France* (New York, 2000), 3.

9. Among other recent works: Louis Fougère, Jean-Pierre Machelon, and François Monnier, eds., *Les communes et le pouvoir de 1789 à nos jours* (Paris, 2002); Annie Bleton-Ruget, Pierre Bodineau, and Jean-Pierre Sylvestre, eds., *"Pays" et territoires. De Vidal de la Blache aux lois d'aménagement et de développement du territoire* (Dijon, 2002); Alban Bensa and Fabre, eds., *Une histoire à soi: figurations du passé et localités* (Paris, 2001); Richard Balme, Alain Faure, and Mabileau, eds., *Les nouvelles politiques locales: dynamiques de l'action publique* (Paris, 1999); and Vincent Dubois and Philippe Poirrier, eds., *Politiques locales et enjeux culturels: les clochers d'une querelle, XIXe-XXe siècles* (Paris, 1998).

des souvenirs locaux). This was a public effort of unprecedented magnitude to resuscitate the local past, instill affection for one's *pays* (or locality), and hence produce a sense of place, a deep emotional and intellectual attachment combining territorial identification with membership in a social or political community. "Much has been written in the provinces these past years," noted one commentator in 1838, and most of it was about "the history of localities." Liberal philosopher Théodore Jouffroy likewise noted that same year that France had finally outgrown an era "in which the lowliest writer conversed about China and knew nothing of Picardy."[10] Seeking to recover the historical spirit of "local places," thousands of French citizens joined learned societies, penned vignettes and monographs, created pantheons of celebrities, and staged the local past through elaborate pageants. More individuals—most of them middling bourgeois men—cultivated such local memories than at any other time in French history. In doing so, they granted the local a tangibility and visibility that pamphlets and treatises, for instance, did not.

Many observers derided these provincials, however, as petty antiquarians or reactionaries who cultivated the local past to flee a chaotic society they could neither grasp nor dominate. All were "foreign to the contemporary world, . . . living only through memories." For radical François Génin, the *pays* was a "barbarous locution" whose popularity signaled a deeper "shrink[ing]" of the minds. The modest *pays* of landed, franchise-paying bourgeois was supplanting the bold *patrie*. "It is by narrowing language," he wrote, "that one progressively narrows ideas."[11] Indeed, the cult of local memories displayed unmistakable ambivalence toward the century's new forms of political expression, its patterns of social movement and urban life, its modes of economic production and consumption, and its relationships to space and time. The sheer quantity of local material that elites collected, their repeated surveys of the *pays* and inventories of its past, their bottomless output of self-reflexive discourse reveal their anxieties before the postrevolutionary landscape. As an effort to preserve artifacts and usages, revive ancient solidarities, and delineate an orderly landscape, this phenomenon signaled, at best, misgivings toward modernity and what Baudelaire called the "thrill [*frisson*]" of the new city.[12] It thus comes as no surprise that, decades later, the New Right of

10. *Musée des familles* 6 (1838): 255; and *Mémoires et documents inédits pour servir à l'histoire de la Franche-Comté publiés par l'Académie de Besançon*, 4 vols. (Besançon, 1838–69), 1:vii.

11. *Extrait du procès-verbal de la séance publique de la Société des Antiquaires de Picardie, dans la grande salle de la mairie d'Amiens, le dimanche 24 juillet 1842* (Amiens, 1842), 4; and Francois Génin, *Des variations du langage français depuis le XIIe siècle, ou recherche des principes qui devraient régler l'orthographe et la prononciation* (Paris, 1845), 417–18.

12. Walter Benjamin, "Sur Baudelaire," in his *Ecrits français*, ed. Jean-Maurice Monnoyer (Paris, 1991), 243–44. The radical theorist Félicité de Lamennais likewise divorced *patrie* and *pays*: see his *Le pays et le gouvernement* (Paris, 1840).

Maurice Barrès and adepts of Vichy's "National Revolution" embraced the local and regional past as a gateway toward immemorial traditions, hierarchy, and homogeneous community.[13]

But the cult of local memories transcended reaction or nostalgia. It also contributed to processes we associate with Western modernity, from the rise of science and state building to civic participation and the formation of new modes of territorial identity. At once autonomous and subordinated to the nation, at once "a whole and . . . part of a whole" (as one *littérateur* put it in 1838), the local was inherently ambiguous and open to multiple uses. For many, "local history" referred interchangeably to the province, city, or *pays*. The local's "very slipperiness," argues anthropologist Deborah Poole, accounts for "its power, its hold on the social and political imagination."[14] In France, local memories captured and promised to allay the indeterminacy of a postrevolutionary era. Without fully espousing the free market, French elites of diverse political leanings commodified local heritage and displayed a grasp of—and a willingness to enter—a modern nexus of tourism and marketing. They self-consciously outlined cultural identities that were local and national—but neither exclusively one nor the other. While steering clear of democracy, they devised civic practices that rested on voluntary and collective action. They also formulated a new pedagogical design that was at once political and apolitical: surreptitious edification through local historical milieus. Born at the confluence of official action and civil society, local memories promised to depoliticize French society—an enticing prospect in this tumultuous era—while, ironically enough, providing new opportunities for political expression. On this plane, the local was not only rural and traditionalist, but also urban and left-wing (predominantly liberal).

The cult of local memories was sufficiently malleable to assuage many of the anxieties and meet pressing needs of this postrevolutionary era. However threatened during this period of political and economic unification, the *pays* and its memories offered contemporaries a promising language and set of practices to imagine and mold a society that many of them both embraced and feared. The cult of local memories would heal wounded psyches, bolster private and public identities, and sustain claims to authority and citizenship. It accordingly belongs to a modernity in

13. Christian Faure, *Le projet culturel de Vichy: folklore et révolution nationale, 1940–1944* (Lyons, 1989); and Jean-Michel Barreau, *Vichy, contre l'école de la République: théoriciens et théories scolaires de la 'Révolution nationale'* (Paris, 2000), 239–47.

14. Alexandre-Armand Bost, *Traité de l'organisation et des attributions des corps municipaux d'après la législation et la jurisprudence actuelles*, 2d ed., 2 vols. (Paris, 1840 [1838]), 1:13; Félix Bourquelot, *Histoire de Provins* (Provins, 1839), 6 and 14; Deborah Poole, *Vision, Race, and Modernity: A Visual Economy of the Andean Image World* (Princeton, N.J., 1997), 216; and Raymond Williams, "Regional," in his *Keywords* (New York, 1976), 264.

which, per Walter Benjamin, the old and new intermingle, "everything is pregnant with its contrary," and individuals at once apprehend and embrace the modern world.[15] Diverse as it was, this turn to the local betrayed a recurring conviction: that local memories would foster a renewed sense of place in provincial France. Early-nineteenth-century publicists began linking territorial contiguity with common interests and sentiments (a shared local spirit, or sense of place) that, in turn, could yield solidarity and civic consciousness. This conceptual marriage soon encompassed the local past, persisted throughout the century, and heralded a true recomposition (as some called it) of France.[16] Rather than the ex nihilo creation of a new society, this was an inherently local effort to renew the existing one. By yielding self-understanding, moral teachings, civic participation, social cohesion, and true national unity, this local sense of place would recompose *pays* and nation alike.

This book thus tells a story of rupture and achievement, in which new aspirations converged around "love of the *pays*" and transformed the French cultural and political landscape. It offers a synthetic tableau of this field—let us call it the field of local memories—and situates it at the confluence of multiple investments: territorial identity, civic assertion, surreptitious pedagogy and politics, new forms of governmental action, and what I will call an imaginary of place and past. Yet the local's indeterminacy makes it unstable and uncontrollable.[17] Little wonder, then, that this phenomenon lends itself to another story—one of hesitancy and unmet expectations. Despite this field's prospects, provincial and Parisian actors were uneasy partners in a joint yet conflicted venture, unable to set the parameters of their relationships. To cultivate local memories furthermore required that one define them on cultural and civic planes. This meant resolving fundamental questions about the modern nation-state: the reach of politics, local difference (internal diversity and cultural identification with a specific place), and local initiative (the respective attributes of civil society and the state).[18] These questions stymied official and nonofficial actors and explain why many ventures were contemplated, de-

15. Benjamin, "Paris, Capital of the Nineteenth Century," in his *Reflections*, ed. Peter Demetz, trans. Edmund Jephcott (New York, 1978), 148; and Marshall Berman, *All That Is Solid Melts into Air: The Experience of Modernity* (New York, 1988), 14 and 23.

16. Marie-Vic Ozouf-Marignier, "Centralisation et lien social: le débat de la première moitié du XIXe siècle en France," in Enrico Iachello and Biagio Salvemini, eds., *Per un Atlante storico del Mezzogiorno e della Sicilia in età moderna* (Naples, 1998), 77–78. On the persistence of such convictions under the Second Empire, see Sudhir Hazareesingh and Vincent Wright, "Le Second Empire," in Fougère et al., *Communes et le pouvoir*, 319–20.

17. Vicente L. Rafael, "Regionalism, Area Studies, and the Accidents of Agency," *American Historical Review* 104, no. 4 (October 1999): 1208.

18. On these implications, see Yvon Lamy, "Le patrimoine culturel public. Réception, désignation, mobilisation," in idem, ed., *Le pouvoir de protéger: approches, acteurs, enjeux du patrimoine en Aquitaine* ([Bordeaux], 1992), 13.

bated, but abandoned or never undertaken. They also preclude facile distinctions between, say, provincial advocates and governmental opponents of local diversity.[19]

Some contemporaries nonetheless grappled self-consciously with these eminently modern questions. Whether they did so explicitly or through hesitations and reversals, they turned this field into a grass-roots arena of experimentation and reflection. It is here—within these tensions and efforts to resolve them—that we uncover this field's fundamental contribution to the era's political culture. If the French Restoration (1815–1830) constituted, per historian Pierre Rosanvallon, a "laboratory of contemporary political thought," the field of local memories that flourished during the following decades may thus be seen as a laboratory of cultural and political practices. The central question remained that of "postrevolutionary politics": the organization of the body politic, the infiltration of politics in everyday life, the reach of official action.[20] But this field's modernity did not reside in doctrine, for its key formative currents—from sensationalism to Doctrinaire liberalism—had indeed taken shape earlier in the century. It was, rather, a modernity of questions and applications, a transplantation into local historical practices of tensions born in the French Revolution (unity and particularism, centralization and citizenship, politics and unanimity). Incipient in the 1820s, this process came into its own after 1830. Innovation, as historian Philippe Minard suggests, often originates in the encounter between conceptual schemes and practical questions that demand resolution.[21] (What memories deserve attention? Who should cultivate them? How should one do so?) Others had cultivated local memories in the past, but these actors were the first to, intentionally or not, turn this field into a space of reflection on territorial identity, citizenship, and governmental authority in a modern nation-state. In this fashion, the local underlay efforts to reimagine a society in flux and delineate the contours of postrevolutionary France.

Recent studies of nineteenth-century France have taught us about history's contribution to nation building, the birth of a historical discipline and profession, and to a lesser degree, the achievements of unsung *littérateurs*.[22]

19. Cf. Jean-Michel Leniaud, "L'Etat, les sociétés savantes et les associations de défense du patrimoine: l'exception française," in Jacques Le Goff, ed., *Patrimoine et passions identitaires* (Paris, 1998), 138–39.

20. Rosanvallon does not suggest, of course, that the Restoration limited itself to theory. See his *Le moment Guizot* (Paris, 1985), 28 and 75–76.

21. Philippe Minard, *La fortune du colbertisme: état et industrie dans la France des Lumières* (Paris, 1998), 12.

22. Within a large historiography, see Robert Gildea, *The Past in French History* (New Haven, 1994); Pim den Boer, *History as a Profession: The Study of History in France, 1818–1914,* trans. Arnold J. Pomerans (Princeton, N.J., 1998); Christian Amalvi, *De l'art et la manière d'acco-*

Literary scholars have illuminated the era's troubled fascination with the past: the efforts to breach the revolutionary divide through history; the new conviction that, given its intrinsic value, time generated progress; but also the anxieties before the evanescence of the past—now seen as a distant and transitional stage.[23] Historians have begun amending the long-accepted portrait of a backward-looking provincial field, dominated by anachronistic clerics, legitimists in "internal exile," or aristocrats pining for the restoration of provincial estates.[24] We are learning about the formation of regional images and the Third Republic's unexpected interest in the local.[25]

We still know little, however, about the cultural and political uses of local memories in modern France: their theatricality, urban visibility, pedagogical uses, and applications as commerce and "philosophical idea."[26] We know little, furthermore, about the creation of a local sense of place—about its inherent promises, its conceptual strains, or the uneasy status of local memories as point of convergence and stake of multiple conflicts. We know little, finally, about the cult of local memories as arena of political and cultural reflection, involving the central state, local officials, and civil society—from profit-driven Parisian editors to modest provincial professors, from landowners to middling professionals (the latter far more numerous). Their cult of local memories—even in middling towns—nuances depictions of languid provinces and a timorous civil society, deadened by an all-controlling state. It fleshes out Jean-Yves Guiomar's claim that the failed emancipation of civil society from the state provoked a renewed politicization of the cultural realm—and, more specifically, the territory and region—after 1789.[27] And it unveils a new dimension of modern French political culture: the discursive and symbolic representations and the social practices (from sociability to topography) through which

---

moder les héros de l'histoire de France (Paris, 1988); and Jo Tollebeek, "L'historiographie en tant qu'élément culturel dans la France du dix-neuvième siècle. Une étude historiographique exploratoire," *Storia della Storiografica* 26 (1994): 59–81.

23. Richard Terdiman, *Present Past: Modernity and the Memory Crisis* (Ithaca, 1993); Claudie Bernard, *Le passé recomposé: le roman historique français du dix-neuvième siècle* (Paris, 1996), 19–20; and Peter Fritzsche, "The Case of Modern Memory," *The Journal of Modern History* 73, no. 1 (March 2001): 87–117.

24. Odile Parsis-Barubé, *Les représentations du Moyen âge au XIXe siècle dans les anciens Pays-Bas français et leurs confins picards. Essai d'historiographie comparée* (Villeneuve d'Ascq, 1999); and Pierre-Yves Saunier, *L'esprit lyonnais, XIXe–XXe siècle: genèse d'une représentation sociale* (Paris, 1995).

25. François Guillet, *Naissance de la Normandie: genèse et épanouissement d'une image régionale en France, 1750–1850* (Caen, 2000); Catherine Bertho, "L'invention de la Bretagne: genèse sociale d'un stéréotype," *Actes de la recherche en sciences sociales* 35 (1980): 45–62; Anne-Marie Thiesse, *Ils apprenaient la France: l'exaltation des régions dans le discours patriotique* (Paris, 1997); and Jean-François Chanet, *L'école républicaine et les petites patries* (Paris, 1996).

26. *Fête du Moyen Age sous Philippe-le-Bon, représentée pour la première fois à Douai, le 14 juillet 1839, par les soins de la Société de bienfaisance* (Douai, n.d. [1839]), 4.

27. Jean-Yves Guiomar, *La nation entre l'histoire et la raison* (Paris, 1990).

actors delineated the body politic, laid claim to power, and gave meaning to their world.[28] The cult of local memories thus constitutes a promising avenue toward broader questions about modern France. Three of them surface repeatedly in this book.

The first relates to the path of modernization in nineteenth-century France. While they differ on its causes, classic accounts describe an inexorable and rather quick unification of the nation, under a centralized government, as market and cultural entity. Affection for the nation progressively but irrevocably superseded local loyalties.[29] Critics of this argument have called attention to the syncretic character of national identity. The latter, they claim, acquired different forms in distinct locales, within an open negotiation that involved the country's multiple memories. Introducing a recent collection on *National and Regional Identities in Europe*, Gerhard Haupt and his coeditors reject the claim that modernity entails the disappearance of local loyalties. Instead, they emphasize the "interpenetration" between national and local sentiments.[30] I confirm their insights by demonstrating that, in this arena, provincials sought by and large to integrate national and local loyalties. Here, French identity was articulated neither in the center nor the provinces, but at the juncture of Paris and the localities. I further argue, however, that, while local memories indeed became "subordinate to the national historical project,"[31] they also acquired a new scope during the nineteenth century. The local thus constituted a central element, or by-product, of modernization. But it was an unwieldy one: at once espoused for its numerous promises and denigrated for its intimations of particularism, fragmentation, or mediocrity. In addition, another philosophical commitment—the universalism of human nature—complicated the binary relationship between the local and the national. From this vantage point, the path of modernization was anything but straightforward in nineteenth-century France.

28. I thus expand on Keith Baker's influential, but overly linguistic, definition. Like him, however, I uncover a single political culture, shaped by opposing claims, rather than concurrent political cultures, originating within political schools or parties. See Keith Michael Baker, *Inventing the French Revolution* (Cambridge, 1990), 4–5; and Ronald P. Formisano, "The Concept of Political Culture," *Journal of Interdisciplinary History* 31, no. 3 (2001): 393–426. Cf. Serge Berstein, ed., *Les cultures politiques en France* (Paris, 1999).

29. See Eugen Weber, *Peasants into Frenchmen: The Modernization of Rural France, 1870–1914* (Stanford, 1976); and Charles Tilly, *Coercion, Capital, and European States, A.D. 990–1990* (Cambridge, Mass., 1990), 107.

30. Heinz-Gerhard Haupt, Michael G. Müller, and Stuart Woolf, Introduction to idem, eds., *Regional and National Identities in Europe in the XIXth and XXth Centuries* (The Hague, 1998), 5–6. Such revisions can be found in Peter Sahlins, *Boundaries: The Making of France and Spain in the Pyrénées* (Berkeley, 1989); Caroline Ford, *Creating the Nation in Provincial France: Religion and Political Identity in Brittany* (Princeton, N.J., 1993); and, from a different vantage point, Susan Carol Rogers, *Shaping Modern Times in Rural France: The Transformation and Reproduction of an Aveyronnais Community* (Princeton, N.J., 1991).

31. Celia Applegate, "A Europe of Regions: Reflections on the Historiography of Sub-National Places in Modern Times," *American Historical Review* 104, no. 4 (October 1999): 1160.

The second question revolves around the contours of the nineteenth-century state and its relationship with provincial elites. By state, I mean a succession of regimes or ministries—with their respective agendas—as well as a set of governmental institutions, agencies, and procedures that acquired semipermanence in the nineteenth century. I use the term broadly to include all designs and initiatives endowed with an official status as well as those local officials—prefects, subprefects, rectors—who represented *le pouvoir* (governmental authority), relayed ministerial directives, and looked to Paris for promotions.[32] The cult of local memories amplifies and nuances recent portrayals of a state that, after 1789, deepened its presence in civil society in order to educate and unify the national citizenry.[33] It uncovers modes of operation and evaluation that typically sought to make governmental presence felt rather than seen in this intellectual realm. Far from castigating local memories, the Ministry of Public Instruction and provincial officials spurred intellectual elites to investigate the local past and deepen what Désiré Nisard called "*l'orgueil du lieu*" (the pride of place).[34] Yet they also struggled to embrace symbols of local individuality and failed to persuade all provincial elites to relinquish authority over their local past. Indeterminate on this plane as well, the cult of local memories was both a new instrument of governmental action and a platform from which to redirect or even subvert this very action.

The third and final question turns around the changing valence of local specificity and diversity in nineteenth-century France. It is best grasped by first considering the French Revolution and First Empire. The revolutionaries struggled to define the place of local difference within the newly emancipated, united, and "indivisible" nation. While Sieyès, Desmoulins, and others castigated particularism in its cultural and corporate forms, the country's diversity of customs and idioms, its affection for the *pays* hampered prevalent dreams of internal homogeneity. The Empire's efforts to produce departmental *statistiques*—these exhaustive surveys of a given territory and its population—likewise failed because they could not subsume local specificity within a homogeneous national tableau. Internal diversity emerged as an incontrovertible, and problematic, reality. Contrast this with the early Third Republic, when politicians, educators, and others celebrated affection for the local as the foundation of a renewed France. How, then, did local diversity—erstwhile obstacle to national unity—become one of its underpinnings? Historians typically

32. As representatives of both the commune and the central authorities, mayors had multiple allegiances. While it is easier to situate them within this state under the Second Empire (which appointed them) than the July Monarchy or Second Republic (which selected them from elected municipal councils), they remained an ambiguous entity.

33. Rosanvallon, *L'Etat en France de 1789 à nos jours* (Paris, 1990).

34. Désiré Nisard, "Les classes moyennes en Angleterre et la bourgeoisie en France" (1849), in his *Etudes de critique littéraire* (Paris, 1858), 225.

emphasize France's desire for renewal and self-understanding in the wake of defeat and civil war in 1870–71. A broader perspective reveals the field of local memories' key role in this story. It was there, inter alia, that contemporaries progressively and sometimes unwittingly elaborated diverse articulations of the local and the national, of diversity and unity. None resonated louder in ensuing decades than the *petite patrie*, gateway to the *grande patrie*.

In apprehending the cult of local memories, I have made decisions about conception and method that require a rapid justification. This book rests on four intertwined propositions. The first holds that representations—be they textual or figurative—are fashioned within multifaceted political and linguistic formations, yet given life in contingent historical situations. Discourse and the social world mutually shape one another. Each one is determined from "without" and from "within" (M. Bakhtin)— and the relationship between them requires close attention.[35] Consideration of a text's intellectual pedigrees—from political theory to, say, the language of decentralization—is thus essential, but insufficient in itself. One must consider at once what is imagined, said, and done. This includes the social and political relations that surround texts as well as their supporting institutions and procedures: in this case, learned and charitable associations, questionnaires, topographies, festivals, and the like. This also includes the discreet actions and public displays through which individuals manipulate and reroute texts toward their own ends.[36] This initial proposition furthermore implies that texts both reflect and transcend human intention. I thus analyze discourse closely to recover the multiple meanings that contemporaries granted to their actions and environment. In this respect, I am drawing on a recognized understanding of discourse and narrative as blueprints for navigating and reordering the social world. That, or whether, an event took place is less important on this level than its meaning for, and depiction by, historical actors.[37] At the same time, the cult of local memories begs analysis as a set of conceptual categories and tensions that escaped contemporaries, be it fully or partially.

35. William H. Sewell, Jr., *A Rhetoric of Bourgeois Revolution: The Abbé Sieyès and "What Is the Third Estate?"* (Durham, N.C., 1994); and Mikhail Bakhtin [P. M. Medvedev], *The Formal Method in Literary Scholarship: A Critical Introduction to Sociological Poetics,* trans. Albert J. Wehrle (Baltimore, 1978 [1928]), 29.

36. This is one of the lessons of speech-act theory. See J. L. Austin, *How to Do Things with Words,* ed. J. O. Urmson and Marinq Sbisà, 2d ed. (Cambridge, Mass., 1962).

37. Hayden White makes this point in "Historical Pluralism," *Critical Inquiry* 12 (spring 1986): 486–87. On actors' representations and narrative, see, respectively, Max Weber, *The Theory of Social and Economic Organization,* ed. Talcott Parsons (New York, 1947), 95–96; and Margaret D. Somers and Gloria D. Gibson, "Reclaiming the Epistemological 'Other': Narrative and the Social Constitution of Identity," in Craig Calhoun, ed., *Social Theory and the Politics of Identity* (Oxford, 1994), 38–39.

The second, and consequent, proposition holds that the field of local memories took shape in constant dialogue with other fields. A vast literature on intertextuality has alerted us to these exchanges between texts and authors, across the physical boundaries of books and other artifacts and the looser boundaries of genres and disciplines.[38] To evoke the *pays* within this field, for instance, was to converse with journalistic or political fields. The term was, from the start, loaded with meanings and political charge. The same is true of genres—literary or, say, festive. Genres evoke not only shared norms and structural traits, but also political and ideological horizons, sedimented visions of social relations that transcend thematic content. They entail set conventions and awaken certain expectations.[39] It thus matters whether one's vocabulary also held a valence in, for instance, religious discourse; whether one articulated it in a periodical or a topography, a historical pageant or a carnival. The cult of local memories accordingly took form within a broad intertextual context, ranging from philanthropy to philology. While some individuals will appear with particular frequency, I have a cast a wide net in order to showcase these intertextual and interpersonal relationships—what, borrowing from Quentin Skinner, one could call "the more general social and intellectual matrix."[40]

Third proposition: the field of local memories was both fragmented and unified. It was fragmented in space according to the geographical location, profession, class, and political leanings of participants. These participants entertained distinct ambitions and often drew from distinct wells of local memories. This field was fragmented in time, moreover, by diverse factors, from the policies of successive regimes to the fortunes of political and philosophical schools, the progress of industrialization, and the advent of new leisure activities. The July Monarchy nonetheless emerges as the most vibrant period in this story.[41] Many of the individuals who shaped the field of local memories belonged to the first postrevolutionary generation. Born between 1785 and 1805, they reached their prime under the late Restoration and early July Monarchy and, with few

38. Bakhtin, "Du discours romanesque," in his *Esthétique et théorie du roman*, trans. Daria Olivier (Paris, 1978), 83–182; and Julia Kristeva, "The Bounded Text," in her *Desire in Language: A Semiotic Approach to Literature and Art*, ed. Leon S. Roudiez, trans. Thomas Gora et al. (New York, 1980), 36–63.

39. I am borrowing elements from William Hanks's work on discursive genres, esp. "Discourse Genres in a Theory of Practice," *American Ethnologist* 14, no. 4 (1987): 670; and Bakhtin, *Formal Method*, 16–17.

40. Quentin Skinner, *The Foundations of Modern Political Thought*, 2 vols. (Cambridge, 1978), 1:x.

41. On the July Monarchy as cultural and political rupture, see, among others, Dominique Kalifa, "L'ère de la culture-marchandise," *Revue d'histoire du dix-neuvième siècle* 19 (1999): 7–14; and Christopher M. Greene, "Romanticism, Cultural Nationalism and Politics in the July Monarchy: The Contribution of Ludovic Vitet," *French History* 4, no. 4 (December 1990): 487–509.

exceptions, commanded this field until the mid-1860s. If this book begins in the 1820s—and pays such attention to the rupture of 1830—it is also because this generation, more than any other in the nineteenth century, espoused local memories as a new means of cultural, political, civic, and pedagogical action. "Generation," as I use the term here, refers to a cohort sharing not a selfsame political engagement, but a common horizon (the French Revolution and political instability). The Revolution of 1830 reactivated the French Revolution's promises, pedagogical ambitions, and civic designs—as well as its memories, both glorious and traumatic. For this generation more than any other, local memories promised to recompose France either through this revolutionary tradition (every French locality has a history and the right to write it) or against it.

Some older individuals, such as Benjamin Constant, had of course glorified the local before 1830. Others, building on ancient historical traditions, had begun investigating the local past under the Empire or the Restoration, with its growing historical curiosity and vibrant debate on decentralization.[42] Yet, 1830—with its looser political constraints, its return to national origins, its yearning for a revolution of the minds, its growing alarm before the social question, its rapid disillusions—marked a rupture in kind and number. Contemporaries coined such neologisms as *localisme* and *localisable*. They commented on the unprecedented visibility of local memories, praising their era for at last investigating the "particular histories" of French towns and villages. They also devised new patrimonial venues while granting others a broader dimension. In 1847, the new Société des sciences historiques et naturelles de l'Yonne thus embraced a "taste" for local history and archaeology that had "spread in France since 1830."[43] It was in the early 1830s, likewise, that French officials first encouraged provincial elites to cultivate local memories.

Distinctive as they were, the late Restoration and July Monarchy yielded a set of institutions, practices, aspirations, anxieties, and tensions that persisted until the early Third Republic. Without neglecting this field's politi-

---

42. See, for instance, Lara Jennifer Moore, "Restoring Order: The Ecole des Chartes and the Organization of Archives and Libraries in France, 1820–1870," Ph.D. diss., Stanford University, 2001; and Rudolph von Thadden, *La centralisation contestée: l'administration napoléonienne, enjeu politique de la Restauration (1814–1830)* (Arles, 1989). For a recent reassessment of the Restoration's political culture, see Sheryl Kroen, *Politics and Theater: The Crisis of Legitimacy in Restoration France, 1815–1830* (Berkeley, 2000).

43. Jean-Baptiste Richard de Radonvilliers, *Enrichissement de la langue française: dictionnaire de mots nouveaux*, 2d ed. (Paris, 1845), 413; Victor Fouque, *Histoire de Chalon-sur-Saône, depuis les temps les plus reculés jusqu'à nos jours* (Chalon-sur-Saône, 1844), 7–8; and *Bulletin de la Société des sciences historiques et naturelles de l'Yonne* 1 (1847): 16 and iii. On the "rise of local history" during these years, see also Guy Thuillier and Jean Tulard, *Histoire locale et régionale* (Paris, 1992), 16–17.

cal and cultural evolution, we should not overlook its continuities during this half-century. The changes that occurred under the early Third Republic proved more significant, in my view, than earlier variations. In sociological terms, this half-century witnessed what Edmond Goblot long ago called the "golden age" of the bourgeoisie. Supplanting a nobility of persisting influence, the bourgeoisie dominated France until the century's closing decades, when it had to share power with a *petite bourgeoisie* of employees, shop owners, petty officials, and the like. In the field of local memories, this social transformation often coincided with (or closely followed) the demise of the earlier generation. The concurrent rise of national institutions—from professional associations to political parties— further weakened the intrinsically local authority and influence of provincial elites. "The local sphere now mattered far less," conclude two historians about the late nineteenth century.[44] In cultural terms, this half-century was one of persisting amateurism, ill-defined disciplines (including history), mediocre universities, and relatively small-scale newspapers. The professionalization of French society, the consolidation of its universities, the development of positivistic science, and the emergence of the mass press altered all of this in the last third of the century.[45]

So did, on the political plane, the durable institution of a republic and the emergence of an exclusionary, nationalist right—both of which, as we will see, directed local memories toward new and distinct ends. The preceding decades had seen liberalism establish itself as the country's leading doctrine, supplying widely held convictions and permeating governmental circles.[46] Liberalism did not, of course, silence other political voices. The nineteenth century was a rich period for political theory. Neither did liberalism represent the same thing to all people. Lucien Jaume, for one, has distinguished between three leading strands: a dominant "liberalism of the notables" that sought to liberalize the Napoleonic system, linking social organization with enlightened political administration; individualistic liberalism, concerned above all with the citizen-subject, political freedom, and constitutional balance; and Catholic liberalism, bent on reconciling Catholic doctrine with modern liberties (press, association, and the like).[47] Several convictions and concerns nonetheless recurred: personal

44. Edmond Goblot, *La barrière et le niveau: étude sociologique sur la bourgeoisie française moderne*, new ed. (Paris, 1967 [1925]), v; and Geoffrey Crossick and Haupt, *The Petite Bourgeoisie in Europe, 1780–1914: Enterprise, Family, and Independence* (London, 1995), 200.

45. Robert Fox, "Learning, Politics and Polite Culture in Provincial France: The Sociétés Savantes in the Nineteenth Century," *Historical Reflections/Réflexions Historiques* 7 (summer–fall 1980): 556–57; and Martyn Lyons, "The Audience for Romanticism: Walter Scott in France, 1815–1851," *European History Quarterly* 14 (1984): 29–30.

46. Alan S. Kahan, *Aristocratic Liberalism: The Social and Political Thought of Jacob Burckhardt, John Stuart Mill, and Alexis de Tocqueville* (New York, 1992), 153–54.

47. Lucien Jaume, *L'individu effacé, ou le paradoxe du libéralisme français* (Paris, 1997).

liberties, the superiority of elites of talent, opinion and influence as privileged means of political action, and a desire to reconcile a doctrine of limited government with the imperatives of governance.

These convictions and concerns attached themselves to political groups as well as regimes (notably the Doctrinaires and July Monarchy). At the same time, they suffused this field throughout these decades. To view the entire Second Empire as liberal, however one defines the term, is a stretch, but some historians have convincingly outlined an "Orleano-Bonapartist" continuum that encompassed July Monarchy and Second Empire.[48] The Empire kept many officials in place, regardless of their earlier political convictions. Jacques Servaux and François-Louis Bellaguet (tutor to the children of liberal historian Barante) thus joined the Ministry of Public Instruction between 1834 and 1840 and retired decades later as high-level functionaries. "Reliable . . . servant[s] of the state" for their superiors, "awful [because dutiful] bureaucrats" according to some provincial elites, these men made a pivotal contribution to the cult of local memories.[49] Alongside them, we find intellectuals such as Jules Desnoyers, who counseled François Guizot on patrimonial issues in the 1830s and pledged his successors the same "dedication" in 1858.[50] Such permanence does not imply absolute doctrinal or political continuity. People change views, after all. Similar pronouncements or initiatives may thus mean different things in different epochs. It does indicate, however, that changes in regime or minister affected but did not utterly reconfigure this landscape. No political school did more to shape the field of local memories than liberalism and none, by the same token, found it more problematic.

My fourth and final proposition holds that a set of perpetually reconfigured relationships underlay the field of local memories. To grasp this field in its complexity thus requires that one integrate local and national analytical scales. Provincial elites read with attention the works of Marchangy or Augustin Thierry. But they also cultivated local memories according to their own ends and needs, fashioning a body of knowledge that maintained an irreducible specificity while responding to national, or

48. Alain Plessis, "Pouvait-on penser librement sous le Second Empire?" and Bernard Ménager, "Le bonapartisme pouvait-il être parlementaire?", in Tulard, ed., *Pourquoi réhabiliter le Second Empire?* (Paris, 1997), 102–3 and 128; and Louis Girard, *Problèmes politiques et constitutionnels du Second Empire* (Paris, 1964).

49. Désiré Nisard, *Souvenirs et notes biographiques*, 2 vols. (Paris, 1888), 1:284; AN F17 21723: Anon. memorandum on Bellaguet, 18 October 1869; and BMA ms. 487: Ernest Prarond to Charles Louandre, 19 April 1880. See also Paul Gerbod, "L'administration de l'Instruction Publique (1815–1870)," in Pierre Bosquet et al., *Histoire de l'administration de l'enseignement en France, 1789–1981* (Geneva, 1981), 20–36.

50. AN F17 2833: Jules Desnoyers to François Guizot, 22 September 1834, and idem to Gustave Rouland, 29 August 1858.

even European forces. The cult of local memories owed as much to Thierry as to small-town notaries. It owed as much, likewise, to official as to vernacular cultures: to "advocates of centralized power" as to a gamut of local interests that sought to articulate personal memories and acquire authority.[51] Although the divide between them proved porous, these categories frame a syncretic project, in which state and civil society, center and periphery appear in their singularity and within a broader "articulation."[52] In this respect, this book departs from *Les Lieux de mémoire*, Pierre Nora's masterful inquiry into the material and symbolic sites of modern French memory. According to Nora, contemporary France has lost the collective memory, the underlying social consensus that integrated all citizens within the nation under the aegis of the republican state. It now falls on *"hommes-mémoires"*—historians such as himself—to uncover the "subconscious organization of collective memory" and "revitalize" the citizen's affective relationship with the nation.[53] The outcome is an editorial venture that, however "pluralist and fragmented" in its last volumes, revolves around national and official memory.[54] As a result, it minimizes internal diversity and tensions and eludes local procedures and investments. Marrying bottom-up and top-down perspectives, I have sought to situate the local in a dynamic of convergence, divergence, and negotiation with official and national memory.

I should nevertheless indicate what this book does *not* set to accomplish. Focusing as it does on elite representations and strategies of production, it says little about reception or the rural *veillées* and urban workshops in which French men and women reportedly passed on local memories and "love of the *pays*."[55] To analyze the latter is to undertake a

---

51. John Bodnar, *Remaking America: Public Memory, Commemoration, and Patriotism in the Twentieth Century* (Princeton, N.J., 1992), 244–45. Studies of decentralization likewise often revolve around parliamentary debates and Paris-based figures. See, for instance, Rainer Riemenschneider, "Décentralisation et régionalisme au milieu du XIXe siècle," *Romantisme* 35 (1982): 115–33.

52. Marc Abélès, "How the Anthropology of France Has Changed Anthropology in France: Assessing New Directions in the Field," *Cultural Anthropology* 14, no. 3 (August 1999): 406.

53. Pierre Nora, "Entre mémoire et histoire," in idem, ed., *Les lieux de mémoire*, 7 vols. (Paris, 1984–92), 1:xxx, xli. See also Jean-Paul Willaime, "De la sacralisation de la France: *Lieux de mémoire* et imaginaire national," *Archives de sciences sociales des religions* 66, no. 1 (July–September 1988): 126; and Avner Ben-Amos, *Funerals, Politics, and Memory in Modern France, 1789–1996* (Oxford, 2000), 3–4.

54. Peter Carrier, "Places, Politics and the Archiving of Contemporary Memory in Pierre Nora's *Les lieux de mémoire*," in Susannah Radstone, ed., *Memory and Methodology* (Oxford, 2000), citation on 37. For similar critiques, see David Bell, "Paris Blues," *The New Republic* (1 September 1997): 32–36; and Steven Englund, "The Ghost of Nation Past," *The Journal of Modern History* 64, no. 2 (June 1992): 303, 318.

55. Edouard Girod, *Esquisse historique, légendaire et descriptive de la ville de Pontarlier* (Pontarlier, 1857), ix. On this topic, see Françoise Zonabend, *La mémoire longue: temps et histoire au village* (Paris, 1980); and Alain Corbin, *Le monde retrouvé de Louis-François Pinagot: sur les traces d'un inconnu 1798–1876* (Paris, 1998), ch. 7.

different project, with its own questions, methodology, and (fleeting) evidence. Nor is this book an exhaustive survey of historical localism in nineteenth-century France. The reader will learn little about historical paintings, heraldry, landscape, fiction, or regional cuisine.[56] What she will find, instead, is a selective but carefully plotted itinerary through this field. Within the huge mass of evidence bequeathed by the cult of local memories, I have paid particular attention to certain strands, including the self-reflexive discourse and contradictions that permeated both blueprints and completed ventures. I have also undertaken a close analysis of six leading sites. Three reached a national audience: the Comité des travaux historiques (CTH), an agency founded by the Ministry of Public Instruction in 1834; the scientific congresses and Institut des provinces, established at the same time; and Parisian periodicals on the provinces and decentralization. Three others, situated in provincial towns, were intrinsically local: learned societies and archeological commissions; historical pageants; and cultural periodicals. I have also examined, though less comprehensively, historical monographs, national and local newspapers, museums, city hall decorations, the Ministry of the Interior's Commission des monuments historiques, and at the end of this period, geographical societies.

This corpus encompasses all French regions. Scientific congresses were held in forty different cities, for instance, while the Ministry of Public Instruction corresponded with provincials from every French department. In addition, I studied the publications of learned societies from twenty cities and followed printed and archival leads in many others, from Amiens to Toulouse.[57] Yet, this project clearly called for an in-depth local study, capable of both recovering the cult of local memories' social life and illuminating the dialectic between center and provinces. I accordingly searched for a significant region, halfway between the urban microstudy and the national canvas. The quest for representativeness strikes me

56. There are, of course, very good works on these topics. See, for instance, Michael Marrinan, *Painting Politics for Louis-Philippe: Art and Ideology in Orléanist France, 1830–1848* (New Haven, 1988); Chrystèle Burgard and Françoise Chenet, eds., *Paysage et identité régionale. De pays rhônalpiens en paysages* (Genouilleux, 1999); Amélie Djourachkovitch and Yvan Leclerc, eds., *Province–Paris: topographies littéraires du XIXe siècle* (Rouen, 2000); and Julia Csergo, "L'émergence des cuisines régionales," in Jean-Louis Flandrin and Massimo Montanari, eds., *Histoire de l'alimentation* (Paris, 1996), 823–41.

57. For each of these twenty cities, I read the associations' periodical publications for the years 1837–38, 1845–46, 1858–59, and 1868 (or the closest available). I selected two societies from Normandy (in Bayeux and Caen), the Northeast (Abbeville, Châlons-sur-Marne), eastern France (Strasbourg, Troyes), Burgundy (Auxerre, Dijon), the center (Clermont-Ferrand, Le Puy), Franche-Comté and Savoie (Besançon, Chambéry), western France (Nantes, Saint-Brieuc), Gascony (Angoulême, Bordeaux), Languedoc (Béziers, Rodez), and Provence (Draguignan, Toulon). For more precise information, please see the bibliography.

FIGURE 1. Map of France, identifying principal cities mentioned in the text.

as dubious, given the irreducibility of local experiences and the historical and economic diversity of French regions. I instead sought to catch a particular place at a revealing moment, when actors put local memories to new uses. I ultimately opted for the department of the Nord, a territory that provides local conclusions while suggesting broader ones.

A narrow expanse alongside the Belgian border, the Nord displayed marked contrasts. Slowly reclaimed from the sea, northern Maritime Flanders (or Westhoek) is a low-lying, coastal land of dunes and canals whose "sad and wild" landscape, broken by church spires and the cranes of Dunkirk, "inspire[d] melancholy sensations" in some observers.[58] This rural region, rich in grain fields, was less populated than the dense Interior Flanders, with its urban centers in Douai and surrounding Lille. Below the Lys River lies an expanse of sandy hills whose fertile topsoil yielded abundant crops of grains and vegetables. In the department's southern half, the Cambrésis, Hainaut, and Avesnois compose a land of chalky plateaus and wide valleys irrigated by the Scarpe and Escaut rivers. The countryside surrounding Cambrai and Valenciennes, this area's largest towns, was rich in wheat and sugar beet fields. The heavily urban Nord began a cycle of demographic and economic growth in the 1810s and, by 1827, included eighteen towns of more than five thousand inhabitants.[59] Small textile and manufacturing workshops were widespread throughout the department. While Maritime Flanders remained predominantly agricultural, Lille and its surrounding area underwent an early transition to industrial capitalism, benefiting from mechanical innovations, a supply of labor and capital, and an enterprising cadre of industrialists. The textile industry, long prominent in this region (linen, batiste, lace), expanded rapidly in Lille and more moderately around Cambrai and Valenciennes. By 1850, the Nord led provincial departments in population density (over 1,100,000 inhabitants), industrial development, and percentage of workers and indigents. Such trends increased under the Second Empire, with the exploitation of the coal basin and the multiplication of sugar refineries as well as chemical and metallurgical plants in the south.[60] Industry thus flourished in a department that remained largely agrarian, producing a mix of economic modernity and tradition that unsettled some residents. This internal disparity encompassed religion and language. Catholicism was deeply ingrained, though less so in the cities and the south than in the countryside and the devout and clerical Westhoek. Flemish remained prevalent, but essentially in the latter's countryside.

In historical terms, the Nord comprises lands from the old counties of Flanders and Hainaut, both formed in the ninth century. Their history during ensuing centuries was one of urban prosperity and bourgeois privileges, but also of social unrest and successive invasions. Both counties en-

58. Eusèbe Girault de Saint Fargeau, "Nord," in his *Dictionnaire géographique, historique, industriel et commercial de toutes les communes de la France et de plus de 20,000 hameaux en dépendant*, 3 vols. (Paris, 1844–46), 2:65.

59. Louis Trénard, "Aux origines de la déchristianisation: le diocèse de Cambrai de 1830 à 1848," *RN* 47 (1965): 400; and Charles du Rozoir, *Relation historique, pittoresque et statistique du voyage de S. M. Charles X dans le département du Nord* (Paris, 1827), 7.

60. André Jardin and André-Jean Tudesq, *La France des notables*, 2 vols. (Paris, 1973), 2:150–70; Claude Fohlen, *L'industrie textile au temps du Second Empire* (Paris, 1956), 223–37; and Emile Coornaert, *La Flandre française de langue flamande* (Paris, 1970).

tered the Duchy of Burgundy then fell into the Spanish Habsburg domain in 1477. Louis XIV incorporated them into France through his military campaigns of the late seventeenth century.[61] The department's cities were idiosyncratic: Douai as a judicial and administrative center, Cambrai as an archbishopric, Dunkirk as one of the oldest French ports. Several common traits nonetheless characterized the Nord during our period, including a dominant bourgeoisie, a weak landed nobility, and an aversion to political extremes. Its elites proved, on the whole, loyal to successive regimes. After 1830, legitimism appealed above all to Catholic landowners, particularly in the Westhoek.[62] The Nord's cities also shared ancient traditions of urban association and festivities as well as urban pride and affection for local liberties. Historical memories thus held a particular resonance in a conquered territory that comprised an ancient *pays d'État*, a territory whose cities had eventful pasts—whether as medieval communes, homes of the counts of Flanders, or strongholds of successive occupants. The Nord, declared a leading Parisian daily in 1851, was "the sole *pays* [with] a remnant of the provincial and communal spirit." It was there, said Thierry, that the bourgeoisie had first acquired urban liberties and it was there that he began searching for archival traces in 1837. Local historiography was, moreover, well established. A local historian commented in 1836 that the department's archives and libraries contained an "infinite . . . number of documents."[63]

With its borderland location and municipal traditions (but weak irredentism),[64] the Nord thus enables us to ask how a peripheral elite delineated its local memories within a national framework. It also illuminates the state's responses to expressions of local individuality. Atypical as it was, finally, it displays longings, tensions, and conceptual reflections that affixed themselves to local memories elsewhere in France. All ultimately demonstrate that, François Génin to the contrary, the narrowing of language may indeed entail the extension of ideas.

61. Cambrai's situation is rather particular, for as an episcopal seat and imperial city, it had a long tradition of neutrality (albeit with close ties to the Austrians by the fifteenth century).

62. Philippe Guignet, *Le pouvoir dans la ville au XVIIIe siècle: pratiques politiques, notabilité et éthique sociale de part et d'autre de la frontière franco-belge* (Paris, 1990), esp. 42–91; Gildea, *Education in Provincial France, 1800–1914: A Study of Three Departments* (Oxford, 1983), 8–12; Ménager, "La vie politique dans le département du Nord de 1851 à 1877," Ph.D. diss., University of Paris IV, 1979; and Proceedings of doctoral thesis defense of Karine Van Wynendaele, "La vie politique dans le département du Nord sous la monarchie constitutionnelle (1815–1848)," Université Charles-de-Gaulle Lille 3 (1999), in *RN* 82, no. 337 (October–December 2000): 789.

63. *Le Constitutionnel,* 13 May 1851; AN F17 3265: Augustin Thierry to prefect Nord, 15 June 1837; and Pierre Clément, *Histoire de la Flandre, depuis l'invasion romaine jusqu'au XIXe siècle* (Lille, 1836), 9.

64. Timothy Baycroft, "Changing Identities in the Franco-Belgian Borderland in the Nineteenth and Twentieth Centuries," *French History* 13, no. 4 (December 1999): 437–38.

PART I: *Le Pays*

ONE

The Field of Local Memories

> If the cult of local traditions and memories is indeed a virtual duty of filial piety, let us not fall short.
>
> ANDRÉ LE GLAY,
> *Programme des faits historiques représentés*
> *par la marche des chars et phaétons,*
> *à la fête communale de Cambrai,*
> *le 15 et le 18 août 1833* (Cambrai, 1833)

THE PRESCRIPTION GIVEN above governed the private and professional life of André Le Glay, the Nord's foremost historian from the 1820s until his death in 1863. Nothing predisposed this man of humble origins, son of a farmer and quitrent collector, to attain such prominence. Born in 1785 in the village of Arleux (pop. 1,072), Le Glay attended school in the middling cities of Douai and Cambrai before studying medicine in Paris. In 1812, aged twenty-seven, he returned to Cambrai to practice his profession. Twice elected to the municipal council, *secrétaire de mairie* in 1817, justice of the peace in 1825: Le Glay soon became an eminent citizen of his town. Between his professional and civic obligations, he managed to offer botany courses, publish works on natural history and public health, and starting in 1826, serve as municipal librarian. By the late 1820s, he was devoting considerable time to "the cult of local traditions and memories." Le Glay eventually wrote dozens of books on local history and archaeology, contributed to periodicals and newspapers, joined numerous learned societies, intervened in scholarly congresses, scripted historical pageants, and pushed for monumental preservation. In 1835, Minister of Public Instruction François Guizot asked the "most active and enlightened" Le Glay to head the Archives of Flanders (or departmental archives). The three-thousand-francs-a-year post entailed a move to Lille, but this did not dampen Le Glay's devotion to place and past. "Do you know anything . . . that better re-

23

FIGURE 2. André Le Glay (1785–1863).

sembles filial piety than love of the *pays?*" he asked a packed auditorium of Lillois in 1842.[1]

Le Glay's unremitting commitment to the local past earned him widespread admiration, the Legion of Honor, and official praise as "an equally modest and learned man."[2] Yet neither his activities nor his arguments on behalf of local memories were atypical within his intellectual circle. He simply did more and spoke with greater eloquence than others. This unassuming yet ubiquitous figure hence constitutes a peerless guide to the field of local memories that emerged in the early nineteenth century. This field was at once discursive, patrimonial, and cultural—and I survey

1. Administrative documents show that Le Glay's name was officially spelled Leglay. Given his capitalization of 'Le,' he probably did not seek to affect noble ancestry. See ADN C 20869: List of communicants and noncommunicants in the parish of Arleux, 17 November 1778; François Guizot to Louis-Philippe, report on the publication of documents on the history of France, 2 December 1835, in Charmes, 44; AN F17 2865: André Le Glay to Min. Pub. Instr., 20 January 1850; *Procès-verbal de la séance générale du 23 février 1842 de l'Association lilloise* (Lille, 1842), 7; Hippolyte Verly, *Essai de biographie lilloise contemporaine, 1800–1869* (Lille, 1869), 134–35; Paul Sénèz, *Le panthéon douaisien,* issue on Le Glay (Douai, 1895), 4; and *MEC* 79 (1932): 172–83.

2. *Rapport à M. le Ministre de l'Intérieur sur les monumens, les bibliothèques, les archives et les musées des départements de l'Oise, de l'Aisne, de la Marne, du Nord et du Pas-de-Calais par M. L. Vitet . . .* (Paris, 1831), 76 and 86; and AN F17 2897: Henri-Adrien de Longpérier, report of 10 November 1864.

each plane in turn in the pages that follow. I do so to orient the reader within an unfamiliar landscape and, most significantly, to lay the groundwork for a more sustained analysis. Even specialists will, I trust, discover an arena of unsuspected breadth, vitality, and complexity.

THE DISCURSIVE FIELD: PLACE AND THE *PAYS*

On a first plane, the field of local memories was a mix of historical and geographical referents. The cult of local memories forced contemporaries to determine on two levels what memories they would delineate. The outcome, unsurprisingly, was a bevy of projects that revolved around distinct eras and territories. Despite this proliferation, two trends—one of them predictable, the other less so—shaped this discursive field.

Much has been written about the nineteenth century's fascination with history and, more pointedly, the Middle Ages. The latter surfaced in the late eighteenth century, flourished in the 1820s (along with translations of Walter Scott's novels), and imprinted French historical writing until the 1870s. While some condemned the Middle Ages' theocratic obscurantism, anarchy, or social inequality, others succumbed to a romantic absorption with the period's spirituality and irrational strangeness. Interest converged on the twelfth and thirteenth centuries—a time of heartfelt Christian devotion; era of troubadours, ladies, and knights; summit of institutional and corporate organization. All of this held a particular appeal to nineteenth-century traditionalists, but others looked to the Middle Ages as well. "Local description," declared one republican *littérateur* in 1849, will unveil "picturesque tableaus, that is, a world of enchanted sites, of monuments, of palaces, of famous dungeons, of citadels, of feudal castles, of churches, of gothic cathedrals, of abbeys, of convents and ruins." It was during the late Middle Ages, also, that freedom-loving bourgeois liberated communes from the aristocratic and clerical yoke.[3] Guizot, Augustin Thierry, and other liberals extolled the liberties that the Third Estate had conquered at that time. These were at once the foundation of a "great middle class" and the premise of a national polity and culture. The latter would now attain a tangible, lasting form, thanks to the French Revolution and the constitutional regime of Louis-Philippe.[4]

---

3. "Nouvelle souscription" (n.d. [1849?]), attached to the BNF copy of Aristide Guilbert, *Histoire des villes de France, avec une introduction générale pour chaque province*, 6 vols. (Paris, 1844–48), vol. 1, 3; Frédéric Martel, "Les historiens du début du XIXe siècle et le Moyen Age occitan: Midi éclairé, Midi martyr ou Midi pittoresque," *Romantisme* 35 (1982): 69; and Jürgen Voss, "Le problème du Moyen Age dans la pensée historique en France (XVIe–XIXe siècle)," *Revue d'histoire moderne et contemporaine* 24 (July–September 1977): 321–40.

4. Guizot, Speech in the public meeting of the Société des antiquaires de Normandie, 2 August 1837, *Mémoires de la Société des antiquaires de Normandie* 11 (1837–39): xlv.

Yet the contours of the nineteenth century's Middle Ages remained blurry. Depending on whom one asked, the period could encompass the Renaissance or—especially under the Second Empire—the Merovingian and Carolingian empires. What is more, fascination with the Middle Ages was less exclusive than commonly depicted. Guizot called for investigations into all periods of national history. Odile Parsis-Barubé's painstaking study of the Pas-de-Calais, Somme, and Nord departments likewise shows that, prior to 1870, the number of articles on the medieval and early modern eras (c. 1550–1800) was comparable in periodicals. More revealingly yet, the largest group of articles cut across historical periods.[5] This was partly because many contemporaries lacked the requisite paleographical training to study the Middle Ages. But other factors came into play. While the Nord's historical fêtes granted the Middle Ages and Renaissance a disproportionate importance, the organizers typically chose moments of local glory rather than particular eras. Some also presented broad narratives of local history. In Cambrai, during the 1820s, Le Glay's programs included counts of Flanders and "the ancient chivalry"—in other words, the Middle Ages and early Renaissance. After 1830, however, they celebrated the Nord's economic resources and artistic or charitable "celebrities." "Our principles are no longer the same," explained the organizers. Counts of Flanders and Flemish knights "must no longer figure in modern celebrations." In subsequent years, most of Cambrai's pageants depicted "the most brilliant scenes of our *pays*'s history."[6]

The first—and least surprising—trend within this discursive field is hence that political considerations influenced such decisions. Until the advent of the Moral Order in the early 1850s, this field displayed remarkable political diversity. Liberals were most numerous and active, alongside a sizable traditionalist bloc, a small number of vocal and nonrevolutionary republicans, and various other radicals. Le Glay was an opportunistic moderate, a social conservative who lauded the Bourbons under the Restoration, endorsed the 1830 revolution and Guizot's brand of liberalism, then submitted to the Second Republic and Second Empire alike. His rejection of medieval knights clearly paralleled his political evolution. The same is true of the territories he extolled. His Restoration programs

5. While rare, investigations of the present era (beginning with the French Revolution) were more common than in the eighteenth century. See Odile Parsis-Barubé, *Représentations du Moyen âge*, 1:222–23 and 281 and 2:352–53 and 588; and Daniel Roche, *Le siècle des Lumières en province: académies et académiciens provinciaux, 1680–1789*, 2 vols. (Paris, 1978), 1: 367.

6. [Le Glay?], *Programme de la fête communale de Cambrai, 15 août 1827* (Cambrai, n.d. [1827?]); Delloye 38/5: "Programme de la fête communale de Cambrai" (20 July 1831), supplement to *La Feuille de Cambrai* (n.d. [July or August 1831]); and [Le Glay], *Programme des faits historiques représentés par la marche des chars et phaétons, à la fête communale de Cambrai, le 15 et le 18 août 1833* (Cambrai, 1833), 8.

opened with a flag bearing the arms of Flanders and ended with a hymn that beckoned: "Flanders, rejoice / Here comes the King of France!" These stanzas vanished in August 1830. The department now claimed "these celebrities in whom the province once took such pride," explained Le Glay.[7]

Indeed, traditionalists commonly celebrated the prerevolutionary province (such as the Languedoc), a political and geographical territory that connoted the authority of aristocratic families, privileges steeped in history, and cultural individuality. The province also evoked organic and oligarchic local communities, a "great family" in which distinctions of rank remained visible. For royalist writer Louis Marchangy in 1825, it embodied "this hierarchy of conditions that granted everyone his rights and hopes." Some associated this idealized society with the Bourbon monarchy. Without demanding the return of provincial estates, others cultivated these memories to denounce a state that, since Louis XIV, had effaced the personalities and confiscated the political or fiscal liberties of historical provinces. In the Nord, where references to the province often invoked the counts of Flanders, this territory appealed especially to legitimists and nobles. Dunkirk's Comité flamand de France (f. 1853) and Lille's *Flandre illustrée* (pub. 1858–59) both glorified the customs and "particular history . . . of our ancient and beautiful Flanders," "our ancient province." Like others, Comité flamand members slipped nimbly between culture and politics to claim that "as far as mores, customs, and dialects go, France will always include Bretons, Normands, Provençaux, Basques, Burgundians and Picards, Alsatians and Flemings."[8]

Liberals sometimes cultivated the province, but tended to favor the commune and department, which denoted acceptance of the postrevolutionary political order. Municipal references extolled the aforementioned bourgeois liberties and the urban framework that underlay the professional and civic existence of most liberal elites. "It is the communes that brought forth our present society," declared Douai magistrate Eugène Tailliar in 1835. Le Glay thus combed the Nord's archives in search of documents on their "history, rights, and privileges."[9] These documents

7. Charles du Rozoir, *Relation historique*, 33; [Le Glay?], *Programme de la fête communale de Cambrai. 15 août 1828* (Cambrai, n.d. [1828?]), quotation on 16; Delloye 37/42: "Programme de la fête communale de Cambrai de 1830," poster (1830); and "Programme de la fête communale de Cambrai" (20 July 1831).

8. By Flanders, the Comité flamand thus meant Maritime (Flemish-speaking) Flanders alone. See Louis de Marchangy, *Tristan le voyageur, ou la France au XIVe siècle*, 6 vols. (Paris, 1825), 1:xxii; *ACF* 1 (1853): 81–82 and 117; Pascal Lange, "Le Comité flamand de 1853 à 1914" (Masters thesis, Université de Lille III, 1971), 149; and *Flandre illustrée* 34 (13 March 1859): 266.

9. Eugène Tailliar, *De l'affranchissement des communes dans le Nord de la France, et des avantages qui en sont résultés* (1835), repr. in *MEC* 15, vol. 2 (1837): 7–10; and Le Glay, "Histoire et description des archives générales du département du Nord, à Lille," in Jacques Joseph

contributed to the Comité des Travaux Historiques's (CTH) largest venture between 1834 and 1853: the *Recueil des monuments inédits de l'histoire du Tiers Etat*, devoted to municipal institutions. While some reformist liberals and radicals agreed with Tailliar, many viewed the commune, not as the birthplace of an enterprising yet benevolent bourgeoisie, but as a "democratic" space in which all citizens could exercise their civic rights, engage in participatory politics, and fulfill the nation's "tendencies and needs."[10] These actors, too, hence turned to the commune throughout these decades. Under the July Monarchy, they also expressed a deep commitment to administrative territories—canton or arrondissement—as spaces of proximate civic activity. The reformist liberals who founded a new learned society in Valenciennes in 1832 thus named it Société d'agriculture, sciences et arts de l'arrondissement de Valenciennes. Without spurning these territories under the Second Empire, radicals nonetheless gravitated toward a commune that, given the advent of universal suffrage (and conservative victories), offered greater hopes of political success.[11]

All of this suggests that contemporaries selected territories and eras with care, aware of their precise meanings. These territorial referents formed a semiotic system, in which each component's value, or meaning, depends on its relationship to the others. The commune, then, was itself, but also *not* the province, *not* the arrondissement. At the same time, members of different political schools cultivated the same territory. While traditionalists converged on the province, for instance, they neither monopolized it nor shunned the department. As François Guillet recently demonstrated, contemporaries of diverse political stripes were increasingly apprehending Normandy or Languedoc not as juridical and historical provinces, but as natural regions, with a common geology and customs.[12] More significantly for us, many contemporaries defined local

---

Champollion-Figeac, ed., *Documents historiques inédits tirés des collections manuscrites de la Bibliothèque Royale et des archives ou des bibliothèques des départements*, 4 vols. (Paris, 1841–48), 2:76. See also Firmin Guichard, *Essai historique sur le cominalat dans la ville de Digne, institution municipale provençale des XIIIe et XIVe siècles*, 2 vols. (Digne, 1846).

10. Prospectus (1843) attached to the BNF copy of Guilbert, *Histoire des villes*, vol. 1, 5. By reformist liberals, I mean the "dynastic" and center-left, or what contemporaries called the Party of Movement.

11. This discussion has benefited from exchanges with Sudhir Hazareesingh. To these territories, let us add the parish and diocese, less prevalent during these decades though increasingly so after midcentury. I discuss the clergy later in this chapter. See Parsis-Barubé, *Représentations du Moyen Âge*, 2:831; and Hazareesingh and Vincent Wright, "Le Second Empire," in Louis Fougère, Jean-Pierre Machelon, and François Monnier, eds., *Communes et le pouvoir*, 312–16.

12. François Guillet, "Naissance de la Normandie (1750–1850): genèse et épanouissement d'une image régionale," *Terrain* 33 (September 1999): 147. On legitimists and the department, see *Annales des Basses-Alpes* 1 (1838): 7–8. The region's heyday came under the Third Republic, however. Only then did it flourish as geographic and ethnographic category; vector of economic development; political and literary movement; architectural style; and focus of a nascent tourism industry. See, for instance, Marie-Claire Robic, "Milieu, région et paysage géo-

memories with startling imprecision. They not only cut across historical periods in their articles and pageants, but also combined seemingly incompatible spatial referents. The 1831 prospectus for Ludovic Vitet's *Histoire des anciennes villes de France* evoked not only "ancient communes," but "provincial histories" and "local" narratives as well.[13] This was a widespread pattern: Le Glay's own projects revolved around the village, city (and commune), arrondissement, department, and province. He and others juxtaposed territorial referents in order to seduce multiple audiences. More important, they cultivated what they called the "spirit of locality and tradition that is the very life of *la province*."[14] Defined in affective rather than precise geographical or administrative terms, communes, provinces, and the like constituted complementary conduits toward an ill-defined but historically grounded local sense of place. This is the second governing trend within this discursive field.

Contemporaries in fact drew increasingly from a set of territorial referents that carried memories but lacked clear boundaries, institutional existence, or political history. Such was the case of *localité*, which denoted a town, village, or a small surrounding expanse. Such was also the case of *contrée*, best translated as "land." The soul only attaches itself to "the history of the *contrée*, the province, the city," Thierry declared in 1820. Three decades later, Victor Derode, founding president of the Société dunkerquoise pour l'encouragement des sciences, des lettres et des arts, called for a "local historical museum, that would contain everything that pertains to the *contrée*." More pervasive yet was the *pays*, derived from the Latin *pagus*. Thierry called for "histor[ies] of one's *pays*" and so did Marchangy, for whom "local customs" and "hereditary traditions" sustained "love of the *pays*." In Derode's museum as elsewhere, the cult of local memories would "illuminate the ancient condition of a *pays* that holds all our affection." It would assemble "all that relates to its history, traditions, and mores."[15]

The origins of the *pays* go back to the Celts and, especially, the Romans,

---

graphique: la synthèse écologique en miettes?," in idem et al., eds., *Du milieu à l'environnement: pratiques et représentations du rapport homme/nature depuis la Renaissance* (Paris, 1992), 167–99; Isabelle Collet, "Les premiers musées d'ethnographie régionale en France," in *Muséologie et ethnologie* (Paris, 1987), 68–99; and Stephen L. Harp, *Marketing Michelin: Advertising and Cultural Identity in Twentieth-Century France* (Baltimore, 2001), chap. 7.

13. Alexandre Mesnier, prospectus for Vitet, *Histoire des anciennes villes de France: recherches sur leurs origines, sur leurs monumens, sur le rôle qu'elles ont joué dans les annales de nos provinces. 1e série. Haute-Normandie. Dieppe* (Paris, n.d. [1831]), 3.

14. Throughout this book, I distinguish *la province*—the French territory outside Paris—from the historical provinces. See Armand-René Du Chatellier, *Du mouvement des études littéraires et scientifiques en province (histoire des congrès)* (Paris, 1865), 21.

15. Augustin Thierry, *Lettres sur l'histoire de France*, 2d ed., repr. in *Oeuvres d'Aug. Thierry* (Brussels, 1839), 422; ASD 1851–52: Proceedings of the Société dunkerquoise, 25 May 1851; Marchangy, *Tristan le voyageur*, 2: 247 and 5: 146; and *Annales de la Société archéologique et historique des Côtes-du-Nord* 1 (1842): 12.

whose three-hundred-odd districts, none larger than a day's round-trip journey by foot, were by and large ethnic territories. It revolved around a city by the Carolingian era and typically had its own customs, patois, and social networks by the sixteenth century. The *pays*'s cultural resonance remained limited within the rural population, but the term progressively spread within nineteenth-century scholarly discourse, from mineralogy and geology to history, archaeology, and finally, geography.[16] By century's end, geographers and historians (Paul Vidal de la Blache, Lucien Gallois, André Siegfried) defined the *pays* yet more systematically as a "natural region," whose geology or customs distinguished it from arbitrary historical or administrative designations, such as the department.[17]

In prior decades, there was the *pays* as country or nation—whose glory one celebrated along with such "illustrious" celebrities as Cuvier—and the *pays légal*, the civic community of elites who, by virtue of their wealth, wisdom, and public devotion, participated in the nation's political life. "My *pays*, how nice that sounds!" said Jérôme Paturot, the fictional hero of Louis Reybaud's 1843 eponymous satire of bourgeois ambition. "The cabinet says it, the opposition says it, everyone says it."[18] At the local level, the *pays* was a "relatively narrow" expanse, smaller than the region or province. It sometimes surrounded a city (Cambrai and the Cambrésis, for instance), always lacked an administrative basis, and for some, possessed an underlying physical, cultural, or (less frequently) economic unity.[19] A *pays* has "a unique geological configuration, climate and customs," explained a dictionary of French institutions and mores in 1855. The conviction that geography, or the nature of the land (*le sol*), related intimately to history and customs had appeared in the late eighteenth century and

16. The term also came to designate tax circumscriptions: *pays d'État* and *pays d'élection*. See Xavier de Planhol with Paul Claval, *Géographie historique de la France* (Paris, 1988), 187–92 and 217–20; Daniel Schweitz, *Histoire des identités de pays en Touraine, XVIe–XXe siècles* (Paris, 2001), 18–24; and Michel Puzelat, "La notion de pays: un parcours historiographique," in Odile Redon, ed., *Savoirs des lieux. Géographies en histoire*, Cahiers de Paris VIII (Saint-Denis, 1996), 89–106.

17. Jean-Claude Chamboredon, "Carte, désignations territoriales, sens commun géographique: les 'noms de pays' selon Lucien Gallois," *Études Rurales* 109 (January–March 1988): 5–54; Didier Gonzalez, "L'idée de pays dans la géographie et la culture française au tournant du siècle," in Claval, ed., *Autour de Vidal de la Blache: la formation de l'Ecole française de géographie* (Paris, 1993), 124; and Marie-Vic Ozouf-Marignier, "Le *Tableau* et la division régionale: de la tradition à la modernité," in Robic, ed., *Le "Tableau de la géographie de la France" de Paul Vidal de la Blache* (Paris, 2000), 158–160 and 169.

18. Popularized by liberals during the late 1820s, the term *pays* was adopted by members of all political schools during the following decade. See *Allocution prononcée, au nom de l'Académie des Sciences de l'Institut de France, par M. Duméril, le 23 août 1835, jour de l'inauguration de la statue de Cuvier, à Montbéliard* (Paris, n.d. [1835?]), 3; and Louis Reybaud, *Jérôme Paturot à la recherche d'une position sociale* (Paris, 1846 [1843]), 361.

19. Francois Génin, *Variations du langage*, 417; and Jean-Jacques Goblot, "*Pays* dans le vocabulaire politique du 19e siècle," in Sylvianne Rémi-Giraud and Pierre Rétat, eds., *Les mots de la nation* (Lyons, 1996), 285–93.

grown increasingly prevalent ever since. Vast unified territories such as Normandy hence contained numerous *pays*—each of which required an investigation of its origins and distinctive features.[20] Yet mid-nineteenth-century dictionaries also emphasized the polysemy of a term that had uncertain origins and boundaries and could denote numerous territories, from the canton to the province.[21] Within the field of local memories, the term thus designated a generic place of residence and belonging, a physical space and a community that encompassed the urban and the rural. A close friend of Le Glay, Valenciennes lawyer and historian Arthur Dinaux, spoke in 1842 of reviving "piety for the *pays*'s glorious memories[,] which tie the resident to the land." Many radicals and traditionalists concurred with this liberal.[22] Beyond political fissures, place was the lure of this discursive field.

THE PATRIMONIAL FIELD, 1: A RECONNAISSANCE

This discourse did not, however, originate in a vacuum. Equally striking were the institutions that Le Glay and others either transformed or created to cultivate local memories. Statements alone would not inspire affection for the *pays*: a more concrete entity—the *patrimoine*—was also required. Coined from the Latin *patrimonium* in the twelfth century, the term long denoted inherited property (typically from one's parents) and the sacred heritage of Church law, embodied in relics and other holy entities. Granting the term a new prefix, the French revolutionaries expressed their "pride [at] seeing a family patrimony become a national patrimony." The latter designated the artistic property, from monuments to archival documents, which now belonged to the sovereign nation.[23] Seeping into common usage during the first half of the nineteenth century, the term

20. This conviction had multiple origins, from the growth of natural science to a physiocratic concern with the resources or population of discrete territories. Constantin-François Volney, for one, had insisted on the necessary correlation between geography and history. See Adolphe Chéruel, *Dictionnaire historique des institutions, moeurs et coutumes de la France*, 2 vols. (Paris, 1855), 1:960; Guillet, *Naissance de la Normandie*, esp. 78–79, 114, and 144; and Daniel Nordman, "Introduction générale: les sciences morales et politiques à l'École normale," in idem, ed., *L'École normale de l'an III. Leçons d'histoire, de géographie, d'économie politique* (Paris, 1994), 14–16.

21. E. D., "Pays," in Eugène Duclerc and Laurent-Antoine Pagnerre, *Dictionnaire politique: encyclopédie du langage et de la science politiques* (Paris, 1842), 699.

22. *AHN* 3 (1841–42): 140. For similar language under the Second Empire, see, for instance, *Souvenirs de la Flandre wallonne* 1 (1861): 2.

23. "Patrimoine," *Trésor de la langue française*, 16 vols. (Paris, 1971–94), 8: 1191; André Desvallées, "Emergence et cheminement du mot patrimoine," *Musées et collections publiques en France* 208 (1995): esp. 8–11; and Edouard Pommier, "Discours iconoclaste, discours culturel, discours national, 1790–1794," in Simone Bernard-Griffiths, Marie-Claude Chemin, and Jean Ehrard, eds., *Révolution française et "vandalisme révolutionnaire"* (Paris, 1992), 304. For a recent overview, see Jean-Marie Leniaud, *Les archipels du passé: le patrimoine et son histoire* (Paris, 2002).

came to encompass national cultural belongings—ideals and values—as well as local ones. Derode's Dunkirk museum would thus hold a "precious [local] patrimony." It is true, of course, that the patrimony constituted a means of self-affirmation rather than a mere material entity.[24] Yet, for most of these actors, one entailed the other. Tangibility was essential and they sought it out by creating, or transforming, a variety of institutions, genres, and practices.[25]

It bears emphasizing that this field both ensued and broke from a long tradition of national and local projects. While the Renaissance's urban narratives or Nicolas de Nicolay's sixteenth-century provincial descriptions constitute modern starting-points, these projects stemmed most directly from the spate of historical enterprises and new geographical curiosity of the seventeenth and, especially, eighteenth centuries.[26] After 1615, bishops commissioned diocesan monographs to establish their rights and privileges. Soon afterward, Maurist monks embraced local monastic history as a hallowed intellectual activity, fit for their leisure time. The congregation's instructions on historical method yielded monographs on Brittany, Languedoc, and other provinces in the late seventeenth and eighteenth centuries.[27] In the mid eighteenth century, secular elites began studying the past and topography *of*—rather than *in*—a particular city or region. Their "discovery of the provinces" (R. Chartier) entailed countless monographs and topographies, local journeys, presentations before provincial academies, and articles in provincial newspapers.[28] In one respect, contemporaries apprehended territories within all-encompassing descriptions of an ordered landscape, which displayed prosperity, progress, and social unity. In another, they started identifying, or reaffirming, the historical and natural specificity of their province. Some *parlement* magistrates and provincial estates idealized the provincial

24. ASD 1851–52: Proceedings of the Société dunkerquoise, 25 May 1851; and Joël Candau, *Mémoire et identité* (Paris, 1998), 162.

25. Guy Thuillier aptly speaks of an "institutionalization" of local history. See his "Les historiens locaux en Nivernais, 1815–1940," in *101e congrès national des sociétés savantes*, section d'histoire moderne (Lille, 1976), 2: esp. 364.

26. Claire Dolan, "L'identité urbaine et les histoires locales publiées du XVIe au XVIIIe siècle en France," *Canadian Journal of History/Annales canadiennes d'histoire* 27 (August 1992): 277–93.

27. Blandine Barret-Kriegel, *L'histoire à l'âge classique*, 4 vols. (Paris, 1988), 3:171–78 and 271, and 4:68; Victor Carrière, *Introduction aux études d'histoire ecclésiastique locale*, 3 vols. (Paris, 1934–40), 1:x–xii and xvi; and Maurice Lecomte, *Les Bénédictins et l'histoire des provinces aux XVIIe et XVIIIe siècles* (Abbaye Saint-Martin de Ligugé, 1928).

28. Roger Chartier, "Les deux France: histoire d'une géographie", *Cahiers d'histoire* 23 (1978): 412–14; Roche, "Les académies et l'histoire," in his *Les républicains des lettres: gens de culture et Lumières au XVIIIe siècle* (Paris, 1988), 175, 189, and 191–99; and Claude Labrosse, "La région dans la presse régionale," in Jean Sgard, ed., *La presse provinciale au XVIIIe siècle* (Grenoble, 1983), 111–20.

past to buttress their claims to authority. Learning and local patriotism—source of virtue and emulation—went hand in hand.[29]

In this domain as in others, the French Revolution was a catalyst and a point of departure. Its reconfiguration of a uniform territory, whose rational circumscriptions would efface provincial particularism, and its efforts to assess the country's regeneration renewed interest in the territory. The "journey in France" emerged as a dominant cultural practice and literary genre. At the same time, destruction of royal, ecclesiastical, and noble property led some revolutionaries to propound a new ethic of monumental preservation. They established national archives and a commission to classify and inventory the nation's newly recovered cultural possessions, from manuscripts to statues. While these initiatives had no inherently local dimension, they helped spread concern with the past, be it national or local. The revolutionaries in fact asked local administrators for "itemized list[s] of all monuments" in their district.[30] This administrative impetus persisted to some extent during ensuing decades. In 1819, for instance, the Ministry of the Interior requested information on "the principal aspects of our annals," with special attention to the "local and, as it were, popular notions." The Académie des inscriptions et belles-lettres' interest in the history of place names (1818) and Alexandre de Laborde's *Monumens de la France* (1818 and 1836) both betrayed and accentuated a growing curiosity. The Revolution, as we will see, also opened a chasm, awakened aspirations, and provoked repudiations that, in different ways, spurred interest in local memories.[31]

By 1828, Bordeaux's Académie des sciences, belles-lettres et arts could thus take pride in its long-standing devotion to "the history of its *pays*." Yet, only in ensuing decades did local memories become one of its leading preoccupations, what some called "a need of our epoch."[32] It was also

---

29. Louis Brion de la Tour, *Coup d'oeil général sur la France* (Paris, 1765), n.p.; Jacques Revel, "La région", in Pierre Nora, ed., *Lieux de mémoire*, 5: 851–83; Guillet, *Naissance de la Normandie*, 47 and 186–203; and Yves Luginbuhl, "Paysage élitaire et paysages ordinaires," *Ethnologie française* 19, no. 3 (July–September 1989): 228–29. On estates and provincial history, see Marie-Laure Legay, *Les états provinciaux dans la construction de l'état moderne aux XVIIe et XVIIIe siècles* (Geneva, 2001), 478–84.

30. Nordman and Ozouf-Marignier, *Le territoire (1): réalités et représentations* (Paris, 1989), vol. 4 of Serge Bonin and Claude Langlois, eds., *Atlas de la Révolution française*, 11 vols. (Paris, 1987–2000), 72; Françoise Choay, *L'allégorie du patrimoine* (Paris, 1992), esp. 76–84, 205, and 223; Chantal Georgel, "L'Etat et 'ses' musées de province ou comment 'concilier la liberté d'initiative des villes et les devoirs de l'Etat,'" *Le mouvement social* 160 (September–July 1992): 67; and Marie-Anne Sire, *La France du patrimoine: les choix de la mémoire* (Paris, 1996), 21.

31. ADN 1 T 250/1: Min. Int. to prefects, circular of 8 April 1819; Pierre de Lagarde, *La mémoire des pierres* (Paris, 1985), 79–85; and Choay, *Allégorie*, 93–96.

32. *Académie des sciences, belles-lettres et arts de Bordeaux. Séance publique du 5 juin 1828* (Bordeaux, 1828), 52; and *MEC* 18 (1843): 9.

then that, owing to the efforts of Victor Hugo and others, concern with monumental preservation made unprecedented (albeit still limited) inroads within the French population. After decades of negligence, contemporaries began establishing or reorganizing archival depots. The liberal ministry of Martignac (1828–29) and the July Monarchy shifted governmental priorities from Parisian to provincial archives, which they sought to clean up and exploit.[33] Representations of traditional costumes and stereotypes also granted French provinces distinct pasts and personalities. The growth of archaeology as a discipline furthermore elicited a vogue of local investigations. Contemporaries hence declared around 1840 that archaeology had still been "in its infancy" a generation earlier. Now, however, "archaeological digs are undertaken everywhere. One plows almost as much for history as for wheat."[34]

Subtle observers sensed, however, that, be it in kind or number, these investigations represented an evolution as much as a rupture. Le Glay's 1836 "New Program" for the historical and archaeological study of the Nord presented nine directions of local study, from patois philology to history. Its evolution from a twelve-page pamphlet on Cambrai in 1820 (date of its first edition) to a 140-page program on the Nord captures this patrimonial field's quantitative transformation. At the same time, Le Glay's comprehensive approach betrays a qualitative progression toward a more rigorous effort to map a historical place and attain collective self-understanding.[35]

This inquiry took place, first, in the realm of print. While history had grown in popularity for several decades, only in the early nineteenth century did it become the largest category of literary production (27.5 percent in 1811–25, up from 18.7 percent in 1784–88 and 10 percent in 1723–27). Local history followed suit.[36] According to the *Catalogue de L'histoire de France*, over eighteen thousand book-length publications on

33. Marie-Paule Arnauld, "Centralisation ou délocalisation: les archives en France de la Révolution à nos jours," in François Furet, ed., *Patrimoine, temps, espace: patrimoine en place, patrimoine déplacé* (Paris, 1997), 175–77; and Lara Jennifer Moore, "Restoring Order," 28–30 and 86–91.

34. Frédéric Maguet and Anne Tricaud, eds., *Parler provinces: des images, des costumes* (Paris, 1994); AN F17 2810/1: Lucien de Rosny to Min. Pub. Instr., 15 August 1842; and *Revue de la province et de Paris* 3 (September 1842): 349. See likewise *Revue archéologique* 1, no. 1 (1844): 140.

35. Le Glay, *Indication des principales recherches à faire sur les antiquités et l'histoire de l'arrondissement de Cambrai* (Cambrai, 1820); and idem, *Nouveau programme d'études historiques et archéologiques sur le département du Nord* (Lille, 1836).

36. Roche, *La France des Lumières* (Paris, 1993), 82; den Boer, *History as a Profession*, 7; and René Grevet, "L'histoire et le pouvoir au XVIIIe siècle. Le discours politique provincial," *RN* 72, no. 288 (October–December 1990): 769–71.

the topic came out between 1825 and 1877—practically one a day. This is more than five times the total output of the preceding three centuries. By the 1860s, local monographs had become the leading subgenre of French history. Local history and archaeology made up 20.2 percent of works on "French history" in the Bibliothèque Nationale's 1897 catalogue.[37] This explosion owed much to the growth of book production during an era of looser constraints in the publishing trade, new printing techniques, and rising literacy. There was, however, something distinctive about this field. In 1834, a journalist described the efforts of young Parisian *littérateurs* to "create what is called a local literature, by evoking the *pays'* memories and legends." Provincials were not outdone during a period that saw countless "devoted men" undertake local "historical investigations."[38]

These investigations yielded, of course, local monographs—these *histoires, recherches, mémoires,* and *précis* that restricted their gaze to the village, town, or *pays.* Le Glay's first publication described the Cambrésis' noteworthy monuments and institutions. His last one, published in 1863, was an archival inventory. In between, he authored biographies, topographical surveys, studies of local buildings and monuments, annotated editions of historical documents, article collections, programs of study, and library catalogues. Prolific as he was, Le Glay eschewed other prevalent genres, including *éphémérides*—or local chronicles—and historical fables. He did not write either poetry or fiction about local memories, but others did, including his son Edward, an archivist and future subprefect. Edward also contributed an article on Valenciennes to Aristide Guilbert's *Histoire des villes de France* (Paris, 1844–48), a collective venture that promised to "decentralize general history in the interest of local history." This enterprise, the "largest . . . which bookselling has dared to undertake these past years," would expose readers to "the memories of [their] *pays*" through 6 weighty volumes, 517 articles, 90 metal engravings, and 133 colored coats of arms. Each article offered a complete historical portrait of the locality.[39]

L'Illustration equated the *Histoire des villes* with "the reawakening of local history." Other press outlets went further still and cultivated local memories themselves. In the Nord as elsewhere in the provinces, newspa-

37. Compiled in the late nineteenth century, the *Catalogue* is a vast bibliography of French publications. I counted works on all local circumscriptions, from the city to the province. Quantifying cultural phenomena is a risk-laden enterprise and I offer such figures to suggest, however hypothetically, the appeal of a genre and a practice. See *Catalogue de l'histoire de France,* 17 vols. (Paris, 1968–72 [1855–95]), vols. 8 and 15; Charles-Olivier Carbonell, *Histoire et historiens: une mutation idéologique des historiens français: 1865–1885* (Toulouse, 1976), 91–92 and 132–33; and den Boer, *History as a Profession,* 13.

38. *Revue d'Alsace* 1 (1834): 36, 48, and 54; and *RN,* 1st ser., 1, no. 3 (March 1835): 373.

39. "Nouvelle souscription" (n.d., 1849?), attached to the BNF copy of Guilbert, *Histoire des villes,* vol. 1.

pers occasionally published articles on local history—from village monographs to serialized municipal histories.[40] The same was true of the cultural periodicals that, beginning in the late 1820s, fed their readers a mix
of local history, archaeology, fiction, and sometimes, commerce and science. Le Glay contributed to the *Revue cambrésienne* (1835–39), Valenciennes's *Archives historiques et littéraires du Nord* (1829–57), Lille's *Revue du
Nord* (1833–40, 1854–57), and others. One Rouen journalist estimated
that sixteen such periodicals were created in the provinces in 1832 and
1833 alone. Many vanished by 1840, but others emerged during the following decades, oftentimes as more erudite publications, better suited to
"an epoch of examination, of analysis." Le Glay also contributed to local
departmental and municipal *annuaires*—annual administrative compendia that included "serious studies of our *pays*' history"—and the periodical
publications of provincial learned societies. By 1886, the latter had reportedly published fifteen thousand volumes—compendia of articles,
speeches, documents, and occasional fiction.[41]

While the capital's newspapers published little on local history, the
same was not true of those Parisian periodicals that, beginning in the mid-
1820s, promised to represent the "rights and interests" of a *province* that
lacked cultural and administrative resources. Some publications saw this
as one of their many tasks; others made it their mission. I have identified
close to twenty such provincialist periodicals as well as prospectuses for a
dozen more between 1828 and 1860. Nearly all involved provincial correspondents, yet the editors and most contributors lived in Paris. A few
sought to implicate *la province* in national affairs. Most purported to restore its reputation, remedy a broader neglect in the Parisian press, and
"establish a greater literary union between Paris and the departments."
They published considerable fiction and poetry, but also identified
provincial resources and riches while providing "a complete and detailed
investigation of our land." *Le Panorama* vowed in the late 1830s to showcase "provinces [that] have their monuments, history, traditions, legends, . . . customs, fêtes." No commune, to be sure, would refuse to in-
scribe its memories in as unprecedented a collection.[42]

The same held true in the associative realm, where contemporaries

40. See, for instance, *L'Impartial du Nord*, 5 January 1840; and *L'Industriel du Nord et du Pas-
de-Calais*, 14 July 1861. See also *L'Illustration* 7, no. 162 (4 April 1846): 78.

41. *Revue de Rouen* 3 (January–June 1834): 56; *RN*, 3d ser., 8, no. 10 (November 1857):
308–9; and *Annuaire de l'arrondisement de Cambrai* (1841): v. See also Simon Jeune, "Les revues
littéraires," in Henri-Jean Martin and Roger Chartier, eds., *Histoire de l'édition française*, 4 vols.
(Paris, 1982–86), 3:415; and Claude-Isabelle Brelot et al., "La Franche-Comté à la recherche de
son histoire (1800–1914)," *Cahiers d'études comtoises* 31 (1982): 95.

42. Prospectus for the *Revue des départemens de la France* (September 1828); *Revue de la
province* 1, no. 1 (1 February 1861): 1; *L'Echo des provinces* 1, no. 1 (22 January 1865): 1; and
Prospectus for *Le Panorama. Histoire-archéologie-littérature-arts-bibliographie* (n.d. [1837?]).

spoke, as early as 1834, of an "astounding multiplication of literary [or learned] societies in the departments." A decade later, the *Revue des deux mondes* noted that this provincial activity had taken off in the early 1830s.[43] While contemporaries offered differing estimates of the phenomenon, all grasped its evolution: thirty-two provincial academies and a small number of other societies prior to 1789; their proscription as corporate bodies in August 1793; and an explosion during the nineteenth century. In 1864, a *littérateur* claimed that 162 *sociétés savantes* had been created between 1789 and 1830 and 363 more between 1830 and 1864. These figures may be disputed, but the proportional ratio stands. Scholars have suggested that France numbered 655 learned societies and 100,000 members by 1885 (80 percent or so in the provinces); 200,000 individuals, they add, joined a society in the nineteenth century. Eighteenth-century provincial academies, in contrast, had attracted but six thousand members.[44]

The *Grand Larousse* defined learned societies as "free societies that take an interest in scientific issues or have been created to serve the public good." This elastic category encompassed a variety of voluntary associations, some of them newly founded, others long established. As associations of more than twenty members, all required an official authorization—or, at minimum, "toleration"—and could petition for the title of *société d'utilité publique* (allowing them to accept willed property). Members of *royal* societies figured on jury lists (after 1827) and were de facto municipal and departmental electors under the July Monarchy.[45] The reconstituted academies proved, on the whole, more aristocratic and less specialized than the societies founded after the revolution. All nonetheless shared an ancient ethos of practical and moral service to city and country, of private solidarity and public self-display, of co-optation and exclusion. They also engaged in similar activities: periodic meetings and public ceremonies, oral and written presentations (generally, of one's investigations or literary production), and public contests. Most resolved to "only address questions of utmost interest to our locality"—be it public hygiene or archaeology. A growing number depicted themselves as "enclo-

43. *La Revue des provinces* 1 (1 November 1834): 3; and Charles Louandre, "De l'association littéraire et scientifique en France. II. Les sociétés savantes et littéraires de la province," *RDM*, new ser., 16 (1846): 817.

44. *CS* 31 (Troyes, 1865), 17–18; Jean-Pierre Chaline, *Sociabilité et érudition: les sociétés savantes en France: XIXe–XXe siècles* (Paris, 1995), 37 and 93–94; idem, "Sociétés savantes et académies de province en France dans la première moitié du XIXe siècle," in Etienne Frantois, ed., *Sociabilité et société bourgeoise en France, en Allemagne et en Suisse, 1750–1850* (Paris, 1987), 170–71; Robert Fox, "The Savant Confronts His Peers: Scientific Societies in France, 1815–1914," in idem and George Weisz, eds., *The Organization of Science and Technology in France 1808–1914* (Cambridge, 1980), 245; and Roche, "Académies et l'histoire."

45. "Société," *Grand Larousse: dictionnaire universel du XIXe siècle*, 17 vols. (Paris, 1866–90?), 13: 802.

sures in which we seek to collect all that pertains to our history."[46] Old Regime academies devoted less than 15 percent of their oral presentations and contest topics to history. In the mid nineteenth century, however, local history and archaeology became the leading sphere of interest of these societies—an interest that could also encompass philology or topography. The Société d'agriculture, sciences, arts et commerce du Puy thus rewarded disquisitions and poems on local monuments and "any facet of the department's history."[47]

Learned societies included resident, corresponding, and honorary members. Le Glay belonged to several, in various capacities, in the Nord. Although the department lacked a prerevolutionary academy, its dozen or so societies ranged from Douai's patrician Société d'agriculture, des sciences et des arts (f. 1799) to the Société d'émulation de Cambrai (f. 1804), a liberal association dedicated to agriculture and "the history of the [local] *patrie.*" Upon moving to Lille in 1835, Le Glay joined the local Société des sciences, d'agriculture et des arts (f. 1802), "devoted to the cult of science in a large, eminently industrial city."[48] A year later, he cofounded the Association lilloise pour l'encouragement des lettres et des arts dans le département du Nord, whose public meetings, concerts, exhibits, and library would instill respect for art and local memories. Le Glay also helped the prefect create an administrative agency devoted to the Nord's monuments, history, and archaeology. Established in Lille in 1839, the Commission historique du Nord was one of eighteen-odd prefectoral agencies founded for this purpose under the July Monarchy (a few others had appeared under the Restoration). In 1841, it numbered forty-four members, most of them holding prominent positions in local learned societies. They met regularly to evaluate the importance of ancient monuments and edifices, make recommendations about subsidy requests, and discuss points of local history or philology. They inherited, as Le Glay told them, the "special mission of glorifying the *pays's* memories."[49]

46. *Bulletin de la Société des sciences, belles-lettres et arts du département du Var* 6, no. 1 (1838): vi; and *Annales de la Société d'agriculture, sciences, arts et commerce du Puy* 12 (1842–46): 10. On the academic ethos of service, see Roger Hahn, *The Anatomy of a Scientific Institution: The Paris Academy of Sciences, 1666–1803* (Berkeley, 1971), 42.

47. Roche, "Académies et l'histoire," 174–83; Keith Michael Baker, "Memory and Practice: Politics and Representation of the Past in Eighteenth-Century France," in his *Inventing the French Revolution,* 32 and 311, n. 4; Chaline, *Sociabilité et érudition,* 43–44; and *Annales de la Société d'agriculture, sciences, arts et commerce du Puy* 9 (1837–38): 27.

48. *MEC* 14 (1833): 6; and ADN 1 T 246/3: President Société royale des sciences, de l'agriculture et des arts de Lille, report of 1 May 1830.

49. I identified commissions in the following cities: Aurillac, Beauvais, Bordeaux, Bourges, Carcassonne, Chalons-sur-Marne, Clermont-Ferrand, Dijon, Evreux, Laon, Le Mans, Le Puy, Lille, Narbonne, Perpignan, Rouen, Saint-Omer, and Vésoul. See ADN 1 T 253/1: Le Glay to prefect Nord, 2 April 1838; and *BCN* 3 (1847–49): 41.

So did the various congresses—these "modern, contemporary, democratic institution[s]"—that surfaced during this period. In the summer of 1834, Le Glay coorganized a "provincial congress" of intellectual elites from the Nord in Douai. They concluded their meetings by inviting the local authorities to appoint more municipal archivists, learned societies to inventory local monuments, and the public to pen monetary and numismatic histories of Flanders and Artois. This was but one of numerous European congresses whose participants discussed their research and various issues of local, national, or international importance. The German Deutscher Naturforscher Versammlung, first held in the early 1820s, was followed by congresses in England, Italy, and—starting in the early 1830s—France.[50]

More significantly, the congress of Douai constituted but a "preparatory meeting" for the forthcoming *Congrès scientifique* of Poitiers. Held annually between 1833 and 1878, these itinerant meetings were the brainchild of a young archaeologist, Arcisse de Caumont (1801–73). The well-off scion of a family of petty nobles, this staunch legitimist had earned a reputation in his twenties for his comparative archaeological method and geological maps. In the 1820s and 1830s, he established several learned societies and periodicals dedicated to the history and natural history of his native Normandy and Calvados department. He also founded the Société française pour la conservation et la description des monuments historiques, whose annual archaeological congresses would further the cause of monumental preservation. In 1833, the first scientific congress attracted 220 registered members in Caen. The main goal of these congresses, Caumont later wrote a friend, was to "create secondary [intellectual] centers in the provinces." Participants—most of them local residents—broached diverse topics, from Gallic religion to rural schooling, over nine or more ten-hour days. In the mornings and afternoons, they broke up into thematic sections; in the evenings, they met for general sessions. In 1839, Caumont founded the Institut des provinces, a permanent "peerage of [between 100 and 350] provincial men of letters and savants" that held annual congresses between 1850 and 1878 and served as a counterpart to the prestigious Institut de France.[51] Caumont and his

50. *Mémoires de la Société des lettres, sciences et arts de l'Aveyron* 1 (1837–38), part 1, xxii; *RN* 2 (July 1834): 283–87; Jack Morrell and Arnold Thackray, *Gentlemen of Science: Early Years of the British Association for the Advancement of Science* (Oxford, 1981); and Fox, "Savant Confronts," 259.

51. I studied all congresses held in the Nord, but limited my national sample to the scientific congresses and the Institut des provinces. The most comprehensive work on Caumont and his circle is Bernard Huchet, "Arcisse de Caumont (1801–1873)" (Thesis, Ecole Nationale des Chartes, 1984), 4 vols. See also Françoise Bercé, "Arcisse de Caumont et les sociétés savantes," in Nora, *Lieux de mémoire*, 3: 533–68; Caumont to J. G. A. Luthereau, 1842, quoted in *La Célébrité*

acolytes ran these operations, but local elites organized their region's congresses. Le Glay directed the scientific congress held in Douai in 1835 as well as the archaeological and historical congress of Lille (1845). In 1857 and 1860, he vetted the programs for the congresses of Cambrai and Dunkirk. Distributed to all attendees, these programs invariably included questions on local topography, monuments, and history, "the most fertile field one could till in the provinces." They also proposed ways of developing "love of local traditions," from local biographies (1833) to renderings of local monuments (1853).[52]

In 1858, scientific congress members helped local dignitaries and elites cover the Burgundian town of Auxerre with flags and banners for a nocturnal ceremony depicting the union of the ancient provinces. This historical pageantry—by no means restricted to congresses—constitutes the most spectacular aspect of this patrimonial field. In 1851, *L'Illustration* noted that historical festivities had spread to the "principal cities of the departments," from Le Havre to Bordeaux. Every town, "as small as it may be, . . . dream[s] of a pageant or tournament," added the Parisian *Journal des départements et colonies* in 1858. No expense is being spared to "honor one's *home* [*chez-soi*]" and, as others remarked, popularize festivals that had long existed in the Nord.[53]

Indeed, the department witnessed the appearance of a new kind of festivity—first in the late 1820s and then, more massively, after 1830. In Cambrai, Le Glay helped transform the annual *fête communale* (an urban procession created in 1220) into a spectacle that mobilized the local past and transformed the urban space to imprint the mind and foster attachment to one's *pays*. By 1833, this seven-float *marche historique* retraced Cambrai's history from its Gallic origins to its incorporation into France (in 1677). Each float anchored a local tableau: the free city under Charlemagne, for instance. On all sides, actors impersonated municipal leaders, mounted knights, countesses, and enfranchised vassals. Their hymns and banners glorified the town's virtues and claims to fame, from its communal liberties to its lasting industriousness. Other pageants re-created the entries of prominent Renaissance rulers. Staged repeatedly in Douai between 1839 and 1849, the 1437 entry of Philip the Good surrounded the duke with archers and municipal magistrates, thirty-two mounted knights and her-

---

4, no. 32 (10 August 1861): 250; *AIP* 1 (1846): 5; and *Revue de la province et de Paris* 4 (November 1842): 130.

52. *Séances générales tenues à Lille, en 1845, par la Société française pour la conservation des monuments historiques* (Caen, 1846); ADN 1 T 248/6: Le Glay to prefect Nord, 23 July 1858; and *CS* 7, 2 vols. (Le Mans, 1839), 2: 96.

53. *CS* 25, 2 vols. (Auxerre, 1859), 1: 80–81; *L'Illustration* 17, no. 424 (11–18 April 1851): 229; and *Journal des départements et des colonies*, 17 July 1858 (italics in the text).

FIGURE 3. "Le congrès scientifique, à Tours," *L'Illustration*, 2 October 1847. Seven hundred people, most of them from Touraine, met in Tours for the fifteenth scientific congress. Held in the city's main courtroom, the inaugural session attracted a sizeable crowd as well as the prefect, archbishop, and other notables. "From all sides, the ground is described, local history is fashioned," declared the organizing committee. Though circumspect about the congress's overabundant program, the popular *L'Illustration* publicized this "image of science" throughout France. Courtesy of the General Research Division, The New York Public Library, Astor, Lenox, and Tilden Foundations.

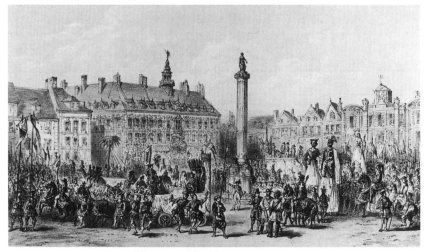

FIGURE 4. "Les fastes de Lille—Kermesse. 20 juin 1852" (1852?). Lithograph of Lille's 1852 historical pageant, an eight-float procession that began with the seventh century and ended with the contemporary era. Courtesy of the Musée de l'Hospice Comtesse (Lille).

alds, forty drums and trumpets, and twenty-nine standard-bearers (see figures 4 and 5).[54] Outside the Nord, cities re-created different events, from Nantes's medieval tournament to the count of Toulouse's departure for the Holy Land in 1098. The result was a "historical representation," a near-veridical spectacle that would (re)introduce spectators and actors to their past.[55]

These pageants surfaced in approximately twenty localities in the Nord between 1825 and 1865. At least thirteen were staged between 1825 and 1829, forty under the July Monarchy, thirteen under the Second Republic, and twenty-five under the Second Empire. Near annual in some towns, episodic elsewhere, they mobilized hundreds of participants and ranged from elaborate, multiple-float festivities to the modest cart procession of Préseau (pop. 1,709).[56] Historical pageants took place in the afternoon or evening—most usually after Mardi-Gras, at the *mi-Carême* (third Thursday

54. *Musée des familles* 1 (1834): 273–80; Albertine Clément née Hémery, *Histoire des fêtes civiles et religieuses, des usages anciens et modernes du département du Nord*, 2nd ed. (Cambrai, 1836), 155–58 and 288; and Pierre Briffaut, *La fête communale de Cambrai* (Cambrai, 1982).

55. *Tournoi et fête équestre de 1850. Notice historique sur la cérémonie du mariage du roi Louis XII et de la reine Anne* (Nantes, n.d. [1850]); *Programme officiel et détaillé des fêtes de charité données à Toulouse les 26, 27, 28, 29, 30 mai 1866*... (Toulouse, 1866); and *Revue cambrésienne* 1 (1835–36): 165.

56. Indicative rather than exhaustive, these numbers are based upon the data I gathered in municipal and departmental archives as well as extant newspapers, periodicals, pageant pro-

FIGURE 5. Lithograph of Douai's 1849 historical pageant: "The Glory of Philip the Good, Count of Flanders." Figures 4 and 5 depict two festive avenues toward the local past: the historical narrative (Lille) and the reenacted Renaissance entry (Douai). This difference aside, both lithographs convey pomp and magnitude. Lille's wicker giants symbolized the urban community since the late fourteenth century. In Douai, the *Gayant* family of giants joined the pageant in 1861. Courtesy of the Bibliothèque Municipale de Douai.

of Lent), around the 15th of August, during the *fête communale*, or on an important date in local history. Municipal commissions or benevolent societies such as the *sociétés de bienfaisance* of Cambrai (f. 1833) and Douai (1838) staged these events. Their emergence in the Nord is unsurprising given its ancient festive traditions and enduring "love of public fêtes." The latter had long dominated the region's cultural repertoire and local residents exploited them more readily than elsewhere. This festive profusion persisted in the nineteenth century, with its processions, carnivals, patronal *fêtes*, and pilgrimages. The historical pageant, in fact, incorporated elements from preexisting festive genres. Prominent among them was the urban parade of constituted bodies, with its civic pride, historical continuity, and show of social unity. The pageant also inherited the religious procession's solemnity and moral tenor as well as the carnival's disguises and twenty-five-feet-high wicker giants. Like the urban entry of Renaissance princes, finally, it represented the city not only to itself, but to ex-

grams, and firsthand accounts. This discussion focuses on the pageants of middling cities and the prefectoral seat, Lille.

ternal gazes as well: those of the ruler and the capital, of neighboring cities and visitors.[57]

Such filiations ought not to obfuscate the novelty of this street spectacle. Historical elements had long figured in urban pageantry, most notably in Renaissance carousels, but within pastoral scenes or alongside mythology, miracles, and allegorical figures (Justice, Strength). These pageants, in contrast, revived "the old usages and ancient glories of the native land." Archival research and self-conscious invention produced an interplay of historical authenticity and artifice, of proximity and distance that organizers duly exploited.[58]

A similar enthusiasm emanated from governmental circles. Le Glay's own devotion to local memories owed much, in fact, to the state. As departmental archivist, he sent his Parisian superiors reports on provincial depots and local monographs that warranted, or not, ministerial subscriptions. As a learned provincial, he likewise answered the Ministry of the Interior's requests for inventories and descriptions of local monuments. Breaking with preceding regimes, the July Monarchy devoted a budgetary chapter to monumental preservation, appointed an inspector general of monuments, and created a Commission des monuments historiques (1838) to protect noteworthy structures and oversee restorations. More significantly, Le Glay was the second of twenty-six men who, between 1833 and 1868, held the title of CTH correspondent in the Nord. Close to 1,250 provincials were CTH correspondents or nonresident members at some point in the century.[59] As such, Le Glay forwarded documents and annual reports on local historical investigations and encouraged mayors to commission archival inventories. He also participated in the CTH's collective ventures, from the monumental inventory of France (late 1830s) to the topographical map of ancient Gaul (1858).[60]

No governmental institution hence played a more important role in this story than the CTH, established by Guizot in July 1834. This agency signals the emergence of what I will call a new intellectual state: a state that, beginning under the July Monarchy, deemed it its mission to oversee

57. Guilbert and Edward Le Glay, "Résumé" of the chapter on Flanders, in Guilbert, *Histoire des villes*, 3: 306–7; Marie-France Gueusquin, *Cités en fête* (Paris, 1992), esp. 68 and 74–75; Henri Platelle et al., *Les pays du Nord: Nord, Pas-de-Calais* (Paris, 1986), 110; and Jacques Le Goff, ed., *Histoire de la France urbaine*, 5 vols. (Paris, 1980–85), 2:592–93.

58. Roy C. Strong, *Art and Power: Renaissance Festivals, 1450–1650* (Berkeley, 1984); and *Gazette de Cambrai*, 5 August 1850.

59. I derive this estimate from Marie-Elisabeth Antoine and Suzanne Olivier, *Inventaire des papiers de la division des sciences et lettres du ministère de l'instruction publique et des services qui en sont issus (sous-série F17)*, 2 vols. (Paris, 1975–81), 2:531–76. See also AN F17 2898: Le Glay, report on Lucien de Rosny, *Des nobles rois de l'épinette*, 16 October 1836.

60. Many of Le Glay's contributions can be found in the dossier under his name in AN F17 2865. See also, for instance, *Annuaire statistique du département du Nord* 12 (1840): 11.

the "intellectual activity" of French elites. A "durable institution in honor of the origins, memories and glory of France," the CTH formed an unprecedented center of governmental direction, verification, and dissemination of national and local memories.[61] Nineteenth-century officials linked their ventures to Jacob-Nicolas Moreau's Cabinet des chartes (f. 1762). By supplying ammunition against aggrieved magistrates and aristocrats who deemed the regime arbitrary, this royal depository of historical documents had sought to bolster the monarchy's historical legitimacy before public opinion. In 1765, *Contrôleur général des finances* Henri-Léonard Bertin asked the intendants to identify specialists of history and public law in their provinces and to push local "men of letters and savants" toward "useful discoveries."[62] While the Old Regime monarchy incorporated historical erudition into its administrative apparatus and launched broad *enquêtes* on the national territory and resources, it did not create—as did the July Monarchy—a "vast framework of investigation . . . in all parts of France," with a central agency, uniform programs of local research, and thousands of provincial operatives.[63] Neither did the regimes that succeeded one another before 1830. Convinced that order and prosperity entailed scientific and literary vitality, the Empire and Restoration did encourage prefects to create learned societies, appoint correspondents to oversee monuments, and invite provincial elites to study local history or inventory antiquities. These sporadic—and essentially statistical—invitations never coalesced into a concerted program, however. The Restoration, for one, celebrated above all those medieval *bonnes villes* that had sworn allegiance to the crown and would presumably remain loyal.[64] Agriculture was "a state's sturdiest support," moreover, and both regimes sought accordingly to create a "system of agricultural societies"—with their traditionalist, land-owning *masses de granit*. Recognizing, in contrast, the social and political value of professional elites as well as landowners, the July Monarchy devised new means of seducing these men.[65]

61. Guizot, *Mémoires pour servir à l'histoire de mon temps*, 8 vols. (Paris, 1858–67), 1: 51.

62. Moreau had proposed a permanent "literary bureau," under royal patronage, in the mid-1760s, but Bertin scuttled these plans. A less formal Comité des chartes met between 1780 and 1784. See Dieter Gembicki, *Histoire et politique à la fin de l'Ancien Régime: Jacob-Nicolas Moreau, 1717–1803* (Paris, 1979), esp. 90–169; Barret-Kriegel, *Historiens*, 1:330–31, and 4: part I; and Baker, "Controlling French History: The Ideological Arsenal of Jacob-Nicolas Moreau," *Inventing the French Revolution*, 77–82.

63. "Chronique de la quinzaine," *RDM*, 4th ser., 15 (July–September 1838): 427.

64. The only large-scale ventures were the all-encompassing departmental *statistiques* that the Ministry of the Interior asked prefects to write under the First Empire. See ADN 1 T 246/2: Min. Int. to prefects, 26 January 1818; Marie-Noëlle Bourguet, *Déchiffrer la France: la statistique départementale à l'époque napoléonienne* (Paris, 1988); and Michel François, "Les bonnes villes," *Compte-rendus de l'Académie des Inscriptions et Belles-lettres* (November–December 1975): 551–60.

65. See Rozoir, *Relation historique*, 60; ADN M 508/1: Min. Int. to prefects, circulars of 14 August and 27 December 1819; and BML, Fonds Humbert XLII/274: Prefect Augustin Laurent de Rémusat, "Sociétés d'agriculture" (n.d. [between 1817 and 1822]).

The CTH came under the supervision of the Ministry of Public Instruction's Bureau des travaux historiques (BTH).[66] Its initial mission was to comb archives and libraries in search of original documents "such as manuscripts, charters, diplomas, chronicles, memoirs, correspondence, even works of philosophy, literature, or art, as long as they reveal a hidden side of the mores and social condition of an epoch in our history." The CTH published collections of historical documents (seventy-eight by 1881) and took steps to protect monuments—all of them mirrors and products of the national spirit. Meeting twice a month, its members examined the documents and reports of provincial correspondents, evaluated nongovernmental propositions for historical publications, edited periodicals (such as the *Revue des sociétés savantes*), and increasingly oversaw scholarly investigations in the provinces.[67]

The CTH would thus furnish the nation with the raw materials of its past and contribute to this vast social history of France that Guizot and Thierry were articulating in their own writings. In creating this agency, Guizot sought to conjugate governmental action with his long-standing devotion to history. His historical activities under the Empire and Restoration are well known: courses at the Sorbonne, pamphlets, articles, monographs, translations, and documentary collections. These activities evince, as Dominique Poulot has shown, a deep-seated resolve to furnish postrevolutionary society with exemplary models and produce an enduring moral repository. "Warm respect for the memory of past generations," Guizot explained in 1838, yielded morality, strength, stability, and progress. According to Guizot's philosophy of history, monuments and archival collections also summarized civilization—the progress of humanity, the growth of freedom and the nation-state, the rise of the bourgeoisie—and displayed a hidden unity. History would bolster the current social order by exemplifying the progress of "reason," the social forces and needs that now expressed themselves through an elite of talents.[68]

66. The CTH's original name was Comité des documents inédits de l'histoire de France. The BTH was one of three bureaus in the ministry's division of scientific and literary instititutions. The other two covered learned societies, libraries, as well as literary subscriptions and "encouragement." Since their responsibilities often overlapped, I include all three in my analysis. See Antoine, "Un service pionnier au XIXe siècle: le Bureau des travaux historiques," *Bulletin de la section d'histoire moderne et comtemporaine du CTH* 10 (1977): 11–37.

67. Guizot to Louis-Philippe, reports of 31 December 1833 and 27 November 1834, in Charmes, 6, 14, and 16; and AN F17 17130: "Tableaux présentant les modifications apportées à la dénomination du 'Comité des Travaux Historiques' de 1834–1885," n. d. [1885]. On the CTH, see Laurent Theis, "Guizot et les institutions de mémoire," in Nora, *Lieux de mémoire*, 3: 568–92; Robert-Henri Bautier, "Le Comité des travaux historiques et scientifiques: passé et présent," *Actes du 115e congrès national des sociétés savantes* (Paris, 1991), 2:381–96; and Rodolphe Leroy, "Le Comité des travaux historiques (1834–1914): entre animation et contrôle du mouvement scientifique en France" (D.E.A. thesis, Ecole Nationale des Chartes, 2001). This thesis became accessible too late for use in this book.

68. Dominique Poulot, "The Birth of Heritage: 'Le Moment Guizot,'" *Oxford Art Journal* 11, no. 2 (1988): 41–42; Furet, "Transformations in the Historiography of the Revolution," in Fer-

The July Monarchy furthermore lacked legitimacy, since its birth involved neither election nor a filiation with an "august race" of monarchs. The CTH would accordingly depict the regime as the culmination of a long historical evolution. It would root it in tradition rather than ratiocination and circumvent its recent, revolutionary origins.[69]

The CTH underwent a clear evolution: an early phase of blueprints, uneven action, and concern with collection (1834–36); a middle phase that, despite some lulls, witnessed growth, a surge of publications, and bureaucratic consolidation (1837–62); and a late phase during which, as will be seen, new scientific and political imperatives challenged earlier convictions and procedures (1862–80s). As table 1 shows, successive ministers put their stamp on the agency. Narcisse de Salvandy instituted a Comité historique des arts et monuments (CHAM)—to inventory all French monuments—and a firmer framework that mirrored the Institut de France's five academies. Victor Cousin simplified the scheme in 1840, but little changed until 1852, when Minister Hippolyte Fortoul directed the CTH toward philology rather than history alone. Whereas the July Monarchy had devoted considerable energy to collecting, classifying, and publishing documents on medieval communes, the early Second Empire broadened its historical and territorial purview. In 1858, Fortouls's successor, Gustave Rouland, returned history and archaeology to their dominant positions and created a scientific section: "There, too, there is . . . much to excavate in the past."[70] While the CTH's investigations ranged from cartularies to Lavoisier's memoirs, they respected the founding injunction to illuminate "our national history." More pertinently, this national history included—and even highlighted— "the patriotic traditions and most generous memories of the local spirit."[71] The French state thus became an outlet of local memories.

THE PATRIMONIAL FIELD, 2: AN ANALYTICAL TABLEAU

The journey described above provides not only a roadmap to this patrimonial field but synthetic conclusions as well. Le Glay's career mirrors a broader pattern: early initiatives in the 1820s, a peak on the eve and morrow of the 1830 Revolution, a slowdown in the early 1840s, and a second

---

enc Féher, ed., *The French Revolution and the Birth of Modernity* (Berkeley, 1990), 264–65; and *Discours prononcé par M. Guizot, directeur de la Société des Antiquaires de Normandie, ancien ministre de l'Instruction publique, dans la séance du 27 août 1838* (Caen, 1840), 7.

69. Bishop of Hermopolis to rectors, circular of 14 April 1825, in *Circulaires et instructions officielles relatives à l'instruction publique*, 12 vols. (Paris, 1863–1900), 1:469; Narcisse de Salvandy to Louis-Philippe, report of 15 April 1847, in Charmes, 128; and Theis, "Guizot et les institutions de mémoire," 578–79.

70. AN F17 3042: Anon. memorandum to Min. Pub. Instr., n.d. [1861]; and Gustave Rouland, speech of 25 November 1861, *RSS*, 2d ser., 6 (2d sem. 1861): 442.

71. Salvandy to presidents of learned societies, circular of 28 July 1845, in Charmes, 105.

TABLE 1. Organization of the Comité des Travaux Historiques.

1834 François Guizot	Committee for the Investigation and Publication of Original Monuments Pertaining to the History of France
1835 François Guizot	1. Committee on Political and Civil History 2. Committee on the History of Literature, Philosophy, Science, and Arts
1837 Narcisse de Salvandy	1. Committee on French Language and Literature 2. Committee on Positive History, or Chronicles, Charters, and Inscriptions 3. Committee on Sciences 4. Historical Committee on Art and Monuments 5. Committee on Moral and Political Sciences
1840 Victor Cousin	1. Committee for the Publication of the Written Monuments of the History of France 2. Historical Committee on Art and Monuments
1852 Hippolyte Fortoul	Committee on French Language, History, and Art
1858 Gustave Rouland	Committee on Historical Investigations and Learned Societies 1. Section of History and Philology 2. Section of Archaeology 3. Section of Science

peak between 1847 and the early 1850s. Political ferment clearly spurred interest in local memories during times of liberalization and contestation. Conservative tendencies did so as well, albeit for different reasons, in the wake of revolutions. Indeed, the insurrections of 1848 and the authoritarian turn of 1851 made this field increasingly conservative. Whereas liberals and radicals had cultivated local memories for diverse political reasons under the July Monarchy, they now perceived them first and foremost as conduits toward local harmony and social order—a "sad" refuge, noted one contemporary, from present-day "uncertainties" and "apprehensions."[72] With more explicitly political priorities before them (including explicit calls for decentralization and municipal governance), republicans grew scarce within this field. Legitimists now searched with renewed ardor

72. Jean Le Pottier, "Histoire et érudition: recherches et documents sur l'histoire et le rôle de l'érudition médiévale dans l'historiographie française du XIXe siècle" (Thesis, Ecole Nationale des Chartes, 1979), 134–36; and Louandre, "Les études historiques et archéologiques en province depuis 1848. I. La Flandre, l'Artois, la Picardie et les provinces de l'Est," *RDM*, new period, 11 (July–Sept. 1851): 922.

for means of social stability and political recovery. The mid-1850s witnessed a second slowdown, linked in part to a Catholic revival that some found more promising. A third peak, between 1857 and 1865, reflected renewed demands for decentralization, the rise of positive history, and new governmental priorities. The early 1830s were clearly pivotal, however. It was then, for reasons that will become clear, that local memories acquired a visible and durable material existence.

In geographical terms, the patrimonial field encompassed the entire *province* save for sparsely populated departments such as the Ardèche. Scientific and archaeological congresses, for instance, took place throughout the country (see figure 6). At the same time, Le Glay's tireless activity embodies the particular vigor of certain regions. Besides the Nord, these include the Pas-de-Calais and Somme, Normandy, Brittany and the center-West, ancient Gascony, the *pays toulousain*, Savoie, Franche-Comté, and Champagne. The wealthier, more literate North was more prolific than the South. Political factors also came into play, for ancient provincial capitals such as Caen and Poitiers proved especially active in this domain. So did, on the whole, peripheral regions.[73] Equally important were a region's degree of urbanization, its cultural and religious infrastructure, and the richness of its past. In the Nord, urban elites witnessed rapid socioeconomic change and sought new means of influence on what, by the early 1830s, they called the "industrial class" (see chapter 3). These aspirations converged on the patrimonial realm—an unsurprising confluence given the department's rich network of libraries, archives, learned societies, periodicals, and pageants. The towns of the Nord furthermore looked back on glorious pasts. The cult of local memories was hence less about outright invention than reactivation. It required a reservoir of historical events, traditions, and customs—ready to be tapped. Conceding as much, the "new" town of Rochefort-sur-Mer (Charente Maritime) staged an episode from Louis XIV's reign in 1862 because it could not "evoke distant memories as in Flanders."[74]

Beyond these variations in time and space, Le Glay's activities reveal a broad gamut of patrimonial practices. The prevalent association of local memories with artifacts—from monuments to documents—produced a first set: identification (trips across the countryside, forays into archival

73. Thierry Gasnier, "Le local: une et indivisible," in Nora, *Lieux de mémoire*, 6: 480; Carbonell, *Histoire et historiens*, 79 and 86–87; and Gonzague Tierny, *Les sociétés savantes du département de la Somme de 1870 à 1914* (Paris, 1987).

74. *L'Illustration* 20, no. 1021 (20 September 1862): 197; and Pierre-Yves Saunier, "La ville comme antidote? ou à la rencontre du troisième type (d'identité régionale)," in Haupt, Müller, and Woolf, eds., *Regional and National Identities*, 143–44. In the Nord, this cult of local memories thus owed much more to urban pride than it did to the department's linguistic diversity. Most pageants in fact took place in its southern, French-speaking half.

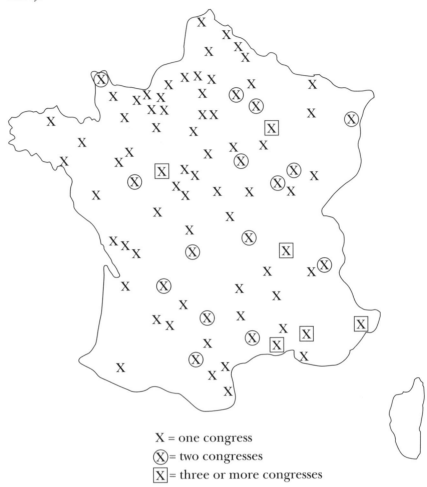

X = one congress

Ⓧ = two congresses

☒ = three or more congresses

FIGURE 6. Scientific and archaeological congresses in France, 1833–1878.

depots or churches), description, preservation (circulars against vandalism), classification, and sometimes, display. The thousands of documents that the CTH collected in Paris were not only about the nation's history, but part of its essence. Provincial elites likewise collected artifacts "relating to the *pays*" as "utterly local monument[s]" for posterity. This yielded compendia (including local bibliographies and patois compilations) as well as permanent institutions, such as libraries and museums. The Société dunkerquoise's library included eight thousand newspapers and periodicals and 1,384 books and manuscripts—nearly all pertaining to local history—in 1854.[75] Local museums saw their number rise from about fifteen in 1800 to thirty in 1815 to nearly six hundred at the end of the century. By 1807, the Ministry of the Interior had placed all "district" museums under the authority of the municipalities, entrusting their success or demise to local elites. The latter typically responded by establishing heteroclite museums that amalgamated local history and natural history. With its historical paintings alongside elephant teeth found in the locality, Cassel's museum (f. 1837) encapsulated the genre.[76]

Contemporaries not only retrieved local memories but also produced textual, spectacular, and plastic representations that would inspire affection for the *pays*. I have already introduced the first two. Plastic representations are best apprehended via the era's fascination for local *illustrations* (celebrities)—the "illustrious men of the *pays*," themselves historical monuments per Chateaubriand. This local "statuomania" surfaced in the 1820s and reached its peak under the July Monarchy. In 1826, Le Glay penned a brochure on Fénelon to accompany the city's monument to the prelate. In 1844, Lille inaugurated a new *hôtel des archives* whose frontispiece—busts of local figures—constituted a monument "in praise of the [*pays*'] eminent celebrities."[77] The Société d'agriculture, sciences et arts de l'arrondissement de Valenciennes sponsored a monument to medieval chronicler Jean Froissart and created, in 1846, a Galerie historique des notabilités, or Galerie valenciennoise. Through portraits, historical paintings, busts, and photographs, this "gallery of local history" showcased fifty local-born celebrities—rulers, administrators, and above all artists and writers. This was not a collection of artifacts, but a local panorama, or shrine, that "perpetuate[d] the memories of the *pays*'s ancient celebrities."[78] The Galerie valenciennoise was also a social space, involving encounters between artists and the public. As such, it reveals a final set of

75. *RAN* 21, no. 10 (October 1867): 361; *Société dunkerquoise pour l'encouragement des sciences, des lettres et des arts. Installation du bureau pour 1854* (Dunkirk, n.d. [1854?]), 5; and *MSDu* 2 (1855): 22. See also Frédéric Barbier, "Les bibliothèques des sociétés savantes," in *Histoire des bibliothèques françaises*, 3 vols. (Paris, 1989–91), 3:455–59.

76. Chantal Georgel, ed., *La jeunesse des musées: les musées de France au XIXe siècle* (Paris, 1994), esp. 35 and 356; Paulette Girodin, "Le musée en France depuis 1815: territoires et fonctions," *Historiens et géographes* 346 (December 1994): 64–65; Poulot, *Musée nation patrimoine 1789–1815* (Paris, 1997), 254–60; and ADN 1 T 241/3: Subprefect Hazebrouck to prefect Nord, 8 November 1838.

77. *Bulletin de la Société des sciences historiques et naturelles de l'Yonne* 1 (1847): 17; Le Glay, *Notice sur le monument élevé à Fénelon, dans l'église cathédrale de Cambrai, etc.* (Cambrai?, 1826); *Département du Nord. Inauguration du nouvel hôtel des archives* (Lille, 1845), 7; and Maurice Agulhon, "La 'statuomanie' et l'histoire," in his *Histoire vagabonde*, 3 vols. (Paris, 1988), 1:137–85.

78. *MSV* 7 (1846): 16–17; *Le Courrier du Nord*, 23 August 1851; *Galerie historique valenciennoise. Catalogue* (Valenciennes, 1858); *RAN* 3, no. 2 (August 1851): 57; and Jean-Claude Poinsignon, "Famille éclatée recherche galerie d'ancêtres. Intérêt des collections artistiques de la Société d'agriculture, sciences et arts de Valenciennes," *Valentiana* 13 (June 1994): 66–68.

practices: elocutionary performances, encounters, discussions, and other "social technologies," as Daniel Roche calls them. Scholarly congresses, the public meetings of learned societies, and public lectures (such as Le Glay's course on local history) all fostered interpersonal communication.[79]

The patrimonial field's novelty hence resided in its multifaceted efforts to preserve (artifacts and "traditions"), to constitute (repositories and representations), to reconstitute (faded sentiments), and to disseminate (affection for the *pays* and its past). What audience, then, did it reach? Print runs and sales figures for monographs, congress proceedings, and periodicals were low. They ranged from fifty copies for Le Glay's *Mélanges historiques et littéraires* (1834) to eight hundred for scientific congress proceedings. The CTH distributed between 475 and 1,000 copies of its publications (to its members, correspondents, cultural institutions, and officials).[80] Rarely did a monograph reach a thousand copies. Such was the nature of nineteenth-century scholarly publishing, with its small print runs and traditional techniques of production. This being said, circles, libraries, and learned societies subscribed to such publications and, hence, broadened their audience. More significantly yet, Parisian journalists noted the "great popularity" of Guilbert's *Histoire des villes* and comparable works. They also reported on the CTH, scholarly congresses, and the public meetings of learned societies. Up to five hundred spectators attended the latter; between 180 and 1,100 people participated each year in scientific congresses.[81] This patrimonial field did not go unnoticed—in more ways than one. Some critics mocked archaeology as narrow, learned societies as anemic, and scholarly congresses as "refuges for mediocrities." Le Glay accordingly defended "all of us archaeologists" in the late 1840s, unaware perhaps that such derision both reflected and reinforced this field's visibility.[82]

Much as literacy expanded during these years (especially in Paris),

79. Roche, *France des Lumières*, 516; and BML, fonds Mahieu B/3: Le Glay, *Discours d'introduction aux conférences sur l'histoire du Nord de la France prononcé en séance générale, le 28 mars 1838* (Lille, n.d. [1838?]).

80. Frontispiece to Le Glay, *Mélanges historiques et littéraires* (Cambrai, 1834); *CS* 28, 5 vols. (Bordeaux, 1862), 1: 457; and ASD 1857–59: Commercial agreement between the Société dunkerquoise and publisher Benjamin Kien, 19 March 1858. On the print runs of the CTH's publications, see AN F17 3319. See also Tierny, *Sociétés savantes*, 86–87.

81. Barbier, "L'édition historique et philologique en France au XIXe siècle," in *Gelehrte Bücher von Humanismus bis zur Gegenwart* (Wiesbaden, 1983), 162; *L'Illustration* 7, no. 162 (4 April 1846): 78; ASD 1853–54: List of invitees to the Société dunkerquoise's 1853 public meeting; *AIP* (1846): 72–73; and *CS* 14 (Marseilles, 1846), 2 vols., 1:5.

82. *Le Charivari*, 9 September 1842; *Le Foyer d'Orléans*, 7 July 1844; Etienne Maurice, *Décentralisation et décentralisateurs* (Paris, 1859), 31; *L'Echo de France (des provinces)* 1, no. 50 (31 December 1865): 2; and *BCN* 3 (1847–49): 181.

these publications and meetings reached a literate class, with considerable leisure time and disposable income. Close to 90 percent of subscribers to local historical monographs defined themselves as members of the legal profession, civil servants, property owners, and the like.[83] The guest book of Jacques Boucher de Perthes's antiquities museum, located in Abbeville, yields similar conclusions for the years 1859–99.[84] Some elites sought, however, to reach a popular audience—notably through historical pageants. Seventy thousand spectators in Douai in 1839, sixty-three thousand from out-of-town in Rouen in the late 1850s, one hundred thousand in Valenciennes in 1866: contemporary estimates are imposing.[85] These pageants attracted local denizens, distant visitors, as well as residents from the surrounding countryside, some of whom had traveled overnight.[86] Ephemeral by nature, they acquired permanence through lithographs that, like this field's paintings or statues, could bypass the written word (see figures 4 and 5). Provincials moreover encountered few cultural alternatives. Theatrical companies were rare, artistic museums "not yet truly established," newspapers often filled with Parisian copy, and traveling fairs and circuses scarce until the second half of the century.[87] Pageants exposed hundreds of thousands of people to the moral and political ideals of local elites—as well as historical events and a territorial referent (the *pays*) of local and national importance. This did not, of course, guarantee approbation. As with other public ceremonies, spectators attended such festivals with diverse motivations (ludic, familial, political) and degrees of attention. Le Glay judged the "*peuple* eager for spectacles and enthralled by ancient memories." Perhaps. After all, a Lille textile worker turned cabaret manager penned pa-

83. The other 10 percent consisted above all of schoolteachers, bailiffs, and solicitors. The same was true of cultural periodicals. I make this claim on the basis of subscription lists in *AHN*, 1st ser., 1 (1829): 4–12; Isidore Lebeau, *Précis de l'histoire d'Avesnes* (Avesnes, 1836), 1–6; E. de Laplane, *Essai sur l'histoire municipale de la ville de Sisteron* (Paris, 1840), 257–63; Z. Piérart, *Recherches historiques sur Maubeuge, son canton et les communes limitrophes* (Maubeuge, 1851), n.p.; as well as Delloye 27/134: "Liste des souscriptions faites au 1er janvier 1845" for Clément, *Histoire des fêtes*. See also James Smith Allen, *Popular French Romanticism: Authors, Readers, and Books in the 19th Century* (Syracuse, 1981), 161–69.

84. Roughly one third of the signatories identified their profession (all of them men). Secondary teachers, lawyers, magistrates, officers, and clergymen were most prevalent—alongside employees and petty civil servants. The relationship between professed and true profession remains obscure. So do the motivations (including shame, perhaps) that led others to keep silent about their professions. Located in Abbeville's municipal library (ms. 324), this guest book deserves closer study.

85. AMD 5 D 38: Mayor to subprefect Douai, 14 October 1839; Charles de Pelleport, *Historique des fêtes bordelaises* (Bordeaux, 1858), 13; and ADN M 161/21: Prefect Nord to Min. Int., 22 June 1866.

86. Louis Legougeux, *Souvenirs lillois. Relation des fêtes qui furent célébrées à Lille les 12, 13, 14 et 15 juin 1825, à l'occasion du sacre de S. M. le roi Charles X . . .* (Lille, 1902), 25.

87. *MSD* 1st ser., 9 (1839–40): 15.

tois songs on the city's pageants.[88] But Cambrai's 1851 pageant elicited some catcalls, a desecrated plaster fountain, and a caustic pamphlet by a petty civil servant.[89] While these formal, didactic processions presumably repelled others as well, traces of public scorn are elusive. Further considerations on this field's impact on French workers or peasants—be it their territorial identities or political consciousness—would accordingly amount to conjecture.

As for the individuals who shaped this field, they formed a select group in their numbers alone (a few thousand over our period). More numerous than in preceding centuries, these intellectual elites still constituted a minute fraction of the population.[90] In the Nord, a core of twenty-five to thirty men proved ubiquitous in this field. Like Le Glay, they cultivated local memories in numerous sites, held most positions of power, and maintained close relations with one another—notably, through favorable book reviews and comparable favors.[91] This was, furthermore, an overwhelmingly male group. In the Nord, women directed neither periodicals nor archaeological commissions nor festive or learned societies. While a few contributed articles or joined learned societies, the vast majority was relegated to the role of observer and spectator: within pageant audiences, in theater boxes during public meetings, as readers and visitors to museums and galleries. Tours's scientific congress opened before "a rather elegant feminine gathering," reported *L'Illustration* in 1847 (see figures 3 and 7).[92] If pageant organizers invited women to parade as historical figures or allegories of their city, it was for reasons of historical authenticity, for their "charm" and "elegance," and because, as in the American parades studied by Mary Ryan, these nonvoting participants embodied local harmony.[93] Women could attend the opening and closing sessions of scholarly congresses, but not their private meetings and "evenings among men." There is no evidence that any presented papers at the scientific

88. Le Glay, *Notice sur les principales fêtes et cérémonies publiques qui ont eu lieu à Cambrai depuis le XIe siècle jusqu'à nos jours*, 2d ed. (Cambrai, n.d. [1827]), 5; and Charles Decottignies, *Les fastes de Lille. Faits historiques racontés en chanson patoise* (Lille, 1863).

89. Delloye 40/67: [Lardeur], "Supplément au Programme de la fête communale de Cambrai du 15 août 1851. Omission signalée dans le programme de la marche triomphale," undated pamphlet [1851]; *La Gazette de Cambrai*, 13 and 20 August 1851; and *L'Echo de la frontière*, 29 August 1851. See also the reflections in Avner Ben-Amos, *Funerals, Politics, and Memory*, 331 and 334.

90. Contemporaries used the expression "intellectual elite": for instance, AN F17 3090/1: Bourneville to Min. Pub. Instr., 30 August 1845. In this book, it will refer to patrimonial activity rather than profession (full-time journalist) or political engagement à la Zola.

91. BNF ms. NAF 24209: Le Glay to Arthur Dinaux, 30 July 1843. Catherine Pellissier arrives at a similar conclusion regarding cultural associations in Lyons: *Loisirs et sociabilités des notables lyonnais au XIXe siècle*, 2 vols. (Lyons, 1996), 1:13.

92. *L'Illustration* 10, no. 240 (2 October 1847): 67.

93. Jean-Yves Guiomar, *Le bretonisme: les historiens bretons au XIXe siècle* (Mayenne, 1987), 341; and Mary Ryan, "The American Parade: Representations of the Nineteenth-Century Social Order," in Lynn Hunt, ed., *The New Cultural History* (Berkeley, 1989), 149–50.

FIGURE 7. Public meeting of the Société impériale des sciences, de l'agriculture et des arts de Lille, depicted in *L'Illustration*, 4 January 1862. Courtesy of the General Research Division, The New York Public Library, Astor, Lenox, and Tilden Foundations.

congresses or Institut des provinces. Some provincialist periodicals alone involved a sizable number of women: twenty-one out of sixty-one contributors to the *Panthéon de la Jeune France* (1841–44), for instance. *France départementale* vowed to showcase the "productions of women that can have such a beneficial influence on provincial emancipation." Yet, the publishers and editors were invariably men who, in some cases, addressed potential contributors as "*Messieurs* the writers of the *province.*" In 1835, *La Revue des provinces* greeted the Société académique de Falaise's decision to admit women as full members with a scathing editorial entitled "Insurrection of women."[94]

This evidence buttresses the view that, by strictly defining the roles and attributes of men and women, the numerous voluntary associations that emerged in nineteenth-century Europe helped demarcate a public and largely male sphere from a largely private, or domestic, female one. These spheres were not impermeable. Some women found ways to politicize this

94. *France départementale* 1 (1834): 137–38; *Album des provinces* 1 (1829): 19; and *La Revue des provinces* 8 (15 February 1835): 253.

private sphere to their advantage; others, like the German women studied by Nancy Reagin, may have expressed territorial identity through "domestic rituals, objects, and practices" they associated with *pays* or nation.[95] Yet, within the field of local memories, men seized local knowledge to speak in their community's name and delineate its past (and, hence, present). Women, of course, acted on the historical field in other capacities: as subscribers and customers, as authors of biographies and historical fiction, or in informal discussions. Bonnie Smith has argued that they were present *en masse* in the nineteenth-century historical field. Barred from full citizenship, numerous professions, and learned institutions, these "amateurs" produced a more cultural and vibrant historical output for the marketplace.[96] Smith evokes, among others, Albertine Clément-Hémery, a writer and educator from Cambrai who had penned feminist pamphlets and edited the *Journal des dames et des modes* under the Directory and Consulate. Indeed, Clément-Hémery's works on local history, celebrities, and geography earned prizes from learned societies in Cambrai, Arras, and elsewhere under the July Monarchy. She joined several societies as a corresponding member and secured an annual allowance from the Ministry of Public Instruction in 1831.[97] One could likewise consider Fanny Dénoix des Vergnes: local historian, contributor to *Flandre illustrée*, member of several learned societies, member also of the 1853 scientific congress—to which she offered a poem, "To the City of Arras." Yet, she and Clément were exceptions. Dénoix des Vergnes was one of three female members of that congress—alongside 421 men. Women published less than 2 percent of historical monographs between 1866 and 1875, for instance.[98] Their subordinate role in this patrimonial field suggests that they struggled to impose themselves within an amateurish realm that participated in a broader program of political exclusion.

This intellectual elite was also one in its socioprofessional composition

95. Leonore Davidoff and Catherine Hall, *Family Fortunes: Men and Women of the English Middle Class, 1780–1850* (Chicago, 1991), chap. 10; Carol E. Harrison, *The Bourgeois Citizen in Nineteenth-Century France: Gender, Sociability, and the Uses of Emulation* (Oxford, 1999); and Nancy Reagin, "The Imagined *Hausfrau*: National Identity, Domesticity, and Colonialism in Imperial Germany," *The Journal of Modern History* 73, no. 1 (March 2001): 54–86, citation on 85–86.

96. Bonnie Smith, *The Gender of History: Men, Women, and Historical Practice* (Cambridge, Mass., 1998). Rosemary Mitchell builds on this argument in her *Picturing the Past: English History in Text and Image, 1830–1870* (Oxford, 2000), chap. 6.

97. Clément-Hémery, *Notice sur les communautés de femmes établies à Cambrai avant la révolution* (Cambrai, 1826); "Extrait de la Biographie des hommes célèbres du département du Pas-de-Calais, par Madame Clément-Hémery," *Mémoires de l'Académie d'Arras, Société royale des sciences, des lettres et des arts* 18 (1838): 54–178; and AN F17 3135: Dossier on Clément-Hémery's ministerial allowances. On Clément-Hémery, see also Annemarie Kleinert, *Le "Journal des dames et des modes," ou la conquête de l'Europe féminine (1797–1839)* (Stuttgart, 2001), 336–37.

98. Fanny Dénoix des Vergnes, "A la ville d'Arras," in her *Coeur et patrie* (Paris, 1855), 296–98; *CS* 20, 2 vols. (Arras, 1853); and Carbonell, *Histoire et historiens*, 177.

and social organization: a network whose members spoke about universal participation while restricting full admission to the city's educated strata. The directing committees of festive societies typically contained a dozen members, learned societies an average of forty resident and two hundred correspondent members. With annual dues between fifteen and thirty francs, the latter were barely less exclusive than provincial *cercles*, those private clubs in which male elites socialized, read newspapers, and found other ways of filling their leisure time. (By comparison, a small working-class house rented for forty francs a year in 1831).[99] Elites rapidly occupied the leading positions in the Nord's festive societies—as they did throughout this field. Some came from the landed aristocracy—especially, but not solely, in the Institut des provinces, reconstituted academies, and those learned societies partial toward agriculture. There, they met *grands notables*, these local leaders who, per André-Jean Tudesq, combined political and social leadership, paid over one thousand francs in annual taxes, and became "the m[e]n of the [cultural] patrimony."[100] Nonaristocratic notables played a leading role in Clermont-Ferrand, for instance, while nobles did so in the Pas-de-Calais and Franche-Comté. Whether their titles dated to the Middles Ages, Old Regime, or early nineteenth century, Franche-Comté nobles equated their familial memories with those of a province that had conferred them dignity—and which they served so well.[101]

Yet while nobles proved active and more numerous in this field than in the general population, they did not prevail. They dominated Autun's Société éduenne des lettres, sciences et arts under the July Monarchy, but not the neighboring Académie des sciences, arts et belles-lettres de Dijon, for instance.[102] In the Nord, nobles were less preponderant than members of liberal professions (doctors, lawyers, notaries); the public service (magistrates, local functionaries, librarians, archivists, professors); an economic class of small and medium-size merchants and factory owners; and,

99. Baron de Morogues, *De la misère des ouvriers et de la marche à suivre pour y rémédier* (Paris, 1832), 62. See also Pieter M. Judson, "Frontiers, Islands, Forests, Stones: Mapping the Geography of a German identity in the Habsburg Monarchy, 1848–1900," in Patricia Yaeger, ed., *The Geography of Identity* (Ann Arbor, 1996), 392.

100. Chaline, *Sociabilité et érudition*, 122–23; André-Jean Tudesq, *Les grands notables en France (1840–1849): étude historique d'une psychologie sociale*, 2 vols. (Paris, 1964), 1: esp. 1:10, 17, and 474–78, and 2: 1232; and idem, preface to Alexis de Tocqueville, *Correspondance et écrits locaux*, ed. Lise Queffélec-Dumasy (Paris, 1995), 10.

101. Charlotte Tacke, "The Nation in the Region. National Movements in Germany and France in the 19th Century," in Justo G. Beramendi, Ramón Máiz, and Xosé M. Núñez, eds. *Nationalism in Europe: Past and Present* (Santiago de Compostela, 1994), 701; Tierny, *Sociétés savantes*, 119–24; Parsis-Barubé, *Représentations du Moyen âge*, 2:383; and Brelot, *La noblesse réinventée: nobles de Franche-Comté de 1814 à 1870*, 2 vols. (Paris, 1992), 1:80–82 and 2:871–79.

102. Pierre Lévêque, *Une société provinciale: la Bourgogne sous la monarchie de Juillet* (Paris, 1983), 377–79.

to a smaller extent, the literary arena (journalists, publishers, full-time authors). These professions furnished more than 60 percent of learned society members prior to 1871—as many as 74 percent in the Commission historique du Nord.[103] Historian Jean-Pierre Chaline has uncovered a similar "bourgeois" preponderance in learned societies throughout the provinces.[104] Scientific congresses rarely tabulated the socioprofessional origins of attendees, but when they did—in 1842, for instance—doctors and university professors were the best-represented groups (27 percent of the 1,525 delegates). Slightly more than 10 percent defined themselves as merchants and industrialists, 6.7 percent as landowners and agronomists.[105] These analytical categories tell us more, it is true, about self-representation than actual occupation and, per Simona Cerutti, mask internal contradictions by imposing a supposed communality of class interests. They nonetheless demonstrate the prevalence of an urban *bourgeoisie capacitaire*, a middling bourgeoisie of talents that subsisted on current income rather than inherited wealth. The financial travails of learned societies bear out the correspondent from Blois who wrote Salvandy in 1847 that "men from a modest background" made up "the nucleus and largest group" in learned societies. "Humble in rank and fortune," echoed a Société des antiquaires de Picardie member in a public address, "my zeal is my unique title."[106] Le Glay's father, for one, bequeathed his two sons an unremarkable 18,627 francs in capital and income. On his own death, Le Glay left his four children a respectable but still unexceptional 41,599 francs. While he and other intellectual elites sat on municipal councils or hygiene commissions, they wielded on the whole moderate economic and political power. Their authority rested upon a less tangible, yet intrinsically local, accretion of education and knowledge, profession, service, reputation, and personal relations.[107]

103. These figures include resident and corresponding members. They rest on the published lists of learned societies, an imperfect yet indicative source.

104. Chaline, *Sociabilité et érudition*, 132–34; and, for similar findings in Normandy, Guillet, *Naissance de la Normandie*, 266–67. Cf. Carbonell, *Histoire et historiens*, 241–42; and Philippe Vigier, "Diffusion d'une langue nationale et résistance des patois, en France, au XIXe siècle," *Romantisme* 25–26 (1979): 199.

105. Notables increased their presence under the Second Empire. See *CS* 10 (Strasbourg, 1843), 610.

106. Simona Cerutti, "La construction des catégories sociales," in Jean Boutier and Dominique Julia, eds., *Passés recomposés: champs et chantiers de l'histoire* (Paris, 1995), 224–34; AN F17 3026: President Société des sciences et lettres de Loir-et-Cher to Salvandy, 27 January 1847; and *Bulletin de la Société des antiquaires de Picardie* 1 (1841–43): 2.

107. ADN 3 Q 3/10: *Déclaration de mutation par décès* of Julien Leglay, 25? November 1838; and ADN 3 Q 3/25 and 318/97: *Déclarations de mutation par décès* of André Leglay, 9 and 12 November 1863. On the bourgeoisie of talents, see Jürgen Kocka, "The Middle Classes in Europe," *The Journal of Modern History* 67, no. 4 (December 1995): 783–806; and Alain Guillemin, "Aristocrates, propriétaires et diplomés: la lutte pour le pouvoir local dans le département de la Manche, 1830–1875," *Actes de la recherche en sciences sociales* 42 (April 1982): 46.

This middling bourgeoisie hence played a leading role alongside other socioprofessional groups. A final one requires mention: the clergy. After 1875—and the reform of higher education—clergymen gave religious history a formidable impetus, publishing a multitude of monastic, parish, and diocesan monographs and biographies. During the preceding decades, their contribution was more modest (despite regional variations), but notable nonetheless. Clergymen steered clear of pageants and contributed sparingly to cultural periodicals, but taught Caumont's theories, attended his archaeological and scientific congresses (9.2 percent of delegates in 1842), and joined learned societies. Their presence in the latter ranged from 2 percent of members (the Nord) to 26 percent (Franche-Comté), or more. It hovered around 6 percent in newer, multidisciplinary societies.[108] Many clergymen bemoaned the degradation of religious edifices in which, like Chateaubriand, they uncovered the "genius" of Christianity, "a kind of shiver and a vague feeling of Divinity" that subordinated pure reason to organic continuity between generations. In the late 1830s, Caumont and the CTH both urged the clergy to preach respect for the architectural and monumental patrimony. Be it in Auch, Beauvais, or Nevers, bishops and archbishops created archaeology courses, called for monumental inventories, published archaeological manuals, and founded commissions, museums, and learned societies (Embrun's Académie flosalpine [1857]).[109] The archbishop of Bordeaux asked priests to respect the religious patrimony, inventory local monuments, and send him "notes" on local history (which he then incorporated into his course on the historical archaeology of "our own *pays*").[110] His Cambrai counterpart (Pierre Giraud) cooperated with Le Glay and the Commission historique du Nord on several historical and archaeological ventures. If Giraud expressed such concern with the destruction of the religious patrimony, it was largely because pious sentiments and local community were vanishing. His pastoral letters accordingly embraced

108. In the Nord, clergymen dominated the Comité flamand alone, furnishing half of its members. See Claude Langlois, "Des études d'histoire ecclésiastique locale à la sociologie religieuse historique. Réflexions sur un siècle de production historiographique," *Revue d'histoire de l'église de France* 62, no. 169 (July–December 1976): 334–37; Carrière, *Introduction aux études*, 1:xxxvi–xliv; Gérard Cholvy, "Régionalisme et clergé catholique au XIXe siècle," in Christian Gras and Georges Livet, eds., *Régions et régionalisme en France: du XVIIIe siècle à nos jours* (Paris, 1977), 199; Den Boer, *History as a Profession*, 30; Parsis-Barubé, *Représentations du Moyen âge*, 2: 390; and Chaline, *Sociabilité et érudition*, 127–28.

109. François-René de Chateaubriand, *Génie du Christianisme* (Paris, 1838), 278; MAP 80/2/1: Caumont to Min. Int., 22 May 1838; *Bulletin du CHAM* 1, no. 1 (1840): 93; AN F17 13269: Proceedings of the CHAM, 25 April 1838, 6 and 23 December 1840, 10 March 1841, and 19 January 1842; and *Bulletin de la Société des Antiquaires de Picardie* 1 (1841–43): 236.

110. Ferdinand Donnet, *Instructions, mandements, lettres et discours de Mgr l'archevêque de Bordeaux, sur les principaux objets de la sollicitude pastorale de 1837 à 1850* (Bordeaux, 1850), 71–80 and 255–56, quotation on 255.

preservation and called for histories of the *pays* that would relate all "events worth remembering [*dignes de mémoire*]."[111]

THE CULTURAL FIELD AND THE MARKET

The cult of local memories involved, finally, the advent of a new field of cultural production. Sociologist Pierre Bourdieu defines such fields—be they literary, artistic, or other—as "network[s], or . . . configuration[s], of objective relations" between social actors. Each individual possesses a particular share of economic, social, cultural, and symbolic capital: financial resources, connections, education (both scholarly and social), and status. This share—whose value is relative to others—determines one's "position" in a given field. Actors accordingly compete for capital and dominant positions, which impart both legitimacy and definitional authority (to determine, for instance, what is an acceptable or superior historical work). All fields operate in this fashion, but each one has its distinctive stakes, procedures of entry, criteria for success, and rites of consecration.[112] Bourdieu's theory tends to reduce all cultural phenomena to structural grids and power relations. It nonetheless displays the field of local memories' novelty as an unstable configuration of aligned and adversarial actors, who manipulated local memories to legitimate their intellectual production, broaden their social networks, and obtain public recognition.

This field of local memories formed a subset of a broader literary field that expanded dramatically during the nineteenth century. This was an era of rising literacy rates, looser constraints in the publishing trade, new techniques of book production, and growing moral and political stature for writers.[113] Booksellers and reading rooms grew increasingly numerous. Responding in part to a glut of educated young men and limited opportunities in the liberal professions, a growing number of French youths entered an increasingly profit-driven literary arena. Many moved from the provinces to Paris, France's undisputed cultural epicenter. Be it in litera-

111. Le Glay, *Cameracum christianum, ou, Histoire ecclésiastique du diocèse de Cambrai* . . . (Lille, 1849); Pierre Giraud, *Instructions et mandements de Mgr l'évêque de Rodez, transféré à l'Archevêché de Cambrai, sur les principaux objets de la sollicitude pastorale*, 2 vols. (Lille, 1842), 1:365; and Louis-François Capelle, *Vie du cardinal P. Giraud, archevêque de Cambrai* (Lille, 1852), 267.

112. Pierre Bourdieu, "The Economics of Linguistic Exchanges," *Social Science Information* 16, no. 6 (1982): 657; idem, "The Field of Cultural Production, or: The Economic World Reversed," in his *The Field of Cultural Production: Essays on Art and Literature*, ed. and trans. Randal Johnson (New York, 1993), 30; and Loïc Wacquant, "Towards a Reflexive Sociology: A Workshop with Pierre Bourdieu," *Sociological Theory* 7 (1989): 39.

113. Martin and Chartier, *Histoire de l'édition française*, 2:526–41, and 3: esp. 8–9 and 158–216; and Jean-Yves Mollier, "Un changement de climat: les nouveaux libraires et les débuts de l'industrialisation," in Barbier et al., *L'Europe et le livre: réseaux et pratiques du négoce de librairie, XVIe–XIXe siècles* ([Paris], 1996), 571–86.

ture, journalism, or higher education, careers were made and unmade in the capital. By 1876, Paris housed 51 percent of French journalists and "men of letters" and published more than 80 percent of books. Competition was fierce and literary professionals scarce: only one author out of ten lived from his or her pen, less so in the provinces, where literary outlets were less numerous and profitable.[114] Le Glay published much, but earned his living as a doctor and archivist. "Outside Paris, it is well-known, there are strictly speaking no *men of letters*," declared Lille *littérateur* and accountant Elie Brun-Lavainne in 1837. The capital's hold over literary institutions and publishing houses increased in ensuing decades, deepening provincial resentment. "In the provinces, literature is not a profession from which one can earn a living," remarked another Lille historian in 1857.[115]

Paris, then, was both an actual place—the chosen destination of many in this literary field—and a symbolic one that represented exclusion, privilege, and sometimes venality. Be it in the 1830s or 1860s, some Paris-based *littérateurs* sought to distinguish themselves from a "Parisian" coterie of authors, editors, and publishers. Whereas the latter produced a morally deleterious "industrial literature"—by and for Parisians—they would "probe the needs, thoughts, desires of all of France." Speaking for the provinces, they promised to embrace French diversity and the hitherto neglected cause of the "native land." *Panthéon de la jeune France* may have originated in Paris, but its commitment to local issues and interests placed it outside the capital's literary and artistic "coteries" (1841).[116] Concern with all things local, including memories, hence enabled one to delineate an expertise and a niche in an increasingly specialized literary field. One's cultural or social identity as a self-styled provincial might owe little to geographical location or origins.

Things were more straightforward in the provinces, where intellectual elites usually cultivated the memories of their place of residence. Here, too, some did so in opposition to the capital's exclusiveness and commercialism—real and perceived. Eugène Bouly (de Lesdain), a historian and pageant organizer from Cambrai, claimed to have freely given his 1842

---

114. Leonore O'Boyle, "The Problem of an Excess of Educated Men in Western Europe, 1800–1850," *The Journal of Modern History* 42, no. 4 (December 1970): 471–95; Christophe Charle, "Région et conscience régionale en France: questions à propos d'un colloque," *Actes de la recherche en sciences sociales* 35 (1980): 40; and idem, *Les intellectuels en Europe au XIXe siècle: essai d'histoire comparée* (Paris, 1996), 160.

115. *RN*, 2d ser., no. 2 (December 1837): 378; Elie Brun-Lavainne, *Mes souvenirs* (Lille, 1855), 248; and Henri Bruneel, "L'homme de lettres en province," *L'Illustration* 30, no. 755 (15 August 1857): 99.

116. Prospectus for *La Province. Journal politique quotidien* (September 1848): 2; *France départementale* 1 (1834): 31; *L'Echo des provinces* 1, no. 13 (16 April 1865): 1–2; and *Panthéon de la jeune France* 7 (15 September 1841): 2.

Histoire de Cambrai et du Cambrésis to a local publisher. Shunning Parisian "speculation," he endowed his work with the purity of provincial selfless-ness and, like other nobles, held dear to amateurism.[117] This utter rejec-tion was unusual and typical of provincials who, like him, had never left their city of origin. More widespread was the trajectory of Brun-Lavainne, an autodidact who embraced the local past after a dispiriting experience in Paris. He attempted twice to establish himself there—as a young man in the 1810s and, again, in 1851—and twice he failed. Sent back to Lille with his manuscripts, he cofounded the Association lilloise, edited the *Revue du Nord*, and helped stage historical pageants. Le Glay and countless others had likewise ventured to Paris in their youth in search of success or a higher education, then returned to their *pays*. Whether they did so will-ingly or not, they joined a growing company of individuals who glimpsed the Parisian stage, but lacked the will, talent, or fortune to succeed as na-tional actors. Having failed to "create a future" for himself in Paris, lawyer Thomas-Alexandre Ladurelle (1804–38) returned to his native Béziers where he sought to "disentangle the chaos of our local history" in his bookshop and the Société archéologique he cofounded. In 1859, the *Fi-garo* derided such geographical and social itineraries: "All these powerless men who fruitlessly expended their youth in seeking admission to the cap-ital's newspapers and theaters—the provincial academy welcomes them."[118] True enough, but the cult of local memories still provided a backdoor entry into this literary field. It established one's commitment to the *pays*, ensured access to local intellectual networks (as consolation or social promotion), and legitimated one's local status as a *littérateur*. It en-abled hopeful authors to "make [themselves] known" and "run after suc-cess." Writing about "provincial mores or history," noted one Parisian journalist in 1838, was "the only way of being useful and acquiring renown."[119]

Provincials and Parisians hence responded to new distributions of power and knowledge, to new linkages between territories and capital (both economic and cultural), by seizing and manipulating local memo-ries. Devotion to, and knowledge of, the latter became a pathway toward public recognition. Success in this field rested on a *savoir local*—rather than specialized training—and the ability to project oneself as apolitical,

117. This claim was, of course, self-legitimating, but there is no reason to disbelieve him. See L. Pihan, *Notice sur Eugène Bouly de Lesdain* (Beauvais, n.d.); Eugène Bouly, *Histoire de Cam-brai et du Cambrésis*, 2 vols. (Cambrai, 1842), 1: 11–12; and, on nobles and amateurism, Brelot, *Noblesse réinventée*, 2: 728–32.

118. Jean-Paul Jourdan, "Perception et composition des élites locales à la fin du XIXe siè-cle: le cas du Lot-et-Garonne," in Sylvie Guillaume, ed., *Les élites fins de siècles, XIXe et XXe siècles* ([Paris], 1992), 20; *Bulletin de la Société archéologique de Béziers* 3 (1839): 6–7; Maurice, *Décentrali-sation*, 10; and Saunier, "Ville comme antidote," 157.

119. Christophe Opoix, *Réponse au Prospectus de l'Histoire de Provins, par M. Bourquelot (Félix), avocat* (Paris, n.d. [1838?]), [2]; and *Musée des familles* 6 (1838): 255.

conscientious, and truly committed to the *pays* or provinces. From this vantage point, the cult of local memories's novelty resides in the relationships, trajectories, and self-representations presented here. It prefigures the behavior of provincial writers who, at century's end, found themselves excluded from the Parisian avant-garde and later produced a regionalist literature—a "literary counter-field," as Anne-Marie Thiesse called it.[120]

The rise of the field of local memories furthermore paralleled the growth of the market. Nineteenth-century France was after all in the midst of a "commercial revolution" that had begun a century earlier. The development of retailing, new opportunities for credit, and improved communications helped produce a larger and increasingly complex domestic market. With greater leisure time at their disposal, ever more sophisticated consumers selected from a growing variety of goods and expected ever more original forms of entertainment. Industries of domestic tourism and urban entertainment grew in tandem from the 1820s.[121]

It is in this context that provincialist *littérateurs* targeted two potential clienteles: provincials who often felt slighted by Parisian literati and, in the capital, newly arrived "departmental citizens, . . . [who sought] means of communication with the[ir]" native *pays*. Here was a customer base for their periodicals, their books on "the history of each part of our country," and their related commercial ventures—the "department library," for instance, that would publish books of local history by "provincial savants and *littérateurs* who cannot find a publisher in Paris."[122] Some of these *littérateurs* were themselves provincials who, unlike Brun-Lavainne, had encountered success in the capital. Samuel-Henry Berthoud, a longtime member of the Société d'émulation de Cambrai, moved to Paris in 1832 and, within two years, edited the popular *Musée des familles*. If he "gave [his readers] much Flanders," it was partly out of affection for his birthplace. He had after all joined a Société du département du Nord à Paris, whose members—all born in the Nord—shared "memories of the native land."[123] More to the point, Berthoud sought to sell copy. The same was

120. Anne-Marie Thiesse, *Ecrire la France: le mouvement littéraire régionaliste de langue française entre la Belle Epoque et la Libération* (Paris, 1991), 11 and 39; and Bourdieu, *Les règles de l'art. Genèse et structure du champ littéraire*, rev. ed. (Paris, 1998), 431–33.

121. The Nord's first railway line was inaugurated in 1838 and most of the leading cities were connected by 1848. On the economic and cultural changes above, see Colin Jones, "Bourgeois Revolution Revivified: 1789 and Social Change," in Colin Lucas, ed., *Rewriting the French Revolution* (Oxford, 1991), 69–118; and Alain Corbin, ed., *L'avènement des loisirs, 1850–1960* (Paris, 1995).

122. Prospectus for *L'Intermédiaire. Revue de Paris et de la province* (1844); *France départementale* 1 (n.d. [1834]): 2; *La Décentralisation littéraire et scientifique* 1, no. 1 (16 October 1863): 5; as well as Nicholas Green, *The Spectacle of Nature: Landscape and Bourgeois Culture in Nineteenth-Century France* (Manchester, 1990), 143–44.

123. Berthoud published numerous articles on Cambrai, its recent past, and its festivities in *Musée des familles* and *La Presse*. See Brun-Lavainne, *Souvenirs*, 248; and Auguste Delsart, *Précis historique des réunions de la Société du Nord à Paris depuis sa fondation, en 1825, jusqu'en 1840* (Valenciennes, 1848), 7.

true in the Nord, where, according to Brun-Lavainne, readers "seem to welcome with greatest pleasure . . . pieces about the *pays*'s history or mores." He and others thus resolved to "localize" their periodicals and recruit more "men of the *pays*." In the 1850s, local publishers likewise produced affordable collections of "indigenous" historical and literary works. The *Bibliothèque lilloise* and *Oeuvres dunkerquoises* would "remind contemporaries what they owe . . . their precursors" while turning a profit.[124]

The commercialization of local memories reached its apex within historical pageantry, an ever-grander form of entertainment meant to serve charity and boost the city's commerce. A charitable campaign for widows and orphans would prove more successful, declared a municipal commission from Dunkirk in 1840, if held jointly with "a festive reproduction of ancient solemnities, still alive in the *pays*'s memories." Other residents of Dunkirk underscored "the indisputable benefits that the great influx of foreigners . . . would provide our city and all its shopkeepers." The Nord's pageant organizers thus offered visitors three-day packages, organized "pleasure trains" from Paris, and commodified the local past. Consider the selection of products for sale in Douai in 1849: lithographs of the pageant (4 francs), a "notice" and panorama of the same (3 francs), a picturesque view and a poem on the fête (50 centimes each), a quadrille for piano (2.25 francs), a guide to Douai and an illustrated map of the city (1.50 francs each), as well as flags bearing the city's coat of arms.[125] The economic outlook was bleak for many medium-size towns, subprefectoral seats that struggled to carve a niche for themselves within an expanding national market. Be it in Douai or Angers, pageant organizers thus spoke of ending the "stagnation of business" and bringing "a few more days of prosperity to [their city's] silent streets and local commerce."[126] Marketing historical specificity and authenticity would furnish such towns with "a second life as exhibitions of themselves."[127]

The literary appeal to the market was sufficiently widespread to elicit denunciations. "Avid speculation" threatened the "pure and disinterested"

124. *RN*, 1st ser., no. 3 (October 1834): 5; *RN*, 3d ser., vol. 3, no. 11 (December 1854): 361; *Flandre illustrée* 22 (19 December 1858): 169; *L'Echo du Nord*, 15 March 1851; and *Oeuvres dunkerquoises*, 4 vols. (Dunkirk, 1853–59).

125. AMDu 2 Q 8: "Fête de bienfaisance qui aura lieu le 29 mars 1840, en faveur des veuves et des enfants des marins péris en 1839," poster dated 18 March 1840; AMDu 1 J 50: Collective letter to municipal council of Dunkirk, 14 August 1849; and *Société de bienfaisance. Programme de la fête et du cortège historiques, réunis au programme de la fête communale* (Douai, n.d. [1849]).

126. *Fête du Moyen Age sous Philippe-le-Bon*, 3; and *Fêtes de charité de la ville d'Angers. Juin 1853* (Angers, 1853), 3.

127. Barbara Kirshenblatt-Gimblett, *Destination Culture: Tourism, Museums, and Heritage* (Berkeley, 1998), 7.

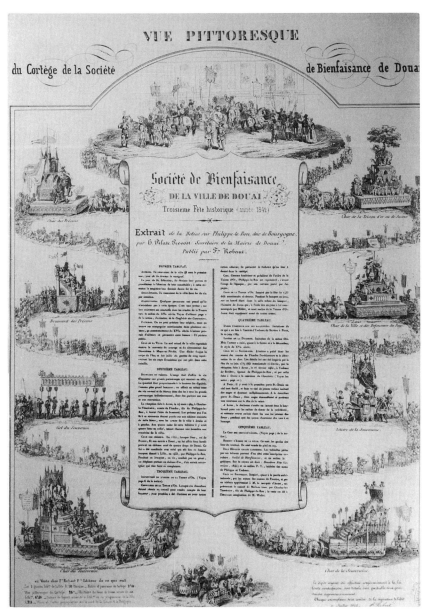

FIGURE 8. "Société de bienfaisance de la ville de Douai. Troisième fête historique (année 1842)." A visual representation of the pageant surrounds excerpts from an article on Philip the Good. The program's scholarship complemented the spectacle's sights and sounds. The pageant clearly targeted various audiences, from the erudite to the illiterate. Printer and future pageant designer Félix Robaut sold this image and other pageant-related products, advertised in the lower left corner. Did such lithographs—at once commodities and pedagogical instruments—decorate domestic interiors? Courtesy of the Bibliothèque Municipale de Douai.

character of history, said Guizot as early as 1837.[128] In the mid nineteenth century, however, the market ultimately failed to support this local output. Provincialist periodicals quickly downscaled their ambitions; the Nord's literary collections remained small; many festive societies went bankrupt (see chapter 3). Some contemporaries understood that local memories had more limited commercial potential than Brun-Lavainne had (perhaps wishfully) posited. Berthoud rejected his submissions in the 1830s because he feared "overfeeding" his readers articles on Flanders. In 1852, the periodical *Martin de Cambrai* observed that provincials bought few books and wondered how many of its readers had embraced local writers who "insist on keeping a local accent [*le goût du terroir*]."[129] Although local memories acquired unprecedented visibility in the realm of print, the unification of the French literary market curtailed both supply and demand. In the 1840s, reading rooms from Cambrai, Valenciennes, and Douai contained not a single publication by Le Glay and other local elites. The lone recurring title on local memories was Berthoud's own *Chroniques et traditions surnaturelles de la Flandre* (1831–34), a collection of vivid stories à la Walter Scott. While this accessible work responded to market forces, most publications on local memories had, like Le Glay's, tenuous commercial prospects.[130] Lawyer Hyacinthe Dusevel thus complained in 1834 that, besides fifty author's copies, he derived no "profit" from his *Histoire de la ville d'Amiens.*[131] Learned societies and scholarly congresses were, by the same token, independent from the market. The latter fertilized this field, but other, more decisive forces nourished the cult of local memories.

INDETERMINACY AND PROMISES

One of these forces, as we have begun to see, was the state. Unlike others, this cultural field failed to emancipate itself from individual, institutional, and most pertinently, governmental patrons. Dusevel (a CTH correspondent) persuaded the Ministry of Public Instruction to subscribe to ten

---

128. Guizot, Speech in the public meeting of the Société des antiquaires de Normandie, 2 August 1837, in *Mémoires de la Société des antiquaires de Normandie* 11 (1837–39): xl. On the comparable reservations of journalists about the market, see William Reddy, *The Invisible Code: Honor and Sentiment in Postrevolutionary France* (Berkeley, 1997), chap. 5.

129. Brun-Lavainne, *Souvenirs*, 248; and *Martin de Cambrai*, 27 August 1862.

130. I consulted the reading room catalogs of Binois de l'Epine (Valenciennes, 1844), Adolphe Obez (Douai, 1844), and Auguste Giard (Cambrai, 1846). They can be found in the BNF, microfilm M2700. Berthoud lauded Scott in his *La France historique, industrielle et pittoresque de la jeunesse* (Paris, 1835), 13. See also Jean-Clément Martin, *La Vendée de la mémoire, 1800–1980* (Paris, 1989), 119; and Franco Moretti, *Atlas of the European Novel, 1800–1900* (London, 1998), 163.

131. BMA ms. 440: Hyacinthe Dusevel to François-César Louandre, 15 June 1834.

copies of his monograph. Le Glay secured ministerial subscriptions to six of his works and, from 1835 on, received an annual subsidy of two to three thousand francs for collaborating with the CTH.[132] All of this displays the striking indeterminacy of a field that, be it on discursive, patrimonial, or cultural planes, took form at the juncture of civil society and governmental action. This political ambivalence—a key factor behind the cult of local memories' allure and contradictions—constitutes a fitting and necessary end to this preliminary journey.

Indeed, the July Monarchy set into motion divergent forces of liberalization and governmental intrusion. On the one hand, its precarious legitimacy and its liberalism (however tenuous) led it to mollify the Bourbons' coarse techniques of rule. It expanded freedom of the press (especially for literary and scientific periodicals); encouraged the multiplication of learned societies; and respected the autonomy of "particular charity." When political unrest led Minister Thiers to curtail the right of association in 1834, he exempted both benevolent and learned societies. In the Nord, the prefect and subprefects kept watch over historical pageants, but neither regulated nor exploited them. Save for isolated mayoral interventions, the authorities allowed Le Glay and others to script their programs with remarkable latitude.[133] Similarly, historical pageants distanced themselves from what Alain Corbin has called the fête of sovereignty: the fête as cult of the regime or reflection of the ruler's glory. The latter had acquired a new scope between the reigns of Louis XIV and Charles X. Witness the multiplication of royal entries and festivities glorifying the monarch under the Old Regime or, during the Restoration, the efforts to reactivate such ceremonies as the oath of Louis XIII.[134] Cambrai's *fêtes* celebrated the monarchy and religion under the Old Regime, then featured predictable themes (virtue, agriculture) during the Revolution. Religion and praise of the regime and ruler returned under the Empire and Restoration. It took the liberal agitation of the late 1820s, the overthrow of the Bourbons, and the advent of a fragile (and rapidly contested) liberal regime for the cult of the sovereign to grow more discrete. "Royalty has be-

132. AN F17 2897: Subscription decrees for books by Le Glay; and AN F17 2865: Anon. memorandum to Min. Pub. Instrc., 18 January 1850. See also Jerrold Seigel, *Bohemian Paris: Culture, Politics, and the Boundaries of Bourgeois Life, 1830–1930* (New York, 1986), 13–14.

133. I make this claim on the basis of extant manuscript and printed sources—documents that would not necessarily display a more covert official influence. See Prince of Monaco, *Du paupérisme en France et des moyens de le détruire* (Paris, 1839), 4; and ADN M 216/5: Adolphe Thiers to prefects, circular of 29 April 1834.

134. Corbin, "La fête de souveraineté," in idem, Noëlle Gérôme and Danielle Tartakowsky, eds., *Les usages politiques des fêtes aux XIXe–XXe siècles* (Paris, 1994), 25–38; Alain-Charles Gruber, *Les grandes fêtes et leurs décors à l'époque de Louis XVI* (Paris, 1972), 2–3; Robert A. Schneider, *The Ceremonial City: Toulouse Observed, 1738–1780* (Princeton, N.J., 1995), esp. chap. 5 and conclusion; and Françoise Waquet, *Les fêtes royales sous la Restauration ou l'Ancien Régime retrouvé* (Paris, 1981).

come so humble," noted famed writer Jules Janin in 1842.[135] In the cities of the Nord, local memories filled this semantic vacuum—tentatively after 1825, in earnest after 1830.

At the same time, one can hardly dismiss the pervasive, if indirect, influence that officials of all ranks exerted on this field. Consider the Nord's learned societies. Under the Consulate, it was the prefect who established Douai's Société d'agriculture, des sciences et des arts, one of many agricultural associations that would soon embrace local memories. In 1845, the Société d'agriculture, sciences et arts de l'arrondissement de Valenciennes not only made its subprefect an honorary member (as was customary), but also asked him to preside over the association. He gladly accepted, he wrote his superior, to "increase my influence and hence serve the government's interests." By 1865, the rector of the *académie* of Douai was presenting himself as the *"patron"* of local learned societies: at once their protector and supervisor. There are many other examples, including the commanding role of a Commission historique du Nord that, as Le Glay reminded his colleagues, "has administrative origins."[136]

All of this situates the field of local memories within an ill-defined realm, in which official action met the initiatives of civil society—sometimes seamlessly, sometimes less so. The Commission historique's 1839 founding decree, which allowed members to name their own president and the prefect to chair meetings at will, captures the ambivalence of these modern voluntary associations—modes of sociability that symbolize free initiative and may welcome critical social forces while broadening governmental prerogatives.[137] The same was true of Cambrai's *fête communale*, whose representations of local history and celebrities were at once a variant and a dilution of the fête of sovereignty. On the one hand, the fête exalted not the ruler per se, but the new sociopolitical order that underlay the July Monarchy: "the institutions guaranteeing a moderate freedom," the elites or *capacités* that helped govern the nation, and the rule of the individual as "predestined King."[138] On the other hand, the *fête communale's* localist rhetoric could serve more radical or conservative political currents. While many elites thus assisted the local or national authorities, few became mere administrative operatives. Their relationship with the state remained unscripted and subject to constant revision; it was a relationship

135. Jules Janin, introduction to *Pictures of the French* (London, 1842), xiii.

136. ADN 1 T 246/6: Subprefect Valenciennes to prefect Nord, 15 January 1846; ADN 2 T 763: Rector Douai to prefect Nord, 28 July 1865; and *BCN* 1 (1843): 4.

137. Dominique Mehl, "Culture et action associatives," *Sociologie du travail* 1 (1982): 24–42; and Robert Cabanes, "Les associations créatrices de la localité," in *L'esprit des lieux: localités et changement social en France* (Paris, 1986), 210–31.

138. "Programme de la fête communale de Cambrai" (20 July 1831); and Corbin, "Impossible présence," in his *Usages politiques des fêtes*, 114.

of concordance but also of trepidation and hesitancy. In cultivating local memories, these contemporaries operated in—and helped form—a new cultural and political realm, a realm that lacked established protocols or firm rules, a realm that the authorities canvassed and sometimes supervised but did not control.[139] It is against this backdrop that we must now explain why Le Glay and others deemed it so important to cultivate local memories.

139. One can situate this hybrid realm within Jürgen Habermas's model of state-civil relations in the nineteenth century: viz., the erosion of a bourgeois public sphere of rational debate and political criticism, made "progressively insignificant" by the extension of a "neomercantilist" state that now intervened in commodity exchange, labor regulation, and other fields. Given Habermas's contention that this transformation occurred decisively after 1873, the preceding decades may be seen as a period of flux between private and public spheres. Missing, however, from Habermas's account are the porosity between these spheres and, per Geoff Eley and others, the conflicting interests and contested meanings that suffused civil society. See Jürgen Habermas, *The Structural Transformation of the Public Sphere: An Inquiry into a Category of Bourgeois Society*, trans. Thomas Burger with Frederick Lawrence (Cambridge, Mass., 1989 [1962]); and Geoff Eley, "Nations, Publics and Political Cultures: Placing Habermas in the Nineteenth Century," in Craig Calhoun, ed., *Habermas and the Public Sphere* (Cambridge, Mass., 1992), 306–7. David Kammerling Smith argues that a blending between state and society characterized the eighteenth century as well. See his "Structuring Politics in Early-Eighteenth-Century France: The Political Innovations of the French Council of Commerce," *Journal of Modern History* 74, no. 3 (September 2002): 490–537.

PART II: *L'Amour du Pays*

TWO

Recomposing Self and Nation

In our midst, love of the *pays* has always been kept up as a cult.

EDOUARD GIROD
*Esquisse historique, légendaire et descriptive
de la ville de Pontarlier* (1857)

IN 1835, ANDRÉ Le Glay wrote a friend about his pride in "cultivating this historical science that is your delight as well as mine." For him as for others, the cult of local memories used scientific procedures and norms to illuminate a local past that buttressed the present era. Inspired by their "love of the *pays* and of science," provincial elites professed to transfer science from an aristocratic coterie to the "public domain." The Société des lettres, sciences et arts de l'Aveyron vowed in 1838 to erect a "scientific edifice . . . for our *pays*." Scientific congresses fulfilled the "sacred duty [of science] to disseminate abundant and truthful lights."[1] With their footnoted programs and "explanatory notes," historical pageants "paid the greatest honor to science."[2] Similar ambitions typified ministerial circles, where, be it under the July Monarchy or Second Empire, one presented the CTH as an agency devoted to "science and history" and congratulated provincial learned societies for "constituting a new science" while reviving "ancient France."[3] Like other European countries, France "witnessed a vast increase in the scale of scientific enterprise, major changes in patterns of scientific organization, and a total reconstruction of scientific education" during the first half of the nineteenth century (T. Kuhn). The number of scientists doubled between

---

1. BNF ms. NAF 24209: André Le Glay to Arthur Dinaux, 11 April 1835; *Bulletin de la Société archéologique et historique de la Charente* 1 (1845): 177; *MSDu* 3 (1856): 34; *Mémoires de la Société des lettres, sciences et arts de l'Aveyron* 1 (1837–38), part I: viii and xlv; and *CS* 10 (Strasbourg, 1842), xix.

2. *Gazette de Picardie*, 8 September 1841; and *Ville de Rambouillet. Fête de bienfaisance. Lundi de Pâques 17 avril 1865. Cavalcade historique organisée par les habitants, etc.* (Rambouillet, n.d. [1865]), 6–8.

3. AN F17 13268: Proceedings of the Committee on chronicles, charters, and inscriptions, 7 August 1837; and *RSS*, 1st ser., no. 2 (1st sem. 1857): 5.

1775 and 1825; disciplines such as biology took form; and a spate of learned and popular practices—from periodicals to fairs—inaugurated a new era in scientific popularization. In 1844, a commentator thus spoke of an "extraordinary renovation of science" that had begun during the French Revolution. Be it as an ideology of boundless progress or gateway toward subjacent laws, as anchor of a social order or set of concrete applications, science became "the fixation of a society" during these decades.[4] While science meant different things to different people, members of the field of local memories equated it early on with "historical faithfulness," painstaking research, the "methodical" study of documents, and a disregard for political passions. "History, daughter of time and truth, must attempt to be veridical in all things," Le Glay explained in the late 1840s.[5]

To ask why contemporaries cultivated local memories at this time is thus to speak about science and method. In 1845, one Dubois-Druelle accordingly addressed his *Douai pittoresque*—a study of local history and monuments—to a learned readership of historians and antiquaries. But he also wrote this book for those local residents who, "find[ing] a study as well as a cult in a fragment of local history," wish to "preserve the memory of [local] monuments."[6] Other historians concurred under the Second Empire that, alongside the "brilliant Muse," there is another history, "simple and more naive, living spirit of the land, friend of the commune and hearth, echo of the familial traditions, that . . . attaches man to the place in which he was born."[7] In this field, science could coexist with emotion—or religion. If contemporaries equated local memories with a "cult" or a "pious" mission, it was also because they nourished a broader Christian duty "of filial love and veneration for the memory of the faithful deceased."[8] Throughout these decades, liberals and traditionalists, clerics and laymen alike embraced local memories as one of many "mode[s] of

4. Nicole and Jean Dhombres, *Naissance d'un nouveau pouvoir: sciences et savants en France 1793–1824* (Paris, 1989); Thomas S. Kuhn, *The Essential Tension: Selected Studies in Scientific Tradition and Change* (Chicago, 1977), 220; *Revue de la province et de Paris* (January 1844): 7–8; and Hippolyte Castille, *Les hommes et les moeurs en France sous le règne de Louis-Philippe* (Paris, 1853), 339.

5. *BCN* 3 (1847–49): 181; *Annales de la Société, royale académique de Nantes et du département de la Loire-Inférieure*, 2d ser., 7 (1846): 367 and 386; and Le Glay, *Chronique d'Arras et de Cambrai, par Baldéric, chantre de Térouane au XIe siècle* (Cambrai, 1841), ix.

6. M. Dubois-Druelle, *Douai pittoresque, ou description des monumens et objets d'antiquité que renferment cette ville et son arrondissement . . .* (Douai, 1845), n.p. [2]. See also M. Renault, *Essai historique sur Coutances* (Saint-Lo, 1847), 45.

7. Léonce de Pontaumont, *Histoire de la ville de Carentan et de ses notables, d'après les monuments paléographiques* (Paris, 1863), n.p. [dedication]; and AMDu 2 R 15: Alexandre Bonvarlet, "Rapport sur le concours d'histoire en 1864," 2 September 1864.

8. *Annales de la Société archéologique et historique des Côtes-du-Nord* 4 (1846): 10; and [Pierre Giraud], *Lettre pastorale de Monseigneur l'Archevêque de Cambrai sur la visite générale des églises de son diocèse qu'il vient de terminer* (Cambrai, n.d. [1845]), 10. I am grateful to Frédéric Vienne, of the Diocesan Archives of Lille, for furnishing me a copy of this document.

initiation to . . . religious sentiments."[9] These memories helped spiritual-
ize an ostensibly irreligious society while feeding a sacred, transcendent
patriotism. Whereas some exalted "religious memories" as the noblest
component of "local patriotism," others noted that, in this modern era, a
new type of religion, "born from the religion of patriotism," complemented or supplanted traditional cults. "What faith produced in the
Middle Ages, love of the *patrie* will renew in the nineteenth century," declared Victor Derode while calling for a historical museum on Dunkirk in
1851.[10] This conviction gained ground in the years that followed.

Fluid and contested, the cult of local memories thus emerges as an interplay of diverse individual aims and sociocultural forces. Alongside science and religion, we find this elite's imaginary: representations and practices that would resolve contradictions, provide psychological solace, and
imbue one's actions and existence with meaning.[11] The latter sometimes
overlapped with a memorial current that mobilized local memories to
deepen affection for a local "place" and delineate territorial identities.
"Love of the *pays* often resides in the memories that relate to it."[12] On a
doctrinal plane, local memories underlay conceptions of citizenship,
political community, or social order derived from contemporary political
philosophies—from liberalism to republicanism and traditionalism. This
concern with political doctrine distinguished this current from an instrumental one, which sought to accumulate power, depoliticize competing
social groups, and produce a putative local harmony. Distinct, intertwined, and equally meaningful, these currents converged within an enterprise of self-creation, an effort to rethink and reorder one's social
world while situating oneself within it. Formed at the intersection of
knowledge, memory, and power (*savoir, mémoire, pouvoir*), this enterprise
also yielded new and promising relationships between local residents, between the national and the local, between France and its *pays*.[13]

THE IMAGINARY OF LOCAL MEMORIES

Narratives, Hayden White wrote in an influential essay, "possess an order
of meaning that they do *not* possess as mere sequence." Historical narra-

9. *Distribution des prix de l'Institut de sourds-muets de Lille, dirigé par les frères de l'instruction chrétienne de Saint-Gabriel et les religieuses de la sagesse* (Lille, 1841), 2.

10. Jean-Joseph Gratien, *Histoire de l'abbaye de Saint-Claude depuis sa fondation jusqu'à son érec-
tion en évêché*, 2 vols. (Lons, 1854–55), 1: 2, quoted in Pierre Lacroix, "Prêtres érudits du Jura
aux XIXe et XXe siècles," *Revue d'histoire de l'église de France* 71 (1985): 49; *Bulletin de la Société
des antiquaires de Picardie* 4 (1850–52): 176; and ASD 1851–1852: Victor Derode, speech to the
Société dunkerquoise, 25 May 1851.

11. Bronislaw Baczko, *Les imaginaires sociaux: mémoires et espoirs collectifs* (Paris, 1984), 25.

12. *MSV* 3 (1841): 280.

13. Gerard Noiriel, *Sur la "crise" de l'histoire* (Paris, 1996), 176–83.

tives, like others, render the external world meaningful by endowing "reality with form and therefore mak[ing] it desirable, imposing upon its processes the formal coherency that only stories possess." But narratives do more than grant events a symbolic order and coherence. They also constitute naming and classifying practices that alter expectations and behavior and reconfigure the external world by altering the way actors interact with it.[14] It is as such that I will first examine the cult of local memories: as a series of texts, genres, and practices that would rename and remold a social world whose meaning had grown opaque. It told a story whose motifs either came to the fore during the French Revolution or responded to this event and the ensuing crisis of meaning and authority.[15] This imaginary—developed by a literate elite—cut across political cleavages, regional disparities, as well as lines of division between the state and civil society. While anxieties were particularly acute following the 1830 and 1848 revolutions, this imaginary also displayed a striking continuity throughout the century's middle decades.

If local memories acquired such resonance, it was largely because they made it possible to imagine a society in flux, prey to political, social, and economic forces that escaped the control of contemporaries. Parisians and provincials used an identical vocabulary to describe "a society without bonds, whose elements, fallen on top of one another, stir haphazardly," a society marked by "disorders of the mind" and "confusion of ideas."[16] The outcome was a "universal malaise," a "moral malaise" that made "an entire country . . . worried and sick, without knowing why." Elites depicted the same shaken social and political order, the same inner turmoil, the same wavering sense of self. "Surrounded by ruins, . . . [the spirit] seek[s] in vain something to hold on to in the universal disturbance." This anxiety surfaced throughout our period, from the "positive, pressing ill" of the late 1820s to the "world in dust" of the late 1860s.[17]

This malaise encompassed and transcended the early century's *mal du siècle*: the ennui and frustrations of Alfred de Musset and other young *littérateurs*. Its main cause escaped no one. "Fifty years of agitation, that is the first cause of the ills," declared the liberal *Revue de l'instruction publique* in

14. Hayden White, "The Value of Narrativity in the Representation of Reality," in W. J. T. Mitchell, ed., *On Narrative* (Chicago, 1981), 5 and 19–20; and Anselm L. Strauss, *Mirrors and Masks: The Search for Identity*, new ed. (New Brunswick, 1997), 24 and 147.

15. Priscilla Parkhurst Ferguson, *Paris as Revolution: Writing the Nineteenth-Century City* (Berkeley, 1997).

16. Philarète Chasles, "Statistique littéraire et intellectuelle de la France pendant l'année 1828," *Revue de Paris* 1, no. 7 (1829): 241; Charles Louandre, "Statistique littéraire de la production intellectuelle en France depuis quinze ans.—Seconde partie," *RDM*, new ser., 20 (October–December 1847): 417; and *RN*, 1st ser., 1 (November 1833): 30.

17. AN F7 6771: Prefect of Nord to Min. Int., 3 March 1827; AN F7 6770: Prefect of Nièvre to Min. Int., 9 June 1828; Narcisse de Salvandy, *Vingt mois, ou la Révolution et le parti révolutionnaire*, new ed. (Paris, 1849), 547–48; *Congrès méridional. 1e session 1834* (Toulouse, 1834), 27–28; *Revue cambrésienne* 1 (1835– 1836): 111; and *CS* 33, 2 vols. (Aix-en-Provence, 1867), 1: 6.

1842, before denouncing a movement that "seizes the men, the laws, the governments, without leaving one principle standing." The French Revolution had unhinged and unseated and opened a void that still threatened to engulf France. The events of 1830 seemed to revive a Revolution that, as Lamartine now grasped, "was not finished." Elites accordingly spoke of an "epoch of transition" in which, as the *Revue des provinces* put it in 1834, "the laws and mores [*moeurs*] of the old centuries no longer exist [and] the mores and laws of the new century are not yet established."[18] The Revolution's most unsettling legacy was an all-encompassing politicization of everyday life, set into motion by its clubs and popular societies, its pamphlets and *journées*.[19] "Politics had impetuously left [its] narrow and specialized sphere" to become "our era's most exclusive need." In 1834, a young liberal *littérateur* from Strasbourg observed that "every literary work nowadays has a political or social meaning; and when the author has not given it one, the crowd nonetheless seeks it out, imagines it, creates it."[20]

Alongside this political upheaval, contemporaries encountered a socioeconomic transformation that grew increasingly visible by the mid-1830s. In 1838, after six years in Paris, editor Samuel-Henry Berthoud made his first return trip to his native Cambrai. He expressed his awe before the town's physical transformation, the multiplication of mills, factories, limited partnerships, and retail outlets. But he was troubled as well, for his *pays'* "antique and naïve physiognomy" was fading. His disquiet responded to a bevy of changes: the landscape's alteration in the wake of urban growth and industrialization, the integration of localities into the national economy, the dislocation of more or less hierarchical local communities, and population movement from countryside to cities.[21] Many of these changes had proved alarming since the mid eighteenth century, but everything was now accelerating. This was an era in which, as Le Glay put it in 1843, "no one is satisfied . . . with the place he occupies." Growing physical and social mobility blurred the boundaries between social groups and forced elites to rethink their position within this unstable landscape.[22] Decades after the Revolution—this attempt "to abolish the memory of . . .

18. *Revue de l'instruction publique* 1, no. 9 (15 December 1842): 139; Alphonse de Lamartine, *Voyage en Orient*, quoted in Gérard Fritz, *L'idée de peuple en France du XVIIe au XIXe siècle* (Strasbourg, 1988), 75; and *La Revue des provinces* 1 (1 September 1834): 7.

19. Lynn Hunt, "The Unstable Boundaries of the French Revolution," in Michelle Perot, ed., *A History of Private Life*, trans. Arthur Goldhammer, 5 vols. (Cambridge, Mass., 1987–91), 4:13–45.

20. Prospectus for E. Duclerc and Laurent-Antoine Pagnerre, *Dictionnaire politique* (Paris, 1842), 1–2; Prospectus in *La France littéraire*, 1st ser., 1 (January 1831): 3; and *Revue d'Alsace* 1 (1834): 35 and 42.

21. Samuel-Henry Berthoud, "Feuilleton: Courrier de la province," *La Presse*, 23 January 1838.

22. Claude Labrosse, "La région dans la presse régionale," in Jean Sgard, ed., *La presse provinciale au XVIIIe siècle* (Grenoble, 1983), 117–18; *BCN* 1 (1843): 384; and Richard Terdiman, *Discourse/Counter-Discourse: The Theory and Practice of Symbolic Resistance in Nineteenth-Century*

ancestors, religion, the laws, the mores"—everything furthermore remained on the verge of vanishing, from "scattered traditions" to "monuments of all kinds." The anguish of loss, present in the eighteenth century within a vision of "corruptive time" (J. Goulemot), now responded to the advent of a leveling modernity.[23]

The recovery, preservation, and production of local memories—themselves at risk of vanishing—both embodied and responded to such trauma. While the comforting function of monumental preservation is well documented, we should appreciate the desperation with which elites sought to collect the "debris of this national life," ensure that monuments survived in all parts of France, and counter "the furor to destroy."[24] Portraying themselves as the "last travelers in a France that will soon have ceased to exist," Charles Nodier and the baron Taylor promised to depict ruins that would have otherwise been lost. Beyond traditionalist gripes about the toppling of the "institutions of our old France," such practices of preservation offered the prospect of resolution: emotional solace and a refuge from politics.[25]

In 1840, residents of the Pas-de-Calais presented the Ministry of Public Instruction with a plan for local "memorials," a necessity given that "for more than half-a-century the political passions [have] absorbed all the ideas." Such disquiet suffused this field. Pageant organizers declared that "politics is too serious for us"; periodical directors promised to avoid polemics; the editors of the *Histoire des villes de France* rejected "the intrusion of politics into the domain of history."[26] Their claims responded partly to a legislation that curtailed the permissible topics for voluntary associations and periodical publications. Returning to an ancient academic ethos, they also reflect a yearning for spatially or temporally bounded apolitical enclosures, refuges from "the sounds of hatred." Political questions

---

France (Ithaca, 1985), 48. On the acceleration of change, see Saunier, "Ville comme antidote," 153.

23. Charles de Montalembert, quoted in G. Baldwin Brown, *The Care of Ancient Monuments* (Cambridge, 1905), 75; Prospectus in *La Revue des provinces* 1 (1 November 1834): 3; Salvandy, edict of 18 December 1837, in Charmes, 64; and Jean-Marie Goulemot, "Bibliothèques, encyclopédisme et angoisses de la perte: l'exhaustivité ambigue des Lumières," in Marc Baratin and Christian Jacob, eds., *Le pouvoir des bibliothèques* (Paris, 1996), 294.

24. Françoise Choay, *L'allégorie du patrimoine* (Paris, 1992), 14; *Discours prononcé par M. Guizot*, 4; Salvandy to correspondents, circular of 1839, in Charmes, 94–95; and AN F17 13268: proceedings of the Committee on chronicles, charters and inscriptions, 19 May 1837.

25. Charles Nodier, Justin Taylor, and Alphonse de Cailleux, *Voyages pittoresque et romantiques dans l'ancienne France*, 17 vols. (Paris: 1820–78), I:8; *Le Panorama* 1 (10 August 1837): 1. On revolutionary trauma and history, see Bonnie Smith, *Gender of History*, 9.

26. AN F17 3021: Du Haÿe to Min. Pub. Instr., 28 September 1840; "Programme de 1835," in *Société de bienfaisance* (Cambrai, n. d. [1839]), 5; BML, fonds Humbert XLI/263: untitled and undated newspaper article [1837]; and Aristide Guilbert, Introduction to idem, *Histoire des villes*, 1: vii.

could "arouse passionate emotions."[27] In Dunkirk, a subcommittee of the new Société dunkerquoise stipulated in 1851 that "if political systems are undeniably important, they also produce *division*, whereas the goal of our institution is to *unite*." Internal "deliberations, discussions, or even conversations" should thus avoid politics. Elites from Angers to Rodez likewise depicted their associations and fêtes as "quiet, pure and dispassionate sphere[s]" in which, freed from the "sad dissension" of politics, local elites recovered "the memory of their unity."[28] Endowed with the neutrality of scholarship, learned activities demonstrated one's remove from politics. None did so better than "the curiosity for local things," seen by many as a diversion from "the bitter science of politics," or even "a reaction against the revolutionary movement."[29] Strasbourg's Société des sciences, agriculture et arts du département du Bas-Rhin thus pledged in 1838 to shun "the vast theories of the impossible" and confine itself to "modest locality interests." Beyond its practical benefits—averting destructive infighting—this apolitical stance promised to assuage the "disruptive fever" that, per Le Glay, was tearing apart "a people given over to political passions."[30]

Before reconciliation, however, came self-understanding. Neglect of the past also fed the malaise of a country that neither knew itself nor, all too often, craved such knowledge. "Our *pays*'s history is hardly known": such laments resounded throughout our period. "There is a need no one can deny," wrote the novelist Frédéric Soulié in 1836, "it is France's need to know herself in greater detail." The newly emancipated nation knew neither what it was nor what it owned nor what it had been (hence, its well-known preoccupation with origins). Its cities and regions did not know one another, its government did not know its citizens, its inhabitants did not know the history and value of the very land they inhabited. "Rich paternal soil, so fecund, and which the crowds only look at indifferently."[31] Archivists were unfamiliar with the documents in their collections; northern France with the economic and intellectual output of the

27. Daniel Roche, *Siècle des Lumières*, 1: 102; *Bulletin de la Société des sciences historiques et naturelles de l'Yonne* 1 (1847): 13; and *Actes de l'Académie des sciences, belles-lettres et arts de Bordeaux* 5 (1843): 257.

28. ASD 1851–52: "Rapport du comité chargé d'élaborer un projet de règlement," 9 March 1851 (italics in the original); *Fêtes de charité de la ville d'Angers. Juin 1853* (Angers, 1853), 9; and *Mémoires de la Société des lettres, sciences et arts de l'Aveyron* 1 (1837–38), part 1: xxxvii.

29. *CS* 44, 2 vols. (Nice, 1878), 1: 37; and *RAN* 10, no. 5 and 6 (November–December 1858): 134.

30. *Nouveaux mémoires de la Société des sciences, agriculture et arts du département du Bas-Rhin* 3, first part (1838): 11; and *MEC* 13 (1833): 9–10.

31. *Mémoires de la Société royale académique de Savoie* 8 (1837): 91; Frédéric Soulié, *Romans historiques du Languedoc*, 2 vols. (Paris, 1836), 1: x; *MSDu* 9 (1864): 22; and Berthoud, *La France historique, industrielle et pittoresque de la jeunesse* (Paris, 1835), 13–14. On this postrevolutionary malaise and the quest for individual self-knowledge, see Alain Girard, *Le journal intime*, 2d ed. (Paris, 1986), xvi–xvii.

South; schoolchildren with the nation's geography. The CTH sought to learn "what we own in terms of monuments, their location and their worth" by sending out questionnaires in 1838, but the responses told an identical story: French men and women were oblivious to their locality's historical riches. The nation was excising segments of its self.[32]

This quest for self-knowledge was an effort—discussed in greater depth in the next chapter—to instill affection for one's place of residence. "This vivifying [local] study will lead us to better understand . . . [and] draw us closer to our *pays*," declared a member of Auxerre's leading learned society in 1847. It also reflected the thirst for knowledge of a bourgeoisie that, per Nicole Mozet, sought symbolic ownership of a territory that it now owned and had to govern. Like others, the modern French state requested ever-increasing information on its resources, population, and local habits.[33] For Doctrinaires, this quest for knowledge and social legibility rested on the conviction, that, in Guizot's words, "the government does not make society, it finds it." A government ruled, not by virtue of a social contract, but in accordance with the historical forces that shaped the body social. Given this "irrigation of governance by society" (L. Jaume), a legitimate government required positive understanding of the country's social forces and collective interests. Only by discerning the inner workings of this new society could the state fulfill its needs and truly represent it.[34]

Beyond this, the cult of local memories displayed the elite's conviction that an internal disorder was gnawing at the nation's insides. If the Commission historique du Nord published arrondissement *statistiques* through which "each commune [would] . . . at last know its origins and history," it was also to stabilize French society by placing it before its historical and social self and granting it a sense of finitude and continuity. Salvandy captured the conservative nature of such ventures when he declared that, since the French Revolution,

> our country . . . has been restless, searching everywhere for stability, seeking its image in all its forms, . . . and constantly disappointed, constantly

32. Adrien-Etienne de Gasparin, report on the CHAM's activities in 1838, in *Budget général des dépenses pour l'exercice 1840* (Paris, 1839), 335; and AN F17 2810/1: Completed questionnaires on monuments, 1838–40.

33. *Bulletin de la Société des sciences historiques et naturelles de l'Yonne* 1 (1847): 109; and Nicole Mozet, "Yvetot vaut Constantinople: littérature et géographie en France au XIXe siècle," *Romantisme* 35 (1982): 91–114. On the curiosity for the interior, see Stéphane Gerson, "Parisian Littérateurs, Provincial Journeys and the Construction of National Unity in Post-Revolutionary France," *Past and Present* 151 (May 1996): 141–73. On the modern state and internal knowledge, see Gilles Palsky, *Des chiffres et des cartes: la cartographie quantitative au XIXe siècle* (Paris, 1996), 9.

34. François Guizot, *Des moyens de gouvernement et d'opposition dans l'état actuel de la France* (Paris, 1821), 127; Lucien Jaume, *Individu effacé*, 141 and 152–53; and Pierre Manent, "The French Revolution and French and English Liberalism," in Ralph C. Hancock and L. Gary Lambert, eds., *The Legacy of the French Revolution* (London, 1996), 64–66.

falling back upon itself of its own weight, because it could not find or recognize within itself these [indispensable] conservative principles, these rest-
ful elements.[35]

Others linked the Revolution to a "disharmony" between French society
and its institutions—a dissonance that one could only elucidate by "com-
paring society with itself during the principal periods of its existence."[36] I
would furthermore emphasize the impact of recognition and historical
self-understanding—"a permanent examination of France by her own
children"—upon the psyches of individuals who stood before a society
that "needs to understand itself . . . [because it] is not even completed
[*faite*]." These words were written in 1829. By the late 1850s, some elites
were noting with pleasure that "the France that did not know herself [has
begun] . . . to study herself."[37] A ministerial circular used, however, a
more tentative present tense: "France wants to interrogate and know herself." Much remained to be done. "Ask a peasant the history of this land of
France that he plows every day," suggested *L'Echo des provinces* in 1865.
"He will remain mute." The same held true for landowners, unable to
identify the medals they discovered in their fields. "No one knows what
the locality in which one resides has been nor what it is."[38] The cult of
local memories remained as urgent as ever.

Indeed, a complex vocabulary of the unknown, the invisible, and the
underground suffused this field. Elites conveyed a wary vision of an unfamiliar territory, invisible forces lurking beneath the surface. Scholars
have drawn attention to the dread of underground perils that appeared in
France in the late eighteenth century. A by-product of urbanization and
anxieties about hygiene, the latter revolved around potential subterranean collapses, defective sewer systems, and mephitic exhalations. More
broadly yet, it was a fear of what Salvandy called "an action at once underground and open, incessant, unpunished"—an action that included the
dark designs of workers who, in cities such as Lille, lived in damp base-
ments.[39] We know more about such fears than about the concomitant al-

35. ADN 1 T 248/6: Edmond de Coussemaker, report to Prefect of Nord, 8 July 1864; and
Salvandy, *Vingt mois*, 106.
36. Marcelin Desloges, *Le Globe* 4, no. 91 (13 March 1827), quoted in Jean-Jacques Goblot,
La Jeune France libérale: "le Globe" et son groupe littéraire, 1824–1830 (Paris, 1995), 277.
37. Chasles, "Statistique littéraire," 242; *MSDu* 6 (1859): 12; and *RSS*, 1st ser., no. 2 (1st
sem. 1857): 5.
38. AN F17 3318: Louandre to presidents of learned societies, circular of 24 May 1857;
L'Echo des provinces 1, no. 3 (5 February 1865): 3; and Florentin Lefils, *Géographie historique et
populaire des communes de l'arrondissement d'Abbeville* (Abbeville, 1868), ii–iii.
39. Similar phantasmagorias underlay the social investigations of Alexandre Parent-
Duchâtelet and others. See Rosanvallon, *Moment Guizot*, 260; Salvandy, *Vingt mois*, xv and 11;
Alain Corbin, *Le miasme et la jonquille: l'odorat et l'imaginaire social XVIIIe–XIXe siècles* (Paris, 1988
[1982]), 25–28, 106; Shelley Rice, *Parisian Views* (Cambridge, Mass., 1997), 158–59; and Antoine Picon and Jean-Paul Robert, *Un atlas parisien: le dessus des cartes* (Paris, 1999), 177.

lure of an underground that, beyond the romantic quest for high emotions, promised to disclose subterranean verities and regenerate the nation.[40] Much in this field seemingly took place below the surface. With its vocation to "illuminate and preserve all the buried monuments of national history," the CTH earned praise for "resuscitat[ing] ... the buried and forgotten France." Officials spoke of "great riches ... [that] remain *interred*"; "*buried*" documents in archival depots; "the voice and teachings of the past within the *depths* of the soil."[41] In the late 1860s, elites from the Nord still promised to study the "various layers of our *pays*'s soil," the "sole depository today of the secrets of our annals and local origins."[42]

Two decades earlier, a CTH correspondent had written the ministry that "Autun's soil ... continues to throw out medals, stilettos, Gallic coins."[43] He, perhaps, could simply gather what the soil regurgitated, but most of these actors felt that a bolder approach was in order. It was up to them to dig, excavate, "study the development of the country in its most intimate and hidden elements." It was up to them to venture beneath this surface and sift the soil, to penetrate an expanse that was both the site of the "ills" and the repository of "national will." The cult of local memories pointed toward subterranean principles and a national or local essence—buried in the soil and in time. Forgotten and hidden from view, the latter would, once unearthed, provide the nation with historical markers and mirrors of its true self. "We will reveal to the *pays* the riches of its entrails, . . . the glorious memories and lofty lessons of its history," promised the secretary of the Société des lettres, sciences et arts de l'Aveyron in 1837. The cult of local memories would venture into "the entrails of society" and, like the nascent geological science, lay bare the nation's "successive sediments."[44]

Everything, of course, did not take place under the surface. Equally important within this imaginary were the exhaustive canvassing, identifica-

40. See, however, Aurélia Gaillard, ed., *L'imaginaire du souterrain* (Paris, 1997); and Claudie Bernard, *Passé recomposé*, 177.

41. The original words were *enfouis* and *ensevelis*. This trope of hidden authenticity would recur during the late nineteenth and twentieth centuries in what Herman Lebovics calls a "vision of True France." See Lebovics, *True France: The Wars Over Cultural Identity, 1900–1945* (Ithaca, 1992), 9; *RSS*, 1st ser., 1 (January 1848): 8; *France littéraire* 9 (1840): 165; Guizot, report to Louis-Philippe, 31 December 1833, in Charmes, 3; Thierry, report to Guizot, 10 March 1837, in Charmes, 54; and *Rapport au roi sur le budget du Ministère de l'instruction publique pour l'exercice 1839* (Paris, 1838), 39. My italics.

42. Prospectus, in *Bulletin scientifique, historique et littéraire du département du Nord et des pays voisins* 1, no. 1 (1869): 2; and *BCN* 11 (1871): 375.

43. AN F17 2810/1: Louis de Rosny to Min. Pub. Instr., 15 August 1842.

44. AN F17 2823: Charles Jourdain et al., memorandum to Gustave Rouland, 22 February 1859; *Mémoires de la Société des lettres, sciences et arts de l'Aveyron* 1 (1837–38), part 1: xlviii; Salvandy, *Vingt mois*, 8; and Eugène Tailliar, *Notice sur l'origine et la formation des villages du Nord de la France* (Douai, 1862), 3. On geology and archaeology, see Antoine Schnapp, *La conquête du passé: aux origines de l'archéologie* (Paris, 1993), 275–81.

tion, and representation of the terrain, or ground. Consider the "topographical index" that has survived in the archives of the Société dunkerquoise. Written between 1855 and 1865, this manuscript notebook is nothing more than a comprehensive alphabetical listing of town and village names from the arrondissement of Dunkirk.[45] We know little about this index—whether it responded to an official request, whether the association commissioned it, whether a member produced it of his own volition. It was done with care, however, and deemed worthy of preservation. Its author(s) presumably found it scientifically useful, a contribution to the *statistical* study of place names and topography that had begun decades earlier. Yet the work is unusually terse. Unlike others produced at the time, it provides neither etymological nor historical information on these toponyms. It nonetheless helps explain the appeal of genres and practices—inventories, topographies, inventories, learned dictionaries, and classificatory tableaus—that had grown prevalent in the eighteenth century and now became ubiquitous within, among others, the field of local memories. Avatars, according to Michel Foucault, of a premodern relationship to the empirical world, a "spatialization" and *quadrillage* that furnished "the possibility of constant order," they also reflected a new desire to capture a civilization in its totality and the rise of an archaeological science, predicated on sequence and series.[46]

Indeed, these genres and practices demonstrate the valence of in situ investigation (*sur les lieux*) within the elite's imaginary. Most ventures in this field rested on the firsthand canvassing of a local territory or a description of the latter and its historical landscape. Provincial archives bear traces of countless questionnaires—official and not—inviting civil servants and learned society members to undertake local journeys in search of data and artifacts.[47] Contributors to the Parisian *Le Panorama* claimed to "interrogate" plains, riverbanks, hills, or other "place[s]" that were imbued with historical memories. "What better means to arrive at truth than to take note of events where they took place?" asked the president of the Société d'émulation de Cambrai in 1843. This conviction persisted under the Second Empire, buttressed by a CTH whose archaeological inventories could "only [be] correctly executed by people who will travel across the *pays* and see for themselves the monuments they describe."[48] The ground required analysis as testimony of economic and political revolu-

45. ASD, box E: "Topographical index" (n.d.).
46. Michel Foucault, *Les mots et les choses* (Paris, 1966), chap. 5, quotations on 144 and 171; and Dominique Poulot, "Birth of Heritage," 48–49 and 52.
47. See, for instance, ADN 1 T 253/3.
48. Prospectus for *Le Panorama* (n.d. [1837?]); *Le Panorama* 3 (n.d. [September 1837]): 83; *MEC* 18 (1843): 8; and AN F17 3307: Anon. CTH member, report on Boyer, "Répertoire archéologique des arrondissements de Sancerre et de Saint Amand" (n.d. [1862]).

tions, whose impact required local observation. Paradoxically, it also displayed the "deep traces" of memories that "civil discord" had failed to erase. This in situ investigation furthermore reflects a broader scientific transformation in which *études de cabinet* gave way to local empirical studies—observation, interviews—that complemented written sources and produced "cumulative" knowledge.[49] Jean-Yves Guiomar has suggested that the growing popularity of geology helped create a new relationship between the surface (or landscape) and the soil, between geography and history in the 1840s. An "intimate bond" linked the *pays*'s "geological structure and the relief of its surface," posited a historian from Bergues in 1858.[50] Each local investigation hence became an avenue into immemorial origins.

At the same time, such in situ knowledge constituted yet another anchor for an era in which things were not necessarily what they seemed. Predicated on thorough procedures, these genres and practices granted the historical and physical landscapes a reassuring seal of concreteness and authenticity. Traditionalists and many liberals agreed that abstract rationalization produced anarchy. Rooted in direct observation and accumulation of facts, archaeological inventories and the like would help "the TRUE gush forth," as Louis-Philippe put it, by undermining the empire of "illusions" and opinions.[51] "In some sense closer to reality," the "provinces" provided an avenue toward "authentic meaning" and "love of all parts of the *sol* [rather than] . . . cold doctrines." Thanks to such local investigations, "truth will soon regain most of its brilliance."[52]

It would do so, most pertinently, through exhaustive collections and classifications of local data—such as Dunkirk's topographical index. The latter represented a legible territory, in which everything was identified, granted meaning, and fitted into clear, explanatory frameworks. It captured the nineteenth century's obsession with ordering and cataloguing—visible in Balzac's *Comédie humaine* as well as the taxonomies of Linnaeus. Like the Swedish naturalist, participants in the field of local memories vowed to draw up all-encompassing nomenclatures. "We will

49. AN F17 3308: Du Mèze, "Répertoire archéologique du département de la Haute-Garonne" (n.d. [1860]); Marie-Noëlle Bourguet, "De la Méditerranée," in idem et al., eds., *L'invention scientifique de la Méditerranée: Egypte, Morée, Algérie* (Paris, 1998), 17; and Jean-Yves Puyo, "Pratiques de l'excursion sous la Troisième République: les forestiers, les naturalistes et les géographes," in Guy Baudelle, Marie-Vic Ozouf-Marignier, and Marie-Claire Robic, eds., *Géographes en pratiques (1870–1945): le terrain, le livre, la cité* (Rennes, 2001), 316–17.

50. Jean-Yves Guiomar, "Le désir d'un tableau," *Le Débat* 24 (1983): 90–106; and *Mémoires de la Société de l'histoire et des beaux-arts de la Flandre Maritime de France* 2 (1858): 6.

51. Louis-Philippe, undated apothegm, in Eugène Paignon, ed., *Code des rois, pensées et opinions d'un prince souverain sur les affaires de l'Etat* (Paris, 1848), 129.

52. *France départementale* 1 (1834): 31; Armand-René Du Chatellier, *Du mouvement des études*, 40–42; and *MSV* 6 (1846): i.

excavate [*fouiller*] our old France to describe, catalogue and reason it," wrote the archaeologist Adolphe-Napoléon Didron in 1834. "The 37,200 communes must be visited, explored from all directions," echoed Salvandy in 1839. "Not a single monument, not a single ruin fragment . . . must go unmentioned."[53] Similar ambitions underlay local monographs—all-encompassing historical narratives that apprehended the *pays* "from all conceivable points of view"—and monumental *statistiques* that would describe "every monument of every canton, without a single exception." Themselves acts of cultural creation, these taxonomic practices illustrate Claude Lévi-Strauss's contention that "any classification is superior to chaos."[54] This elite's yearning for transparency, order, and certitude explains in large part the appeal of "totalizing" practices, of all-purpose analytical grids that left no site uninspected, no artifact unexamined, no hamlet unaccounted for.

These places and artifacts were not only tabulated, but also linked to one another within representations of unified territories and communities, cleansed of singular, atypical phenomena. "Unity! Unity! Everything invokes it, everything asks for it anew," cried out a *littérateur* from the Nord in 1838. Following a prevalent Catholic framework, local memories and association were avenues toward a broader moral and spiritual unity: the unity of Providence, transcending "the variety of things and events"; the "unity of thought, expressed implicitly by the word Faith"; the "unity of sentiment, expressed implicitly by the word Charity."[55] This concern with unity—and its correlatives: harmony, synthesis, reconciliation—also constitutes, for Raoul Girardet, one of the four leading "mythological" configurations of nineteenth- and twentieth-century political thought. It sprang from the widespread conviction of living through a "crisis of civilization." By the same token, the revolutionary fixation with national unification lost little of its resonance in ensuing decades.[56] Just as the new "administration essentially need[ed] unity," so the CTH's historical ventures retraced the historical progression of a united nation, beyond the political strife of times past. According to a Second Empire official, they

53. AN 42 AP 21: Didron, "Ce que doit être et ce que doit faire l'archéologue," November 1834; and Salvandy to correspondents, circular of 1 March 1839, in Charmes, 96. On the influence of natural history on local history and archaeology, see Françoise Bercé, "Arcisse de Caumont et les sociétés savantes," in Pierre Nora, ed., *Lieux de Mémoire*, 3: 539–40.

54. *MSDu* 18 (1875): xxxiii; *AIP* (1851): 199–204; and Claude Lévi-Strauss, *La pensée sauvage* (Paris, 1962), 24. On the Enlightenment origins of such "taxonomic efforts," see Roche, *France des lumières*, 35.

55. *RN*, 3rd ser. (April 1838): 116; *RN*, 3rd ser. (June 1839): 231; and *MSDu* 6 (1859): 10.

56. Raoul Girardet, *Mythes et mythologies politiques* (Paris, 1986), esp. section 4, quotation on 168; Anne-Marie Thiesse, *La création des identités nationales. Europe, XVIIIe–XXe siècle* (Paris, 1999), 178; and Georges Gusdorf, *Les sciences humaines et la pensée occidentale*, 12 vols. (Paris, 1966–82), 9: *Fondements du savoir romantique*, 400.

glorified a regime whose "parts were in solidarity with one another [and interwoven in a] marvelous unity."[57] On a more concrete level, they also hinged on the cooperation of North and South, Paris and provinces, and state and civil society—all of them equal contributors to a common cause.

The same held true outside ministerial offices. Did the cult of local memories not rest on voluntary association, "reciprocal affection" between local residents, a "spirit" that assimilated all "intelligences, . . . all wills"?[58] The Académie du Gard's greatest merit, according to its secretary, was to "give the example of deep-seated concord to a most divided population." Genres such as the *statistique* and the dictionary likewise incorporated all branches of learning in a common framework, while scientific congresses united "all savants through a common bond."[59] The ubiquitous use of correspondents—by the CTH, Parisian *littérateurs*, and provincial learned societies—would anchor Frenchmen within unifying networks. For Saint-Simonians as for others, the conceptual appeal of networks fed and paralleled their material extension during this era (telegraphs, sewers, railroad lines). They promised to regularize and order a fragmented and chaotic society, dominated by individualism (a term coined in 1825 in France) and egoism (included in a French *Dictionary of New Words* in 1842). In addition to political rights and romantic subjectivity, individualism denoted economic self-interest and personal ambition. Charles de Rémusat spoke for many when he linked the predicament of postrevolutionary France to the rupture of personal ties, the abolition of permanent social functions, and a wanting spiritual authority. Freed from all political, corporate, or religious moorings, atomized individuals wandered aimlessly, prey to what Le Glay called "the individual pride that circulates within society to dissolve it." The cult of local memories—this collective, orderly, transcendental venture—would benefit an age of "individual strife."[60]

Ultimately, the cult of local memories pointed toward the reconciliation that undergirded all others: the reconciliation of ideas. Some contemporaries, it is true, entered this field to recover an idealized commu-

---

57. ADN M 137/37: Min. Int. to prefects, circular of 23 September 1836; and AN F17 2649/2: Rector Douai to Min. Pub. Instr., 15 November 1858.

58. *La Guienne* (Bordeaux), 7 May 1852; and *Mémoires de la Société d'agriculture, sciences, arts et belles-lettres de Bayeux* 1 (1842): 4.

59. AN F17 3318: Secretary Académie du Gard to Min. Pub. Instr., 6 April 1858; and *CS* 1 [Caen] (Rouen, 1833), x–xi.

60. Koenraad W. Swart, " 'Individualism' in the Mid-Nineteenth Century (1826–1860)," *Journal of the History of Ideas* 23, no. 1 (1962): 77–90; Richard de Radonvilliers, *Enrichissement de la langue française*, 161; Darío Roldán, *Charles de Rémusat: certitudes et impasses du libéralisme doctrinaire* (Paris, 1999), 75; and *Procès-verbal de la séance générale du 23 février 1842 de l'Association lilloise*, 2.

nity that, in their eyes, the French Revolution had torn asunder and industrial progress now threatened to destroy. One should not underestimate their presence and impact. In an era of "moral decrepitude" and corruptive equality, an era in which hordes "from all countries and professions" infested a once glorious Paris, local history depicted "times of order" and respect for one's social station.[61] Yet, what Amiens's mayor called the "resuscit[ation] of the past" transcended misoneism to outline a broader social and political transformation.[62] The vocabulary emanating from this field is suggestive:

"We *recompose* the history of this region" (Le Glay, 1833).
"To *restore* to life our *pays's* history" (*Revue cambrésienne*, 1837).
"The *reconstruction* of local history" (Prefect of the Cantal, 1858).[63]

The rhetoric of recomposition captures this field's twin dimensions—ostensibly conflicting yet inseparable. We find, on the one hand, an urge to salvage and record the nation's "debris," to capture a physical remnant or image of what once had been; on the other, a desire to reconstruct and renew, to build a new society on recovered historical foundations. The fusion of present and past would yield a new amalgam and reinvigorate the country. A double connection with the French Revolution was at play. Elites reestablished historical threads that the latter had severed, but they also co-opted revolutionary discourse and aspirations by inaugurating an "era of regeneration."[64] To recompose meant to rebuild what had been toppled, but also to create something new. This was, however, a recomposition through, rather than against, history and, on this plane, against rather than through politics. The cult of local memories thus seduced many of these elites because of the weight they attached to social harmony—to be realized within the *pays*—and an intellectual realm that promised to heal and reform French society. It would furnish true self-understanding, allow reason to express itself, depoliticize postrevolutionary France, and operate a moral rapprochement. Decades after 1789, the time had come for the nation to undertake the indispensable intellectual and moral revolution: the revolution that would tell France what it was and, hence, end all revolutions.

61. BMA ms. 440: Sanson de Pongerville to François-César Louandre, 28 September 1847 and 28 November 18[?].
62. Municipal Archives of Amiens, 1 D 1–31: Proceedings of the Municipal Council of Amiens, 11 March 1841 On the idealization of medieval community as palliative to industrial materialism, see Lionel Gossman, *Medievalism and the Ideologies of the Enlightenment: The World and Work of La Curne de Sainte-Palaye* (Baltimore, 1968), 333 and 357–58.
63. Delloye 38/16: Le Glay, speech of 8 January 1833; *Revue cambrésienne* 2 (June 1837): 303; and AN F17 2811: Prefect of Cantal to Min. Pub. Instr., 13 May 1858 (my italics).
64. *MSV* 6 (1846): i; and *CS* 10 (Strasbourg, 1842), xxii.

"TO MY PAYS"

While contemporaries entertained such ambitions regardless of where they lived, provincials were also cultivating the personal memories of their *pays* of birth or residence. Their inventories and monographs embodied acute memorial aspirations and what Lucy Lippard eloquently termed topographical intimacy. Be it in Melun, Béziers, or Bordeaux, these actors sought not only to pacify and regenerate, but also to retrieve personal memories (even childhood ones), "honor themselves," and tell "posterity who our predecessors were, who we will have been."[65] Dedicating her monograph on Beauvais "to my *pays*," Fanny Dénoix des Vergnes promised to "reaffirm our old renown, our young grandeur." She and others delineated a "collective individuality," a local personality whose traits—be it perseverance or courage—had a long history.[66] "When my memory reminds me of the events and men who, in other times, honored the *pays*," declared a member of the Association lilloise in 1841, "I confess to feeling pride" in belonging to the said *pays*. The cult of local memories clearly revolved around personal and collective identities—the recovery and amplification of forgotten or missing sentiments.[67]

Excessive references to "identity" in academic parlance and popular culture have eroded its analytical precision.[68] I nonetheless use it here to capture these actors' own intentions and because I take seriously the contention that meaning production and authority—what Bronislaw Baczko calls "interpretative schemes" and "valorization"—are intertwined. As a heuristic, identity makes it possible to apprehend these overlapping yet distinct domains in a single analysis. First, territorial identity will refer to self-representation and meaning production, the constitution and expression of an individual and collective sense of self—anchored in space and history, inherently singular, and defined against other social groups. One thinks and depicts a social world that is legible and provides a meaningful and more or less firm location. Second, the term will denote strategic ef-

65. Lucy R. Lippard, *The Lure of the Local: Senses of Place in a Multicentered Society* (New York, 1997), 33; H. G. Nicolet, *Histoire de Melun depuis son origine jusqu'à nos jours* (Melun, 1845), 349; *Bulletin de la Société archéologique de Béziers* 3 (1839): 179; and *Actes de l'Académie royale des sciences, belles-lettres et arts de Bordeaux* 21 (1859): 273.

66. Fanny Dénoix des Vergnes, *Beauvais* (Paris, 1858), n.p. [iii]; and Victor de Courmaceul, *Etude statistique sur l'arrondissement de Valenciennes et considérations sur son état ancien et moderne et sur ses progrès au XIXe siècle* (Dunkirk, 1860), 56–57.

67. BML, fonds Godefroy 14688: Anon., quoted in "Association lilloise. Séance du 21 juin 1841. Discours de M. Le Glay, président" (Lille, 1841), 8. See also Patrick Garcia, *Le bicentenaire de la Révolution française: pratiques sociales d'une commémoration* (Paris, 2000), 189.

68. See John Gillis, "Memory and Identity: The History of a Relationship," in idem, ed., *Commemorations: The Politics of National Identity* (Princeton, N.J., 1994), 3–24; and Rogers Brubaker, "Au-delà de l'identité," *Actes de la recherche en sciences sociales* 139 (September 2001): 66–85.

forts to attain more explicitly political objectives: status, influence, and authority.[69] Following Pierre Bourdieu, this is not only the authority to devise and impose classificatory grids and categories, but also the political and cultural authority to name and define, to propound a "vision of the social world," to "mobiliz[e] groups."[70]

It is from this dual vantage point that I would approach compilations of local data that, like Dunkirk's topographical index, betray a puzzling concern with the minutiae and historical specificity of one's *pays*. The *sol* was not only a geographical expanse, but also "a ground into which our fathers' steps have imprinted memories."[71] If these elites deemed it so important to canvass the latter, name it, and retrieve its singular memories, it was largely to tailor their self-representation (both private and public), to discover and let others know who they were. It was also to shore up their position and affirm their continuing relevance in a changing environment. Their overlapping identities—as residents of a particular locale; as men of learning and, in some cases, professionals; as eminent urban citizens and natural leaders; as arbiters of the *pays*'s history and topography—rested on a renewed sense of place. They hinged on clearly articulated local relations—both horizontal and vertical—and the survival of "local differences and nuances" that they alone knew and could delineate. This was true of those nobles who legitimated their patronage and authority by inscribing their familial ancestry in provincial memories.[72] It was also true of the middling elites who, unlike notables and some nobles, rarely benefited from a wide (national or international) social network or participated in supralocal alliances, whether social, economic, or political. Leading provincial industrialists and traders deepened their presence in Paris during the first half of the century, but not these elites. They were closer to what anthropologist Robert Redfield termed *literati*—a literate stratum protective of local specificity and prerogatives—than the worldlier *intelligentsia*.[73]

Widespread following the advent of the railroad, anxieties about the loss

69. This definition betrays a concern with identity as construct (rather than essence) and with the *public* constitution of self, place, and authority—rather than with private and more elusive identifications. I have drawn in part from John Bodnar, *Remaking America*, 42–43; and John Money, *Experience and Identity: Birmingham and the West Midlands, 1760–1800* (Manchester, 1977), 75. See also Baczko, *Imaginaires sociaux*, 35.

70. Pierre Bourdieu, "L'identité et la représentation: éléments pour une réflexion critique sur l'idée de région," *Actes de la recherche en sciences sociales* 35 (1980): 63–66 and 69; and idem, *La distinction: critique sociale du jugement* (Paris, 1979), 556–60.

71. *Mémoires de la Société d'agriculture, sciences, arts et belles-lettres de Bayeux* 1 (1842): 10.

72. Claude-Isabelle Brelot, *Noblesse réinventée*, 2: 645 and 877; and David Higgs, *Nobles in Nineteenth-Century France: The Practice of Inegalitarianism* (Baltimore, 1987), esp. 9–10, 19, and 142.

73. Robert Redfield, *The Primitive World and Its Transformations* (Ithaca, 1953), 43–44. I borrow the term *supralocal alliance* from Giovanni Levi, *Inheriting Power: The Story of an Exorcist*, trans. Lydia G. Cochrane (Chicago, 1988), 131–35.

FIGURE 9. Cambrai around 1835: a middling agricultural and textile center comprising eighteen thousand inhabitants, eight hundred eligible voters, four newspapers, and a municipal library of twenty-seven thousand volumes. Industrialization had begun—with its textile factories and coal mines—but Cambrai still retained much of its middling-town physiognomy. Courtesy of the Cabinet des Estampes, Bibliothèque Nationale de France (Paris).

of "provincial originalities"—physical configuration, talents, monuments and memories—thus afflicted these circles more than others. At a time in which urban residents often linked their personal well-being to their city's, they proved especially acute in middling towns whose prospects were stymied by the growing economic monopolies of Paris and regional centers (see figure 9).[74] Cambrai and Douai thus staged historical pageants, not only to sell themselves, but also to recover "at least a portion of the splendor that [their] isolation causes [them] to lose each day." All that remained, perhaps, was the glory of their past, "the apogee of Douai's grandeur" that, in 1861, pageant organizers claimed to capture by reenacting the 1405 entry of John the Fearless, duke of Burgundy. Had this not been an era of commercial vigor, the town's heyday as political center of a powerful dynasty? By enabling "the elite of Douai's youth" to impersonate vigorous burghers, these organizers reclaimed this long-standing splendor and bolstered their sense of self-worth as *douaisiens*. But all elites did not celebrate their place of birth and a familial patrimony. Of greater import

74. *Revue d'Alsace* 1 (1834): 49; Wolfgang Schivelbusch, *The Railway Journey: The Industrialization of Time and Space in the 19th Century* (Berkeley, 1977); and Theodore Koditschek, *Class Formation and Urban-Industrial Society: Bradford, 1750–1850* (Cambridge, 1990), 23.

for some was the elevation of a territorial community "to which we belong by [birth] or adoption, through the heart."[75] The Galerie valenciennoise's sponsors did not care whether contributing artists were from Valenciennes or not as long as they glorified the town's past, reaffirmed its qualities, and established its preeminence over its neighbors. Like the town's pageants, the gallery would serve as a model for "all other cities."[76]

No one better captured the self-comforting dimension of such memorial ventures than Friedrich Nietzsche. "The history of the city becomes for [the antiquarian] the history of his self," he wrote in 1874. "He understands the wall, the turreted gate . . . and finds himself, his strength . . . , the happiness of knowing oneself not to be wholly arbitrary and accidental." Local history "imbue[d] modest, coarse, even wretched conditions," Nietzsche added, with "a simple touching feeling of pleasure and contentment." At stake, in addition to inner serenity, was one's power and influence, rooted in social function, tradition, or allegiance.[77] Local memories and their institutional supports—from associations to publications—constituted a clear means of social demarcation. To be sure, entry into a provincial learned society did not denote social and cultural leadership as clearly as it had a century earlier. These voluntary associations were exclusive enough, however, to forge social ties among their members and separate them from the laboring class. While some amalgamated nobles and bourgeois, others allowed middling professional elites to distinguish themselves from the nobility, notables, or even the commercial bourgeoisie. Like pageants or congresses, they provided a platform from which to delineate the local territory and its past, rule on all branches of local knowledge, distribute rewards, and speak for the community before local and national audiences alike.[78] The cult of local memories was also about collective self-affirmation and hegemony—about discreetly imposing a dominant vision of the social world.

75. *Gazette de Cambrai*, 21 August 1850; Bonnard, *Récit historique et détaillé de l'entrée de Jean-sans-Peur en la ville de Douai, en l'an 1405, fait d'après les documents les plus avérés* (Douai, n.d. [1861]), 1, 4, and 8; and *Annales de la Société d'agriculture, sciences, arts et commerce du Puy* 21 (1857–58): 129.

76. Urban rivalries were an ancient theme—with symbolic as well as material implications (including official subsidies). On such concerns in Valenciennes, for instance, see *MSV* 3 (1841): 286; and AMV 3 II 42: Proceedings of the Société des Incas, 6 November 1851. See also Ted Margadant, *Urban Rivalries in the French Revolution* (Princeton, N.J., 1992).

77. Friedrich Nietzsche, *On the Advantage and Disadvantage of History for Life*, trans. Peter Preuss (Indianapolis, 1980 [1874]), 19–20; and Robert A. Nisbet, *The Sociological Tradition*, 2d ed. (New Brunswick, 1993 [1966]), 6.

78. Robert Fox, "Learning, Politics and Polite Culture," 254–55; and Carol Harrison, *Bourgeois Citizen*, 3 and 51. On voluntary association and bourgeois class formation, see also R .J. Morris, "Voluntary Societies and British Urban Elites, 1780–1850: An Analysis," *The Historical Journal* 26, no. 1 (1983): 109–10; and Philippa Levine, *The Amateur and the Professional: Antiquarians, Historians, and Archaeologists in Victorian England, 1838–1886* (Cambridge, 1986), 11.

The scientific status of local memories was crucial on this plane as well. Science has long functioned as a means of social advancement in Western Europe, providing material resources, prestige, influence, and moral authority. This was especially true for these middling male elites who, like the German "Mandarins" studied by Fritz Ringer, occupied a tenuous terrain between aristocrats of birth and technical specialists. The slow but inexorable professionalization of French science—underway since the Revolution—progressively marginalized these amateurs.[79] To assert their relevance before the scientific establishment and buttress their local authority, these "dominated among the dominant" depicted themselves as the most diligent and eminent local scientists. Their expertise rested on their intimate knowledge of the locality, in situ observation, meticulous procedures, and selfless devotion to the *pays*.[80] Ostensibly apolitical practices, such as historical monographs, "legitimate[d their authors] in the enlightened world," liberal Léon Saladin wrote his friend Salvandy in 1825. Men of science and talent, who rejected "coteries" and favored "the public good over . . . empty restlessness and intrigues," could lay claim to "intellectual leadership."[81] Theirs was a gendered leadership—all the more so in these congresses and learned societies. Their annual public meetings reaffirmed—before a largely female audience—the masculine qualities of male elites: selfless devotion to the locality, fraternity, rigor (but also imagination), industriousness, the inner fortitude to complete arid investigations, the "courage" to "risk one's sight and health while consulting immense archives."[82] Speakers apologized when addressing topics they deemed too dry or technical for women. They asked the latter for their "indulgence" and "patronage." And they operated a predictable division of labor: practical and rational matters to men, spiritual and emotional ones ("the maternal heart") to women.[83]

Underlying this local identity, finally, was the premise that outsiders lacked the knowledge and legitimacy to demarcate one's *pays* and its past.[84]

79. Maurice Crosland, "The Development of a Professional Career in Science in France," in idem, ed., *The Emergence of Science in Western Europe* (New York, 1976), 140–41.

80. Fritz K. Ringer, *The Decline of the German Mandarins: The German Academic Community, 1890–1933* (Cambridge, Mass., 1969), 7; Alex Dolby, "Afterword: Scientific Knowledge, Power and Space," in Crosbie Smith and Jon Agar, eds., *Making Space for Science: Territorial Themes in the Shaping of Knowledge* (New York, 1998), 335; and Bourdieu, "Field of Power, Literary Field and Habitus," in his *Field of Cultural Production*, 164–65. On science and cultural legitimation, see Steven A. Shapin, "The Pottery Philosophical Society, 1819–1835: An Examination of the Cultural Uses of Provincial Science," *Science Studies* 2 (1972): 311–336.

81. AN 152 AP 2: Léon Saladin to Salvandy, 7 January 1825; *MSV* 7 (1846): 41–42; and *Annales de la Société royale académique de Nantes et du département de la Loire-Inférieure* 8 (1837): 81.

82. *RN*, 1st ser., 1, no. 3 (March 1835): 373; and Le Glay, *Chronique d'Arras*, ix.

83. *MSDu* 7 (1861): 32; *MSDu* 3 (1856):17; *MSDu* 19 (1876): xviii; and Harrison, *Bourgeois Citizen*, esp. 12 and 66–68.

84. On this theme in Lyons and Florence, see Saunier, "Ville comme antidote?" 157–59.

Elites from Angoulême thus denounced the errors regarding "local traditions" and history in Parisian guides and dictionaries about their region. Other elites defended their *pays*'s historical glory, seeking to prove that "no region in France is richer than ours in historical memories." It was "a duty of honor to . . . rehabilitate" oneself and a *pays* that Parisian travelers such as Etienne de Jouy and Mérimée had "mistreated"—that is, ridiculed or condemned to obscurity.[85] In the Nord, elites acknowledged the disastrous impact of successive wars on local monuments, but they likewise upheld the reputation of Joan of Constantinople (1188–1244), countess of Flanders and Hainaut. Responding to Henri Martin and the other Paris-based historians who blamed her for her father's death, they extolled her Christian charity, municipal leadership, and commitment to communal charters. To denigrate her was to "rob" local residents of their "own patrimony, a sacred heritage to all of us, her children."[86]

POLITICS AND CITIZENSHIP

This was, no doubt, both a cultural and a political question. We know that history (national or local) had long sustained a discourse of virtue and patriotism as well as political demands for liberties and responsibility in France, that it became "the school of the true citizen" (D. Roche) by the late eighteenth century. This trend intensified during the early nineteenth century, be it in texts or on the stage.[87] We know less, however, about the growing political resonance of local memories during the century's middle decades. Reclaiming the legacy of 1789, the July Monarchy not only renewed interest in the origins of the nation and the bourgeois order, but heightened expectations for a more equitable distribution of political power and an extension of civic responsibilities (notably at the local level). In 1833, a journalist from Rouen defined "the great intellectual insurrection of the departments" as a triumphant "political revolution." A decade later, the legitimist *Gazette du Languedoc* noted that "innovators" were seizing morals, philosophy, and history. "The latter, above all,

85. *Bulletin de la Société archéologique et historique de la Charente* 1 (1845): 23; *Mémoires de la Société des lettres, sciences et arts de l'Aveyron* 1 (1837–38), part 1: xxxiii–iv; and Albertine Clément-Hémery, *Promenades dans l'arrondissement d'Avesnes*, 2 vols. (Valenciennes, 1829), 1:3–4. Other regions, such as the Perche, had to battle Parisian indifference rather than derision: Corbin, *Monde retrouvé*, 37.

86. Edward Le Glay, *Histoire de Jeanne de Constantinople, comtesse de Flandre et de Hainaut* (Lille, 1841); Jules Deligne, *Eloge de Jeanne de Constantinople, comtesse de Flandre et de Hainaut* (Lille, 1844), 22; *Association lilloise. Ouverture des conférences hebdomadaires de 1844* (Lille, 1844), 8; and *AHN*, 3d ser., 5 (1855): 440–41.

87. Roche, *France des lumières*, 97; and Régis Bertrand, "Erudits et historiens de Haute-Provence depuis le XVIIe siècle," *Provence historique* 38, no. 151 (January–March 1988): 309. See also Stanley Mellon, *The Political Uses of History: A Study of Historians in the French Restoration* (Stanford, 1958); and Tollebeek, "Historiographie en tant qu'élément culturel," 60–65.

seemed to offer new conquests. Every village, every small departmental subdivision has had its chronicler [of late]."[88] Indeed, the cult of local memories reveals a broader politicization of the local as past and territory. Political modernity meant that history belonged to all, and should include all. The lowliest locality could now lay claim to a personal glory, take pride in its political history, and hence contribute to a truly national history. In doing so, it fulfilled the promises of the French Revolution. The latter, as liberal Félix Bourquelot explained in his 1839 *Histoire de Provins*, had turned an individual history into a collective one, thereby illustrating "the intimate link between general history and local history." If Frédéric Soulié deemed it essential to pen historical narratives on the Languedoc in 1836, it was also because local monographs now constituted stories of freedom, rather than enslavement. For *littérateur* Aristide Guilbert as well, every locality, every province had "memories of might, grandeur, and glory." He accordingly sought to restore the "individuality" of French towns, "these one thousand powerful aggregations of citizens who, for fourteen hundred years, have formed our nation's most advanced element."[89]

At the same time, this period rapidly became one of disillusion—be it in the mid-1830s, when the regime curtailed political participation and intensified censorship, or following the Second Republic's turn to the right. Restrictions on political expression and association were severe enough to nourish discretion, yet loose enough for new political arenas to emerge. This further explains the appeal of local memories—of a localist rhetoric that could express oppositional designs, of voluntary associations or congresses whose "suggested names[,] . . . allegorical forms" and procedures (elections, petitions, discussions) could serve hidden political purposes.[90] This intellectual elite after all included numerous editors, pamphleteers, *Conseil général* members, and others whose civic and political commitments were as heartfelt as their desire to escape politics.[91] Elie Brun-Lavainne's 1836 speech on women in medieval and Renaissance Lille captures their rhetorical strategies. Contrasting the chivalrous order of the late Middle Ages with the Renaissance, Brun-Lavainne posited that the lat-

---

88. *Revue de Rouen* 2 (10 July–10 December 1833): 383–84; and *Gazette du Languedoc*, 26 July 1842.

89. H. Piers, *Histoire de la ville de Bergues-Saint-Winoc* (Saint-Omer, 1833), 71; Félix Bourquelot, *Histoire de Provins* (Provins, 1839), 5; Soulié, *Romans historiques*, 1:xi; Guilbert, *Histoire des villes*, 1: xii; and Prospectus for *Histoire des villes* (n.d. [1844?]). This conviction persisted in later decades: see *MEC* 31 (1870), 2 vols., 1:27–28. On the policitization of the territory at this time, see Paule Petitier, *La géographie de Michelet: territoire et modèles naturels dans les premières oeuvres de Michelet* (Paris, 1997), 217–18.

90. Catherine Duprat, "Des Lumières au premier XIXe siècle. Voie française de la philanthropie," in Colette Bec et al., eds., *Philanthropies et politiques sociales en Europe (XVIIIe–XXe siècles)* (Paris, 1994), 14–15.

91. Line Skorka, "Les sociétés savantes de l'Yonne et le pouvoir politique," presentation to the Colloque de l'Association Bourguignonne des Sociétés Savantes, Sens, 1 October 1994.

ter had seen the "genius of art" die out, skepticism poison philosophy, and the condition of women deteriorate. "This is where we will stop," he then declared. "It is in the past alone that we have sought to draw lessons. The present and the future are outside our domain." This paralipsis clearly yielded a political commentary on the contemporary era. Brun-Lavainne drew a boundary between past and present, history and politics to expose its artificiality, tiptoe around it, and then implicitly cross it.[92] A decade later, a liberal historian from Valenciennes explained that he had replaced "pretentious genealogies" by popular revolutions in his historical topography of the town. For the secretary of the Société d'agriculture, sciences et arts de l'arrondissement de Valenciennes, nothing better illustrated this historian's "democratic sentiments" and origins in a "middle class that had always dominated . . . our *pays* of old franchises."[93]

Countless other texts and speeches furnished tacit yet hardly opaque commentaries on the social and political order. The same was true of historical pageants, whose contents—and omissions—reflected their organizers' political views. Rancorous debates sometimes followed. In Cambrai, traditionalists condemned the "narrow partisan spirit" of liberals who had evacuated knights from the fête's program. Reformist liberals, in turn, accused the former of "falsifying the spirit of history" by allowing political sentiments to dominate their own pageant programs. They also accused traditionalists and aristocrats of pining for organic, local communities that, like the "ancient peers of the Cambrésis," they would dominate as their fiefs.[94] In 1851, the increasingly conservative *fête communale* polarized Cambrai's leading newspapers. What the pro-Order *Gazette de Cambrai* saw as an "homage to the memory of those who preceded us in life," the republican-liberal *Echo de Cambrai* castigated as a return to "feudal monarchy" that "humiliated the people in their dearest memories." The pageant belittled "the great movement of communal emancipation" and the French Revolution (represented by a lone, sad float). As elsewhere in France, competing political groups battled for control of the local past.[95]

This politicization took another form. "At a time in which provincial patriotism awakens," Le Glay declared in 1834, "it is natural that each *contrée* . . . discover what it was when it had an independent existence and did

---

92. Elie Brun-Lavainne, "De la condition des femmes dans l'ancienne Châtellenie de Lille," in *Association Lilloise pour l'encouragement des lettres et des arts dans le département du Nord. Séance d'installation du 17 décembre 1836* (Lille, 1836), 32.

93. *MSV* 6 (1846): iii; and *MSV* 7 (1846): 64.

94. Delloye 39/110: Clippings from *L'Emancipateur*, n.d. [1838]; Delloye 39/13: Clipping from *La Feuille de Cambrai*, n. d. [March 1839]; and [Fidèle Delcroix], *Programme de la marche triomphale des chars, cavalcades, etc. à la fête communale de Cambrai. 15 et 17 août 1838* (Cambrai, 1838), 4.

95. *La Gazette de Cambrai*, 28 July 1851; and *L'Echo de Cambrai*, 21 August 1851. On similar debates in Franche-Comté, see Brelot, *Noblesse réinventée*, 2: 636–37.

not constitute a suburb of Paris." Douai's pageant organizers extolled the newfangled interest of French cities for "their ancient institutions" and "individuality" at a time of growing "Parisian centralization." A few years later, a history professor from Montpellier devoted several pages of his urban monograph to "the necessity of reviving municipal institutions against the excesses of administrative centralization."[96] Such statements were not in themselves bellicose, but they rested on an ill-defined and fundamentally political vocabulary of local emancipation, franchises, and decentralization. Steeped in historical references and ubiquitous from the 1820s on, this vocabulary seduced most political schools.[97] *Emancipation* typically referred to the enfranchisement of medieval towns from the yoke of feudal lords as well as the seizure of local liberties—now in need of reaffirmation. It also came to denote a broader distancing from the state. *Décentralisation* and *décentraliser*, along with less successful neologisms such as *décentralité*, emerged between the late 1820s and 1845 to denote devolution—of administrative responsibilities, political rights, or cultural resources—from Paris to the provinces.[98] They underlay broad demands for intellectual "deconcentration" (source of provincial apathy); traditionalist claims to local preeminence before governmental authority; as well as reformist demands for bourgeois self-government within a state of law. Eugène Bouly—a visceral opponent of the July Monarchy—thus made Le Glay's statement on provincial patriotism the epigraph to his *Histoire de Cambrai* in 1842. He went further yet by contrasting in a pageant program the "emancipation of the communes" with the "slavery of centralization." Fifteenth-century Cambrai was not a mediocre subprefectoral seat, but a free city "whose *bourgeois*, proud of their franchises, told the Kings, when they so desired: be on your way."[99]

The language of municipal emancipation lost some of its resonance with the demise of the Orleanists and the center-left's difficulties to find a

---

96. Le Glay, *Chronique d'Arras*, x; *Fête du Moyen Age sous Philippe-le-Bon*, 3; and A. Germain, *Histoire de la commune de Montpellier*, 3 vols. (Montpellier, 1851), 1: ix–xii, citation on ix.

97. While it emerged throughout the provinces, this language was especially prominent in northern and western France, Alsace, and parts of Burgundy and the Southwest. For a rigorous analysis of the various conceptions of decentralization, see Sudhir Hazareesingh, *From Subject to Citizen: The Second Empire and the Emergence of Modern French Democracy* (Princeton, N.J., 1998).

98. *Centralité* had appeared in 1793, *centraliser* a year later. See *Trésor de la langue française*, 16 vols. (Paris, 1971–94), 6: 808; Vivien Schmidt, *Democratizing France: The Political and Administrative History of Decentralization* (Cambridge, 1990), 22; and François Burdeau, *Liberté, libertés locales chéries* (Paris, 1983), 49.

99. Brelot, "Le sentiment provincial en Franche-Comté pendant la première partie du XIXe siècle: persistances et sociologie," in *Annales littéraires de l'Université de Besançon* 216 (1979): 117–18; Delloye 38/100: Eugène Bouly, "Littérature locale. Programme de la fête communale. 15 août 1838" (n.p., 1838), 2; and *Gazette de Cambrai*, 12 March 1839 (italics in the original).

platform under the Second Empire. Cries for decentralization grew yet more forceful, however, after the events of June 1848—further proof of the capital's degeneration. Indeed, republican, liberal, and legitimist opponents of the Empire rapidly gravitated toward the rhetoric of decentralization, a "magical word" that escaped definition. By playing at once on political and nonpolitical registers, decentralization made it possible to portray oneself as a true representative of the nation, request local responsibilities and civic reform, and contest an unconstitutional regime without seeming overly antagonistic.[100] Indeed, then as earlier, intellectual elites exploited, with strategic intent, the semantic porosity between this vocabulary and local memories. Brun-Lavainne recalled in 1855 that "by uttering the cry of decentralization [in the 1830s], I was certain of finding favorable echoes during a time when, wherever one turned, people searched for the ancient titles of communal liberties." In Paris, provincialist periodicals likewise amalgamated the recovery of "our old local memories" with denunciations of an "administration" that—regardless of the regime—had "impose[d] everywhere its iron will" and nearly annihilated local "energy" since the Revolution. Showcasing the overlap between the political and historical fields, Guilbert complained that, in both of them, "one has overdone centralization, that is, one has vitiated an excellent principle through exaggeration."[101]

In many instances, however, the cult of local memories was politicized, but not necessarily because—or how—these actors intended it. "Communal emancipation," for example, meant different things in the historical and political fields, in erudite periodicals and parliamentary debates. At the same time, each utterance expressed—at least, for informed readers and auditors—this vocabulary's entire semantic register. In such cases, the cult of local memories was political as an intertextual operation. We cannot, for instance, divorce Le Glay's earlier statement on local independence and individuality from the political life of Lille. Few questions proved more contentious under the July Monarchy than the administrative status of mayors and the attributions of departmental and municipal councils. Contemporaries commonly framed these questions in the language of emancipation and decentralization. In 1843, Mayor Louis-Dominique Bigo-Danel delivered a resounding speech on "communal

100. *La décentralisation littéraire et scientifique* 1, no. 1 (16 October 1863): 2; and Steven D. Kale, *Legitimism and the Reconstruction of French Society, 1852–1883* (Baton Rouge, 1992), esp. chaps. 3 and 4. See also Gustave Flaubert, *L'éducation sentimentale*, ed. S. de Sacy (Paris, 1965), 421.

101. Brun-Lavainne, *Mes souvenirs*, 161; *La Revue des provinces* 3 (1 December 1834): 89–90; *France départementale* 6 (1839): 2; *Revue provinciale* 2, no. 6 (15 August 1849): 404–5; and Guilbert, public letter to provincial residents, 15 March 1842, appended to the BNF copy of *Histoire des villes*.

franchises." As a conservative liberal (or *constitutionnel*), he sought to buttress and widen the municipal rights secured after 1830 while maintaining the central state's administrative authority.[102] Local initiative and central rule were compatible, he said, as long as the latter did not "encroach" on the "communal system." "While professing religious respect for governmental prerogatives," he added, "we cannot help but look after the preservation of the commune's franchises with a jealous attention." Whether Le Glay shared Bigo-Danel's conception of communal franchises or not is, to some degree, inconsequential. The key point is that any use of this vocabulary—be it historical or not—pointed toward citizenship and political organization.

When it came to two pressing civic questions, however, contemporaries fused local memories and political recriminations to attain precise objectives under the July Monarchy. The regime's property-based electoral system dashed hopes for a "truly civic system" by linking voting rights to income and, hence, privileging landowners, Parisian administrators, and businessmen.[103] A disenfranchised bourgeoisie of talents voiced its frustrations and demands within the field of local memories. Denouncing the "fiction that political *capacité* resides in money," Brun-Lavainne requested electoral rights for the "intellectual *capacités*": "the savant, the man of letters, the virtuous and capable citizen."[104] Liberal members of scientific congresses similarly called for broader rights for the "true *capacités*." Here, too, their political claims paralleled historical descriptions of cities such as Poitiers as "land[s] of freedom and franchises" with "a political existence"—cities whose residents, by virtue of these glorious precedents, deserved full membership in the body politic.[105]

The second question was national tax collection. Elites of differing political leanings criticized what they perceived as an arbitrary procedure, imposed from above without consultation of municipal councils. On the right, Lille's *Gazette de Flandre et d'Artois* glorified ancient "communal rights" to better denounce a "taxation [that] was set by successive legislative cabals, . . . often by ministerial whims." On the left, Guilbert cofounded a *Revue générale de l'impôt* in January 1842, weeks before launch-

102. According to the law of 21 May 1831, for example, municipal councillors were elected rather than appointed and mayors were selected from these councils. See Louis-Dominique Bigo-Daniel, speech of August 1843, in *Journal de Lille*, 29 August 1843.

103. Pierre-Joseph-Spiridion Dufey (de l'Yonne), *Histoire des communes de France et législation municipale, depuis la fin du XIe siècle jusqu'à nos jours* (Paris, 1828), 325–26.

104. Thirty-eight percent of the Nord's 6,768 eligible voters were traders or industrialists in 1837. See *RN*, 1st ser., 5 (January 1836): 243–55, quotation on 247; *RN*, 1st ser., 4 (September 1835): 378; Christophe Charle, *Histoire sociale de la France au XIXe siècle* (Paris, 1991), 47–50; and André-Jean Tudesq, "La bourgeoisie du Nord au milieu de la monarchie de Juillet," *RN* 41, no. 164 (October–December 1959): 278–79.

105. *CS* 2 (Poitiers, 1834), 15 and 488–89.

ing the *Histoire des villes de France*. His two publications participated in a single civic endeavor. Whereas the *Histoire* lauded local franchises and asked the state to "return some of their ancient communal attributions to the municipalities," the *Revue* castigated a "fiscal inquisition" that denied French people the right to discuss and vote taxation.[106] A year earlier, left and right had banded in opposition to Finance Minister Jean-Georges Humann's inventory of all taxable property. This apparent ukase provoked riots (especially in southern France) and passionate defenses of the historical "rights of the *pays*." In Toulouse, where the agitation began, the *Gazette du Languedoc* praised the municipal authorities for opposing Humann and thereby exemplifying "this old municipal spirit, . . . last palladium of communal privileges, . . . [that] has always risen against . . . a centralizing government." Around this time, the newspaper published historical articles extolling "communal association . . . [this] palladium of freedom."[107] Local memories and political protest were, here again, irrevocably entwined.

PAYS TO NATION

The cult of local memories mystifies us because it promised so much—from psychological solace and self-understanding to cultural authority and a new civic order. At the same time, we grasp the appeal of rootedness, exhaustive surveys, and unity during eras of transition (or perceived as such), eras in which local identities seem threatened by forces from above and below. We recognize a mode of territorial self-affirmation that hinges on collective ownership of the past, the affirmation of local singularity, the recovery and defense of an endangered identity. We understand why these ostensibly apolitical representations of the local past elicited political aspirations and debates. We recognize, moreover, an underlying contradiction between tradition and innovation. Local historical pageants after all presented themselves as both gateways to the past and "new spectacle[s]." Amalgamating past and present, authenticity and imagination, this ersatz reality promised what Walter Benjamin called a "wishful fan-

106. *Gazette de Flandre et d'Artois*, 10–11 December 1838; Guilbert, Introduction to *Histoire des villes*, I: xxi; and Guilbert, Auguste Billiard, and Henri Cauvin, *Revue générale de l'impôt: organe des intérêts et des réclamations des contribuables publiée par une réunion d'anciens employés des finances, d'économistes et de jurisconsultes* 1 (January 1842): 1–3.

107. Félix Ponteil, "Le ministre des finances Georges Humann et les émeutes antifiscales en 1841," *Revue historique* 179 (1937): 311–54; *Gazette du Midi*, n.d. [June 1841], quoted in Ponteil, "Le ministre des finances Georges Humann," 323; and *Gazette du Languedoc*, 5 August 1840 and 6 July 1841. On these riots, see Jean-Claude Caron, *Un été rouge: chronique de la révolte populaire en France (1841)* (Paris, 2002).

tas[y]" for a mended social order and, we will soon see, a classless utopia.[108]

As emblem of a new era of freedom and means of bridging the revolutionary chasm, the cult of local memories furthermore provided nineteenth-century elites with a new platform and language to define the body politic and their own civic responsibilities. To delineate place and past was in part a public posturing, a means of compensating for lack of power in other arenas. "Most French provincials," a Parisian *littérateur* noted in 1856, "will gladly decry the abuses of centralization until the day when, hopping onto a carriage, they will in turn come to centralize." It was also, however, to comment on the shape of one's local and national communities. It was to engage in civic practices: grassroots action and collective projects on behalf of one's community. For liberals and others, it was ultimately—by design or not—to recompose France through local practices and modes of territorial representation that conformed best to a "civilization" that was "still too new, too caught up in confusion" to have attained its definitive form.[109] The French "social state" still lacked a corresponding "intellectual state," explained Guizot. "Revolutions do not change the internal and moral world as promptly as they do the external and material world." In 1838, a learned society member from Nantes spoke likewise of an "intellectual emancipation" that would at last complete the "political emancipation" of 1789.[110]

Contemporaries thus cultivated local memories as autonomous ends. Their monographs, inventories, or pageants referred to the *pays*, city, or department alone. Only by "describing it on its own, by isolating it from others" can one know a *pays* well, declared one author from Eure-et-Loir in 1836. Yet, during this era of nation formation, few could ignore the relationship between the locality and the nation-state. This relationship was highly charged, but it was also promising to elites from diverse political schools, who both elaborated new configurations and amplified prerevolutionary ones.[111] In one respect, the proximate and authentic "local" would bolster or stabilize the new national edifice by shoring up its foundations. Local monographs, these inherently "particular" narratives, fur-

---

108. Walter Benjamin, "Paris, Capital of the Nineteenth Century," in his *Reflections*, ed. Peter Demetz, trans. Edmund Jephcott (New York, 1978), 148.

109. Paul de Musset, "Parisiens et parisiennes," in *Paris et les parisiens au XIXe siècle. Moeurs, arts et monuments* (Paris, 1856), 403; and *CS* 10 (Strasbourg, 1842), xxii.

110. François Guizot, quoted in "Cours préliminaire," *Encyclopédie des gens du monde, répertoire universel des sciences, des lettres et des arts*, 22 vols. (Paris, 1833–1844), 1: i; and *Annales de la Société royale académique de Nantes et du département de la Loire-Inférieure* 9 (1838): 329–30.

111. On the latter, see, for instance, David A. Bell, *The Cult of the Nation in France: Inventing Nationalism, 1680–1800* (Cambridge, Mass., 2001), 118–19. See also François-Jules Doublet de Boisthibault, *Eure-et-Loir* (Paris, 1836), vol. 1 of V.-A. Loriol, ed., *La France. Description géographique, statistique et topographique . . .* 7 vols. (Paris, 1834–36), 1.

nished the necessary groundwork for "the complete interpretation of general history." Statues of local figures, such as seventeenth-century Dunkirk privateer Jean Bart, consecrated "name[s] that glorify France."[112] The editors of a prospective history of France—suggestively titled *La France ou histoire nationale des départements*—assured readers in 1844 that their interplay of communal and national histories would "easily progress, through a series of natural junctions, toward the center, toward the heart of the nation."[113] In another respect, the local was the obligatory conduit toward a veritable reconfiguration of France. The *pays* would learn about themselves; they would learn about one another; and France would discover its identity as a diverse yet united nation. The conciliation of "provincial originalities" and local narratives alone would uncover France's "true physiognomy." "Make Normandy known to the *Normands,* Brittany to the *Bretons,* and each province to all the others," enjoined the *Revue de Rouen* in 1834. "Substitute a more authentic unity to the material and still somewhat artificial unity of contemporary France."[114] Two decades later, Victor Derode praised his Société dunkerquoise colleagues for having "consolidated the *patrie*'s moral unity and the solidarity that unites the various provinces." The recomposition of France "on her true foundations"[115] transited through the locality—as indispensable as the patriotic elites who recovered memories that were both their own and the nation's.

112. Pierre Legrand, *Dictionnaire du patois de Lille,* 2d ed. (Lille, 1856), xiii; *Mémoires de la Société royale d'émulation d'Abbeville* (1836–37): 78; AN F21 4388: Benjamin Morel to Min. Int., 5 April 1844; and Alain Cabantous, "Jean Bart ou les figures du mythe et de la réalité," *De Franse Nederlanden/Les Pays-Bas français* 5 (1980): esp. 35–39.

113. Alexandre Ducourneau and Amans-Alexis Monteil, prospectus for *La France ou histoire nationale des départements* (Paris, 1844), 2.

114. *RN,* 1st ser., 3 (March 1835): 374; M. Dartois, "Importance de l'étude des patois en général; coup d'oeil spécial sur ceux de la Franche-Comté" (n.p., n.d. [1837?]); and *Revue de Rouen* 3 (January–June 1834): 117.

115. *MSDu* 6 (1859): 39; and *MSDu* 2 (1855): 10.

THREE

The Pedagogy of Place

> Imbue the inferior ranks with this filial cult of memories . . .
> [that] not only . . . display the *pays's* history, [but] also put science to
> moral use.
>
>

*Mémoires de la Société d'agriculture,
sciences, arts et belles-lettres de Bayeux (1842)*

I F RESIDENTS OF Montargis resolved in 1841 to commemorate
"the famous men born in the *pays*," it was largely to remind
themselves—and a broader audience—of who they were. In
this small town as elsewhere in France, a voluntary association of elites
cultivated local memories to "glorify [them]selves," secure cultural recognition, and reaffirm their authority.[1] But there was more to it. No less
pressing was the urge to tell other local residents, regardless of their social
provenance, who *they* were. The great room of Montargis's city hall—site
of this permanent commemoration—was after all one of the city's foremost public spaces, "in which festivals are held, weddings celebrated, *collège* and school awards given." Neither exclusive nor restricted to self-
display, the room existed for the use and enjoyment of the entire
arrondissement. So did the *Notice biographique des illustrations de Montargis*,
the collection of biographical sketches that complemented this endeavor.
Encompassing celebrities as well as ordinary residents, it cost an affordable fifty centimes—save for schoolteachers, who received it free of
charge for collective classroom readings. All of this displays entwined ambitions to reactivate the adult population's memories of the local past and
"speak graciously to our grandchildren about their ancestors' doings." In
the small town of Montargis, the cult of local memories was also—perhaps
primarily—a pedagogical undertaking, capable of inspiring individuals to
exclaim: " 'This famous man, he was from my *pays!* ' "[2]

---

1. AMM M A 13: "Souscription pour les Illustrations locales de Montargis" (Montargis, n.d.
[1842?]); and [Louis-Marie de Cormenin], *Notice biographique des illustrations de Montargis* (Montargis, 1844), iii.

2. Cormenin, *Notice biographique*, n.p. and iii; *Le Loing*, 10 November 1843; and "Souscription pour les Illustrations locales."

Three convictions prevailed in Montargis: that concrete local and historical spaces offered the best hope of disseminating local memories; that such memories could instill a sense of place (a deep affection for a locale, a community, and the latter's values); and finally, that this sense of place would buttress French society by fostering self-understanding, social cohesion, and civic participation. It is no surprise that, by the 1840s, these elites were either espousing a pedagogy of the great man or linking physical transformation with moral and social improvement. Their venture owed much to the Enlightenment's cult of secular and civilian *illustrations,* those virtuous figures who served the *patrie* and derived their worth from their talent and benevolence—rather than military glory, birth, or canonization.[3] It owed much to the utopian festivals and museums of the French Revolution, with their unremitting desire to transform public spaces, neutralize and harness potent historical signs, and devise new tools of civic education. For the revolutionaries, such cultural undertakings would revitalize French society and sustain posterity by conveying eternal verities and acting on all citizens at once.[4] Montargis's venture captured, finally, an old confidence in the edifying powers of 'good memories'—they "uplift the soul and make it proud"—and a more recent embrace of openness and diffusion of knowledge. These impulses underlay the countless statues of local celebrities that appeared throughout France and embodied the *pays's* distinctive spirit.[5]

And, yet, Montargis's redecorated great room marked a departure. "It is not enough to have . . . monuments whose spires dart toward the skies," explained one of its sponsors in 1844. "One must also introduce [citizens] to the names and actions of those individuals who honored their place of birth or adoption." Monuments, including statues, had a limited reach on their own. Other modes of pedagogical action were needed, not only to "popularize," but also to seize the population's imagination. This meant integrating local memories and physicality to produce, in a most literal fashion, what historian Pierre Nora has called *lieux de mémoire*—places of memory. From the conceptual resonance of the ground and underground we thus move to the transformative powers of local historical spaces: decorated rooms, artistic galleries devoted to glorious local predecessors, re-

3. Jean-Claude Bonnet, *Naissance du Panthéon: essai sur le culte des grands hommes* (Paris, 1998), 32–34; David A. Bell, *Cult of the Nation,* 112–21 and 134–36; and Mona Ozouf, "Le Panthéon: l'école normale des morts," in Pierre Nora, ed. *Lieux de Mémoire,* 1:139–66.

4. Ozouf, *La fête révolutionnaire, 1789–1799* (Paris, 1976); and Edouard Pommier, "Discours iconoclaste, discours culturel, discours national, 1790–1794," in Simone Bernard-Griffiths et al., eds., *Révolution française,* 313.

5. *Bulletin de la Société des sciences historiques et naturelles de l'Yonne* 14 (1860): liv; Françoise Waquet, "La communication des livres dans les bibliothèques d'Ancien Régime," in Frédéric Barbier et al., *Le livre et l'historien: études offertes en l'honneur du professeur Henri-Jean Martin* (Geneva, 1997), 378–79; and Catherine-Bertho Lavenir, *La roue et le stylo: comment nous sommes devenus touristes* (Paris, 1999), 48.

configured outdoor expanses, and historical pageants. All would, like Bordeaux's historical festivals, "unite" local residents "with their place of birth . . . [by] presenting habits and memories."[6] First glimpsed under the late Restoration, this pedagogical model was articulated under the July Monarchy and given a new scope under the early Third Republic. Its story is not, however, one of sudden and all-encompassing change, in which large segments of the population transformed the French landscape. At once more modest and more complex, it is a story of fitful advances and experimentation: the uneasy emergence of a loose model whose underlying tenets encountered opposition. The tensions of the field of local memories, we will begin to see, are ultimately as revealing as its material achievements.

BIRTH OF A PEDAGOGICAL MODEL

This pedagogical model lacks both a precise birth date and a single parental figure. Proposals and ventures surfaced, often independently, during the late 1820s and 1830s and grew more numerous, first, during the early-to-mid 1840s and, later, following the social turmoil of June 1848. This activity persisted, with less intensity, under the Second Empire, then underwent a resurgence in the early 1880s. By then, this model had taken numerous forms. Rather than enumerating them, I will undertake a selective, loosely chronological journey through this field—with stops in Montargis, the Nord, Paris, and other towns. This itinerary captures this model's historical evolution, its formal variety, and the blend of aspirations that equated local memories with moral and civic renewal.

"Convinced of the utility of noble examples, an association has recently opened a subscription to place, in the city hall's great room, busts [and] crowns for the famous men born in the arrondissement." This announcement, published in Montargis's leading newspaper (*Le Loing*) in 1841, introduced local residents to a venture without precedent in the town's history. The subscription opened in a local bookstore, several notarial studies, and six neighboring towns. What was Montargis at that time? An ancient Roman city, once capital of the Gatinais, it was now a "well-paved" subprefectoral seat of nearly eight thousand inhabitants, thirty miles east of Orléans. Traversed by the Loing and Ouanne rivers, proud of its ancient castle and riverside tanneries, it dominated a land of forests, vine-

---

6. ADN 3 T 853: Cormenin, "Note pour les illustrations d'arrondissement," petition to the *Conseil général* of the Loiret, session of 5 September 1844; and Charles de Pelleport, *Historique des fêtes bordelaises*, 15–16. See also William Cohen, "Symbols of Power: Statues in Nineteenth-Century Provincial France," *Comparative Studies in Society and History* 31, no. 3 (July 1989): esp. 495–96.

18 — Montargis (Loiret) - Le Canal et le Château

Edition F. F.

FIGURE 10. Postcard of Montargis at century's end. Courtesy of the Cabinet des Estampes, Bibliothèque Nationale de France (Paris).

yards, and cereal fields—an arrondissement whose commerce and "industrial state" were on the decline. Described as "well-off" rather than "rich," Montargis numbered five bankers, five earthenware producers, and a large artisan population in 1843. A new rubber factory and the arrival of the railroad boosted the local economy in the 1850s. Social unrest was apparently limited, but the town's fifteen hundred indigents (in 1847) betrayed an unmistakable "social problem." A prototypical small town in this respect as in others, Montargis furnished the model for Louis-Benoît Picard's "La petite ville," one of the era's most popular melodramas (see figure 10).[7]

In 1837, the local castle's clock tower collapsed. Here as elsewhere, neglect and destruction of civil and religious monuments convinced some residents that local memories would soon vanish. This concern led Antoine Boivin, a forty-year-old bookseller and librarian, to spearhead the great room's redecoration. He drew on his profession, historical knowledge, and political connections to compile a list of historical celebrities, coordinate the subscription, and win the financial and political backing of

7. *Le Loing*, 20 December 1841. This description of Montargis is derived from Boyard, *Statistique agricole, commerciale, intellectuelle de l'arrondissement de Montargis* (Orléans, 1836); Louis Nottin, *Orléans et Montargis au début de la monarchie de juillet* (Orléans, 1931); and Paul Gache, *Les grandes heures de Montargis* (Roanne, 1980).

local officials.[8] By 1842, the legitimist Boivin, the liberal Alexandre Périer (brother of Minister Casimir Périer), and four other municipal councilors had formed an organizing commission. A year later, they found an unexpected ally: radical deputy Louis-Marie de Cormenin, one of the era's most renowned and prolix *publicistes*. Born in a family of royalist nobles, Cormenin served Napoleon and the Bourbons before winning election to parliament in Orléans, as a liberal, in 1828. His views soon gravitated toward republicanism: universal male suffrage, free and compulsory primary education, suppression of the peerage. A defender of political centralization, Cormenin also endorsed broader municipal attributions and self-administration. "Let us centralize important questions; let us decentralize small ones."[9] The leading author of the 1848 decree on universal suffrage, Cormenin was also a staunch Catholic, whose "genius for charitable works" earned the Abbé Migne's praise. Both currents, we will see, sparked his interest in Montargis's "pantheon of our celebrities." While Cormenin joined the venture in obscure circumstances, he contributed generously, donating a bust of Mirabeau, writing the *Notice biographique des illustrations*, and petitioning the *Conseil général* of the Loiret for a subsidy. He also praised the venture in Aristide Guilbert's *Histoire des villes de France* and his own *Entretiens de village* (1845), a prize-winning compendium of moral essays.[10]

By that time, the project neared completion. The great room, which one entered through a double door, was painted in antique yellow marble. On the far wall, a large inscription proclaimed in golden letters: "*Illustrations* of the arrondissement of Montargis." On the near wall, bronze, starred crowns surmounted six panels, which supplied biographical information on local celebrities (see figure 11). These figures of national renown, all of them deceased, ranged from politics and the military (Mirabeau, Coligny) to literature and fine arts (poet Guillaume of Lorris, romantic painter Girodet). Between the panels, visitors encountered the names of unheralded residents who had performed "good deed[s]." The

8. AMM M A 13: Antoine Boivin to mayor of Montargis, 8 November 1842; and AMM: Proceedings of the Municipal Council of Montargis, 17 November 1842. See also T. Pinard, "Montargis, son château, ses seigneurs," *Revue archéologique* 10, no. 2 (1853–54): 603–8.

9. Cormenin, *Droit administratif*, 5th rev. ed., (Paris, 1840 [1822]), xix; and idem, *Manuel du contentieux de l'administration municipale. Exposé de législation et des règles de jurisprudence administrative et judiciaire qui président à l'administration des communes*, 2d ed. (Paris, 1841). On Cormenin, see also Charles Louandre, "Louis-Marie de Cormenin," in Cormenin (Timon), *Livre des orateurs*, 2 vols., 18th ed. (Paris, n.d. [1869?]), 1:4–18; and Paul Bastid, *Un juriste pamphlétaire: Cormenin, précurseur et constituant de 1848* (Paris, 1948).

10. Alain Garrigou, "Le brouillon du suffrage universel: archéologie du décret du 5 mars 1848," *Genèses* 6 (1991): 161–78; Jacques-Paul Migne, "Economie charitable," in his *Encyclopédie théologique, ou série de Dictionnaires sur toutes les parties de la Science religieuse*, 168 vols. (Paris, 1845–73), 8: 421; *Le Loing*, 10 November 1843; and Eugène de Mirecourt, *Portraits et silhouettes au XIXe siècle. Cormenin* (Paris, 1868), 59.

ILLUSTRATIONS DE L' ARRONDISSEMENT DE MONTARGIS.

COLIGNY GAILLARDIN | GUILLAUME (DE LORRIS). | MIRABEAU | NESME | VASSENT | GIRODET. | CASTELLIER DUDIN. | Mᵐᵉ GUYON LANTARA.

FIGURE 11. The great room of Montargis's City Hall. Cormenin and his fellow organizers commissioned this lithograph and included a reproduction in their *Notice biographique des illustrations de Montargis.* "The entire *arrondissement*" would thereby encounter its illustrious ancestors. Courtesy of the Bibliothèque Municipale de Montargis.

room also contained the busts of four local *illustrations*, or celebrities. More had been planned, but funds proved insufficient.[11] The great room nonetheless called to mind the portrait galleries of illustrious men that first appeared in sixteenth-century princely courts. Richelieu's gallery, one of the most renowned, interspersed portraits and statues to display his glory and inculcate virtues.[12]

Much nonetheless distinguished Montargis's great room from Richelieu's gallery, starting with its location in a public edifice and the substitution of panels for portraits. The sponsors furthermore amplified this venture by publishing the *Notice biographique,* a sixty-page pantheon of local

11. Proceedings of the *Conseil général* of the Loiret, 5 September 1844, in *Conseil général du département du Loiret. Procès-verbal de la session de 1844* (Orléans, 1844), 198; Cormenin, *Notice biographique;* AMM M A 13: Expenditures for the decoration of the great room, 6 February and 21 December 1844; and *Le Loing,* 20 September 1845.

12. Margaret MacGowan, "Le phénomène de la galerie des portraits des illustres," in Roland Mousnier and Jean Mesnard, eds., *L'Age d'or du mécénat (1598–1661)* (Paris, 1985), 416–17.

celebrities and admirable individuals. To the "famous" and national persons above, they added two local celebrities—a fifteenth-century knight and an eighteenth-century mayor—as well as twenty-two "notable" and "commendable" individuals (doctors, philanthropists, scientists) and eleven ordinary residents (deceased and alive) who had shown uncommon bravery or generosity. While most of the celebrities were men, one also finds two women: an aristocrat who had sheltered Protestants during the Wars of Religion and Madame Guyon, the quietist poet who was close to Fénelon. Two women also figured among the praiseworthy ordinary residents. Comprising Catholics as well as Protestants, monarchists as well as Bonapartists, this pantheon represented a political and social middle ground, free from extremism. Local hero Gaillardin had defended Montargis during the Hundred Years' War; Coligny had died a Protestant martyr; the "sincere patriot" Girodet had impressed both Napoleon and Louis XVIII. Even the revolutionaries were moderates: a local doctor who had sat in the Legislative Assembly as well as Mirabeau, a favorite of liberals and moderate republicans, the constitutional monarchist who had "hastened" the Revolution before seeking to contain it.[13] The venture celebrated public service and private virtues: courage, duty, charity, simplicity, and love of the *pays*. The result was a paean to "good deeds" and "talent" born in the local soil. Directed at both men and women, this glorification of the new, postrevolutionary society of merit was modern, following Maurice Agulhon's line of argument, in its embrace of utility, service, patriotism, and middle-class values.[14] It was modern, moreover, as a self-consciously local venture that linked extraordinary achievement and ordinary virtue on a moral plane. It would recompose France by exposing the population to the individual "virtues" of their "ancestors" and the collective virtue of the citizenry. In this guise, the cult of local memories integrated the era's yearning for "great men" with an egalitarian regard for the greatness of simple folk.[15]

The great room was modern, finally, as a complex pedagogical under-

---

13. Cormenin, *Notice biographique*, 12 and 34; and, on Mirabeau's appeal in the 1840s, Ronald Gosselin, *Les almanachs républicains: traditions révolutionnaires et culture politique des masses populaires de Paris (1840–1851)* (Paris, 1992), 101.

14. The venture distantly echoes, however, royal publicist Jacob-Nicolas Moreau's efforts to bolster patriotism in 1760. Let us recognize, he exhorted, those "good citizens and useful men" who have given "great examples" and remain all too often forgotten in their province. See Moreau, "De l'avantage qu'on peut tirer des écrits" (1760), in idem and Gabriel François Coyer, *Ecrits sur le patriotisme, l'esprit public et la propagande au milieu du XVIIIe siècle*, ed. Edmond Dziembowski (La Rochelle, 1997), 73–74; Maurice Agulhon, "La 'statuomanie' et l'histoire," in his *Histoire vagabonde*, 1: 147–48; and Ozouf, "Panthéon," 159 and 162.

15. Cormenin before the *Conseil général* of the Loiret, 5 September 1844; and Jacques Neefs, "La 'haine des grands hommes' au XIXe siècle," *MLN* 116, no. 4 (September 2001): 764.

taking. Local residents would (re)encounter their *pays*'s memories on multiple planes:

1. *Spatial:* (Repeated) visits to the great room and viewings of panels and busts.
2. *Festive and ritual:* The celebration marking the inauguration of the redecorated great room; weddings and ceremonies in the city hall.
3. *Textual:* Subscription requests, newspaper articles, Cormenin's *Notice biographique,* and other publications.
4. *Figurative:* The lithograph.
5. *Auditive:* Classroom readings of the *Notice biographique.*

All of this made it possible to seize individuals through their senses and transform them. This conviction was shared outside Montargis. In June 1845, the prefect of the Nord wrote his Loiret colleague for information on the great room—a venture now being considered "in numerous departments." He was following in the footsteps of his predecessor, Gabriel Rousseau de Saint-Aignan. This amateur archaeologist vowed in 1843 to instill appreciation for the "benevolent people" and "all the circumstances that mark the history of . . . the Nord's communes." To do so, he asked the Commission historique du Nord to draw up plans for historical *tableaux d'honneur.* In rural communes, wooden panels would hang outside the church and present the locality's history, institutions (church, school), celebrities, and virtuous or charitable citizens. These panels would eventually include the names of admirable civil servants—thus linking past and present. Urban panels (made of stone) would convey similar information outside the city hall. Additional panels would focus around urban institutions, from schools to hospitals. The Commission historique embraced a project that would teach every local resident "to love the place in which he was born." André Le Glay even suggested that each commune keep a *livret d'honneur,* a vellum-bound record of its memorable events and admirable denizens. Solemn readings would take place during the annual *fête communale.*[16]

This project was thus a brainchild of the prefect and local intellectual elites of diverse political persuasions. Despite predictable differences— the prefect's efforts to inspire affection for "enlightened" officials, the elites' interest in private charity—all of them sought to glorify talent and the ordinary virtues above by imbuing local spaces with historical mean-

---

16. ADN 3 T 853: Maurice Duval to prefect Loiret, 18 June 1845; ADN 3 T 853: Gabriel de Saint-Aignan to Commission historique du Nord, 8 March 1843; and *BCN* 1 (1843): 383 and 399. On the *livre(t) d'honneur*'s sixteenth-century antecedents, see Arlette Jouanna, *Ordre social, mythes et hiérarchies dans la France du XVIe siècle* (Paris, 1977), 170–71.

ing. They shared this ambition with Montargis, but would fulfill it through different routes. In Montargis, elites targeted a single city: the *arrondissement*'s political center. They also created an artificial space within a building—city hall—that held symbolic value but not necessarily historical importance. Without fully rejecting this focus on emblematic spaces, Saint-Aignan and the Commission historique called above all for in situ action. Rather than limiting themselves to a single local pantheon, they sought, first, to modify the entire urban and rural landscape and, second, to establish a correspondence between the representation—such as the panel—and its historical referent. "It is good to remember [local events and people] *sur les lieux*," explained Le Glay.[17] The same conviction led some contemporaries to place "commemorative inscriptions" on battlefields and the homes of local celebrities.[18]

Both approaches had visible results in the Nord, although financial difficulties apparently stymied the *tableaux d'honneur*. Emblematic spaces included the Galerie valenciennoise and the theaters that learned societies decorated with historical flags, portraits, and escutcheons for their annual public meetings.[19] These ventures seem modest, however, beside the Nord's historical pageants, far more ambitious efforts to imprint the urban environment in situ. Organizers neglected nothing to transport spectators across time. Weeks in advance, they advertised the pageant on city walls, in the Nord's dailies, and as far as Paris and London. They published detailed programs of their fête as well as numerous brochures, newspaper articles, and learned historical *notices* (sometimes read aloud before the procession). Spectators not only learned about their own past, but also received an "introduction," or key, to coded historical processions that lasted as long as ten hours and transformed the city.[20] Banners and flags displaying local colors, costumes and music, adorned facades, medieval jousts and games: all of this created mental associations between the urban landscape and a shared past (figure 12). Pageants were thus usually held twice, following slightly divergent itineraries in order to imprint the entire urban grid and prolong a spatial transformation that was at once temporary and permanent. Staging this pageant outside its

17. *BCN* 3 (1847–49): 169.
18. *Mémoires de la Société des antiquaires de Normandie* 9 (1835): 580–84; *Le Glaneur*, 12 June 1841; *MSDu* 1 (1853): 8; and David Lowenthal, *The Past Is a Foreign Country* (Cambridge, 1985), 265.
19. *MSV* 8 (1847): 179; and *MSDu* 4 (1857): 6.
20. *Le Mémorial de la Scarpe*, 29 August 1840; *La Gazette de Cambrai*, 5 August 1850; and *Notice historique sur Philippe-le-Bon, contenant le programme détaillé de la troisième fête, avec addition de nouvelles notes, la proclamation, l'itinéraire, l'amour du pays, pièce inédite de Mme Desbordes-Valmore* (Douai, 1842). See also the articles on Charles the Bold in *L'Echo de la frontière*, September 1847; and Valentine Camescasse, *Souvenirs de Madame Camescasse. Douai au XIXe siècle, salons parlementaires sous la IIIe République*, 3d ed. (Paris, 1924), 25.

FIGURE 12. The medieval jousts of Douai in 1849, part of a five-day festival that included nocturnal and diurnal pageants, a medieval "Flemish fête," and nautical games. Courtesy of the Bibliothèque Municipale de Douai.

original context, organizers exploited the distance between the actual event and its representation to fuse historical verisimilitude and communal dream. They appealed to the intellect—witness the footnoted programs—as well as the senses and the personal experience of a realm that was at once foreign and familiar. Exactitude was a springboard toward imaginary reconstitution in a fête that, like scientific history, rested on temporal distance yet, like memory, sought to erase it.[21]

Memory, or more precisely, "the religion of memories," likewise underlay the sole ministerial intervention in this pedagogical domain. On 1 December 1848—months after the June riots and well into the Second Republic's conservative period—the Minister of Public Instruction asked his prefects to encourage the creation of pantheons of local celebrities throughout France. The said minister was one Alexandre Freslon, a lawyer and prosecutor who had won election to parliament as a moderate republican. The republic, he wrote, was duty-bound to uphold the memory of illustrious national figures, but it could not do so for "all the deserving names." This endeavor thus had to be local. "It is above all in one's province that one should gather, before their fellow citizens, the names and examples of the men who have brought fame to their *native pays.*" Prefects would confer with mayors, school directors, and the presidents of learned societies to duplicate Montargis's "patriotic" enterprise and re-

21. I follow the discussion of history and memory in Joël Candau, *Mémoire et identité*, 127–28.

decorate their city hall. In doing so, they would draw inspiration from Cormenin's *Notice biographique* and its lithograph (appended to Freslon's circular). Cormenin had claimed a few years earlier that the ministry approved his venture and endorsed his *Notice* for public school readings.[22] Although corroborating evidence is lacking, the ministry clearly amalgamated his design with prefectoral oversight while seeking to inspire reverence for local memories beyond Montargis. The matter was increasingly pressing during this era of change and uncertainty, an era that saw the new republican regime admit modest individuals to immortality and make growing civic use of fêtes, public readings, and other schemes promoting the nation's "political education."[23]

This sense of urgency led a member of the Institut des provinces to propose, in 1850, turning the nation's city halls into "local pantheon[s] open to all virtues, all glories." Lille's Commission historique likewise seized on Freslon's circular to reactivate its earlier blueprint. Historical panels would strengthen "the bond that unites each French person to the place in which he was born," *littérateur* Henri Bruneel told the Nord's mayors. "The safety of the *patrie* and society may well be linked to this noble effort."[24] Bruneel also wrote the program for Lille's 1852 historical pageant. Urban elites, provincial journalists, Parisian *littérateurs*—all now agreed with the organizers that such spectacles would revive an evanescent "local patriotism" during an era of social and political turmoil.[25]

Pageant organizers took yet other steps to transform public space at this time. In Cambrai, they erected sixteen plaster monuments in 1851: statues, triumphal arches, columns, and fountains celebrating communal liberties and prominent historical figures—often in front of their original homes. The town would thus recover its authentic "historical physiognomy."[26] So would Valenciennes, where, that same year, elites organized a nocturnal ceremony before laying the foundation stone of the monument to Jean Froissart. They covered the city with flags and trophies, a monumental arch, and illuminations. Medals rewarded residents who placed historical transparencies or allegories on the facades of their homes.

22. AN F17 2831: Alexandre Freslon to prefects, circular of 1 December 1848; Cormenin, "Note pour les illustrations"; and idem, *Notice biographique*, cover.

23. Avner Ben-Amos, *Funerals, Politics, and Memory*, 266; Hippolyte Carnot, *Le Ministère de l'Instruction Publique et des Cultes, depuis le 24 février jusqu'au 5 juillet 1848* (Paris, 1848), 22; and Rémi Dalisson, "Fête publique et citoyenneté: 1848, une tentative de régénération civique par la fête," *Revue d'histoire du XIXe siècle* 18, no. 1 (1999): 63.

24. *Congrès des délégués des sociétés savantes des départements, sous la direction de l'Institut des provinces. Session de 1850. Bulletin* 1: 11; and *BCN* 3 (1847–49): 173–74.

25. *Journal de Lille*, 18 March 1851; *L'Echo de la frontière*, 1 March 1851; and *Le Constitutionnel*, 6 September 1848.

26. MMC ms. 1439: Victor Delattre, "M. Eugène de Bouly de Lesdain, historien de Cambrai. Sa vie—ses travaux" (1885), 72; and Eugène Bouly, *Programme de la fête communale de Cambrai et de la marche historique qui aura lieu pendant cette fête* (Cambrai, 1851), 4.

FIGURE 13. The inauguration of Valenciennes's monument to Jean Froissart, in *L'Illustration*, 23 May 1851. Courtesy of the General Research Division, The New York Public Library, Astor, Lenox, and Tilden Foundations.

Medallions representing ten of Froissart's contemporaries also surrounded his statue, forming a pantheon of local celebrities (see figures 13 and 14). Local denizens and others would thus enter a protected shrine devoted to "the free city of Valenciennes," a permanent and autonomous historical space that facilitated direct communion with the town's memories and immemorial virtues.[27] Finalized by the end of the Second Republic, this pedagogical model underwent little modification until the late 1870s.

IMPERCEPTIBLE ACTION

The pedagogy of place took form at the confluence of several cultural forces. It owed much to the rise of romantic history, with its affection for the Middle Ages; its mix of erudition and imagination; its novels, *histori-*

27. *L'Illustration* 17, no. 433 (12 June 1851): 378; *Courrier du Nord*, 26 April 1851; *RAN* 8, no. 3 (November 1856): 106; and Casimir Pétiaux, *Monument à Jehan Froissart, chroniqueur et historien au XIVe siècle* (Valenciennes, 1858).

FIGURE 14. "Valenciennes. Monument Froissart": end-of-the-century postcard.
Courtesy of the Cabinet des Estampes, Bibliothèque Nationale de France (Paris).

ettes, and picturesque accounts; its concurrent desires to experience, understand, and halt the passage of time. A journalist from Douai wrote lyrically about pageants that, in 1839, awakened "this intimate feeling, these interior voices, as Victor Hugo calls them, that spoke to your soul [and] brought you back to ancient Flanders." Likewise in Aups, in 1857: "We were no longer in the nineteenth century, but back in the Middle Ages."[28] Pageants furthermore capture the era's fascination with historical spectacle. Witness the popularity of panoramas, these dimly lit circular paintings whose scenes were sometimes historical. Witness, also, the Western European craze for *tableaux vivants*, these living reconstitutions of mythological, literary, and historical scenes that were staged during play intermissions, at "respectable" social gatherings, or as preambles to photographic compositions. Like the pageant's "history lesson in tableaux," they yielded a seemingly unmediated encounter with the past. Similar yearnings were visible on French stages. The mid-1820s saw the emergence of the historical scene, a new genre whose prose dialogues dramatized key events in French history. Prosper Mérimée, George Sand, and

28. *Le Mémorial de la Scarpe*, 16 July 1839; and *Fêtes d'Aups à l'occasion de la Saint-Pancrace. Bravade et entrée historique de Charles, comte d'Anjou et de Provence* (Aix, 1857), 8.

other romantic playwrights put costumes and processions at the service of historical representation and a visual spectacle that was at once moral, political, and pedagogical.[29]

At the same time, this cult of local memories participated in a wider democratization of history—in terms of its authors (see chapter 1), but also of its audience and contents. In one respect, the expansion of the press, publishing houses, and pageantry meant that history, like other emerging disciplines, reached a broader public. Some elites targeted a broad audience, be it the "masses" or "young students." Penning short historical accounts under the Flemish pseudonym Landsvriend (friend of the land), Bruneel and Edward Le Glay likened themselves to minstrels, roaming their region to "teach the *peuple* its history and lead it to love its *pays*." Be it in Montargis, the Nord, or Second Republic ministerial offices, elites sought to arouse "a generous emulation among the new generation."[30] In another respect, they broadened the very concept of legitimate memories. Revolutions and time had taken their toll on ancient monuments and buildings, leading some contemporaries to value the "minor patrimony"—from furniture to flags. In this modern and more liberal era, moreover, historically significant places and objects could be found in the most unassuming places. "History consists of . . . great and small things," contended Cormenin and others. The nation's ordinary and ostensibly trivial places now carried social and political meaning.[31]

This evolution paralleled a growing interweaving of space, memories, and imperceptible education. The Galerie valenciennoise promised to disseminate local history—"an efficient means of moralization"—among a "*peuple*" that read little. Historical pageants, these "history lesson[s] for the *pays*," likewise told the *peuple* "anew . . . [a] history that it was forget-

29. Some circuses likewise re-created historical or current military scenes. See Quentin Bajeac, *Tableaux vivants: fantaisies photographiques victoriennes (1840–1880)* (Paris, 1999); Martin Meisel, *Realizations: Narrative, Pictorial, and Theatrical Arts in Nineteenth-Century England* (Princeton, N.J., 1983), 47–49; *La cavalcade du Cateau au profit des pauvres. Notice sur les fêtes du dimanche 27 et du lundi 28 juin 1869* (Le Cateau, 1869), 3; and Jacqueline de Jomaron, ed., *Le théâtre en France*, 2 vols., 2d ed. (Paris, 1992), 2:44, 50–52, 101, and 111–17. I thank Andy Shanken for directing me toward the *tableaux vivants*.

30. *RN* 2 (July 1834): 286; Pierre Clément, *Histoire de la Flandre*, 11; H. E. Landsvriend, *Bouchard d'Avesnes* (Paris, 1841), vii; and Freslon to prefects, op. cit. *Peuple* meant many things in the nineteenth-century, from the nation to virtuous laborers to an unstable working class. Michelet evoked "these obscure masses that . . . [are] France," but noted in 1846 that, for most bourgeois, *peuple* referred first and foremost to factory workers. See Jules Michelet, "L'héroïsme de l'esprit," in his *Oeuvres complètes*, ed. Paul Viallaneix, 21 vols. (Paris, 1971–82), 4:36; Idem, *Le peuple*, ed. Viallaneix (Paris, 1974 [1846]), 152; and Fritz, *Idée de peuple*.

31. Claude-Isabelle Brelot, "La mémoire héraldique de la ville: armoiries urbaines du XIXe siècle," in Attilio Bartoli Langeli and Gérald Chaix, eds., *La mémoire de la cité: modèles antiques et réalisations renaissantes* (Naples, 1997), 301; Bertho-Lavenir, "L'invention du monument historique," *Quarante-huit/Quatorze* 4 (1992): 21; and Cormenin, feuilleton in *Le National*, 4 June 1844.

ting, or, perhaps, had never known."[32] "Easy to grasp [and] intelligible to all" at a time of persisting illiteracy, such spectacles offered a most promising means of communication. Indeed, they display the pedagogical appeal of images—an appeal that had been steadily rising since the sixteenth century.[33] Like other historical spaces, they also constituted what André Micoud calls *hauts lieux*, symbolic sites that provide models of exemplarity and the prospect of a new "social space," transcending current contradictions.[34] One of the era's most prominent *hauts lieux* was the national gallery of historical paintings that Louis-Philippe inaugurated in Versailles in 1837. Accessible to all French citizens, its historical narrative would unite all factions around his person, thereby erasing political differences. Offering only a grand display of national grandeur, centered on battles, it said nothing, however, about people's daily lives.[35] These local historical spaces, in contrast, revolved around local events and figures that were more familiar to their targeted audience. They invested buildings and landscapes that were part of the population's everyday life. As such, they constituted a more ambitious and promising pedagogical device.

These spaces also display a preoccupation with place and the physical and "social milieu" that began permeating France in the late eighteenth century. Archaeologists, art critics, and others (including Chateaubriand) insisted, for one, that monuments lost their essence outside their original physical and spiritual landscape. Architect Viollet-le-Duc "pit[ied] those works that were torn from their womb, weaned from their native soil." *Idéologues* such as Daunou likewise drew the consequences of their sensationalist conception of the self, shaped by the chemical reactions triggered by sensory experiences of the material world. They articulated both an optimistic vision of humanity—perfectible through environmental modifications—and a concrete program for social improvement. This

---

32. *RAN* 11, no. 5 (November 1859): 147; *Le Courrier du Nord*, 31 March 1840; and Delloye 38/72: Clipping from *L'Emancipateur*, n.d. [1839].

33. Delloye 38/100: Bouly, "Littérature locale. Programme de la fête communale. 15 août 1838" (n.p., 1838), 1; *L'Artiste* 1, no. 41 (March 16, 1851): 333; and Jean Adhémar, "L'enseignement par l'image," *Gazette des beaux-arts*, 6th period, 97 (1981): 53–62.

34. André Micoud, ed., *Des hauts lieux: la construction sociale de l'exemplarité* (Paris, 1991), quotation on 63.

35. The same was true of another historical *haut lieu*: the *Chambre des pairs*, decorated with busts and statues of military and civilian *illustrations* in 1840. Interestingly, I could not locate a single reference to the Versailles gallery by pageant sponsors. See Thomas W. Gaehtgens, *Versailles: de la résidence royale au musée historique* (Paris, 1984), 41 and 63; Michael M. Marrinan, "Historical Vision and the Writing of History at Louis-Philippe's Versailles," in Petra Ten-Doesschate Chu and Gabriel P. Weisberg, eds., *The Popularization of Images: Visual Culture under the July Monarchy* (Princeton, N.J., 1994), 120–21; and Pierre Karila-Cohen, "Charles de Rémusat et l'impossible refondation du régime de juillet," *Revue d'histoire moderne et contemporaine* 33, no. 3 (July–September 1997): 413–14.

credo fused with other convictions—the moral force of habitual practices, a vision of society as "an object sui generis, with its own laws, its own science" (P. Rabinow)—to couple physical transformation, social reform, and moral renewal.[36] Statisticians accordingly began their investigations by studying territories and social environments; penal reformers emphasized the corrective force of milieus and habits; architects decorated museum walls with ornaments to create didactic facades.[37] Some contemporaries furthermore extolled festivals as an all-encompassing milieu whose "demonstrations . . ., by striking the senses, must awaken the same ideas within a large mass of men." Festivals could "rekindle the soul and . . . restore health."[38] The milieu fused with memory, finally, to create potent historical spaces. In 1816, *littérateur* and future liberal deputy Laurent-Pierre de Jussieu devised plans for a "Historical gallery" of paintings that, given "the power of signs" on the senses and imagination, would create permanent memories. In the provinces, schoolteacher Théodore de Rive captured the promise of intrinsically local spaces in 1858, when he asked fellow members of the Société d'agriculture, sciences et arts de l'arrondissement de Valenciennes to produce panels on local celebrities, botany, and the like for elementary school classrooms. "The best of teachers," he explained, "is . . . as fitting a milieu as possible, one that acts imperceptibly upon beings, just as the atmosphere contributes to the renewal of the productions of the vegetable kingdom."[39]

The lure of imperceptible action ultimately explains, better than any other factor, the appeal of this pedagogical model throughout these decades. The organizers of Cambrai's pageant were candid in 1839: "What [workers] neglected in the classroom, they now do without thinking: they study the history of their native city and *pays* . . . [and] treat the present as a serious matter." Without citing Rousseau, pageant organizers thus endorsed his conviction that public festivals would foster "public fraternity"

---

36. Eugène Viollet-le-Duc, quoted in Marie-Anne Sire, *France du patrimoine*, 59; Paul Rabinow, *French Modern: Norms and Forms of the Social Environment* (Cambridge, 1989), quotation on 11; Dominique Poulot, *Musée nation*, 367–69; and Gaehtgens, "Présentation historique de la problématique du contexte XIX–XXe siècle," in François Furet, ed., *Patrimoine, temps, espace*, 48.

37. Bernard Lepetit, "Missions scientifiques et expéditions militaires: remarques sur leurs modalités d'articulation," in Marie-Noëlle Bourguet et al., *Invention scientifique*, 103; and Abel Blouet, *Projet de prison cellulaire pour 585 condamnés, précédé d'observations sur le système pénitentiaire* (Paris, 1843).

38. "Fêtes," in Pierre Leroux and Jean Reynaud, eds., *Encyclopédie nouvelle, ou dictionnaire philosophique, scientifique, littéraire et industriel offrant le tableau des connaissances humaines au dix-neuvième siècle*, 6 vols. (Paris, 1836–42), 5: 287.

39. Laurent-Pierre de Jussieu, prospectus for *Galerie historique ou cours d'histoire générale par tableaux* [1816], repr. in Gaehtgens, *Versailles*, 381, as well as Gaehtgens's exegesis on 65–67; and *RAN* 9, no. 12 (June 1858): 371.

and yield memories that, "engraved in . . . the heart," attached residents to their land.[40] In this era of ubiquitous politicization, an era that yearned for intellectual renewal as well as social stasis, the pedagogy of place held boundless promises of discreet recomposition.

"THE MOST ENCHANTING OF DREAMS"

This pedagogy yielded civic as well as ideological designs—where civic action denotes participation in the national body politic and ideology denotes a group-specific set of values, perception of one's environment, and blueprint for the organization of social relations.[41] With its urge to depoliticize and its concern with social and geographic immobility, this ideological design displayed an affinity for in situ action (such as historical pageants). With its urge to politicize and its appeal to reason and voluntary initiative, the civic design favored, in contrast, emblematic spaces (such as Montargis's great room). Strands of both designs occasionally permeated the same venture.

The ideological design appealed to all political schools—but none more than conservative liberals and traditionalists. It rested on the conviction that France's social problem—unrest, the *peuple*'s social and political aspirations, pauperism—was most amenable to moral solutions. Scientific congresses vowed to spread the "liking for moral and intellectual pleasures" while learned societies devoted themselves to "the moral and physical improvement of the working classes."[42] Paris's image as a degenerate fulcrum further contributed to the (self-) depiction of *la province* and its elites as the last bastion of French morality. "These hard-working men retired in the depths of their province" could, better than anyone, inculcate what Le Glay called "moral being, peace of the soul, submission to the laws, respect for authority, universal fraternity."[43]

They would do so, most notably, by disseminating local memories. These elites were certainly not the first to equate historical monuments

40. According to Rousseau, affection for the *pays natal* was a prerequisite for civic sentiment. See Delloye 26/27: *Société de bienfaisance* (Cambrai, n.d. [1839?]); Marc Balissa, *Fraternité universelle et intérêt national (1713–1795): les cosmopolitiques du droit des gens* (Paris, 1998), 55–57; and Jean-Jacques Rousseau, *Politics and the Arts: Letter to M. d'Alembert on the Theatre*, ed. and trans. Allan Bloom (Ithaca, 1960), 132–33. I have inverted the order of this quotation.

41. I am drawing on Louis Dumont, *Essays on Individualism: Modern Ideology in Anthropological Perspective* (Chicago, 1986).

42. AN F17 3090/1: De Bourneville to subprefect Reims, 15 December 1845; and Alfred Morel, *Des établissements d'instruction publique, de prévoyance, d'assistance et de réforme à Dunkerque, 1820–1862* (Dunkirk, 1863), 5.

43. BNF Z 41001: Le Glay, speech in the Association lilloise's public meeting of 10 June 1839, untitled brochure (Lille, n.d. [1839]), 59.

with moral lessons or to claim that "memories are practically humankind's entire moral realm." They were apparently the first, however, to invest *local* memories with such potent force: the capacity to transform human beings. They depicted local history lessons as "effective means of moralization," a source of "true notions" that spoke directly to the heart.[44] They embraced local museums that, however mediocre their collections, exerted a "moralizing influence." They furthermore contended that street names derived from local history constituted a "new mode of education." By instilling "respect for the men and the things of the past," explained a Commission historique member in 1863, such street names would "calm the ardor that sweeps one towards an uncertain future." This mode of pedagogical action was perfectly adapted to its time. "Today's *peuple*" after all "likes to educate itself."[45]

In a department such as the Nord, moreover, this was an era of rapid industrial and social change, increasing physical and social mobility, and working-class politicization. Urban centers teemed with destitute migrants. One resident of Lille out of three relied on the welfare office in 1833. City streets were the scenes of social contestation: "coalitions" and seditious cries; nocturnal outbreaks of workers singing the *Marseillaise;* demonstrations by striking miners and textile workers. Numerous bankruptcies and growing unemployment characterized the early 1840s. As elsewhere, the 1846–51 crisis exacerbated the situation, provoking hunger riots, reformist banquets, and plantings of liberty trees. In 1851, the Nord's public prosecutor wrote Paris about a "wretched parade" in Lille that had lured two hundred spectators and ended with a mock execution of the president.[46] The department also witnessed disquieting working-class festivities that, like the metal and leather workers' Saint-Eloi fêtes, mixed ribaldry and religion. Making matters worst, drinking establishments (*cabarets*) multiplied: from 1 per 137 inhabitants in Lille in 1830 to 1 per 70 in 1851. Open from 3:00 A.M. in the summer, they not

---

44. Claude-Charles Pierquin de Gembloux, *Histoire monétaire et philologique du Berry* (Bourges, 1840), iii; *RAN* 11, no. 5 (November 1859): 147; and François Morand, letter of 24 July 1838, in his *Lettres à Augustin Thierry et autres documents relatifs à un projet de constitution des archives communales, proposée en 1838 et années suivantes* (Paris, 1877), 5.

45. *Congrès des délégués des sociétés savantes . . . 1850. Bulletin* 1: 10; and *BCN* 7 (1863): 116.

46. *Souvenirs à l'usage des habitants de Douai, ou notes pour faire suite à l'ouvrage de M. Plouvain sur l'histoire de cette ville, depuis le 1er janvier 1822 jusqu'au 30 novembre 1842* (Douai, 1843), 177; Etienne Durand (Hippolyte Verly), *Les tablettes d'un bourgeois de Lille* (Lille, 1874), 263; AN BB 30/377: Public prosecutor of Douai to Minister of Justice, 12 April 1851; *Histoire des Pays-Bas français: Flandre, Artois, Hainaut, Boulonnais, Cambrésis* (Toulouse, 1972), 406; idem, ed., *Histoire de Lille*, 3 vols. (Toulouse, 1991), 3: 428–29; idem, ed., *Histoire de Cambrai* (Lille, 1982), 223–24; Henri Platelle, ed., *Histoire de Valenciennes* (Lille, 1982), 202–3; and Philippe Guignet, "L'émeute des quatre sous d'Anzin," *RN* 55 (1973): 347–64.

only served alcohol, but also facilitated covert meetings and political debates.[47]

Elites thus felt a pressing need to mold the masses and instill both obedience and acceptance of one's social fate. It was equally vital to halt the exodus of unskilled rural laborers to cities. Outside the moral constraints of enclosed rural communities, the latter inevitably succumbed to depravity. Le Glay thus denounced, from the 1830s on, the flight of peasants who abandoned the "paternal home" in search of a higher social position. For many elites, the best way of quenching this "moral disease" was to encourage agriculture and hence tie residents to "to the soil of the *patrie.*"[48] But if the likes of Bruneel saw agriculture as an "anchor of . . . social peace," they also grasped its limitations before a "pathological ambition" that produced pauperism, despair, and "street riots."[49] Something else—something more affective—was needed. Bruneel endorsed "any new attraction that tends to restore harmony in this chaos" by pinning down this "restless population." The attraction in question was the Commission historique's historical panels. In Montargis, Cormenin likewise reminded the *Conseil général* that people "do not grow attached to the native land through well-being alone, but also through their memories." Minister Freslon wrote the prefects in 1848 that memories of local *illustrations* would maintain "their descendants around a generous hearth of sorts, in which souls both enlighten and warm one another."[50] Historical pageants served identical purposes. By reminding rural residents that "they were not born yesterday," explained Le Glay, they fostered love of a *pays* one no longer sought to leave. "On this same land, and in this same city, great things have been accomplished." We recognize here a traditionalist worldview, but also Guizot's conviction that "in order to believe in itself, society cannot have been born yesterday."[51]

To understand how the pedagogy of place was expected to root and moralize the *peuple*, let us take a closer look at these pageants—focusing on Cambrai, Douai, and Valenciennes. They may not have responded di-

47. Pierre Pierrard, *Les diocèses de Cambrai et de Lille* (Paris, 1978), 215; idem, *La vie ouvrière à Lille sous le Second Empire* (Paris, 1965), 281–89; Bernard Ménager, "Vie politique," 3: 1129–30; and Trénard, *Histoire de Lille,* 463–64.

48. The Nord underwent a slower rate of rural depopulation than many other departments, however. See *MSL* (1837): 408; *MEC* 16 (1840): 4; Robert Gildea, *Education in Provincial France,* 326–29; and Steven D. Kale, *Legitimism and the Reconstruction of French Society,* 236.

49. *BCN* 3 (1847–49): 173. See also Fanny Dénoix des Vergnes, "Emigration des campagnes vers les cités," in her *Çà et là: études historiques* (Paris, 1865), 26.

50. *BCN* 3 (1847–49): 173; Cormenin, "Note pour les illustrations"; and Freslon to prefects, op. cit.

51. [Le Glay], *Programme des faits historiques représentés par la marche des chars et phaétons à la fête communale de Cambrai, le 15 et le 18 août 1833,* 7–8; and François Guizot, *Du gouvernement de la France depuis la Restauration, et du ministère actuel* (Paris, 1820), 206, cited in Rosanvallon, *Moment Guizot,* 194.

rectly to perceived wantonness or street demonstrations, but they "smack[ed] of neither the orgy nor the cabaret" and reflected pervasive concern with organized and spontaneous uses of urban space. All fêtes, according to one contemporary encyclopedia, "momentarily efface social disparities."[52] Historical pageants promised to soothe a "sick nation" by involving "all the classes" at once in a celebration of community, continuity and unanimity, a "touching union that turns several thousand inhabitants into one great family."[53] This was true, first of all, of their representations. Pageant organizers hoped to moralize local residents by exposing them to suggestive images. Banners and inscriptions such as "As did our fathers" "prevent[ed] the eye of the spectator from losing sight of . . . the political, moral, and religious verities we owe to each of the periods represented."[54] These spectacles excised the participation of working people in medieval uprisings and depicted an idealized urban past, a cohesive and patriarchal local community. Predicated on vertical relations, governed by benevolent elites, the latter was also uncontaminated by external influences, social strife, and for some, the market. All residents knew their place and duties in this harmonious world: "nobles and bourgeois, clergy and guilds, warriors and artisans, in other words the entire society." Such representations would attenuate social conflict by spreading ideals of familial solidarity, social reconciliation, and territorial identity that transcended class membership.[55]

Pageant organizers furthermore encouraged participation in collective celebrations that would reorder social relations and mend a divided society. A festive genre, we know, frames a space that is saturated with meaning and invites particular patterns of behavior. Born of learned procedures, but well nigh religious in their aspirations, historical pageants would generate the "perception of shared emotional states" that Victor Turner has called *communitas.*[56] Elites scripted the historical narratives, but also recruited hundreds of skilled and unskilled laborers—young men and women "from the class of the *peuple*"—to build the floats, decorate the city, collect donations, and above all parade alongside them. Unlike other

52. Elzéar Blaze, *Fête triomphale des Incas à Valenciennes, le 29 mars 1840* (Valenciennes, 1840), 4; and *Encyclopédie des jeunes étudiants et des gens du monde, ou Dictionnaire raisonné des connaissances humaines, des moeurs et des passions,* 2 vols. (Paris, 1838), 1: 296.

53. Municipal bylaw of 5 October 1838, repr. in *Statuts de la Société de bienfaisance de la ville de Douai* (Douai, 1839), 18; and *Flandre illustrée* 23 (26 December 1858): 184.

54. AMV 3 II 9*: Henri-Etienne Caffiaux, proceedings of the Société des Incas, 16 December 1864 (I inverted the order of this quotation).

55. Like other European rituals and ceremonies, these "(re)invented traditions" evoked and reconstituted an idealized, harmonious past. See Eric Hobsbawm and Terence Ranger, eds., *The Invention of Tradition* (New York, 1983); and *La Revue des provinces* 3 (1 December 1834): 92–93.

56. Victor Turner, Introduction to idem, ed., *Celebration: Studies in Festivity and Ritual* (Washington, D.C., 1982), 21.

bourgeois associations, these benevolent societies rarely limited their membership. Commenting on the Société de bienfaisance de Cambrai's 1839 pageant, a local journalist emphasized the abundance of "young workers."[57] This orderly choreography—workers in historical attire— would reassure well-to-do spectators and "amuse the *peuple* while educating it and developing its intellectual and moral instincts." Most important, it would edify the participants themselves. In 1851, a poem praised a festive event for which an "entire *peuple* rises. Everyone sets to work, invents, seeks, dreams." Such, perhaps, was the main attraction of a festive genre that hinged on popular participation rather than passive spectacle.[58]

Indeed, this fête would transform the minds and souls of laborers who devoted countless hours to preparations and, in Douai, received the "exclusive right to impersonate [each year] the figure that the [directing] Committee will have assigned." Like stage actors, they were expected to manufacture their own historical costumes. This entailed research and, presumably, growing identification with the city, its illustrious ancestors, and their orderly values. "The worker who will have worn the knight's insignia, will have more dignity and urbanity." Added the organizers of Valenciennes' 1866 pageant: "In order to imbibe the spirit of their role, to render it with a scrupulous exactitude, all of our members, . . . including the most humble, have had to find or receive certain indispensable facts, all of which carry some lessons." The pageant would thus prompt a personal *prise de conscience* of the local past, instill "love of the *pays*," and impart the qualities of scholarly practice: painstaking effort, forethought, modesty, collective endeavor, and factual truth rather than speculation and passion.[59] This fête would moreover civilize and pacify. Participants would forego "crude pleasures," grow more docile and mild-mannered, and lack the time for political activity. The Société de bienfaisance de Douai made it its "moral goal" to rid "a certain class of the taste for debauchery." In 1839, the mayor wrote his subprefect that the Société sought to "draw away from politics the artisans and workers who care about it too much." It encouraged them instead to devote "all of their leisure time to the preparation of a historical fête."[60]

<hr />

57. Charles du Rozoir, *Relation historique*, 33; and Delloye 39/2: Clipping from *L'Emancipateur*, n.d. [August 1839].

58. Delloye 40/54: Maréchal, intervention before the municipal council of Cambrai, 22 August 1851, quoted in Bouly, "Notice anecdotique sur le Programme de la fête de Cambrai composé par Eugène Bouly," n.d. [1852?]; and *RAN* 3, no. 4 (October 1851): 132–33.

59. *Statuts de la Société de bienfaisance de Douai*, 11; Delloye 39/10: Clipping from *L'Emancipateur*, n.d. [1838]; and *Société de bienfaisance dite des Incas. Souvenir de la marche qui a eu lieu à Valenciennes les dimanche et mardi 17 & 19 juin et noms des sociétaires qui ont représenté les principaux personnages* (Valenciennes, 1866), 6.

60. *Souvenirs à l'usage des habitants*, 152; and AMD 5 D 38: Mayor to subprefect Douai, 14 October 1839. A parallel may be drawn with England: see Peter Bailey, *Leisure and Class in Victorian England: Rational Recreation and the Contest for Control, 1830–1885* (London, 1978), esp. 41–54 and 170.

Actors and spectators would thus experience the emotional depths of a project that began as archival research, culminated in communal celebration, and ended as spiritual epiphany. This ceremonial and performative ritual provided an intimate and atemporal encounter with one's fathers and moral ancestors. Fusing "the world as lived and the world as imagined" (C. Geertz), it required a willing suspension of disbelief and yielded "this ancient fraternity of neighborliness" that united everyone, "poor or rich, artisan or artist, illiterate or learned."[61] In this fashion, the localist pageant also fulfilled the goals of romantic history: history as strong emotion, collective self-understanding, and dialectic between dream and reality. No one would emerge unchanged from a festivity predicated on self-forgetting and self-recovery. This catharsis was open to all, but the historical pageant's true worth resided in its hold over a *peuple* that was physically and emotionally available. It spoke "a language that [these workers] can understand: it is their heart, above all, that one must educate."[62] Educating the heart, instructing the mind, awakening the soul: *littérateurs* and pageant organizers alike blurred the lines between the emotional, the rational, and the moral as they described the lasting effect of this unique pedagogy.

These ideological objectives governed the pageants' very organization. While pageants granted workers a more prominent role than Old Regime urban parades, they also forced them to adopt a borrowed persona. Unlike these parades, whose participants marched as members of a corporate or political body (thereby displaying their own *qualité* or *état*), historical pageants prevented local residents from asserting their social identity—even in the context of a local hierarchy.[63] According to the organizers' logic, the participants did exhibit their selves, but it was an authentic, collective self that they had at last recaptured. As in the festivals of the French Revolution, the aim was less to represent institutional hierarchy than to produce virtue and harmony and create a shared moment whose memory would linger in all minds. Revolutionaries such as Rabaut de Saint-Etienne had after all outlined a "revolution in heads and hearts," fusing learning (books, schools) with education of the heart (festivals,

---

61. *Fête du Moyen Age sous Philippe-le-Bon*, 3; and *Gazette de Cambrai*, 21 August 1850. On the pageant and the public ceremony as ritual, see Clifford Geertz, "Religion as a Cultural System," in his *The Interpretation of Cultures* (New York, 1973), 87–125, quotation on 112; and David Glassberg, *American Historical Pageantry: The Uses of Tradition in the Early Twentieth Century* (Chapel Hill, N.C., 1990), 148–50.

62. Delloye 38/110: Clipping from *L'Emancipateur*, n.d. [1838].

63. Lille's pageants constituted exceptions in the mid-1820s, for municipal employees ended the parades. Historical floats on agriculture and industry also grew more prevalent under the Second Empire—a predictable development given the regime's paternalism and concern with industrial development. See, for instance, Kergestain Lucien Merlet, *Cavalcade historique représentant l'entrée du roi Henri IV dans la ville de Chartres, lorsqu'il vint s'y faire sacrer Roi de France* (Chartres, 1860), iv.

games). They had targeted "the senses, the imagination, memory, reasoning, all the faculties that man possesses."[64] Like revolutionary festivals, these pageants were "rite[s] of unanimity and fraternity" that, per Bronislaw Baczko, imprinted their values on all imaginations and hence stirred participants to action. Historical pageants thus reactivated an Enlightenment-era vision of the fête as an orderly, utopian moment with a transformative potential.[65]

This optimism links the pedagogy of place to the broader development of lay philanthropy in post-Napoleonic Europe. While urban fêtes had entertained such charitable purposes since the Middle Ages, the discovery of "pauperism," the state's reduced commitment to charity, and the momentary eclipse of the clergy (in France) spurred traditionalist and liberal elites alike to enter this domain more actively. This explains the multiplication of benevolent societies—some of them festive—that would help the needy. Bordeaux's "philanthropic" historical pageant provided hundreds of local "workers" with work and distributed 4,500 francs to local charities in 1851. "For this beautiful and noble charity," sang a *chansonnier* from Lille regarding the city's 1858 pageant, "thank you! thank you! for the worker."[66]

What is more, leading social philanthropists such as Joseph de Gérando and Eugène Buret sought to cure the social question through moral reform rather than economic action, penal repression, or forceful governmental intervention. If the *peuple* proved aggressive, lazy, or depraved, if it threatened the social order, it was due to moral deprivation rather than an inherently evil nature. Despite their doctrinal differences, these philanthropists thus resolved to fill its leisure time with good books, gymnastics, historical panels, and other uplifting recreations. "This is how one creates mores," explained François Marbeau in 1847. The working class needed moral edification, sensory stimulation, sociability outside the family, and spiritual comfort. Catholic ceremonies no longer constituted the "museum and opera of the people," declared Buret. The age thus called for a new type of pedagogy, capable of acting upon "man as a creature subject to physical influences." One Victor Modeste called for local museums and public readings, since "all these spectacles for the eyes, all these sounds for the ears" could reach a population governed by its senses

---

64. Bell, *Cult of the Nation,* 2 and 162.

65. Bronislaw Baczko, *Utopian Lights: The Evolution of the Idea of Social Progress,* trans. Judith L. Greenberg (New York, 1989), 177–90, quotation on 186; and Ozouf, *Fête révolutionnaire,* 20, 215, 284, 350, and 354–56.

66. Pelleport, *Historique des fêtes bordelaises,* 8–9, 39, and 44; and Charles Decottignies, *La cavalcade des fastes de Lille. Faits historiques. Chanson patoise* (Lille, 1858), n.p. [4]. On the development of philanthropy, see Colette Bec et. al., *Philanthropies et politiques sociales en Europe (XVIIIe–XXe siècles)* (Paris, 1994).

rather than "the life of the intellect."[67] Secular festivals furthermore provoked "intense emotion" outside the riot. If Gérando endorsed local fêtes and commemorations, it was because such "means of improvement for the human creature" agreed perfectly with his erstwhile *Idéologue* sensationalism. (Building on Locke, Condillac, and others, he elaborated an epistemology founded on experience and sensations, source of all "primitive materials" for the mind). These festivals thus promised to cleanse and regulate society by altering the environment, overwhelming participants and spectators, and subjugating their passions. They would generate a "community of purpose, emotion, interest."[68]

Some clerics and devout Catholics also sought to moralize the *peuple* through its senses. Decorated public spaces and festivities were, after all, ancient Catholic practices.[69] In a century "in which everything is materialized," wrote a priest from the Nord in 1852, "one must speak to the *peuple* through the eyes; many men must first be brought back to religion through the senses, since it was through the senses that they moved away from it."[70] Pageant organizers included liberal or social Catholics who sought to mend social ills and, in some instances, consolidate their paternalistic hold on the *peuple*. Saint-Aignan and Le Glay embraced historical panels as one of many "new modes of charity" that "must fight the constant and disastrous effects of pauperism." Panels would "moralize the population" and instill "within all social ranks a soft and moral education, suited to everyone's situation" (see figure 15).[71] Cormenin concurred: like popular libraries or courses for adults, the great room would disseminate the message of the Gospels and "moralize the . . . *peuple*."[72]

Historical pageants held one final ideological promise: to supplant car-

---

67. Eugène Buret, *De la misère des classes laborieuses en Angleterre et en France*, 2 vols. (Paris, 1840), 1: 306–9, and 2: 461–62 and 466; François Marbeau, *Du paupérisme en France et des moyens d'y remédier* (Paris, 1847), 124; Victor Modeste, *Du paupérisme en France: état actuel—causes—remèdes possibles* (Paris, 1858), 357–58 and 511–12; and Gustave de Gérando, *Des récréations populaires considérées comme un des moyens les plus efficaces de détourner les ouvriers des cabarets* (Paris, 1857), quotation on 12. See also Olivier Ihl, *La fête républicaine* (Paris, 1996), 65; and Jean-Baptiste Duroselle, *Les débuts du catholicisme social en France, 1822–1870* (Paris, 1951), 59–79.

68. Joseph-Marie de Gérando, *De la bienfaisance publique*, 4 vols. (Paris, 1839), 3:387–97, quotations on 393 and 397; and idem, *De la génération des connaissances humaines* (Paris, 1990 [1802]).

69. Robert A. Schneider, *The Ceremonial City: Toulouse Observed, 1738–1780* (Princeton, N.J., 1995), 124; and Sheryl Kroen, *Politics and Theater*, 78 and 90–91.

70. Louis-François Capelle, *Vie du cardinal P. Giraud, archevêque de Cambrai* (Lille, 1852), 218.

71. *MEC* 14 (1833): 10–11; Le Glay, *Mémoire sur les bibliothèques publiques et les principales bibliothèques particulières du département du Nord* (Lille, 1841), 227; and Saint-Aignan to the Commission historique du Nord, 8 March 1843.

72. Proceedings of the *Conseil général* of the Loiret, 5 September 1844. See also Isabelle Olivero, *L'invention de la collection: de la diffusion de la littérature et des savoirs à la formation du citoyen au XIXe siècle* (Paris, 1999), 34.

DÉDIÉ AUX MEMBRES DES SOCIÉTÉS DE BIENFAISANCE.

FIGURE 15. Sisterhood and beneficence permeate this ethereal scene of 1849–
50, another lithograph by Félix Robaut. Neighboring towns and benevolent
associations come together under the protective arms of a Christian matron. The
viewer's gaze converges toward the motto of the Société de bienfaisance de
Douai—"The poor are our brothers"—and the open book exalting history and
charity (the pietà). United in their facial traits, clothing, and physical gestures,
these allegorical figures display the elite's concord before the social problem.
Courtesy of the Bibliothèque Municipale de Douai.

nivals, the era's most immoral festivity. In the Nord, those pageants that
had begun as carnivals had, with few exceptions, curtailed or eliminated
this component by the mid-1830s.[73] The carnival's short and ritualized suspension of normalcy may, as some social scientists argue, buttress a social
order whose return is never questioned. This did not make it any less suspect to contemporaries, who expressed their contempt for such unruly
revelry and the popular mores it set loose.[74] Increasingly numerous and
menacing under the July Monarchy and Second Republic, carnivals could

73. The divorce from the carnival was sometimes incomplete, however. Some pageants retained carnivalesque attributes and some carnivals included lone historical floats. See, for instance, *Ville de Comines. Programme détaillé du cortège-cavalcade augmenté d'une notice historique pour
servir d'explication aux différentes scènes représentées au Cortège* (Lille, 1853).

74. AMDu 1 J 50: Municipal ordinance of 21 January 1839; and Pierrard, *La vie quotidienne
dans le Nord au XIXe siècle: Artois, Flandre, Hainaut, Picardie* (Paris, 1976), 107–10. On the "ritual
of status reversal' " and the preservation of social order, see Turner, *The Ritual Process: Structure
and Anti-Structure* (Chicago, 1969).

serve as launching pads for political statements and skirmishes from the left and, less often, from the right.[75] The historical pageant hence became the antithesis and palliative to these "vile farces," unbefitting "as serious an epoch as ours." The distinction between both fêtes was plain. Where the carnival polarized the population, the historical pageant projected an ostensibly spontaneous unanimity; where the carnival hinged on obfuscation, anonymity, and escape from one's self, the pageant provided clarity, authenticity, and self-recovery; where the carnival, finally, invited participants to transgress boundaries, the pageant offered—like Old Regime processions—fixed roles and a bounded journey through the urban space. The regulations of Bourg's historical cavalcade were unequivocal: "*On no account* shall anyone abandon his allotted place, so as to maintain perfect order."[76]

No wonder, then, that the Compagnie des mines d'Anzin and the Nord's railroad company each donated pageant organizers from Valenciennes a thousand francs in May 1851. No wonder that Parisian journalists praised the latter for "enlightening" and "distract[ing] . . . the minds of the masses." No wonder, finally, that contemporaries urged the government to stage similar fêtes in Paris. These pedagogical ventures demonstrated "the potential influence of popular entertainment upon politics." They provided a new pathway toward "the most enchanting of dreams, the concord of all."[77]

CIVIC EDUCATION

This "enchanting dream" was clearly one of depoliticization: a harmonious community in which all remained in their place. The other design behind the pedagogy of place was, in contrast, decidedly political. Without inviting factional, partisan activity, it nonetheless sought to ease the *peuple*'s entry into the civic sphere. The individuals who articulated this civic design were essentially republicans and reformist liberals, joined by a few conservative liberals. The cult of secular great men—of will and achievement, be it local or national—found most of its adherents on the left. Cormenin's *Notice biographique* thus evokes the *Recueil des actions*

75. On the dangers of the nineteenth-century carnival, see Edward Berenson, *Populist Religion and Left-Wing Politics in France, 1830–1852* (Princeton, N.J., 1984), 207–13; and Robert J. Bezucha, "Masks of Revolution: A Study of Popular Culture during the Second French Republic," in Roger Price, ed., *Revolution and Reaction: 1848 and the Second French Republic* (New York, 1975), esp. 242–43.

76. *Revue cambrésienne* 1 (1835–1836): 165; Delloye 39/17: Clipping from *La Feuille de Cambrai*, March 1839; and *Grande fête de charité donnée à Bourg au profit des pauvres de la ville. Cavalcade historique et promenade en char. Règlement approuvé par l'autorité municipale* (Bourg, n.d. [1863]), 1–2, italics in the original.

77. *Le Courrier du Nord*, 6 May 1851; *Le Constitutionnel*, 13 May 1851; *L'Illustration*, 23 May and 12 June 1851; and Léon Méhédin, *Projet de fêtes publiques à Paris* (Paris, 1852), 19–20.

héroiques et civiques des républicains français, a compendium of actions that French revolutionaries deemed sufficiently inspiring to warrant public readings in schools and assemblies.[78] Behind the *Notice's* localism, we find the conviction that affection for one's *pays* would lead residents to identify with, and participate in the national political community. In the 1810s and early 1820s, liberal thinker Benjamin Constant had criticized a modern era in which isolated individuals, "lacking contact with the past, . . . remove themselves from a *patrie* they cannot see anywhere." Broader political prerogatives for communes and *arrondissements* would make the *patrie* more visible. So would local "habits and memories," which alone could create this "patriotism of the locality" that "especially today, is the only true one." Reformist liberal Paul-François Dubois agreed in 1825: "To reactivate the memories of each locality is to make patriots."[79] For Constant and Dubois, citizenship was necessarily restricted to educated, independent elites. Republican Aristide Guilbert articulated a broader conception of the polity in the 1840s. His *Histoire des villes de France*, he insisted, was the first to furnish French citizens—including workers and artisans—with their local "memories of might, grandeur and glory." A portrait of "the nation's personality," his undertaking was "deeply national in its democratic spirit."[80]

Democratic as it was, this venture targeted a literate audience. Others fused local memories and civic action in a more sweeping fashion. In 1851, for instance, a member of Amiens's Société des antiquaires de Picardie noted that an "immense crowd" had attended the festivities marking the inauguration of a statue depicting a famous sculptor from Noyon. In doing so, he said, local residents asserted their "right to say . . . we, too, matter in the *patrie*."[81] This civic design acquired yet a greater scope in Montargis. The redecorated great room was a civic project in its very location: city hall, the edifice that witnessed all public deeds relating to the local population's "official existence." Elections also took place in the great room—a fact that Cormenin and his colleagues duly emphasized. Their venture was civic, furthermore, in its recourse to a public subscription. Subscriptions served economic purposes, of course, but they also involved "the greatest possible number of arrondissement citizens." Everyone "brought his offering" to a room that rested on the "voluntary

78. Dominique Julia, *Les trois couleurs du tableau noir: la Révolution* (Paris, 1981), 208–13.

79. Benjamin Constant, *Principes de politique* (Paris, 1872), 102–3; and *Le Globe* 2, no. 116 (4 June 1825), cited in Jean-Jacques Goblot, *Jeune France libérale*, 342. For similar views, see J. C. L. de Sismondi, *Etudes sur les constitutions des peuples libres* (Paris, 1836).

80. Aristide Guilbert, prospectus for his *Histoire des villes*, appended to the BNF's copy of vol. 1; idem, Introduction to *Histoire des villes*, 1: i and xviii; and Guilbert, public letter to provincial residents, 15 March 1842, appended to the BNF copy of *Histoire des villes*.

81. *Bulletin de la Société des antiquaires de Picardie* 4 (1850–52): 242.

contribution of the entire *pays*." The great room is "truly ours," said Cormenin.[82] The venture was civic, finally, in its thematics: a cult of *illustrations* that belonged to the arrondissement and the nation and captured republican civic qualities: simplicity, devotion to the community and the common good, and independence of mind. "Examples form citizens," declared Cormenin.[83] The organizing commission, it is true, selected these *illustrations* without consulting the public or generating a democratic debate. Yet its historical *tableaux d'honneur* were ultimately counterparts to the *tableaux-lois* that Cormenin devised in 1843. These large-type reproductions of civil, administrative, and criminal laws of local interest hung in classrooms and municipal council meeting rooms. They contributed to a broader decentralization by educating elected officials and preparing the youth to one day "administer the commune."[84] The redecorated great room hence embodied a republican conception of freedom as voluntary participation in issues of collective importance. The *pays*'s public life schooled citizens in the ways of participatory politics.

These civic implications clearly drew Minister Freslon to Montargis's historical panels. He promised to consecrate the "memory of great citizens" and develop "emulation . . . of public and private virtues." He also referred to these decorated rooms as "local *prytanées*," a term that denoted Revolution-era secondary schools and institutions for deserving citizens. In ancient Greece, the *prytanée* had been a meeting place for important magistrates and the edifice in which the polis rewarded virtuous and patriotic citizens. This civic design also surfaced in the Nord, where Saint-Aignan sought to include in his historical panels those citizens who had displayed "civic courage."[85]

The pedagogy of place hence captured yet another relationship between the local and the national. Following this configuration, the local was not merely the foundation of a national scientific edifice or a source of national self-understanding (see chapter 2). It was also the proximate setting in which citizens learned to love a place and a political community.

82. "Hôtel de ville," in André Berthelot, ed., *La Grande Encyclopédie: inventaire raisonné des sciences, des lettres et des arts par une société de savants et de gens de lettres,* 31 vols. (Paris, 1886–1902), 20: 297; "Souscription pour les Illustrations locales"; *Le Loing,* 20 September 1845; and Cormenin, *Entretiens de village,* 6th ed. (Paris, 1846 [1845]), 269–70. On nineteenth-century subscriptions and their designs, see Chantal Martinet, "La souscription," in *La sculpture française au XIXe siècle* (Paris, 1986), 231–39.

83. *Notice biographique,* 12, 41, and passim; Cormenin, "Notes pour les illustrations"; and Bell, *Cult of the Nation,* 126.

84. I have found little information on the fate of these *tableaux-lois* besides Cormenin's claim that ten thousand French communes owned one by 1846. See BNF Fr 75: [Cormenin], "Tableaux-lois. Lois sur l'administration municipale du 18 juillet 1837" (Paris, 1843); and idem, *Entretiens de village,* 232–37.

85. Freslon to prefects, op. cit.; and Saint-Aignan to the Commission historique du Nord, 8 March 1843.

Implicit in Constant's earlier statements, this relationship surfaced in *France départementale*, a liberal periodical that, in 1838, extolled "love" of the commune and land "in which we took our first steps"—a land that now witnessed local elections. Founded on local sentiments and solidarity, this sense of place anchored individuals in their *pays*, fostered social cohesion, and led them to look beyond their personal circumstances. It would eventually yield "true national love" and, hence, revitalize the French "public spirit." In 1852, the liberal reformist Auguste Vivien likewise defined "local patriotism" as the "initiation to the *patrie*'s noble love of herself." Cormenin, Bruneel, and their colleagues granted such views a tangible form through their historical practices. By cultivating affection for one's place of birth, said Bruneel in 1849, historical panels would "contribute to the development of national patriotism." He continued: "Love of the *patrie*" consists merely of those "tender sentiments that tie the child to the family, the adolescent to the paternal home, the grown man to the commune in which he exercises his rights and fulfills his civic duties." Cormenin and Freslon went further, sketching new ways of political participation and a relationship between a *grande patrie* (the nation) and a *petite patrie*, "the *arrondissement* in which we were born, in which we live, in which our possessions, our families, all our dearest interests, our most tender memories are established."[86] The result was a pedagogical model that, by fusing affective and familial referents with a civic rhetoric, promised to recompose the nation through its local memories.

IMPEDIMENTS

Such promises did not, however, render the pedagogy of place ubiquitous. While some French elites embraced this model, many demurred, however much they endorsed local memories in other forms. Montargis's great room drew interest, but yielded few duplicates. Neither Cormenin nor the Nord's Commission historique managed to secure a subsidy from their *Conseil général*. Historical pageants emerged throughout France, but had become scarce by the mid-1860s. In the Nord, they failed to establish themselves in some towns, were held on an irregular basis in others, and secured neither the unwavering support of the authorities nor the backing of all local elites. One key limiting factor—misgivings about local self-identification—will be discussed at length in part III of this book. The most basic impediment, however, was cost. Historical panels, redecorated rooms, monographs, and historical pageants rested, as we have seen, on subscriptions—a new practice that remained foreign to many and often failed to cover the sometimes considerable expenses. With its two thou-

---

86. *France départementale* 5 (1838): 88–89; Auguste Vivien, *Etudes administratives*, 2 vols. (Paris, 1852), 2: 16; *BCN* 3 (1847–49): 174; and Freslon to prefects, op. cit.

sand swords, shields, and other accessories, Douai's Entry of Philip the Good cost more than twenty thousand francs in 1839, but donations barely topped two thousand francs.[87] Growing familiarity with such spectacles also attenuated their novelty. During the second half of the nineteenth century, new forms of entertainment—traveling circuses, amusement parks, universal exhibitions—competed with the pageant and underscored its traditionalism (processions and the like).[88] Most of the Nord's festive societies had gone bankrupt by the mid-1850s.

Indifference toward history and the patrimony also surfaced, as I have suggested, at all levels of society. Active and productive as some intellectual elites were, their public contests, courses, and pageants did not always attract as many participants as hoped.[89] Such disinterest reveals the tenuous hold of high culture on many French men and women as well as the erudite bent of many intellectual elites. What is more, a prevalent current—"industrialism"—denounced pageants and other such leisure activities as "sterile interruption[s] of work," a brake on material production. Such views help explain the parsimony of many *Conseils généraux* regarding cultural matters.[90] Some political economists moreover condemned all fêtes as corruptive of the poor, a maladapted response to a growing social problem. If the Société des fêtes de charité de Bordeaux vanished in the 1850s, explained its ex-secretary, it was mainly because many residents had refused to "confer a high degree of social utility" to such charitable undertakings.[91] Other traditionalist elites agreed, after 1848, that codified ceremonies were needed to moralize and depoliticize workers, but—unlike Buret and other philanthropists—they believed that Catholic rituals would prove most successful and combat religious indifference as well. This is but one explanation for the growth of Marian devotions and pilgrimage—"recalling an age of medieval splendor and pageantry," per historian Ruth Harris—during the second half of the century.[92]

More significantly yet, the pedagogy of place's ideological conviction—

87. *Bulletin de la Société archéologique de Béziers* 3 (1839): 180; AMD 5 D 38: Mayor to subprefect Douai, 14 October 1839; AMD 5 D 41: [Jean-Baptiste?] Wallez, "Rapport fait à la commission administrative des fêtes historiques par son président dans la séance du 1er mai 1841"; and *Mémorial de la Scarpe*, 16 July 1839.

88. See the complaints in *Revue de l'Escaut* 3, no. 106 (21 August 1859): 3; as well as Vanessa R. Schwartz, *Spectacular Realities: Early Mass Culture in Fin-de-Siècle Paris* (Berkeley, 1998).

89. See, for instance, *L'Orléanais*, 29 June 1845; and *Société des fêtes de charité de Rochefort-sur-Mer 16–17–18 août 1862* (Rochefort-sur-Mer, n.d. [1862]), 2.

90. "Fêtes," in *Encyclopédie nouvelle*, 5: 284; and, regarding the *Conseils généraux*, AN F17 2847: President Commission historique du Nord to president CHAM, April 1843. See also Daniel J. Sherman, *Worthy Monuments: Art Museums and the Politics of Culture in Nineteenth-Century France* (Cambridge, Mass., 1989), 111–13.

91. Pelleport, *Historique des fêtes bordelaises*, 8; and, for instance, R. Marchand, *Du paupérisme* (Paris, 1845).

92. Ruth Harris, *Lourdes: Body and Spirit in the Secular Age* (New York, 1999), 255. Other elites deemed organized sports a most promising means of social control.

social and moral action can reform the *peuple*—and its civic one—local citizenship deserves expansion—contradicted the era's dominant philosophical and political tenets. On an ideological plane, this pedagogical model held that human beings were moldable and perfectible. Although its sponsors rarely publicized this kinship, it owed much, as we have seen, to the sensationalism of the Enlightenment and the *Idéologues*. For its many critics, the latter degenerated easily into (atheistic or agnostic) materialism. Many of these critics were spiritualists who, under the aegis of Victor Cousin and Doctrinaires such as Guizot, sought to amalgamate sensations with a deeper rationalist base. Human beings derived certain ideas from experience, but, most important, they possessed a self, or *moi*, that predated external stimuli. Self-knowledge hinged, first and foremost, on introspection and rational observation of one's mind. Sensationalism, as this school saw it, produced perpetual psychological reconfiguration and endemic social movement, thus endangering the self's autonomy and unity as well as elite control over the social order. The conflict pitting the spiritualist and sensationalist schools was particularly acute in the 1820s, when Cousin accused the "sad [empirical] philosophy" of Condillac and Locke of feeding "the demagogic party." In the mid-1840s, the Cousinian *Dictionnaire des sciences philosophiques* still equated "sensualism" with moral relativism and skepticism.[93] By then, France was "taking the path of spiritualism," as one observer noted. Indeed, the latter now constituted a quasi-official philosophy. Distrusting human malleability, endless perfectibility, and the redeeming quality of the social environment (a reprehensible determinism), the pessimistic spiritualist paradigm questioned the possibility of rehabilitating the *peuple* through historical panels and other forms of moral action.[94]

The Doctrinaire school entertained similar misgivings. The *peuple* required sufficient moral education to distinguish good from evil, but the *capacités* alone were capable of sober, rational reflection and civic partici-

---

93. This hegemony persisted under the Second Empire. See Jan Goldstein, "Mutations of the Self in Old Regime and Post-Revolutionary France: From Ame to *Moi* to *le Moi*," in Lorraine Daston, ed., *Biographies of Scientific Objects: A Historical Ontology* (Chicago, 2000), esp. 101–109; Victor Cousin, 1826 preface, *Fragments philosophiques*, 2d ed., 2 vols. (Paris, 1838), 1:81; "Sensualisme," in Adolphe Franck, ed., *Dictionnaire des sciences philosophiques*, 2d ed. (Paris, 1875 [1844–45]), 1593–94; and Dudley C. Barksdale, "Liberal Politics and Nascent Social Science in France: The Academy of Moral and Political Sciences, 1803–1852" (Ph.D. diss., University of North Carolina–Chapel Hill, 1986), 202–13 and 350.

94. Yvonne Knibiehler, *Naissance des sciences humaines: Mignet et l'histoire philosophique au XIXe siècle* (Paris, 1973), 310–11; Abbé Louis Bautain, "De l'enseignement de la philosophie en France, au dix-neuvième siècle," (1833), quoted in Stéphane Douailler et al., eds., *La philosophie saisie par l'état* (Paris, 1988), 219; and Rosanvallon, *Moment Guizot*, 242–55. William M. Reddy analyzes the relationship between this perception of the self and exclusion in his "Maine de Biran and His Doubles: The Cultural Consequences of Exclusion," paper presented at the conference, "Alain Corbin and the Writing of History," New York University, 27 September 2002.

pation. History, according to an ancient view, merely furnished moral ex-
emplars for an elite of future leaders. "Truth is for all, science for the few,"
declared Cousin in 1826. Culture and civic responsibility thus had to
match social rank and "intelligence," for the risk of misuse—and, again,
social disorder—was great.[95] Such convictions explain why many learned
societies neglected vulgarization. Those provincial elites who embraced
the pedagogy of place did so, more often than not, for its ideological
rather than civic promises. The Commission historique du Nord's decision to place its historical panels in communes, rather than cantonal
seats, in 1849 is a case in point. The canton would have been an eminently
civic choice. Legally instituted in 1790 as an electoral and judicial circum-
scription but deprived of all responsibilities by the Consulate, this intermediary territory became a rallying point for oppositional pamphleteers
under the July Monarchy. Cantonal elections would both widen the electoral franchise and prevent aristocrats from reestablishing, in the smaller
commune, a stronghold over the *peuple*. The 1848 constitution granted
the canton and its council a political role—regarding jury lists, distribution of the contingent, hygiene, charity—that, as one commission member explained, "the commune no longer has." Universal suffrage would
furthermore draw huge crowds to the canton seat for elections.[96] It was
there, insisted some Commission members, that historical panels should
introduce the population to its local memories. Without denying the canton's growing "reality," Le Glay and others argued that this political construct held no emotional resonance for local residents. Most cared about
their commune alone. Some contemporaries perceived the commune as
the first plane of political action, but not these elites. As the "expression
and expansion of the family," the commune simply had "an importance
that no legislation could destroy." A contemporary dictionary developed
this distinction: whereas the commune evoked "a complete body," a self-
enclosed, organic community, the canton was "an integral part of a
body"—of the national body politic.[97] The Commission's selection of the
commune hence reflects an unwillingness to embrace a national, civic
pedagogy.

95. Den Boer, *History as a Profession*, 122–23; Jean Imbert, Introduction to Pierre Bosquet et
al., *Histoire de l'administration de l'enseignement*, 2–3; Patrice Vermeren, *Victor Cousin: le jeu de la
philosophie et de l'état* (Paris, 1995), 182; and Cousin, *Fragments philosophiques*, 130.

96. The Second Republic never passed the law endowing the canton with the provisions
above. On the canton, see Marie-Vic Ozouf-Marignier, "Centralisation et lien social," 84–85;
Jacqueline Lalouette, "L'éducation populaire au canton. Edmond Groult et les musées cantonaux," in *Jean Jaurès cahiers trimestriels* 152 (April–June 1999): 91–92; and Jean-Marc Guislin,
"La dynamique d'une géographie administrative: sous-préfectures et cantons, XIXe–XXe siècles," *RN* 82, no. 335 (April–September 2000): 435–71.

97. *BCN* 3 (1847–49): 167–69; and Auguste Billiard, "Canton," in Duclerc and Pagnerre,
Dictionnaire politique, 183.

FROM UTOPIA TO REPUBLICAN PEDAGOGY

The *pays* we encountered in the preceding pages was, in one respect, a rural territory: a small, harmonious community shaped by Catholic sentiments, wholesome agricultural labor, and attachment to the land. Bergues's Société de l'histoire et des beaux-arts de la Flandre maritime de France thus promised to spread "love of serious studies and the best agricultural methods" in the late 1850s. Its founder, the Social Catholic Louis Debaecker, extolled the Flemings' ancient love for agriculture, rural sayings, and affection for his place of birth.[98] This rural localism resonated among conservatives and traditionalists, alarmed by depopulation and the social and moral breakdown of the countryside in the wake of industrialization. The cult of local memories thus anticipated the late-nineteenth-century agrarian movement, or *retour à la terre*, of Christian Democrats such as the Abbé Lemire (himself a local historian and member of the Comité flamand de France). Wedded to his land and hearth, the sedentary, hard-working, land-owning peasant provided a safeguard against the industrial proletariat and socialism.[99] Yet, the cult of local memories did not restrict itself to this idealized countryside—even in the heavily agricultural Nord. The *pays* was also, and less predictably, an urban expanse, a conduit toward professional success and civic participation. This *pays* resonated above all among liberals and radicals—most of them urban residents. Cormenin's efforts on behalf of Montargis's great room thus demonstrate the import of the "local" in his thought and action. Republican municipalism, we know, apprehended the individual as a citizen rather than a bearer of private interests, endowed him with new responsibilities, and perceived local public life as a civic school and a catalyst for public spirit.[100] Prior to the Third Republic, some republicans expressed such ideas by cultivating local memories within pedagogical ventures.

Rural and urban conceptions of the *pays* betrayed to an extent distinct political visions of French history and society. They were not necessarily antagonistic, however. The liberal Société d'émulation de Cambrai, for one, investigated its urban past and medieval communes during these decades—but it also devoted itself to agriculture, the history of surrounding villages, and rural sayings. The countryside sustained public prosperity and—here as well—"social order," morality, and familial quietude. "The farmers who listen to me love their station in life," declared the

98. AN F17 3034: Louis Debaecker to Min. Pub. Instr., 1 September 1855; and *Mémoires de la Société de la Flandre maritime* 2 (1858).

99. Kale, *Legitimism*, 138–40; Jean-Marie Mayeur, *Un prêtre démocrate: l'abbé Lemire, 1853–1928* (Paris, 1968), 197–205; and Shanny Peer, *France on Display: Peasants, Provincials, and Folklore in the 1937 Paris World's Fair* (Albany, 1998), 103–5.

100. Hazareesingh, *From Subject to Citizen*, 290–97.

Société's president in 1847. "They will not leave the village for the city."[101] For many provincial elites, affection for the *pays* transcended the political cleavage between city and countryside. Directed toward different audiences, urban and rural memories melded into a common sense of place.

In conceptual terms, the pedagogy of place also fused the utopian aspirations of the Enlightenment and French Revolution with a grounded language of place and past. Without seducing all contemporary elites, this synthesis proved resilient enough to underlay the early Third Republic's own cult of local memories. Indeed, this pedagogy's startling extension after 1870 constitutes this chapter's natural end-point. The educators and *couches nouvelles* members who came to control many learned societies in the mid-1860s displayed a greater interest in pedagogy than had their predecessors. They began rewarding "popular" monographs that would introduce their "young fellow citizens" to the local past's "beautiful examples of virtue." In 1881, Lille's mayor named several streets after local historical figures—a departure from previous usage. A year later, twelve newly founded geographical societies from the Nord and surrounding departments federated into a Union géographique du Nord de la France. While its three thousand members entertained different geographical interests, many sought to familiarize schoolchildren with local geography. One cultivates love of the *patrie* "by attaching the citizen to the place in which he was born," explained one member in 1883.[102]

Lawyer and historian Edmond Groult shared this conviction. In 1876, this staunch republican founded a new kind of museum in Lisieux (Normandy): the *musée cantonal*. Seventy-six such museums reportedly existed by 1893. Geared toward "our countryside's hard-working and honest inhabitants," they mobilized all aspects of "local and regional" life to deepen affection for one's place of residence.[103] History received special attention. On the museums' walls, historical panels and portraits of local celebrities adjoined historical escutcheons and photographs of the canton's monuments. Conferences, guided tours for schoolchildren, and

101. ADN 1 T 246/1: Statutes of the Société d'émulation de Cambrai, November 1820; *MEC* 16 (1840): 4–5; and *MEC* 21 (1847): 22–23.

102. *MEC* 32, no. 1 (1873): 283; Emile Bouchet, *Histoire populaire de Dunkerque* (Dunkirk, 1871), ii; AN F 1c I 161: Municipal decree of 4 July 1881; and *BUGN* 4 (1883): 6. Such localism also marked the cult of celebrities in other regions. On Normandy and Burgundy, for instance, see Philippe Poirrier and Loïc Vadelorge, "La statuaire provinciale sous la Troisième République. Une étude comparée: Rouen et Dijon," *Revue d'histoire moderne et contemporaine* 42, no. 2 (April–June 1995): 242–69; and Pierre Ardaillon, "La mémoire des morts en Seine-Inférieure sous la Troisième République: les hommages publics aux grands hommes et aux figures locales," in Olivier Dumoulin and Françoise Thelamon, eds., *Autour des morts: mémoire et identité* (Rouen, 2001), 279–95.

103. Edmond Groult, *La France des musées cantonaux en 1891* (Lisieux, n.d. [1893?]), 5; idem, *Lettre à messieurs les délégués des sociétés savantes à la Sorbonne* (Paris, 1877), 4; and idem, *Principales différences entre les musées cantonaux et les musées scolaires* (Caen, 1886), 3.

local festivals further honored "the memory of the land's saints and heroes, of all the illustrious citizens."[104] At once emblematic spaces and modes of in situ action, these pedagogical ventures were ideological in their aspirations to social harmony: "a concert of thankful voices" in which all "forget their mutual mistrust." As their subscriptions, reliance on "men of initiative," and focus on the canton demonstrate, they were also civic. Held on 14 July, local festivals would "develop *patriotic sentiments* within all classes." The venture's impeccable republican credentials included a gold medal at the 1889 universal exhibition and the endorsements of republican leaders, including Jules Ferry, Paul Bert, and Léon Gambetta. All lauded an effort to "deepen love of the native land."[105]

Indeed, the pedagogy of place now benefited from unprecedented governmental support. Jean-François Chanet and Anne-Marie Thiesse have recently shown that, far from imposing French and an indivisible vision of France on its pupils, the Third Republic tolerated local idioms, adapted its educational programs to local circumstances, and inculcated a local sense of belonging.[106] The Ministry of Public Instruction rewarded those teachers who introduced pupils to their *pays*'s historical and natural riches. In 1880, Bert asked schoolteachers to sensitize their pupils to a tangible local environment that included "the history told by the plants and the land itself." That same year, the Ministry of Public Instruction's new Comité des Sociétés des beaux-arts endorsed the creation of small "archeological museum[s] . . . [that] would teach students to appreciate local art." In 1882, Minister of Public Instruction Jules Ferry urged members of provincial learned societies to temporarily shelve their learned ventures and instead pen accessible monographs for schoolteachers: "the history of each province."[107] This was a radical departure: from Guizot to Duruy, none of Ferry's predecessors had allowed pedagogy to overshadow erudition in this field.

104. Groult, *Les oeuvres patriotiques cantonales* (Caen, 1883), 14; and idem, *Fêtes nationales et patriotiques: projet présenté à M. le Ministre de l'Instruction publique, le 23 juin 1879* (Caen, n.d. [1879?]), 5. On the importance of "historical memories" in such museums, see also Georges Wickham, *Les musées cantonaux* (Paris, 1879), 19.

105. Groult, *Fêtes nationales,* 1 and 6, italics in the original; and AD Calvados T 2345: idem to prefect Calvados, 2 April 1881. See also Jacqueline Lalouette's rich article on Groult, "L'éducation populaire au canton," 91–104.

106. Anne-Marie Thiesse, *Ils apprenaient;* and Jean-François Chanet, *Ecole républicaine.* Patois remained contentious, however, given the religious battles of the era: see Caroline Ford, *Creating the Nation,* 23–24.

107. Paul Bert, "L'instruction dans une démocratie," in his *Leçons, discours et conférences* (Paris, 1880), 398; *Instructions du Comité des sociétés des beaux-arts des départements* (Paris, 1880), 7; Ferry, speech before the Sorbonne congress of learned societies, 15 April 1882, in *Journal officiel de la République française,* 16 April 1882; and Claude Bernard, "L'enseignement de l'histoire, en France, au XIXe siècle (selon les ministres de l'instruction publique)" (Ph.D. diss., University of Paris VIII, 1976), 184.

This rupture owed much to the Third Republic's new pedagogical doctrine, with its recuperation of sensationalistic strands and belief in the impact of "milieus," of "all that comes from the senses" on a malleable citizenry. Children "belong in full to the phenomena of the surrounding world: all [their] senses are open," explained the regime's educators, emphasizing the mutual dependence of soul and body, of moral and physical education.[108] As Louis Legrand showed in his classic study, the regime's conceptual foundations also included positivism. One consequence was an acute wariness of "irrational and unhealthy utopia[s]." In the social realm, explained Ferry, "one does not substitute what could be for what is." His pedagogical reforms rested on the well-known conviction that *leçons de choses* (lessons of things)—or *l'enseignement par l'aspect* (teaching through appearance)—had to replace strict "lessons of words." Students learned better—and developed independent judgment—through concrete examples and personal experience than through "abstraction" and memorization. Ferry thus urged learned society members to eschew dates in favor of "the familiar, intuitive, experimental method" in their local monographs.[109] For republican pedagogue Ferdinand Buisson and others, this method integrated sensual, "mental," and "moral" intuitions (sensations, judgments, and the action of the heart and conscience). Buisson, too, called for lessons of things: "a visit to the *musée cantonal*, an industrial establishment, a historical monument, or a topographical walk." Three decades later, Minister Maurice Faure was still asking French rectors to favor local history and geography in primary classrooms. "Situated, not in an imprecise and vague setting, but in their very milieu, facts will become more impressive, individuals more real." The best teaching progressed from the "known to the unknown," the proximate to the distant, the concrete to the abstract, the local to the national.[110]

Their unease before utopias meant that, without abandoning artificial spaces such as the local pantheon of celebrities, these republicans gave in situ action a new dimension. They modified the preceding model by exploiting the existing milieu—at once geographical, natural, and histori-

108. Marie Pape-Carpantier, "L'éducation des sens," *Revue pédagogique* (1st sem. 1878): 548; Octave Gréard, *Education et instruction: enseignement primaire*, 2d ed. (Paris, 1889), 4–5; and Gabriel Compayré, *Histoire critique des doctrines de l'éducation en France depuis le seizième siècle*, 2 vols. (Paris, 1879), 2: 427–33.

109. Louis Legrand, *L'influence du positivisme dans l'oeuvre scolaire de Jules Ferry: les origines de la laïcité* (Paris, 1961); Jules Ferry, "Marcel Roulleaux et la Philosophie positive" (1867), cited in Pierre Barral, ed., *Les fondateurs de la Troisième République* (Paris, 1968), 247; and *Bulletin scolaire du Nord* 2, no. 5 (May 1876): 75–76.

110. Ferry, speech of 16 April 1882; Ferdinand Buisson, "L'enseignement intuitif," *Revue pédagogique* (2d sem. 1878): 452, 461, and 464; and Maurice Faure to the rectors, circular of 25 February 1911, repr. in Chanet, "L'école républicaine et les petites patries: enseignement primaire et sentiment d'appartenance sous la Troisième République (1879–1940)" (Ph.D. diss., University of Paris I, 1994), 1338.

cal—and directing their attention toward the countryside. An 1872 circular added "topographical walks," with attention to historical sites, into the school curriculum. A decade later, a school inspector from Laon commented that "the best pedagogues recommend beginning geographical study with the *pays* in which one resides."[111]

These philosophical changes thus made the pedagogy of place conceivable. What made it so urgent was the sense of crisis—but also the hope of renewal—that now suffused France. Defeat in the Franco-Prussian War and working-class insurrection in Paris inspired renewed contempt for the degenerate capital and revealed the French army's inadequate grasp of the terrain. These "unfortunate events" showed all too clearly that, as one Société dunkerquoise member put it, "the French do not know their country well enough." One could not love what one did not know: French patriotism hence required revitalization, notably through education. The events of 1870–71 also made explicit France's decline on the European scene. The German alliance of pedagogy and patriotism had much to teach France, Ferry declared in 1882.[112] At the same time, rural depopulation proved more alarming than ever to urban elites (even if the number of migrants did not jump dramatically).[113] These anxieties gave this model's ideological and civic designs a new resonance. Knowledge of local topography and memories would keep people in place, "fill the deep gulf" separating the "classes" (Groult), revive a "mutilated" country by linking "the living and the dead," and constitute the necessary prelude to national self-understanding.[114] German *Heimatkunde*, one educator declared in 1878, had progressed incrementally from the classroom to the local milieu, the region, the nation. Schoolbooks such as the *Tour de la France par deux enfants* (like contemporary regional novels) thus extolled rooted authenticity and geographical self-understanding to incorporate the *peuple* into bourgeois society. Integrating *illustrations* and the milieu, the *Tour de la France* embodied, per its author, a "new kind of morality in action, that . . . involves the description of the very places in which great men were born."[115]

---

111. André Meynier, *Histoire de la pensée géographique en France (1872–1869)* (Paris, 1969), 9; and *BUGN* 6 (1885): 90.

112. ASD, dossier E: Anon., "Géographie de l'arrondissement de Dunkerque pouvant servir d'introduction à l'étude de la géographie dans les écoles primaires," undated manuscript (after 1870); and Ferry, speech of 16 April 1882.

113. Denis Bertholet, *Le bourgeois dans tous ses états: le roman familial de la Belle Epoque* (Paris, 1987), 195.

114. *Annuaire des musées cantonaux et des autres institutions cantonales patriotiques d'initiative privée* 1 (1880): 3–4; and *BUGN* 6 (1885): 91 and 101.

115. Emile Levasseur, "L'enseignement de la géographie dans l'école primaire," *Revue pédagogique* (2d sem. 1878): 249–51; and *Le tour de la France par deux enfants: cours moyen par G. Bruno*, repr. (Paris, 1992 [1904 ed.?]), n. p. [4]. See also Paul Claval, "Le thème régional dans la littérature française," *L'espace géographique* 1 (1987): 67; Chanet, *Ecole républicaine*, 287; Ozouf, "Unité nationale et unité de la pensée de Jules Ferry," in François Furet, ed., *Jules Ferry,*

On a civic plane, Ferry believed that schoolchildren developed "piety for the *patrie*" through a mix of sentiment and "knowledge." That was why the teaching of history, beginning with the tangible *pays*, was "destined to play a great educational role in our country." The better pupils knew the *pays* and its past, the better they would grasp the French past and love their *patrie*. "The child's soul [would] move effortlessly from knowledge of the *petite patrie* to knowledge and love of the *grande*." Local memories, added Bert, would ensure that "love of France" did not remain an "abstract formula."[116] The Third Republic clearly recuperated and expanded the civic model of Cormenin and Freslon: knowledge and love of the *pays* now unequivocally underlay love of and participation in the nation.

This civic amplification reflected in one respect the doctrinal convictions of opportunist republicans, who held a more positive view of political participation (both local and national) than Orleanists or Bonapartists. They defined politics, not as the uncontrollable play of passions and factions, but as an indispensable space of male citizenship—a space of participation, initiative, free expression, debates, and negotiations. It was here that national opinion took form. The state thus had to root its action in majority opinion rather than elite influences alone. It had to educate this opinion and help it express itself—especially in the countryside, whose residents had not been taught about their civic rights and duties.[117] "The Republic will be peasantlike [*paysannesque*] or will not be," Ferry asserted in 1877. This republican education rested, in turn, on close attention to the specific configurations of French *pays*, including their customs, past, and geography. "Let us disseminate geography," declared Gambetta in 1877, and thereby bring to light "the titles of each commune, each canton, each department."[118] The regime's local pedagogy reflected more down-to-earth needs as well. Public education, after all, was "also a question of politics and the great interest of society." Its tasks were to unify the "public spirit," moralize French citizens without resorting to Catholic doctrine, and prepare each individual, per Auguste

---

fondateur de la république (Paris, 1985), 64–65; and Thiesse, *La création des identités nationales. Europe, XVIIIe-XXe siècle* (Paris, 1999), 237–38.

116. Ferry, speech of 15 April 1882; idem, speech before the Pedagogical Congress, 2 April 1880, in *Discours et opinions de Jules Ferry*, ed. Paul Robiquet, 7 vols. (Paris, 1894–98?), 3:521; and Bert, *L'instruction civique à l'école (notions fondamentales)*, 6th ed. (Paris, 1882), 6. See also Henry Lemonnier, *L'enseignement de l'histoire dans les écoles primaires* (Paris, 1889), 36 and 46; and Thiesse, *Ils apprenaient*, 9 and 85.

117. François Ewald, "La politique sociale des Opportunistes, 1879–1885," in Serge Berstein and Odile Rudelle, eds., *Le modèle républicain* (Paris, 1992), 182; Claude Nicolet, *L'idée républicaine en France (1789–1924): essai d'histoire critique* (Paris, 1982), 257–58 and 496–97; and Antoine Prost, "La contribution de l'école primaire républicaine à l'identité française," in Haupt, Müller, and Woolf, eds., *Regional and National Identities*, 259–60.

118. Jules Ferry to Charles Ferry, 16 April 1875, quoted in Jérôme Grévy, *La République des opportunistes, 1870–1885* (Paris, 1998), 66; and *La République française*, 11 June 1877, quoted in ibid., 132.

Comte, for his or her "particular destination" within the social order.[119] Gambetta's well-known quip that "the republic will be won in the town halls [*mairies*]" did not only mean that the new regime had to conquer a rural electorate that had supported the Second Empire. It also expressed the pragmatic conviction that, to meet its doctrinal and more instrumental objectives, it needed to find ways of seducing diverse audiences, addressing their local concerns, and converting them to its political project.[120]

Between 1875 and 1900, France witnessed renewed right-wing interest in local traditions. Pilgrims to Lourdes, for one, expressed their political and religious sentiments by donning the costumes and carrying the flags of historical provinces. A growing number of clergymen entered the field of local memories—for some, as a gateway toward federalist and regionalist designs.[121] At the same time, the New Right of Maurice Barrès and Charles Maurras challenged the Republic's abstract nationalism by articulating—around the region—a deterministic, ethnic, and exclusive conception of the nation. The New Right's *petite patrie* thus had its own, distinctive contours. It underlay a federal blueprint, in which provinces—this "multitude of small, natural, autonomous, groupings"—would revitalize the centralized nation.[122] And it refuted the republic's Kantian universalism—whose abstraction negated "individual differences"—by rooting individuals in their historical and geographical milieu. Only in the provinces could one recover one's true identity (*la terre et les morts*), develop durable social ties, and become a true patriot. All of this led some republicans and liberals to shy away from an increasingly suspect localism.[123]

But not all. The republican cult of local memories promised to anchor

119. Compayré, *Histoire critique*, 2: 421; "Géographie de l'arrondissement de Dunkerque"; Legrand, *Influence du positivisme*, 22 and 46; and Auguste Comte, *Considérations sur le pouvoir spirituel* (1826), quoted in Pierre Arnaud, ed., *Auguste Comte: textes choisis* (1968), 59.

120. Corbin, *Les cloches de la terre: paysage sonore et culture sensible dans les campagnes au XIXe siècle* (Paris, 1994), 206; and Philippe Martel, "Les gauches félibréennes," *Jean Jaurès cahiers trimestriels* 152 (April–June 1999): 22. I am grateful to Torbjörn Wandel for helping me think through this argument.

121. Barbara Corrado Pope, "Immaculate and Powerful: The Marian Revival in the Nineteenth Century," in Clarissa W. Atkinson et al., eds., *Immaculate and Powerful: The Female in Sacred Image and Social Reality* (Boston, 1985), 188; and Gérard Cholvy, "Régionalisme et clergé catholique au XIXe siècle," in Christian Gras and Georges Livet, eds., *Régions et régionalisme*, 196–98.

122. Charles Maurras, *De la politique naturelle au nationalisme intégral*, ed. François Natter and Claude Rousseau (Paris, 1972), 171. On Maurras and federalism, see Gildea, *Past in French History*, 180–81.

123. Maurice Barrès, *Scènes et doctrines du nationalisme* (Paris, 1902), 56; Ford, *Creating the Nation*, 19–24; and Zeev Sternhell, *Maurice Barrès et le nationalisme français* (Brussels, 1985 [1972]), 325–28. See also Ford, "Which Nation? Language, Identity and Republican Politics in Post-Revolutionary France," *History of European Ideas* 17, no. 1 (1993): 31–46.

the regime by displaying its concern with the local and rooting it in rural virtue.[124] It promised to form citizens, moralize individuals, yield social harmony, and in this fashion, respond to the era's social and political needs. It is under the early Third Republic, then, that the local became primarily, and widely, defined in terms of its affective relationship with the nation. For numerous officials and elites, it became the optimal conduit toward community, civic participation, and national recomposition. This cult of local memories thus buttresses a recent historiographical turn that emphasizes neither the regime's rigidity nor the centralizing tendencies of French republicanism, but its concern with local political culture. By the 1870s, many republican elites understood that "the conquest of national power was intimately linked with local politics" (S. Hazareesingh). They accordingly tailored their discourse to local circumstances and granted local (especially municipal) institutions and sociability a key role within their project.[125] As I have sought to show, this "moment" constituted the culmination of a fifty-year evolution that built on Enlightenment, revolutionary, and Catholic convictions. Much changed after 1870: the Republic's use of classrooms and concern with civic education, its rural focus, the nation's omnipresence, a stronger emphasis on internal diversity. Yet the Third Republic did not elaborate its pedagogy ex nihilo. Its localist policy hinged on a now familiar language of historical self-understanding, territorial affection, and local initiative; a confidence in the transformative powers of place; and a mix of civic aspirations and ideological designs that anchored the national in the local. All had surfaced in Republican and nonrepublican circles alike during the preceding decades—nowhere more tangibly than in the field of local memories. The conviction that place and past provided discreet means of civic and ideological action was also, accordingly, one of this field's key legacies.

124. Thiesse, *Ils apprenaient*, 5 and 87–88.
125. Hazareesingh, "The Société d'Instruction Républicaine and the Propagation of Civic Republicanism in Provincial and Rural France, 1870–1877," *The Journal of Modern History* 71, no. 2 (June 1999): 271–307, citation on 273.

FOUR

Local Memories and the Governing of the Minds

> To study the monuments and historical documents of Maritime Flanders, is that not to comply, Monsieur le Ministre, with [your] instructions . . . recommending *the study of local history?*
>
> EDMOND DE COUSSEMAKER (Dunkirk)
> to Victor Duruy, 17 January 1866 [italics in the original]

P RIOR TO THE Third Republic, the French state was all but absent from this pedagogical domain. Some members of the Comité des travaux historiques promised to spread "archaeological knowledge in all villages"; others, along with correspondents, urged the Ministry of Public Instruction to sponsor local "memorials" and install plaques on the birth homes of illustrious provincial figures.[1] To no avail. Beyond the 1848 initiative of Minister Alexandre Freslon, I have uncovered an 1844 circular asking that departmental *annuaires* end with pieces on "local traditions" or celebrities, and little more. Governmental subsidies for monuments to local celebrities proved scarce.[2] School curricula likewise eschewed local memories. History made slow inroads into classrooms, due in part to an overfilled syllabus, the dominance of classics, and a lack of teachers. Introduced into primary schools in 1834, French history was taught in less than one school out of five in much of the Nord until 1867, at which time it became required.[3] The fate of local history was grimmer yet. In July 1851, the Second Republic urged teachers to impart lessons on departmental history, monuments, geography, and industry. This exceptional measure had limited repercussions and, by

1. AN F17 13268: Proceedings of the CHAM, 7 March 1840 and 14 February 1838; and AN F17 3021: Du Haye to Min. Pub. Instr., 28 September 1840.
2. AN F1a 44: Min. Int. to prefects, circular of 26 September 1844; AN F21 4388: Dossier on Dunkirk's statue to Jean Bart; and BMA ms. 487: Gédéon de Forceville to Charles Louandre, 17 August 1873.
3. Pim den Boer, *History as a Profession*, 118–74; Joël Ravier, "Les inspecteurs primaires du département du Nord durant la monarchie de juillet: réflexions et conseils en matière pédagogique," *RN* 81, no. 330 (April–June 1999): 299; and Paul Gerbod, "La place de l'histoire dans l'enseignement secondaire de 1802 à 1880," *Information historique* (June 1965): 125.

all indications, no parallels. Arguments that local history would "contribute to the *peuple*'s intellectual and moral emancipation" convinced few ministerial officials. Students learned about ancient Greece and Rome, but not the "history of the province, city or even village in which each school is established."[4]

All of this enhances the novelty of the "cultural state" that, by all accounts, emerged under the Third Republic. Despite this state's formal evolution (from Jules Ferry to the Popular Front to Jack Lang's ministry), we find a persisting effort to reach "the widest audience possible," a growing reliance on local leaders, and a belief in the unifying, if not emancipating, potential of a national culture.[5] Should we, accordingly, dismiss the preceding decades and speak of a "near complete cultural abstention of the liberal state"?[6] This state's early and enduring embrace of local memories suggests, on the contrary, that ministerial officials, CTH members, and local administrators devised new forms of governmental action in this realm. With national history and "local erudition" at its core and provincial elites as its target, these actors fashioned a cultural policy around a benign local knowledge that, not unlike the pedagogy of place, promised new means of surreptitious action.[7] Pedagogy and democracy were epiphenomenal, but a clear cultural—and political—agenda this was nonetheless. This was a double agenda: first, to constitute a body of largely historical knowledge and, second, to weave "frequent and regular relations" with provincial elites and learned societies. Thanks to "the government's enlightened protection," a provincial journalist wrote in 1859, "studies in local history have acquired a greater importance than in any previous era." The success of this "governing of the minds"—and what I called an intellectual state—is open to debate but not, as we will see, its impact in the provinces.[8]

---

4. A. Lécruselle, *Précis de l'histoire de Cambrai et du Cambrésis depuis les temps les plus reculés jusqu'à nos jours* (Cambrai, 1872), 6; Florentin Lefils, *Géographie historique et populaire*, x; and *MEC* 27, vol. 3 (1865): 50–51.

5. Mission statement of the French Ministry of Culture (February 1959), quoted in David L. Looseley, *The Politics of Fun: Cultural Policy and Debate in Contemporary France* (Oxford, 1995), 37. See also, for instance, Pascal Ory, *La belle illusion: culture et politique sous le signe du Front populaire, 1935–1938* (Paris, 1994); Jean-Pierre Rioux, ed., *La vie culturelle sous Vichy* (Brussels, 1990); Herman Lebovics, *Mona Lisa's Escort: André Malraux and the Reinvention of French Culture* (Ithaca, 1999); and Philippe Urfalino, *L'invention de la politique culturelle* (Paris, 1996), 280.

6. André-Hubert Mesnard, *L'action culturelle des pouvoirs publics* (Paris, 1969), 155. See also Serge Reneau, "L'Etat et le patrimoine en France de la Révolution à nos jours," *Trames* 2 (1997): 28; and Tony Bennett, *The Birth of the Museum: History, Theory, Politics* (London, 1995), 142. Compare, however, Ory, "Politiques culturelles avant la lettre: trois lignes françaises, de la Révolution au Front populaire," in Raymonde Moulin, ed., *Sociologie de l'art*, 2d ed. (Paris, 1999), 25.

7. AN F17 3302: Rector Rennes to Min. Pub. Instr., 29 October 1858.

8. François Guizot to presidents of learned societies, circular of 23 July 1834, in Charmes, 10–11; *RAN* 11, no. 5 (May 1859): 147; and Guizot, *Mémoires*, 3: 14.

INVESTIGATIVE MODALITIES

Anthropologist Bernard Cohn coined the term *investigative modalities* to denote the procedures by which a body of knowledge is defined, collected, classified, and transformed into such "usable forms" as histories and encyclopedias.[9] Included, as well, are institutional frameworks and networks, criteria of evaluation, and modes of reward and validation. To explicate the official cult of local memories, we must first apprehend this intellectual state in such terms—beginning with the distribution of power within the Ministry of Public Instruction. If the CTH constituted this state's scientific arm, then the BTH was its political one. This ministerial bureau made all important decisions regarding collective projects, publications, financial matters, and the vetting of correspondents. "The committee proposes, and the Minister decides," noted a CTH member in 1837. Under the Second Empire, the ministry granted BTH officials such as Jacques Servaux growing responsibilities within the CTH. In addition to drafting ministerial speeches, they sat on CTH meetings and oversaw publications, subsidies, and subscriptions. The ministry, moreover, eliminated those CTH commissions "looking to . . . substitute their action for the administration's."[10] The relationship between both parties remained loosely defined and sometimes contested, but little was undertaken without the ministry's approval.

The CTH nonetheless fulfilled key functions within this official framework. Members of the Académie des beaux-arts noted as much in 1838, identifying two sets of attributions.[11] The first revolved around a body of knowledge and artifacts. The CTH "ma[d]e contact" with provincial learned societies to preserve national monuments and manuscripts and coordinate, among other ventures, an archaeological map and *statistique* of France. It determined what "local investigations" these societies should undertake and how they should do so. The CTH either approached provincial elites directly or through local agents: prefects, subprefects, and—under the Second Empire—university rectors. It sent these elites letters and circulars as well as an unprecedented number of printed instructions and questionnaires. A stand-alone genre since the

---

9. Bernard S. Cohn, *Colonialism and Its Forms of Knowledge: The British in India* (Princeton, N.J., 1996), 5.

10. AN F17 13268: Charles Lenormant, intervention before the CHAM, 19 June 1837; and AN F17 2831: Anon., "Observations générales sur les travaux du Comité de la langue, etc.," n.d. [October–November 1852?].

11. Archives de l'Académie Royale des Beaux-Arts, 5 E 26: "Rapport de l'Académie Royale des Beaux-Arts à la réunion des bureaux des cinq académies de l'Institut," 24 February 1838.

sixteenth century, the instruction initially directed the gaze of distant travelers, ensuring an optimal moral and pedagogical experience. By the eighteenth century, increasingly specialized instructions encompassed topical matters, research methods, and writing technique. They accordingly transformed personal journeys into objective expeditions, meant to collect data and verify hypotheses. Some instructions thus transmogrified into comprehensive questionnaires, often penned by royal administrators in quest of statistical information and "general descriptions" of France.[12] Until the late nineteenth century, the state and learned institutions alike relied on educated amateurs for such knowledge. "No geographical, statistical, ethnographic investigation will yield satisfactory results without the collaboration of many friends of science," explained the Société de géographie in 1824. "A collection of printed questions is the best means of succeeding."[13] Lacking expertise, these acolytes would prove most useful by supplying factual data and answering simple questions.

Dominant within ministerial circles, this conviction helps explain why officials and CTH members deemed it so important to enroll elites in collective projects that were conceived and published in the capital. This impetus culminated in the late 1850s with a tripartite survey of the French historical territory, department by department. Geographical dictionaries would identify local *lieux-dits*—those ancient territories, peoples, and natural sites whose names were linked to "historical memor[ies]." Archaeological inventories would locate and describe the department's monuments. Scientific descriptions would detail the department's geology, *statistique*, zoology, anthropology, botany, mineral waters, and meteorology. These genres capture the state's favored mode of operation. Following its "detailed and precise" instructions, provincial elites would contribute data and artifacts to a broader, national enterprise.[14] Writing the minister on behalf of a local resident in 1858, the prefect of the Creuse discussed at length, not the latter's historical publications, but the local data he had collected and would now make available.[15]

12. Philippe Minard, "Volonté de savoir et emprise d'Etat: aux origines de la statistique industrielle dans la France d'Ancien Régime," *Actes de la recherche en sciences sociales* 133 (June 2000): 63–71; Victor Carrière, *Introduction aux études d'histoire*, 1: xxiii–xvi; and Claude Blanckaert, ed., *Le terrain des sciences humaines: instructions et enquêtes (XVIIIe–XXe siècles)* (Paris, 1996), esp. the articles by Blanckaert, Silvia Collini, and Antonella Vannoni.

13. René Dussaud, *La nouvelle académie des inscriptions et belles-lettres (1795–1914)*, 2 vols. (Paris, 1946), 1:109–11, 178, and 194; and *Bulletin de la Société de géographie* 2 (1824): 71.

14. AN F17 3298: Proceedings of the Commission of the Geographical dictionary, 12 June 1858; AN F17 3312: Min. Pub. Instr. to Louis Debaecker, 2 July 1860; and Gustave Rouland to presidents of learned societies, circular of 10 December 1859, in Charmes, 210.

15. AN F17 2811: Prefect Creuse to Min. Pub. Instr., 15 April 1858.

This modus operandi was, of course, found in other administrative spheres as well. The CTH's nomenclatures and inventories reflect the era's enthusiasm for *statistique*, a yearning for scientific understanding of little-known territories, and the conviction that physical and social milieus constituted knowable series of facts. Here as elsewhere—including the colonies—a desire for epistemological legibility integrated territory and history. In 1838, members of the Commission de l'Exploration scientifique de l'Algérie called for a survey of "all points in this land that are under French domination," as well as a "topographical brigade," whose members would identify all ancient place names.[16] Be it in Algeria or in metropolitan France, this quest for legibility converged on topographical and archaeological maps, this "most useful instrument for the civilization and colonization of Africa and for historical investigations." With their apolitical stance and claims to universality and objective rationality, these maps exemplify the political dimension of topography—an inherent "science of domination" per one scholar. Bernard Cohn has spoken of a British vision of India as "a vast museum, its countryside filled with ruins"—a reassuring, pacified territory, ready for the taking. A similar vision underlay both the CTH's archaeological map of France and its archaeological inventories, which arranged all departments into identical grids. The reader moves rapidly from one locale to another, one monument to another, never stopping for long in any one place.[17] In this respect, the venture shared much with the Ministry of State's 1858 "Map of the Historical Monuments of France" (see figure 16). The latter was, to be sure, an instrument of analysis, resting on efficient spatial representation (symbols depicted abbeys, castles, and the like). Yet, here too, the central government integrated past and place to depict metropolitan and colonial France as a peaceful and uniform territory, an innocuous field of antiquities, so pleasing to the eye.

If, at various junctures in this book, I draw out the kinship between the official cult of local memories and colonial science (focusing on Algeria), it is not to describe a colonization of the interior, a modernizing state bent

16. Jacques Cheyronnaud, Introduction to *Instructions pour un Recueil général des poésies populaires de la France (1852–1857)* (Paris, 1997), 19; Blanckaert, "Histoire du terrain entre savoirs et savoir-faire," in *Terrain des sciences humaines,* 39; Picon and Robert, *Atlas parisien,* 190; and *Rapports de la commission chargée de rédiger des instructions pour l'exploration scientifique de l'Algérie* (n.p, n.d. [1838]), 6 and 52.

17. Minister of War, missive of 18 November 1833, quoted in Monique Dondin-Payre, *La commission d'exploration scientifique de l'Algérie. Une héritière méconnue de la commission d'Egypte* (Abbeville, 1994), 22; James Duncan, "Introduction: Representing the Place of Culture," in Duncan and David Ley, eds., *Place/Culture/Representation* (London, 1993), 1; Cohn, *Colonialism,* 3, 7, 9; and Thierry Gasnier, "Le local: une et indivisible," in Pierre Nora, ed., *Lieux de mémoire,* 6: 473–74. On geography and power in the nineteenth century, see also Anne-Marie Claire Godlewska, *Geography Unbound: French Geographical Science from Cassini to Humboldt* (Chicago, 1999), chap. 5.

FIGURE 16. "Carte des Monuments historiques de la France, dressée par ordre
de Son Excellence M. A. Fould, ministre d'Etat et de la maison de l'Empereur,
par I. Rigaud, géographe" (Paris, 1858). Courtesy of the Archives
Départementales du Loiret (cote 10 T 2), Orléans.

on imposing its rule and culture.[18] The metropolitan situation differed in important respects from the colonial one: a greater tendency to apply persuasion rather than coercion; dealings with full citizens rather than subjects of different races; a concern with elites alone; oversight by the Ministry of Public Instruction rather than the Ministry of War.[19] This cautious parallel nonetheless situates this intellectual state within a nexus of concurrent, and sometimes intertwined, domestic and colonial investigations. The Ministry of War's 1837 call to "investigate all the accessible areas of [Algeria], and gather all that concerns the *contrée*'s history and geography" more than echoes, after all, ministerial circulars to provincial learned societies. Many BTH and CTH members furthermore encouraged, or participated in, such colonial ventures as the Exploration scientifique de l'Algérie. In 1838, Salvandy not only reached out to provincial elites, but also created a commission for the scientific investigation and "conquest" of Africa. Fourteen years later, BTH acolyte Charles Louandre rejoiced that France, a country that was "often unknown to itself," now learned so much about its Algerian colony, now divided into three departments. "In the midst of this scientific invasion, everyone has seized a province, a city or a ruin."[20] Beyond their differences, these colonial and metropolitan ventures shared the same yearning for comprehensive description and inventory, the same concern with topography and past, the same references to an "ascending" French civilization, and finally, the same dual status as "operation of intervention and experience of understanding" (M.-N. Bourguet).[21] They took shape in tandem and hence illuminate one another.

The CTH held a second set of attributions: to help the ministry determine which provincial elites deserved, by virtue of their contributions,

18. See, from different perspectives, Eugen Weber, *Peasants into Frenchmen;* and Robert Lafont, *Autonomie: de la région à l'autogestion* (Paris, 1976), 12.

19. Ranajit Guha, *Dominance without Hegemony: History and Power in Colonial India* (Cambridge, 1997), xii; Daniel Nordman, "Science géographique française et expansion coloniale en Afrique du Nord au XIXe siècle," in his *Profils du Maghreb: frontières, figures et territoires (XVIIIe–XXe siècle)* (Rabat, 1996), 183; and Timothy Mitchell, *Colonizing Egypt* (Berkeley, 1988), 167–71.

20. Minister of War to the Académie Royale des Inscriptions et Belles-Lettres, 28 November 1837, quoted in Dondin-Payre, *Commission d'exploration,* 29; BNF Lk 8 989: Raymond Thomassy, "Des recherches scientifiques sur l'Algérie et de sa colonisation," unidentified article (n.p., n.d.), 178; Narcisse de Salvandy, speech of 1 December 1838, in *Bulletin de la Société de géographie* 10 (1838): 309–10; and Charles Louandre, "La statistique et l'archéologie dans l'Afrique française," *RDM,* new period, 15 (July–September 1852): 1196–99.

21. Marie-Noëlle Bourguet, "De la Méditerranée," in Bourguet et al., eds., *Invention scientifique,* 15; and Thomassy, *Le Maroc et ses caravanes, ou relations de la France avec cet Empire,* 2d ed. (Paris, 1845), 427–28. On nineteenth-century "colonial knowledge" as a central component of colonial domination and "laborator[y] for metropolitan experimentation," see Nicholas B. Dirks, *Castes of Mind: Colonialism and the Making of Modern India* (Princeton, N.J., 2001), quotation on 314.

"public homage" and rewards. The latter included books and periodicals, public praise in official speeches and periodicals, ministerial publication of one's work, subscriptions and subsidies, as well as the titles of correspondent or *royal* (later *national* then *imperial*) learned society. Starting in 1861, the ministry invited "the luminaries of the provinces" to present papers at annual congresses, held in the Sorbonne University. There, laureates of the CTH's public contests donned black coat and white tie to receive medals and ministerial congratulations before their assembled peers. Fifty-six learned societies and 237 individuals were honored in this fashion between 1861 and 1880.[22]

How did one obtain such recognition? Hippolyte Crozes, a magistrate from Albi, in southwestern France, illustrates one path. In May 1859, five weeks after Gustave Rouland issued his first circular on the archaeological inventory of France, Crozes promised the minister his participation. One of the first to do so, he forwarded his manuscript "Archaeological Inventory of the Tarn" to the CTH that October. Seven months later, in May 1860, BTH official Jacques Servaux invited him to expand some sections while abridging others and limiting himself to "descriptions and factual recordings." Crozes sent in a second version two months later, was asked for further revisions, and submitted a third draft in 1862. This time, he insisted that his work duly followed official directives. It was "exact" and "complete," the result of his personal observations. Its presentation did not depart "in the slightest detail" from the CTH's sample. Free of any literary flourish, finally, its style likewise displayed "clarity, simplicity, and concision." Louis De Mas Latrie, a prominent archivist and CTH member, congratulated Crozes personally. Crozes received a medal at the 1863 Sorbonne congress and the Imprimerie impériale published his work in 1865, "one of the best" the ministry had received.[23]

This sequence, like the other investigative modalities we have encountered, uncovers a new regulative and normative rationality, an incipient bureaucratization of intellectual practices. Beginning in the mid-1830s, new centers of decision and evaluation surfaced in the capital; a preexisting network of officials was mobilized to oversee a new network of elites; a framework of erudite practices and rewards furthered the cause of science and historical memories. At once arbiter of provincial investigations and sponsor of collective projects, the ministry and CTH apportioned intellectual labor, centralized authority, and, as we have begun to see, rewarded conformity to their directives. Their investigative modalities were not nec-

---

22. The ministry spent more than 111,000 francs on these congresses between 1861 and 1866 alone. See AN F17 3048: Manuscript note, 8 January 1867; *RSS*, 2d ser., 6 (2d sem. 1861): 444; AN F17 2815: Three lists of "laureates," n.d.; and AN F17 3042: Anon., "Institution du concours entre les sociétés savantes des départements. Fondation de prix annuels," n.d.

23. This account is based on a dossier in AN F17 3315 (file on the Tarn).

essarily new in official circles: inventories and topographies, questionnaires and inventories, instructions and correspondents were well-
established practices since the seventeenth century. They were found in
statistical surveys, geographical descriptions, the *mémoires* that provincial
intendants penned for Louis XIV, and the reports of the *Inspection des
manufactures.*[24] This intellectual state did not invent these modalities, but
it brought them together within an institutional armature that it tailored
to provincial elites. By the 1880s, an official could conclude that, from a
"simple commission that published original documents," the CTH had
rapidly "become a kind of tutor for [provincial] learned societies."[25] In so
doing, it had granted local memories an unprecedented importance
within the French administrative framework.

THE OFFICIAL CULT OF LOCAL MEMORIES

Recapitulating the CTH's accomplishments in 1903, a ministerial official
evoked Guizot's vision of a "vast learned society that encompasses all of
France, . . . [and] welcome[s] with interest articles on all aspects of local
history, philology, or archaeology." These were the official's words, but
Guizot's were close enough. Decades earlier, he had lauded provincial
elites for studying the "history of their *patrie*, be it general or local" and remaining "the sole guardians of ancient local traditions."[26] His successors
concurred. Salvandy instructed the CTH to serve as "a link with the departmental societies" and direct them toward "the [most useful] local investigations." In 1857, Rouland likewise invited provincial elites "to
attach themselves exclusively to the *pays* in which they live [and to under-
take] . . . local studies."[27]

   The July Monarchy, as Alain Corbin has shown, instituted a lenient and
"realistic" approach to local *usages*, from village bells to local festivities.
Many of its officials believed that governmental ukases could not eradi-
cate deep-rooted local customs. Not unlike Eugène Buret and the philanthropists we encountered earlier, these officials sought to govern by considering "local usages and tastes" rather than imposing "ordinances."[28] To

   24. Comte de Boulainvilliers, *Etat de la France, etc.* (London, 1727); Alain Desrosières, *The
Politics of Large Numbers: A History of Statistical Reasoning*, trans. Camille Naish (Cambridge,
Mass., 1998), 26–28; and Philippe Minard, *Fortune du colbertisme*, 63–71.
   25. AN F17 17130: Anon., "Tableaux présentant les modifications apportées à la dénomination du 'Comité des travaux historiques et scientifiques' de 1834 à 1885" (n.d. [1885?]).
   26. AN F17 2765: Draft of a circular to prefects, n.d. (1903?); and Guizot to presidents of
learned societies, circular of 23 July 1834, in Charmes, 10.
   27. Guizot, *Mémoires*, 2: 184; Salvandy, Decree of 18 December 1837, in Charmes, 64; AN
F17 13268: Proceedings of the Committee on sciences, 18 January 1838; and Rouland to rectors, circular of 20 May 1857, in Charmes, 180.
   28. Alain Corbin, *Cloches de la terre*, 68, 121, and 182; ADN M 137/61: Prefect to subprefects
and mayors of the Nord, circular of 15 July 1831; and Eugène Buret, *Question d'Afrique. De la
double conquête de l'Algérie par la guerre et la colonisation* (Paris, 1842), 89 and 112.

tolerate local customs was one thing. To encourage elites to cultivate local memories was, however, another. We thus uncover the birth of a new cultural policy, a political will—diffuse but undeniable—that transcended regimes and had far-reaching results, even in peripheral departments such as the Nord. A rapid journey through the department will illustrate its reach.

In Lille, Prefect Gabriel de Saint-Aignan and the prefectoral secretary founded the Commission historique du Nord on their own initiative but within a favorable ministerial climate in 1839. Created with archaeology and preservation as its ends, the commission soon broadened its mandate to include "the general history of the *pays*, communes, local institutions and somewhat famous figures." This prefectoral validation of historical localism was not lost on Commission members, who returned to their respective towns after their monthly meetings.[29] In Cambrai, official encouragement led the Société d'émulation to dedicate itself yet more assiduously to local history and archaeology. Its long-time president, Alcibiade Wilbert, assured the ministry repeatedly that his association was duly undertaking "historical investigations that have revolved around the *pays*'s history in its relation to the general history of France." Responding to the subprefect's "desire," it instituted a research commission on the ancient monuments of the Cambrésis in 1838. In 1856, Wilbert ended his presidential address by citing the rector's praise for learned societies, these "centers that preserve, along with the intelligent cult of the province's particular traditions, sincere love of the *pays*." Seven years later, the ministry's *Revue des sociétés savantes* lauded the association's local character.[30]

The official cult of local memories had a deeper impact yet in neighboring Valenciennes, whose Société d'agriculture, sciences et arts was split between two factions: one literary and historical, the other agricultural and industrial. The latter dominated until the summer of 1845, when the Société received a circular from Salvandy celebrating the "patriotic traditions and generous memories of the local spirit." A year later, its members heard their subprefect—and new president—declare that ministerial esteem and future subsidies hinged on their compliance with this program. Within a few months, they had devised new ventures, and jump-started older ones, revolving around local memories. Among them: the Galerie valenciennoise, public contests on the local past, and vignettes on local historical figures in its periodical publications. The subprefect accordingly backed the association's (ultimately successful) requests for sub-

29. *BCN* 1 (1843): 1–2; and ADN 1 T 248/6: André Le Glay, Report on the activities of the Commission historique du Nord in 1857–58, 23 July 1858.

30. AN F17 3034: Alcibiade Wilbert to Min. Pub. Instr., 13 August 1850 and 13 September 1864; ADN 1 T 253/1: "Premier rapport fait par M. Alc. Wilbert sur les principaux monuments de l'arrondissement de Cambrai. 7 février 1838," *MEC* 25, vol. 1 (1857): 22; and *RSS*, 3d ser., 1 (1st sem. 1863): 406.

sidies and the title of *société d'utilité publique*. Under the Second Empire, visits by local officials and articles in the *Revue des sociétés savantes* further linked "governmental approbation and aid" to the Société's continued commitment to local history. Its members endorsed Rouland's call for "investigations into all that concerns local history" in 1858 and, a few years later, launched a series of *Mémoires historiques sur l'arrondissement de Valenciennes* that captured the ministry's "generous views."[31]

In Dunkirk, finally, the subprefect attended the newly founded Société dunkerquoise's private meetings in the early 1850s to convey the ministry's wish that it investigate any "documents that could bear on our local history." He urged its members to establish a museum of local archaeological artifacts, create a *Galerie historique* resembling Valenciennes's, and publish annotated volumes of local historical sources. His successor likewise praised the Société for "investigating the past of the *pays* in which one lives."[32] Similar evidence can be marshaled from other regions. In Toulouse, for instance, the rector instructed his academy's learned societies in 1857 to restrict themselves "to the thorough [and historical] study of the[ir] *contrée*."[33] Here as elsewhere, the cult of local memories owed much to official support. Rather than targeting any one region, the central government directed all provincial elites toward the ill-defined *pays* and *contrée*. Other territorial referents studded official discourse, of course: the department and arrondissement throughout this period, the bourgeois commune under the July Monarchy, the ancient provinces under the Second Empire. But to grasp this state's main drive, we need to listen to officials talk about local studies and, as Augustin Thierry put it in 1837, "this praiseworthy spirit of patriotism that wishes to revive and popularize the memories of the native land."[34] Defined with remarkable laxity, these memories sprang from documents and monuments as well as patois and spatial journeys across one's *pays*.[35] Theirs was the neutral, apo-

---

31. *MSV* 7 (1846): 294; *RAN* 10, no. 5 and 6 (November–December 1858): 98, 112, 119, and 132–34; ADN 1 T 246/3: Edouard Grar to rector Douai, 25 June 1858; *RSS*, 1st ser., 5 (2d sem. 1858): 200; and *Mémoires historiques sur l'arrondissement de Valenciennes* 1 (1865): vi.

32. ASD 1851–52: Subprefect Dunkirk to president of the Société dunkerquoise, 29 March 1852; ASD 1853–54: Proceedings of the Société dunkerquoise, 9 January 1853 and 11 June 1854; *L'Autorité*, 1 March 1855; and ASD 1855–56: Proceedings of the Société dunkerquoise's commission on contest topics, 22 June 1855.

33. Rector Toulouse, circular of 13 June 1857, quoted in *Société des lettres, sciences et arts de l'Aveyron. Procès-verbal de la séance du 30 juillet 1857* (Rodez, 1857), 3.

34. Augustin Thierry, report to Salvandy, 10 March 1837, in Charmes, 54.

35. We find a similar, though less pronounced, concern with local past and space in Second Empire Algeria, where each *Bureau arabe* was expected to include local historical, geographical, and other studies by officers and civilians. See BMA ms. 440: Jérome Napoléon to public functionaries of Algeria, "Envoi d'instructions relatives aux recherches archéologiques" (31 December 1858), *Moniteur de la colonisation*, n.d. [January 1859?]; and Kenneth J. Perkins, *Qaids, Captains, and Colons: French Military Administration in the Colonial Maghrib, 1844–1934* (New York, 1981), 61–62.

litical cult of local memories of sedentary provincials, familiar with the past and layout of the narrow territory they happily inhabited and served.

New and far-reaching, this policy was neither codified nor fully coherent. Like other governmental ventures, it constituted a loose, often improvised program, which followed different routes and progressed at a different pace in various towns. Much ultimately depended on local officials. Some did little; others diligently relayed ministerial directives; others yet took initiatives that, while in accordance with these directives, originated outside Paris. Such, to cite but one example, was the Cher's Commission et Musée d'antiquités départementales: "a monument . . . in honor of the *pays*" that the prefect established in 1834.[36] The official cult of local memories thus constituted a heterogeneous and unsettled interplay of ministerial direction and initiatives by local officials, who were both subordinated to, and independent from, their Parisian superiors.

Why did Parisian and provincial officials now deem it so important to cultivate local memories? One must begin, once again, with the romantic sensibility that permeated early nineteenth-century France. When Thierry declared that the time had come for French "annals" to "embrace in their variety the diverse memories of all the provinces," he captured the romantic predilection for geographical and historical specificity—what novelist Louis Reybaud mocked as "this divinity we call local color." In one respect, Thierry and others sought to recapture national history through its "multiple developments and its various transformations."[37] Beyond this, this romantic history rested on a succession of particular, exemplary case studies that carried lessons of broader import. Wilhelm von Humboldt hence urged historians to study the particular, or "individuality," in order to retrieve a universal, or at least national, principle. Guizot's long-lasting friendship and correspondence with Humboldt (from 1807 until 1850) are part of the intellectual backdrop against which he and other officials cultivated local memories during these decades.[38] While this romanticism waned during the second half of the century, the increasingly rigorous and austere history that progressively supplanted it could value local history as foundation of a national edifice. "Monitoring by local societies is indispensable," explained a CTH member in 1862, "to

---

36. AN F17 3026: Prefect to subprefects and mayors of the Cher, circular of 30 June 1834.

37. Thierry, *Lettres sur l'histoire de France*, 2d ed., repr. in *Oeuvres d'Aug. Thierry* (Brussels, 1839), 424; Louis Reybaud, *Jérôme Paturot à la recherche d'une position sociale*, 8; and Aristide Guilbert, Introduction to idem, ed., *Histoire des villes*, 1: xxii.

38. Marcel Gauchet, "Les *Lettres sur l'histoire de France* d'Augustin Thierry," in Nora, ed., *Lieux de Mémoire* 2:276–78; Wilhelm von Humboldt, "On the historian's task" (1821), quoted in Gérard Noiriel, *Sur la "crise" de l'histoire* (Paris, 1996), 52–53; and Michael Werner, "Les correspondants allemands de François Guizot," *Cahiers d'études germaniques* 13 (1987): 117.

avoid the omissions that residents of the *pays* alone can spot." Down-to-earth considerations likewise came into play—especially under the July Monarchy. During an era of budgetary constraints and difficult travel conditions, the state had much to gain, as CTH member Jules Desnoyers told Guizot in 1834, from the "people from the localities themselves." Given their location and familiarity with their *pays*, the latter would provide local data and thereby save the ministry expensive and time-consuming "missions."[39]

To fully understand this policy, however, we must return to the conviction that knowledge [*le savoir, l'intelligence*] was a central dimension of governmental action in the modern era. European states had long understood this, but the July Monarchy deemed it increasingly important. Freed from clerical and aristocratic control since the French Revolution, "intelligence and science could not lay outside the government of society," Guizot posited in a well-known statement. Good government—control over and encouragement of civil society—required that the state fill this vacuum. Around 1854, a ministerial official wrote that the "new government [of Napoleon III] . . . must view the governing of the minds as one of the most indispensable attributes of its authority."[40] Uttered in different contexts, these statements reveal the doctrinal and instrumental allure of the intellectual realm and, more precisely, local and historical knowledge. It was here that the state would regenerate a far too "immobile" society; affiliate the influential acolytes that would both support it in this endeavor and fortify its rule; and discreetly depoliticize unreliable elites. Despite variations in time, this agenda imprinted the official cult of local memories throughout this period.

IN SEARCH OF ACOLYTES

Whenever they commented on the condition of intellectual life and the patrimony in the provinces, officials and Parisian *littérateurs* alike drew a bleak picture of decrepitude and disregard. Particularly acute during the first half of the century, this concern persisted during subsequent decades. In 1840, the inspector general of public libraries, Félix Ravaisson, wrote Salvandy about the sights he had witnessed: the rich library of Dol, "locked up, prey to rats"; innumerable "imperiled . . . treasures"; a "municipal materialism" that discounted all things intellectual.[41] Others

39. AN F17 3307: Anon. report on the archaeological inventory of Sancerre and Saint-Amand, n.d. [late 1862]; and AN F17 2833: Jules Denoyers to Guizot, 22 September 1834.

40. Guizot, *Mémoires*, 3: 14 and 16; and AN 246 AP 19: Anon. official to Fortoul, "Note sur l'Institut," n.d. [ca. 1854].

41. AN 152 AP 2: Félix Ravaisson to Salvandy, 14 June 1840.

bemoaned museums and archives that were "left to perish," priests who sold precious religious artifacts, and widespread destruction of historical edifices. Two intertwined concerns surfaced: the disappearance of France's heritage and a deep-seated "slumber of the minds"—an apathy that was both intellectual and civic.[42] Equally important for Guizot and others was the revolution of the minds that, we will recall, hinged on national self-understanding. For the intellectual realm to undergo "a progress analogous to that which occurred in the social and popular realm at the time of the revolution," declared Charles Louandre in 1847, the state had to rouse the provinces.[43]

To meet these objectives, it turned to provincial learned societies. Officials and Parisian *littérateurs* observed their proliferation "with pleasure," contrasting their intellectual vitality and commitment to local affairs with *la province*'s "numbness and torpor." The Ministry of the Interior perceived them in 1839 as invaluable contributors to its Commission des monuments historiques.[44] Others were less sanguine. One prominent Commission member, Charles Lenormant, warned that "no one is responsible" in such societies. Victor Hugo blamed "provincial academicians" for ill-conceived restorations of precious monuments. Other critics accused them of producing repetitive, "almost general[ly] useless" work due to their elitism, ignorance, and isolation. While such appraisals were severe, numerous observers concurred with Salvandy that "many of these academies lack life and activity."[45] For the minister, this was "due less to a want of capable and learned men than to insufficient stimulation and guidance." It thus fell on the ministry to revitalize these associations by directing them toward useful pursuits, publicizing their work, and linking them to one another and the capital.[46] In exchange for research assistance and reports on their activities, Guizot promised these societies financial assistance and free services (such as postage expenses).

42. AN F17 13269: Proceedings of the CHAM, 6 December 1840 and 13 January 1841; AN F17 3291: Eugène de Certain to Min. Pub. Instr., received on 9 November 1839; Victor Hugo, "France et Belgique" and "Alpes et Pyrénées," in his *Voyages*, ed. Claude Gély (Paris, 1987), 519, 576, and 721; and *Revue de l'Instruction publique* 23, no. 4 (23 April 1863): 60.

43. Louandre, "Statistique littéraire de la production intellectuelle en France depuis quinze ans.—Première partie," *RDM*, new ser., 20 (October–December 1847): 257.

44. *La Revue des provinces* (1 February 1834): 222; *Panthéon de la jeune France* (15 November 1841): 48; *La Gazette littéraire, artistique et scientifique* 1 (30 April 1864): 3; and MAP 80/2/1: Min. Int. to prefects, circular of 11 May 1839.

45. Proceedings of the Commission des monuments historiques, 28 January 1842, in Françoise Bercé, *Les premiers travaux de la commission des monuments historiques, 1837–1848* (Paris, 1979), 170; Hugo, *Choses vues: souvenirs, journaux, cahiers*, 4 vols., ed. Hubert Juin, (Paris, 1972), 1: 432; *La Revue des provinces* (1 November 1834): 2; *France départementale* 2 (1835): 434; *Revue de l'Instruction publique*, 15 June 1845; and *AIP* 8 (1856): 125–26.

46. AN F17 13268: Proceedings of the Committee on sciences, 18 January 1838. Guizot expressed similar views in his circular of 23 July 1834, in Charmes, 8–9.

The state would thus help these elites fulfill their potential as conduits of reason and architects of this revolution of the minds. In this respect, these provincials were the *ends* of a governmental intervention that furthered the cause of decentralization. The cult of local memories schooled young elites in the arts of thought, patience, and humility. Republican *littérateur* Eugène Pelletan accordingly praised the ministry in 1840 for steering the country's future leaders "toward historical studies" that would build their character.[47] More significantly, this policy reflects the disquiet of certain liberals before the apathy of those enlightened, rational individuals best suited to represent and help administer the nongovernmental realm. According to this doctrinal current, modern societies governed themselves through a synthesis of voluntary action by educated elites and governmental direction by the nation's elected representatives—complementary social forces who, through their reason, experience, and education, both grasped and advanced France's broader interests. The French Revolution had abolished most local intermediary institutions, but many of the elites expected to take over were too passive and indecisive, too egoistic, too caught up in their personal occupations to devote themselves to "public affairs."[48] And yet, as Thierry explained in 1820, France's "wish . . . must originate, not in the country's center, but in all the diverse points." By joining such voluntary associations and retrieving "the old titles of our local liberties," local elites would exercise their initiative, deepen their sense of place, and hence involve themselves in local affairs. They would not only retrace the history of a compromise between monarchy and society, but also display the synthesis of civil society and state by collaborating with the CTH.[49] Prominent CTH member (and chief archives inspector) Francis Wey expressed similar views in 1862: knowledge of municipal history alone would battle provincial "inertia," revive "local patriotism," and thereby fuel the peaceful growth of France.[50]

In another respect, however, these elites were not ends but *means*, governmental acolytes who would further broad social and political objectives. This policy originated in a conception of intellectual knowledge and activity that liberals derived from the Enlightenment. Guizot expressed it most cogently in articles on encyclopedias and digests (*abrégés*), two gen-

47. A friend of Aristide Guilbert, Pelletan later contributed to his *Histoire des villes de France*. See Eugène Pelletan, "Troisième lettre à M. le ministre de l'Instruction Publique. Des encouragements littéraires II," *France littéraire* 9, 3d trim. (1840): 165.

48. Pierre Rosanvallon, *Moment Guizot*, 170; and Pierre Manent, *Histoire intellectuelle du libéralisme: dix leçons* (Paris, 1987), 205–6.

49. Thierry, *Dix ans d'études historiques*, in *Oeuvres d'Aug. Thierry*, 626; and Jacques Neefs, "Augustin Thierry: le moment de la 'véritable' histoire de France," *Romantisme* 28–29 (1980): 294–95.

50. Francis Wey, *Dick Moon en France, journal d'un Anglais de Paris* (Paris, 1862), 288 and 294–95; and, on this little-known text, Lara Jennifer Moore, "Restoring Order," 236.

res that fell outside the domain of pure science yet fulfilled a crucial task. Whereas scientists sought to uncover an abstract truth, these "practical work[s]" articulated "a design that was applicable to the external world." Whereas scientists wrote for their peers alone, the latter reached a "vast audience." Whereas scientists worked alone, finally, the latter constituted collective endeavors. Transcending "noble curiosity," encyclopedias and the like disseminated knowledge on "all things." The "learned aristocracy's" monopoly over knowledge had given way to a free play involving "varied, original, independent minds."[51]

This free play involved provincial learned societies, these autonomous "centers of study and intellectual life," immersed in civil society. They were all the more necessary now that so many provincials, "eminent by virtue of their knowledge . . . [and] social situation," were emigrating to Paris or regional centers. Their members would not, granted, make key discoveries or pen epochal works. With proper guidance, however, they could contribute to a "fecund circulation" of ideas and clarify the regime's principles.[52] Dispersed throughout the country, they formed both intermediaries and potential geysers of knowledge, drawing freely from a reservoir of reason, morality, and wisdom to irrigate their locality and counter nefarious influences (clerical or traditionalist, for instance). The official cult of local memories did not attempt to transform individuals (as did the pedagogy of place). Instead, it sought to disseminate useful information and set an example of dedication and commitment to the locality. In 1832, the prefect of the Finistère thus commended the new Société d'émulation de la ville de Quimper for both "study[ing] the localities" and "spread[ing] instruction among the inferior classes." For many officials, this "bourgeoisie of the intellectual world" was a bridge and a "means of civilization."[53]

Governing the minds thus called for a network of official auxiliaries—men who, without necessarily being civil servants, would nonetheless serve and bolster the state in this intellectual realm. This yearning was not intrinsically new—consider, for instance, the participation of elites in local

51. Guizot, "Encyclopédie" and "Abrégé," in *Encyclopédie progressive, ou collection de traités sur l'histoire, l'état actuel et les progrès des connaissances humaines* (Paris, 1826), 9–17 and 306–8; and idem, *Mémoires*, 3: 137.

52. Guizot, *Encyclopédie progressive*, 137–38; and Rosanvallon, *Moment Guizot*, 230 and 234. For similar views, see ADN M 508/1: Minister of Commerce and Public Works to prefects, circular of 15 November 1833; and ADN M137/37: Min. Int. to prefects, circular of 23 September 1836.

53. AN F17 3028: Prefect Finistère to Min. Pub. Instrc., 15 December 1832; *RSS* 1 (January 1848): 10; and AN F17 3318: Louandre to presidents of provincial learned societies, circular of 24 May 1857.

54. Isser Woloch, *The New Regime: Transformations of the French Civic Order, 1789–1820s* (New York, 1994), 218–20.

committees of public education from the 1810s on.[54] Yet it revealed novel ambitions, including those of a young Ministry of Public Instruction (f. 1832) that sought to revamp, regularize, "extend the relations" at all levels, and locate additional means of action. The BTH and CTH would turn intellectual elites and learned societies into officious state operatives, "additional workers" who generated emulation and a public "harmony of views" between "administrators" and "simple citizens."[55]

If these elites proved so enticing, it was, of course, because they were not simple citizens. Guizot described members of learned societies in 1834 as an "elite of men remarkable for their education, their social position, their enlightened taste for the sciences and letters." Twenty years later, the CTH spoke of "societies that have attracted into their midst the elite of a department or province." The Second Empire targeted "new" industrial and commercial elites with greater ardor than it did mere *capacités*.[56] Nonetheless, both regimes sought to develop new patterns of cooperation with well-connected provincials—bourgeois and nobles of various political backgrounds who could serve as political bulwarks. Such elites could help officials understand an opaque society by grasping its underlying forces and collective interests. They could gauge and respond to local transformations and needs. They could "fight listlessness, indifference" and project the image of a beneficent regime. They could, finally, facilitate a reform of the nation "in its opinions, civil institutions, political institutions, sentiments toward religion and toward all the rest." They could do all this due to their talents, "personal influence," and attachment to a locality they knew and mastered.[57]

The quest for influence permeated this governmental venture—as it did others throughout our period. In 1835, Prefect Saint-Aignan advised the Minister of the Interior to exploit all instruments at its disposal, including local elites and voluntary associations, whose "influence . . . is necessarily greater than that of the administration left to itself." A few months later, liberal publicist Henri Fonfrède presented Guizot with a detailed plan for the forthcoming elections. The government, he explained, had to respond to the "democratic" attempt to lessen the "direction [of] social intelligence, which resides in the enlightened and moral classes of the nation alone." To succeed, he urged Guizot to ally key provincial "influences" to

55. *Journal officiel de l'instruction publique*, 22 November 1832; and Paul Gerbod, "L'administration de l'instruction publique (1815–1870)," in Pierre Bousquet et al., *Histoire de l'administration de l'enseignement en France, 1789–1981* (Geneva, 1983), 25–35.

56. Guizot to provincial learned societies, circular of 23 July 1834, in Charmes, 11; F17 3318: Brochure advertising the *Bulletin des sociétés savantes* (Paris, 1854); Theodore Zeldin, *The Political System of Napoleon III* (London, 1958), 164–65; and Corbin, *Monde retrouvé*, 252.

57. Guizot to Charles Lenormant, 11 January 1849, in *Les années de retraite de M. Guizot. Lettres à M. et Mme Charles Lenormant* (Paris, 1902), 21; Salvandy, *Vingt mois*, 590; and Lucien Jaume, *Individu effacé*, 138.

his cause. Do so through "all the means that the constitution does not outlaw," he counseled, including "the distribution of positions, favors, rewards, ranks, honors."[58] Such advice was well taken, but probably superfluous. In 1830, as Minister of the Interior, Guizot had urged prefects to surround themselves with "the *pays*'s natural and active *influences*." One means of doing so, he said, was to direct the latter toward learned societies.[59] Salvandy likewise described the latter as "a new means of influence and authority for the central administration"—a perception that proved enduring within the ministry. Provincial learned societies "have an eminent personnel, by their numbers, their merit, and, even more, by their social relations, their family situation," a high official wrote the minister in the late 1850s. "It is important that the Government encourage the[m]."[60]

If such officials publicly embraced local memories, it was in part because the local represented civil society. A government that addressed local concerns was close to its citizenry. But the official cult of local memories was also good politics. It would flatter and affiliate fickle yet indispensable provincial allies. Guizot spoke for his colleagues and successors when he urged local officials in 1835 to convince these elites of the "superior administration's" regard for their contribution and concerns. "Nothing is more hurtful and discouraging to the notable men, who in each locality freely assist the administration, than" the latter's disregard for "the local events or facts they bring to its attention."[61] On this plane, officials merely echoed and validated what they perceived to be provincial priorities.

The case of Simon-Jude Honnorat (1783–1852), a doctor, former postal official, and amateur philologist from southeastern France, is illuminating. In 1839, the prefect of Basses-Alpes submitted his name to the Commission des monuments historiques as a potential correspondent. In vain: he "presents no particular title," concluded the Commission (apparently unaware, however, that the legitimist Honnorat had refused to swear allegiance to the regime). Five years later, Honnorat asked the Ministry of Public Instruction to subscribe to his *Dictionnaire provençal-français*, a massive work on "living dialects" and "the dead languages of troubadours" that had impressed several provincial learned societies. Following its stan-

58. ADN M 137/39: Gabriel de Saint-Aignan to Min. Int., 22 August 1835; and AN 42 AP 241: Henri Fonfrède to Guizot, 20 December 1835. See also André-Jean Tudesq, *Grands notables*, 1:118.

59. Guizot to Amédée Thierry, 14 September 1830, quoted in his *Mémoires*, 2: 57; idem to Amédée Thierry, repr. in A. Augustin-Thierry, *Augustin Thierry (1795–1856), d'après sa correspondance et ses papiers de famille* (Paris, 1922), 111; and AN F1a 62: idem to prefects, circular of 29 October 1830.

60. Salvandy, report to the king, 31 December 1838, in *Budget général des dépenses pour l'exercice 1840*, 74; and AN F17 17130: Anon. memorandum to Min. Pub. Instr., n.d. (1857?).

61. Guizot to prefects, rectors, and primary school inspectors, circular of 13 August 1835, in *Circulaires et instructions*, 2: 366.

dard procedure (the ministry only subscribed to completed, and hence verifiable, works), a BTH official drafted a letter postponing the decision. Once again, scientific considerations prevailed. But another official observed that Honnorat was "a very influential man in the department of Basses-Alpes"—one for whom the prefect had asked that "something be done." Five months later, the BTH endorsed the subscription. "The author's social position and scientific excellence grant him a great influence in the department," an unnamed official wrote the minister. The ministry ultimately subscribed for one hundred copies of Honnorat's dictionary—an unusually large number.[62]

PERILS OF THE INTELLECTUAL REALM

Influential and morally upright, these provincial elites would hence strengthen the regime and constitute front-line corps in a battle against the "spirit of disorganization" that, in Salvandy's words, had "invaded everything: politics and literature, newspapers and theaters, the streets and government." Using a fittingly bellicose vocabulary, Guizot urged the Société des Antiquaires de Normandie in 1838 to ward off this "basely skeptical spirit . . . that would like us to doubt ourselves completely . . . Let us defend ourselves, gentlemen, against this new enemy." Influence could be misused, however. These men also posed dangers. The July Monarchy after all encountered the "hostility of a notable part of the enlightened, well-read, acting, influential public," Salvandy noted in 1831.[63] Politics had not bypassed the intellectual realm. Were droves of provincial youths not undertaking literary careers that led all too easily to politics? Did Republicans not promise to initiate "to the language of publicists and the mechanism of governments, these interesting generations of young people whom the University deposits in such high numbers on the forum of our big cities"? A Second Empire official spoke of "restless, worried minds, seeking to show themselves off, to write, to gain their share of notoriety and renown" since the July Monarchy. The internal emigration of legitimists after 1830 and their enthusiasm for intellectual pursuits; the agitation of "Saint-Simonians," republican opuscules, and anarchists; and the post-1851 rancor of erstwhile Orleanists and others meant that "sterile or dangerous minds," as Hippolyte Fortoul called them, could surface anywhere.[64]

---

62. This account is based on a dossier on Honnorat, held in AN F17 2896. See also MAP 80/2/1: Tableau entitled "Réponses de MM. les préfets à la circulaire du 11 mai 1839"; and Prospectus for Simon-Jude Honnorat, *Dictionnaire provençal-français ou dictionnaire de la langue d'Oc, ancienne et moderne* (Marseilles, 1842), 1–2.

63. Salvandy, *Vingt mois*, 1; and *Discours prononcé par M. Guizot*, 6.

64. Prospectus for Duclerc and Pagnerre, *Dictionnaire politique*, 3; Anon. Memorandum to Min. Pub. Instr. [1857?], op. cit.; and Fortoul, "Rapport au prince président de la République

"Particular associations"—a category ranging from mutual aid societies to freemasonry lodges—were especially suspect. "Association" may have constituted "a great promise made to humanity," as a liberal journalist asserted in 1834, yet it was an unpredictable force, liable to contest the state or usurp its natural prerogatives.[65] Salvandy's excoriation of associations "forming a city within the city, a state within the state" thus responded largely to radical agitation, a proliferation of overt and secret societies that contested the regime's authority, and blueprints that, like Charles Fourier's, outlined new forms of "association."[66] But suspicion ran deeper. In 1839, a subprefect relayed ministerial concern about the Société de bienfaisance de Douai, a "private and nonauthorized association" that could no longer remain "unregulated, . . . unseen, without surveillance or control." The same held true of provincial learned societies. Without perceiving them as hotbeds of political opposition, the authorities remained wary. In 1843, the prefect transmitted a ministerial circular warning local agents against "abuses" by, among others, "scientific and literary meetings." Vigilance was in order for, like other voluntary associations that fulfilled multiple functions, the latter could easily become "centers of political intrigue."[67] In 1860, the rector of Besançon contrasted the city's reliable Académie des sciences, belles-lettres et arts with the younger (and less aristocratic) Société d'émulation du département du Doubs, "refuge" of local "literary demagogues." In 1866, Douai's subprefect wrote his superior that agricultural associations could likewise become "seat[s] of hostility against the state." The many societies that, in Douai and elsewhere, combined agricultural and learned interests hence required even closer watch.[68]

So did the various Catholic currents that permeated learned societies. Jacques Gadille and Jean-Marie Mayeur have shown that liberal Catholics exploited such societies as well as congresses and scholarship to articulate

et décret sur le plan d'étude des établissements publics," 10 April 1852, in his *Réforme de l'enseignement, ou Recueil des décrets, arrêtés, circulaires, instructions et notes ministerielles concernant les modifications apportées à l'instruction publique depuis le 2 décembre 1851 jusqu'au 31 décembre 1853*, 2 vols. (Paris, 1854–56), 1:34.

65. *La Revue des provinces* (1 November 1834): 8.

66. Salvandy, Intervention in the parliamentary session of 25 March 1834, in J. Madival and E. Laurent, eds., *Archives parlementaires de 1787 à 1860: recueil complet des débats législatifs et politiques des chambres françaises*, 2d ser. (1800–1860), 127 vols. (Paris, 1862–1913), 88:30; Charles Fourier, *Harmonious Man: Selected Writings of Charles Fourier*, ed. Mark Poster (Garden City, 1971), 54; and Pamela Pilbeam, *The 1830 Revolution in France* (New York, 1991), chap. 8.

67. AMD 5 D 38: Subprefect Douai to mayor Douai, 28 September 1839; ADN M 216/1: Prefect Nord to police commissioner Lille, 18 March 1843; and Raymond Huard, "Political Association in Nineteenth-Century France: Legislation and Practice," in Nancy Bermeo and Philip Nord, eds., *Civil Society Before Democracy: Lessons from Nineteenth-Century Europe* (Lanham, Md., 2000), 137–39.

68. AN F17 3300: Rector Besançon to Min. Pub. Instr., 13 October 1860; and ADN M 510/8: Subprefect Douai to prefect Nord, 12 March 1866.

their vision of a Christian Europe and, occasionally, contest the supremacy of Paris. The era's "Catholic science" furthermore challenged its secular counterpart from the mid-1820s on for control of scientific and cultural knowledge.[69] Clerical designs were more worrisome yet—especially under the July Monarchy and around 1860, when the Second Empire's break with Rome fueled tensions with ultramontanists and a clerical party that openly criticized the regime. Rouland was one of the architects of the regime's new ecclesiastical policy, advocating a moderate but firm response. His concomitant overtures to provincial learned societies may well have responded to similar imperatives: a discreet search for secular allies and oversight over such associations. After all, ultramontanists and other social Catholics formed a significant minority within these associations. Many of these men were legitimists who sought to reorganize French society according to a regional, corporative, and clerical model.[70] Some joined suspect charitable associations—such as the Société de Saint-Vincent-de-Paul—or legitimist societies of good books that sought to moralize workers and peasants through wholesome readings. The overlap between these associations and learned societies could be patent. At least five of the Société dunkerquoise's thirty-five members belonged to Dunkirk's Société de Saint-Vincent-de-Paul in 1854. In 1836, more pointedly, Lille's Société des bons livres (Society of Good Books) had become the aforementioned Association lilloise. Le Glay interwove charity, science, "religious fervor," and "the spirit of communal association" in his presidential addresses. This moderate assured the prefect in 1837 that "Christian sentiment" did not a clerical association make: "All that pertains to dogma and precepts lies outside our purview." The Association lilloise nonetheless numbered ultramontanist Louis Veuillot among its corresponding members and shared an address with the legitimist Société Saint-Joseph. Some Lille residents even spoke of the "Association lilloise dite de Saint-Joseph."[71] The relationship between both associations remains murky, but there was cause for concern.

69. Jacques Gadille and Jean-Marie Mayeur, "Les milieux catholiques libéraux en France: continuité et diversité d'une tradition," in *Les catholiques libéraux au XIXe siècle: actes du colloque international d'histoire religieuse de Grenoble* (Grenoble, 1974), 187–93; and Claude Bénichou, "L'ignorance des savoirs," in Claude Langlois and François Laplanche, eds., *La science catholique: "l'encyclopédie théologique" de Migne (1844–1873) entre apologétique et vulgarisation* (Paris, 1992), 102.

70. Jean Maurain, *La politique ecclésiastique du Second Empire de 1852 à 1869* (Paris, 1930); Mayeur, "Démocratie chrétienne et régionalisme en France," in his *Catholicisme social et démocratie chrétienne* (Paris, 1986), 225–27; and Bercé, "Arcisse de Caumont et les sociétés savantes," in Nora, ed., *Lieux de mémoire*, 3: 549.

71. Claude Savart, *Les catholiques en France au XIXe siècle: le témoignage du livre religieux* (Paris, 1985), 380–436; Le Glay, *Discours d'introduction aux conférences sur l'histoire du Nord de la France prononcé en séance générale le 28 mars 1838* (Lille, n.d. [1838?]), 5–6; *Association lilloise. Séance du 21 avril 1841. Discours de M. Le Glay, président* (Lille, 1841), 4; ADN M 137/49: Le Glay to prefect Nord, 23 May 1837; and ADN M 140/5: André [sic] to Min. Int., 12 December 1851.

Making matters worse, hundreds of learned society members participated in Arcisse de Caumont's scientific congresses and Institut des provinces. These "assemblies of enlightened men" claimed the role of national guide and counsel, whose judgments ought to influence legislation and governmental decisions. The very organization of scientific congresses—directing committee, a passing resemblance to legislative sessions, platformlike lists of "wishes"—betrayed their ambitions. This "constitutive assembly for science and letters" would admonish the state when necessary, Caumont wrote a colleague in 1848. It also sought to extend its authority over provincial learned societies, formulating blueprints for a General Council of the Academies of the Kingdom that would "defend the[ir] . . . interests before the government."[72] Most of its presentations and discussions seemed harmless—but not all. In the early 1830s, congress members debated such topics as freedom of education. This intrusion into the "domain of politics" displeased some—both inside and outside the congresses—and the social economy section vanished in 1837.[73] Four years later, the program of Lyons's congress nonetheless included questions on the organization of labor and the merits of Fourier's *école sociétaire*. *Fouriériste* Victor Considérant's speech was so well received—despite rumblings by Caumont and other conservatives—that he described scientific congresses as "good battlefield[s]." They were not always battlefields, but they could become so—and this sufficed to make them dangerous.[74] Officials took note of the changing political dimension of Caumont's network. Under the July Monarchy, some officials worried about the "bold innovators" who sought to disseminate "liberal propaganda" through "so-called scientific congresses." In the late 1840s, their concern shifted toward the Institut des provinces and the network's commitment to legitimism. Throughout this period, they distrusted congresses that "did not fear to cast blame on the administration's actions."[75]

72. *CS* 4 (Blois, 1837), xxiv; BNF ms. NAF 11144: Arcisse de Caumont to Raymond Bordeaux, 6 March 1848; F17 3026: Charles Richelet to Salvandy, 10 April 1847; and H. Lecocq and J.-B. Bouillet, *Plan d'association entre les principales académies départementales* (Clermont-Ferrand, 1838).

73. *La Revue des provinces* 4 (15 December 1834): 133.

74. The battlefield in question was also Alsace, a *Fouriérist* stronghold. See *CS* 9, 2 vols. (Lyons, 1842), esp. 1:lii–liii, 374, 377, and 390; Alphonse Tamisier, *Théorie générale de Fourier. Mémoire de M*** lu dans la 5e section du Congrès, le 5 septembre 1841, par M. Victor Considérant, pour répondre à cette question du programme: 'Exposer et discuter la valeur des principes de l'Ecole sociétaire fondée par M. Fourier'* (Lyons, 1841); and Fourier to Jaenger, 24 September 1841, quoted in Paul Leuilliot, "Congrès scientifique ou congrès fouriériste à Strasbourg en 1842?", *Actes du 92e congrès des sociétés savantes* (Paris, 1967), 163.

75. AN F17 3090/1: Adrien-Etienne de Gasparin to Guizot, 29 August 1835; AN BB 18 1233: idem to Minister of Justice, 30 August 1835 (minute); and MAP 80/1/56: Proceedings of the Commission des monuments historiques, 25 March 1854. See also Robert-Henri Bautier: "Le Comité des travaux historiques," 383–86; and Marcel Baudot, "Trente ans de coordination des sociétés savantes (1831–1861)," *Actes du 100e Congrès national des sociétés savantes* (Paris, 1976), esp. 13–19.

All of these perils converged within the language of decentralization and provincial emancipation. By 1838, a learned society member from Nantes could note that "for some years now, the ideas of centralization . . . have acquired . . . a truly revolutionary tendency." This war *"of emancipation of communes"* had transformed *"la province's* artistic and literary physiognomy."* Members of Caumont's circle made ample use of this language, denouncing the state, in 1864, as a "tyrant . . . that seeks to impose its will and even its whims upon all." Such accusations struck some of their colleagues as excessive. As word and idea, they objected, "decentralization" raised regrettable "questions of administration and politics."[76] French officials had long figured this out for themselves.

THE PEACEFUL INVESTIGATIONS OF LOCAL ERUDITION

Situated against this backdrop, the official cult of local memories was not only an outreach to faithful servants, but also a tenuous incursion into a treacherous territory, a hazardous attempt to counter the perils above by depoliticizing and controlling provincial learned societies. We cannot, as the preceding pages show, reduce the BTH or CTH to instrumental ambitions, a mere desire for authority.[77] Yet neither can we ignore this political dimension nor restrict it to the "authoritarian" Second Empire, as if the July Monarchy had spurned such crass aspirations.[78] To incorporate the latter into our analysis is to uncover the multiple, overlapping layers of an intellectual state that, on this plane, displayed striking continuity between one regime and the next.[79]

A ministerial official presented this instrumental design with remarkable candor in the late 1850s.[80] In a confidential memorandum to Rouland, the (unidentified) author outlined the CTH's instrumental po-

---

76. *Annales de la Société royale académique de Nantes et du département de la Loire-Inférieure* 9 (1838): 315–16 (italics in the original); *AIP* 17 (1865): 298; and *CS* 31 (Troyes, 1865), 616.

77. Cf. Jean-Michel Leniaud, "L'Etat, les sociétés savantes et les associations de défense du patrimoine: l'exception française," in Jacques Le Goff, ed., *Patrimoine et passions*, 143; and—regarding Guizot—Charles-Olivier Carbonell, "Guizot, homme d'Etat, et le mouvement historiographique français du XIXe siècle," in *Actes du colloque François Guizot (Paris, 22–25 octobre 1974)* (Paris, 1976), 233–35.

78. Cf. Dominique Poulot, "Birth of Heritage," 43 and 50–51. On the Second Empire's instrumentalist designs, see Robert Fox, "Science, the University, and the State in Nineteenth-Century France," in Gerald L. Geison, ed., *Professions and the French State, 1700–1900* (Philadelphia, 1984), 83–84 and 90–92. On Salvandy's "purely scientific history, free from . . . political concerns," see Camille Jullian, ed., *Extraits des historiens français du XIXe siècle* (Paris, 1897), lxxvii, cited and endorsed in Louis Trénard, *Salvandy en son temps, 1795–1856* (Lille, 1968), 694.

79. See the probing reflections of Jean Davallon, "Lecture stratégique, lecture symbolique du fait social: enjeu d'une politologie historique," in idem et al., eds., *Politique de la mémoire: commémorer la Révolution* (Lyons, 1993), 204 and 210–216.

80. Anon. memorandum to Min. Pub. Instr. (1857?).

tential. The July Monarchy had wisely created this agency and reached out to provincial elites, he wrote, to "diminish the number of recruits of the militant press [and] encourage those serious works that could not offend the government." It had achieved this by facilitating "the organization and development of learned societies, which supplied local vanities with a theater and an audience, and direct[ing] them imperceptibly toward the path that the state wanted them to tread." Rather than entrusting the "supervision of this [new] literary, historical, archaeological movement" to the semiautonomous Institut de France, Orleanist officials had established a new agency, a "more docile agent of [their] will." Such concerns were all the more pressing in the 1850s, a decade of frequent run-ins between the regime and a politically diverse Institut.[81] The official thus advised Rouland to follow in the July Monarchy's footsteps and "increase its influence on these associations that are too removed from its sphere of action."

The continuity with the July Monarchy is evident. The Second Empire's first objective was to consolidate its authority—in this instance, through ventures that would carry "[the ministry's] name." Guizot had likewise grasped the importance of scientific authority for a state that exercised ambiguous functions of support, regulation, and surveillance. Witness his 1833 statement that functionaries would only accept the decisions of the royal Council of Public Instruction if they "emanate[d] from men whose scientific authority they recognize."[82] More significantly, the blueprint above evinces a yearning for "imperceptible" action that, while in accordance with an increasingly liberal Empire, had surfaced in prior decades. Good government, for some officials, was first and foremost discreet government. In his 1835 letter to the Ministry of the Interior, Saint-Aignan noted that "here as elsewhere, people are tormented by a moral malaise, doubt suffuses the souls." The solution, he said, was a stronger government, but not a more visible one, for "everyone recognize[d]" that freedom had never "been greater, a government less noticed, an administration less inconvenient." Other officials spoke of local *statistiques* that did not resemble "official investigation[s]," of an educational system in which "moral and educational" action was preferable to "external and material" discipline.[83]

81. On the ministry's antagonism with the Institut under the Second Empire and its use of the CTH, see Paul Raphaël and Maurice Gontard, *Hippolyte Fortoul, 1851–1856: un ministre de l'instruction publique sous l'Empire autoritaire* (Paris, 1975), 283–96; and François Dutacq, *Gustave Rouland, ministre de l'instruction publique, 1856–1863* (Tulle, 1910), esp. 34–37, 130–31, and 283.

82. Guizot to the king, report of 31 December 1833, in Charmes, 27.

83. Saint-Aignan to Min. Int., 22 August 1835; AN F1a 40: Min. Commerce, Agriculture, etc. to prefects, circular of 18 June 1834; Salvandy to rectors, circular of 31 May 1838, in *Circulaires et instructions*, 2:607–8; and Salvandy to headmasters, circular of 28 April 1838, quoted in Trénard, *Salvandy*, 415.

The official cult of local memories, Rouland declared in 1858, would likewise "*imperceptibly* and without pressure bring the learned societies to receive and follow the government's inspirations." It would attract to the state "industrious and distinguished minds that may well have lost their way had they not found this valuable use of their time and activities," explained BTH official Charles Jourdain in 1857.[84] The title of CTH correspondent validated its holders publicly as the "intellectual and scientific elite[s] of our provinces" while subtly reaffirming the ministry's scientific and political primacy. For the prefect of the Ariège, this title "may well be the first tie that bound" to the regime a notorious republican from Tarascon.[85] Present within the governmental agenda since the early 1830s, this desire for surreptitious affiliation took new forms in the 1850s. "Kind judgments" and short pieces by provincial learned societies took precedence over critical appraisals and substantive articles in the *Revue des sociétés savantes.* "We must merely show that the minister is interested in the publications of the learned societies," explained one official.[86] Jourdain likewise acknowledged in 1870 that the Sorbonne congresses sought above all to reward provincials and demonstrate the regime's commitment to intellectual decentralization.[87] Participation prevailed over scholarship.

Benign erudition, by the same token, prevailed over analysis. The CTH's circulars and instructions guided elites toward what Jourdain called "the peaceful study of manuscripts and ancient monuments." They instructed elites to collect, describe, copy. While some contemporaries redefined erudition as a rapprochement between historical study and contemporary institutions,[88] the CTH promoted an interest in reiteration rather than rational deduction, an aversion to criticism, and a readiness to remain within a narrow domain, renounce claims to "notoriety and renown," follow instructions, and subsume individual aspirations to collective efforts. Prerevolutionary instructions and early-nineteenth-century *statistiques* had commonly expected such compliance and self-effacement from their acolytes.[89] The key point is that such procedures now shaped the intellectual state's relationship with provincial intellectual elites.

84. Rouland to rectors, circular of 29 March 1858, in Charmes, 191 (my italics); and Charles Jourdain, *Le budget de l'instruction publique et des établissements scientifiques et littéraires depuis la fondation de l'université impériale jusqu'à nos jours* (Paris, 1857), 269–70.

85. Anatole Chabouillet, *Répertoire archéologique de la France. Programme lu et adopté dans la séance du 17 janvier 1859* (Paris, 1859), 7; and AN F17 2811: Prefect Ariège to Min. Pub. Instr., 14 April 1858.

86. AN F17 3015/2: Anon. memorandum to Min. Pub. Instr., n.d. [1862?]; AN F17 3019: Vincent, memorandum to Min. Pub. Instr., 7 December 1853; and Rouland to rectors, circular of 30 May 1857, in Charmes, 183.

87. AN F17 2815: Jourdain, report to the Sorbonne Congress, 23 April 1870.

88. Jourdain, *La Société de l'histoire de France de 1833 à 1884* (Paris, 1884), 1; and *Mémoires de la Société des antiquaires de Normandie* 11 (1837–39): lxiii.

89. Emma C. Spary, *Utopia's Garden: French Natural History from Old Regime to Revolution* (Chicago, 2000), 84.

Erudition had by then long denoted obscure and often barren investigations. Seventeenth-century gentlemen and eighteenth-century *philosophes* had defined themselves against pedantic *érudits*, whose footnotes and textual comparisons hampered true narrative history. Without disqualifying erudition, this inexhaustible "province of erudition and facts," *encyclopédiste* d'Alembert nonetheless distinguished it from the productive "province of reason and discoveries." Nineteenth-century *littérateurs* furthermore denounced antiquarians whose only achievement was "the reprint of an obscure book, the translation of an old chronicle or manuscript." Counseled Flaubert: "Despise [erudition] as the sign of a narrow mind."[90] Yet, such erudite procedures also promised scholarly benefits. Within this state's two-tier apparatus of great Parisian minds and provincial operatives, the latter's task was simply to facilitate the former's syntheses. Condorcet himself had, after all, advised provincial academies to "simply collect, take note of facts upon which one could then attempt to erect a true science." The first half of the century furthermore witnessed a resurgence of "erudition" as patient, critical study of documents. Many provincials concurred that, given their limited training and talents, "Benedictine" tasks suited them better than analysis.[91]

At the same time, these procedures would yield a placid, well-ordered sphere in which fulfilling one's allotted task prevailed over critical exchanges. In 1837, the CTH encouraged a correspondent to "give much greater care to the search for original documents than to their historical appreciation"; three decades later, a contemporary remarked that in the Sorbonne congresses "one listened to lectures" whereas "in other meetings, one discussed issues [*on discutait*]."[92] This was a sphere in which direction resided in the center and provincial elites were subordinates rather than interlocutors. The CTH sought out compliant associates who, like Hippolyte Crozes, followed governmental instructions to the letter. In 1862, it accordingly praised the Société philomathique de Verdun for "scrupulously compl[ying]" with its instructions, but rejected

90. Paul Hazard, *La crise de la conscience européenne, 1680–1715* (Paris, 1961), 55; Jean d'Alembert, "Discours préliminaire," in Denis Diderot and Jean Le Rond d'Alembert, eds., *L'Encyclopédie, ou dictionnaire raisonné des sciences, des arts et des métiers,* repr., 35 vols. (Stuttgart-Bad Cannstatt, 1966 [1751–80]), 1: xx, quoted in Blandine Barret-Kriegel, *Histoire à l'âge classique,* 2: 307; "Erudition," in *Encyclopédie,* ed. Diderot and d'Alembert, 5: 914–18; Charles Philipon, "Le floueur," in *Les physiologies parisiennes* (Paris, 1850), 9; and Gustave Flaubert, *Dictionnaire des idées reçues,* in his *Oeuvres complètes,* 2 vols. (Paris, 1964), 2: 308. See also Anne Goldgar, *Impolite Learning: Conduct and Community in the Republic of Letters, 1680–1750* (New Haven, 1995), 239.

91. Marquis de Condorcet, "Essai sur la constitution et les fonctions des assemblées provinciales" (1788), in *Oeuvres de Condorcet,* ed. A. Condorcet O'Connor and François Arago, 12 vols. (Paris, 1847–49), 8: 483; and Jean Le Pottier, "Histoire et érudition," part 2.

92. AN F17 13268: Proceedings of the Committee on French language and literature, 31 July 1837; and *Annuaire des sociétés savantes de la France et de l'étranger,* 2 vols. (Paris, 1863–64), 2:xxv.

the geographical dictionary of the Société d'émulation du département des Vosges because it had "not sufficiently imbued the [governmental] plan."[93]

This was a sphere, finally, that rewarded description and nomenclature. The ministry's predilection for dictionaries—a genre that, in this erudite form, called for descriptive notices rather than opinions—is revealing. So is its penchant for topographical surveys, given geography's status as an "essentially descriptive" discipline that merely furnished others with pertinent data.[94] Ultimately, these erudite practices had little use for individual interpretation. This was characteristic of French science—centralized, bureaucratic, and resistant to innovation.[95] Doctrinal convictions also came into play. According to Victor Cousin, "serious studies" calmed the "nervous ardor" of "young minds" by drawing them away from "purely abstract questions, [before which] one can easily . . . lose oneself in purely sterile dreams." A single opinion required years of erudite study. The result was a philosophy that, per its critic Joseph Ferrari, "described, compiled, commented."[96] For BTH official Désiré Nisard, the essence of French literature resided likewise in what he called "reason": the "predominance of discipline over freedom[,] . . . imagination and the senses." Dismissing theoretical suppositions, Nisard praised "precious erudition" and assigned literature a moralizing and disciplinary function, complementing "the examples of the domestic hearth, religion, the laws of the fatherland."[97] Neither thinker encouraged self-affirmation. Nisard's reason countered "the literary *moi*, so superb and so odious, which scorns the great ancestors" and turns literature into "cerebral overexcitement." While Cousin claimed to have rooted his philosophy in individual freedom and free will, he subsumed the latter to a transcendent, "impersonal reason" that was "the contrary of individuality." Social stability and consensus ultimately curtailed individual autonomy and originality.[98]

So did a more blatantly instrumental yearning for "peaceful tastes" and

93. AN F17 3304/2: Min. Pub. Instr. to Charton (member Société d'émulation des Vosges), 31 December 1862; and AN F17 3302: Secretary BTH to secretary Société philomathique de Verdun, 7 March 1862.

94. Some sought to make geography explanatory rather than descriptive, but they remained a minority. See "Topographie," in *La Grande Encyclopédie*, 31: 171–72; and Numa Broc, "Quelques débats dans la géographie française avant Vidal de la Blache," in Paul Claval, ed., *Autour de Vidal de la Blache: la formation de l'Ecole française de géographie* (Paris, 1993), 37.

95. Lewis Pyenson, *Civilizing Mission: Exact Sciences and French Overseas Expansion, 1830–1940* (Baltimore, 1993).

96. Victor Cousin, *Fragments littéraires* (Paris, 1843), 51, quoted in Patrice Vermeren, *Victor Cousin*, 184–85; and Joseph Ferrari, *Les philosophes salariés*, pref. Stéphane Douaillier and Vermeren (Paris, 1983 [1849]), 170.

97. Désiré Nisard, "Manifeste contre la littérature facile," in his *Etudes de critique littéraire*, 4; idem, *Histoire de la littérature française*, 4 vols. (Paris, 1844–61), 1:iii and 19; and Zeldin, *A History of French Passions, 1848–1945*, 2 vols. (Oxford, 1977), 2:412–13.

98. Nisard, *Précis de l'histoire de la littérature française depuis ses premiers monuments jusqu'à nos jours* (Paris, 1841), 383; idem, "Manifeste," 13–14; Cousin, Preface of 1826, *Fragments*

an apolitical body of knowledge—as neutral as science itself. Responding to the perils that traversed this intellectual realm, ministerial officials hoped to depoliticize provincial elites as surreptitiously as they affiliated them. The aforementioned memorandum to Rouland praised the July Monarchy's efforts to "extinguish, within the peaceful investigations of erudition, an ardor for controversy, a taste for polemics that granted a passionate and dangerous character to contemporary questions."[99] While the Institut could look toward the future, the CTH and its acolytes had to confine themselves to the past, Salvandy explained in 1838. Without fully condemning reason, the minister contrasted a reassuringly distant past with rampant "speculation." Such "positive" investigations grew more urgent under the early Second Empire—as a response to "vague theories" and the national histories written by the regime's Orleanist and republican critics. The ministry did not turn to history in earnest until the late 1850s—Fortoul, for one, distrusted history almost as much as he did philosophy—but it did grant the CTH and "the peaceful investigations of erudition" a new scope. Study of the past, Duruy declared in 1863, could calm "the *impatients*."[100]

Such considerations further illuminate the ministry's interest in "studious investigations" that displayed an "essentially local character." *Local*, as we have seen, meant apolitical on one discursive register. A "thoroughly local" political debate, as Salvandy wrote Guizot in 1830, was one without "political color."[101] During the following years, officials commonly distinguished an apolitical sphere of "local interests" from the (national) arena of "political passions." *Conseils généraux* could not withdraw too much "into the local spirit" and busy themselves with local concerns, from roads to hygiene. The locality—and, by extension, *la province*—constituted a soothing alternative to the capital, this caldron in which young provincial "minds," who had left their *pays* with vast ambitions, encountered students, journalists, pamphleteers, and political refugees.[102] Local erudition would anchor these elites within a reassuringly apolitical local

---

philosophiques (Paris, 1838 [1826]), 103 and 106; Jaume, *Individu effacé*, 11 and 147; and Jan Goldstein, "Mutations of the Self," 113.

99. AN F17 3090/1: Anon., report to Guizot, 11 June 1836; and Anon. memorandum to Min. Pub. Instr. [1857?], op. cit.

100. AN F17 13268: Proceedings of the Committee on sciences, 18 January 1838; *Revue de l'Instruction publique* 8, no. 132 (15 April 1849): 1479–81; AN 246 AP 19: Anon. to Fortoul, n.d.; and Duruy (24 September 1863), quoted in Armand Du Mesnil, *Souvenirs de lectures. Histoire et morale* (Paris, 1894), 87. See also Stuart L. Campbell, *The Second Empire Revisited: A Study in French Historiography* (New Brunswick, 1978), 33–37.

101. Rouland to learned society presidents, circular of 22 February 1858, in Charmes, 191; and AN 42 AP 212: Salvandy to Guizot, 22 October 1830.

102. AN F1a 39: Thiers to prefects, circular of 27 April 1833; Anon., *De l'importance des communes et des départements, et de la nécessité d'accroître les ressources communales et départementales* (Tulle, 1844), 31; *La Presse*, 24 August 1841; and Christophe Charle, *Les intellectuels en Europe au XIXe siècle* (Paris, 1996), 43, 108–13, and 160.

habitat—free from speculation. Often tacit, the correlation between such views and the official cult of local memories grew more explicit under the Second Empire. "General" historians, explained the *Revue des sociétés savantes* in 1863, were "sometimes devoted to a system, if not party or sect spirit."[103] The ministry thus sought to draw provincial elites out of "the generalities in which they have all too often lost themselves [and] lead them imperceptibly toward local investigations . . . the terrain they know, which they can explore without danger." It valued these elites as local observers, "who renounc[ed] general theories" to tackle "these questions that can only be resolved on site," in a *pays* that fulfilled their aspirations.[104]

In doing so, officials also sought to defuse the ominous discourse of emancipation and decentralization and prevent its opponents from seizing ownership of words such as *pays* or province. Prefect Saint-Aignan is, again, a case in point. His activities on behalf of local memories acquire another dimension when correlated with his confidential political reports on the Nord. No development alarmed him more than the "municipal spirit" of certain center-left municipalities. This spirit, he wrote his superior in 1841, "tends unflaggingly to dominate and even destroy the spirit of centralization." Certain mayors viewed themselves, "not as intermediaries between the superior authority and the communes, but as representatives of these communes, and hence, adversaries . . . of the central authority." While Saint-Aignan linked this spirit to "ancient prejudices" in cities such as Lille, he also denounced a far-ranging municipalism, too "egoistic" to dedicate itself to "the consolidation of governmental or general interests." At base, he was concerned with the state's feeble roots in civil society and underlying patterns of loyalty and service.[105] These reports illuminate Saint-Aignan's support for the Commission historique du Nord, which he aided with his personal funds when needed. Rather than systematically denouncing localism, Saint-Aignan sought to transform municipal allegiance into a more neutral local erudition. He helped establish an administrative framework—at once patrimonial and discursive—that redefined and neutralized such referents as "decentralization." The commission did not involve all proponents of the "municipal spirit," but it constituted a discreet attempt to confiscate a dangerous vocabulary. The official cult of local memories would instill veneration for one's place of

103. *RSS*, 3d ser., 1 (1st se. 1863): 534.

104. AN F17 3318: Anon. memorandum on the *Revue des sociétés savantes*, n.d. (1857?); and Rouland to rectors, circular of 29 March 1858, in Charmes, 189. See also Bercé, "Arcisse de Caumont et les sociétés savantes," in Nora, ed., *Lieux de mémoire*, 3: 549 and 564.

105. The preceding account is based on ADN M 137/39: Saint-Aignan to Min. Int., reports dated 6 November 1839, 5 October 1841, 19 October 1841, and 31 December 1844. See also *Journal de Lille*, 23 May 1845; and ADN M 6/8: Personnel dossier of Saint-Aignan.

residence and deference before the administration. For the likes of Saint-Aignan, it would pacify the intellectual realm and, indirectly, the country.

This governmental effort to regenerate, affiliate, and depoliticize provincial elites through local memories mirrors these elites' own efforts to moralize, edify, and depoliticize the *peuple*. Though no contemporary made the connection, these distinct yet intertwined ventures shared an identical yearning for discretion. These elites thus occupied a paradoxical position, at once sponsors and targets of an imperceptible mode of action. Dominant before the *peuple*, they confronted a state that conferred them some responsibility, but not what, speaking of colonial India, Bernard Cohn called "the authoritative voice in determining what was useful knowledge." Indeed, these interpersonal relations, too, unveil scientific and political procedures that took form in the nexus of colonies and *métropole*. In one as in the other, the authorities turned to local informants who, like the Kabiles recruited by Captain E. Carette in the 1840s, knew their locality but displayed intellectual limitations. Kept within "the horizon of their locality," the latter collected data from which others would "deduce the laws . . . whose appreciation always escapes natives." In Algeria as in metropolitan France, the authorities granted their local acolytes few opportunities to delineate memories, identify monuments, label places, or produce cultural artifacts outside official confines.[106] Scholars have described the Exploration scientifique de l'Algérie's uniform representations as a "geographical and symbolic seizure" of a land and a people whom the state did not fully control, but whose "cultural and historical dimensions" it now "appropriat[ed]."[107] Back in mainland France, such instrumental designs likewise combined with scientific and doctrinal aspirations to shape the state's relationship with local memories and intellectual elites.

GOVERNMENTAL MODERNITY AND VICISSITUDES

While shunning local pedagogy, this intellectual state by no means rejected localism in toto. Reaching out to men it both needed and distrusted, it embedded itself yet more deeply in a social realm that, per

106. Cohn, "The Command of Language and the Language of Command," in his *Colonialism*, 51; and E. Carette, *Etudes sur la Kabilie proprement dite*, 2 vols. (Paris, 1848), 1:4–5. On such practices and scientific missions, see Paul Edison, "Latinizing America: The French Scientific Study of Mexico, 1830–1930," Ph.D. diss., Columbia University, 1999, 207–9.

107. Nordman, "Mission de savants et occupation: l'Exploration scientifique de l'Algérie (vers 1840–1860)," in Loukia Droulia and Vasso Mentzou, eds., *Vers l'Orient par la Grèce: avec Nerval et d'autres voyageurs* (Paris, 1993), 84; and Nabila Oulebsir, "La découverte des monuments de l'Algérie: les missions d'Amable Ravoisié et d'Edmond Duthoit (1840–1880)," *Revue du monde musulman et de la Méditerranée* 73/74 (1994): 57–74, citation on 59.

Pierre Rosanvallon, it sought to govern and harmonize. Its cult of local memories hence illustrates the inception of a "new 'governmental' relation to culture" in which, following Tony Bennett, cultural artifacts are deployed to "reshap[e] general norms of social behavior." Indeed, such governmental practices as collection, copy, and exhaustive inventory evoke the disciplinary procedures that, following Michel Foucault, constitute the "dark side" of the modern liberal state. The official cult of local memories could be described as an instrument of control and normalization, instilling habits and modes of behavior while, self-consciously and not, "subjugat[ing] the individual" to ubiquitous authority.[108] Unlike the panopticon or the asylum, however, this realm of civil society could not be governed by "habits [and] rules." "Obedience" was not the end-all. The ministry sought to penetrate, steer, and oversee a realm of knowledge production that was at once suspect and indispensable, decrepit and full of new possibilities; a realm that required governmental intervention but whose greatest strengths were, and had to remain, autonomy and spontaneity. An official hence wrote the Minister of Public Instruction in 1873 that "what has made the committee [CTH] so strong and granted the ministry a broad influence over these departmental societies is that at no time have we meddled in their internal affairs." Succeeding regimes did, however, search for more discreet entryways into this realm, for new and not-so-new means of "mak[ing] their presence felt in all places," as Guizot had put it.[109] Be it under the July Monarchy or the Second Empire, we thus uncover the same desire to make one's presence felt rather than seen, to avoid imposition and the appearance of imposition.

And yet, the portrait I have drawn so far remains partial. Missing is the uneasy interplay between, on the one hand, this state's growing presence and ambitions and, on the other, its striking frailty. Its accomplishments, from its institutional framework to its accumulation of data, are plain. The *Monuments de l'histoire de France* alone yielded thirty-five cartons and forty-six boxes of data on 3,500 localities.[110] Eugène Pelletan nonetheless regretted in 1840 that "due to ministerial vicissitudes, this enterprise

---

108. Bennett takes issues with aspects of Foucault's interpretation, emphasizing the public dimension of governmentality and the ways in which actors consensually though unwittingly participate in their own 'policing.' However, both scholars analyze such cultural phenomena in terms of power and normalization. See Rosanvallon, *Etat en France;* Bennett, *Birth of the Museum,* 6; and Michel Foucault, *Discipline and Punish: The Birth of the Prison,* 2d American ed., trans. Alan Sheridan (New York, 1995), 128–29 and 222.

109. AN F17 3318: Anon., "Notes pour les réunions d'avril 1873," 5 April 1873; and Guizot, report to the Chamber of deputies, 11 September 1830, in *Histoire parlementaire de France: recueil complet des discours prononcés dans les chambres de 1819 à 1848 par M. Guizot,* 5 vols. (Paris, 1863), 1: 64.

110. Fox, "Science," 128; and Bautier, "Le Recueil des Monuments de l'histoire du Tiers-Etat et l'utilisation des matériaux réunis par Augustin Thierry," *Annuaire-Bulletin de la Société de l'histoire de France* (1944): 102–4.

lacked unity, sustained direction." A CTH correspondent from Lille complained that same year that, six months after his appointment, he still awaited an "instruction" or circular from Paris. Two years later, a scientific congress member implored the government to contribute more forcefully to the creation of new provincial learned societies. Echoed an historian from Picardie in 1863: "The Ministry of Public Instruction has not always provided [provincial learned societies] with the support, the opportunities for communication and the publicity that it grants them today." This author identified a pattern of governmental deficiencies that proved more enduring than he cared to admit.[111] Such shortcomings owed much to the central state's poverty. A journalist noted in 1842 that debt payment, operational costs, and military expenses took up 85 percent of the annual budget. The Ministry of Public Instruction suffered disproportionately. Forced to "reduce as much as possible the extraordinary expenses in the budget of historical investigations," the CTH shrunk its print runs and trimmed its lists of periodical recipients. Whenever possible, it sought to print historical documents "without incurring expenses for the state." When the president of the Société archéologique de l'Orléanais inquired in 1866 about the fate of his much-praised archeological inventory, he learned that "mediocre allocations" had postponed its publication.[112]

Equally important were the deficiencies of a bureaucratic structure in which quarrels between ministries and services were commonplace. Because of a "conflict" with the Ministry of Finances, the BTH had to curtail its shipment of periodicals to provincial societies in the 1840s. In 1839, it only authorized the CTH's *Bulletin* after receiving guarantees that "the administration will always have the upper hand" in this venture. Officials and CTH members moreover misplaced letters from provincials, struggled to match specific ventures with budgetary chapters, and took months to evaluate archaeological inventories. Mail could transit for weeks in ministerial offices before reaching the CTH, whose poorly classified archives were dispersed throughout the ministry. The CTH, declared member François Génin in 1845, is "the faithful image of chaos"—a chaos and an excess of administrative demands that, according to one Parisian *littérateur*, weakened the "zeal" of provincial elites.[113] The situation improved somewhat

111. Pelletan, "Troisième lettre,"165; AN F17 2847: Antoine de Contencin to Min. Pub. Instr., 19 January 1840; *CS* 10 (Strasbourg, 1842), 392; and *Annuaire des sociétés savantes de la France et de l'étranger*, 1: 24.

112. *Revue générale de l'impôt* 2 (February 1842): 75–76; Gerbod, "L'action culturelle de l'Etat au XIXe siècle (à travers les divers chapitres du budget général)," *Revue historique* 270, no. 2 (1983): 390; AN F17 3245: Anon. memoranda, 10 July 1857 and n.d. [1860?]; and AN F17 3309: Min. Pub. Instr. to President Société archéologique de l'Orléanais, 27 April 1866 (minute).

113. F17 3029: Marginal annotation in letter from Secretary Académie des Jeux Floraux to Min. Pub. Instrc., 20 June 1846; AN F17 13268: Charles de Montalembert, intervention before

under the Second Empire, but not communication lapses between Parisian offices and local officials, whose political acumen and familiarity with local societies often went to waste.[114] Although a subprefect belonged to the new Société d'études d'Avallon, the BTH was startled to discover its existence in 1860. Seven months later, the rector of Besançon chastised the ministry for tardily replying to a local professor: "Such negligence has helped to throw [him] into the opposition."[115]

All of this uncovers a more precarious intellectual state than Rosanvallon's or Foucault's narratives allow.[116] It also highlights a final correlation between metropolitan France and the colonial realm. In France as in the colonies, officials put "intelligence" and historical practices to new uses without fully exploiting the political potential of their scientific ventures. Like the British administrators of India, these officials failed to fully grasp this potential—or else doubted the efficacy of their own ventures. In France as in the colonies, moreover, this intellectual state rested on what anthropologist Nicholas Dirks has called "the ill-coordinated nature of power," an unwieldy mix of actors and designs.[117] In the late 1850s, officials thus voiced different views of amateurish provincials. Setting high scientific standards, some BTH officials rebuffed such associations as the new Conférence littéraire de Douai, however admirable their "social situation" and "political sentiments." Others were more lenient. "Mr. de Gourgue [a CTH correspondent] holds a name that honors the *pays*'s history," reported the prefect of Dordogne. "I do not recall that he has zealously undertaken historical investigations, but his support could nonetheless be useful."[118] By evoking a uniform governmental project, we thus run the risk of effacing this intellectual state's complexity. Likewise, the Guizot who emerges from this chapter was neither an earnest philosopher-king nor a master political strategist,

---

the CHAM, 22 May 1839; AN F17 3317: President Société dunkerquoise to Min. Pub. Instr., 18 July 1860; Francois Génin, *Variations du langage*, xx–xxi; *Panthéon de la jeune France* 12 (15 February 1842): 253; and Yvonne Knibiehler, *Naissance des sciences*, 291.

114. On this theme, see Karl Appuhn, "Inventing Nature: Forest, Forestry, and State Power in Renaissance Venise," *The Journal of Modern History* 72, no. 4 (December 2000): 888.

115. AN F17 3315: Marginal annotation in letter from President Société des sciences historiques et naturelles de l'Yonne to Min. Pub. Instrc., 4 March 1860; and AN F17 3300: Rector Besançon to Min. Pub. Instrc., 13 October 1860.

116. But it dovetails with, for instance, Ruth Harris's portrayal of the Second Empire: see her *Lourdes*, 134. See also Vincent Wright, *Le Conseil d'Etat sous le Second Empire* (Paris, 1972).

117. Dirks, foreword to Cohn, *Colonialism*, xvi–xvii. On the material difficulties of the Algerian *Exploration*, see Nordman, "L'exploration scientifique de l'Algérie: le terrain et le texte," in Bourguet, *Invention scientifique*, 76–81.

118. Viscount Alexis de Gourgue(s) [1805–85]: prominent aristocrat, elected to the *Conseil général* in 1849, member of the Institut des provinces. See ADN 1 T 246/2: Min. Pub. Instr. to prefect Nord, 2 March 1859; and AN F17 2811: Prefect Dordogne to Min. Pub. Instr, 3 December 1855.

but a figure who sought to reconcile doctrinal convictions and scientific ambitions with instrumental imperatives. Other officials and elites found themselves in the same situation. Their efforts and struggles to fulfill these diverse agendas were also, as we will now see, efforts and struggles to delineate the cultural and political contours of postrevolutionary France.

PART III: *Le Mal du Pays*

FIVE

Town, Nation, or Humanity?

> One cannot reprove love of the *pays* when it stops short of idolatry, of contempt for all other places.
>
> *Mémoires de la Société des lettres,*
> *sciences et arts de l'Aveyron* (1846–47)

AMBRAI'S HISTORICAL PAGEANTRY reached an apex in the mid-1830s. In February came the Société de bienfaisance's Renaissance entry, a reconstituted ceremony featuring Emperor Charles V or French King Francis I (see figure 17). In August followed the municipality's *marche historique,* a vast tableau of local history staged during the *fête communale.* Both pageants told different stories, but shared an identical goal: to inspire widespread affection for the *pays* and its memories. This unanimity was shattered in 1838, when Cambrai's mayor and other liberals turned the *marche historique* into an unprecedented "fête of intelligence." "This year's program differs completely from all others," explained Fidèle Delcroix, the tax collector who headed the organizing committee. "It is the development of a new idea that suits the progress of the human mind." The opening banner—"Utility! Progress!"—set the tone. The fête of intelligence would mine world history for those "discoveries and institutions that proved useful to humanity," from Egyptian agriculture to steam engines. The pageant's traditional "hymn to Flanders" gave way to a deistic paean to law, freedom, and natural reason. Thanks to political advances and "modern discoveries," explained Delcroix, "the great human family tends increasingly to know itself." His pageant would accordingly depict universal reason and the "fusion of the peoples" (see figure 18).[1]

Delcroix and his colleagues found inspiration eighteen miles to the northeast, in Valenciennes. Two decades earlier, a group of young liberals had formed a festive association they named Société des Incas. With "Union, Pleasure, Humanity" as their motto, their pageants were dazzling

---

1. [Fidèle Delcroix], *Programme de la marche triomphale des chars, cavalcades, etc. à la fête communale de Cambrai. 15 et 17 août 1838* (Cambrai, 1838).

FIGURE 17. The Société de bienfaisance de Cambrai's 1837 pageant, representing Francis I's entry into Cambrai in 1529 (illustration from *Le Musée des familles*, 1838). Notice the nineteenth-century spectators toward the right. Courtesy of the Bibliothèque Royale de Belgique (Brussels).

nocturnal ensembles, involving Peruvian dignitaries as well as Polish warriors, African tribesmen, Scottish clan heads, and motley other authentic and imaginary figures. By 1838, the *marche des Incas* included 11 floats, 73 groups or figures, 300 torch-carrying "savages," 225 musicians, and 100 donation collectors in Mexican attire. In 1840, it featured a ceremony set in sixteenth-century Peru. Responding to European aggression, the Inca monarch convoked all nations to a "universal congress," complete with Sacred Fire and sacrificed lamb. Gathered around the throne of the Sun, representatives of the five continents sealed "the reconciliation of the great human family and . . . the holy pact of universal peace" (see figure 19).[2]

The *marches des Incas* and fête of intelligence shared much, on ideological grounds, with the Nord's other historical pageants. Delcroix was after all a close friend of André Le Glay, architect of Cambrai's earlier *marches*

2. I will henceforth use italics to distinguish these festive Incas from the peoples they impersonated. See BNF 8 Li31 256: "Marche des Incas," pamphlet describing the pageant of 25 March 1838; and "Fête triomphale des Incas. Programme," supplement to *L'Echo de la frontière*, 19 March 1840.

FIGURE 18. "Américain," "Egyptien," and "Ancien Grec" in *Programme de la marche triomphale des chars, cavalcades, etc. à la fête communale de Cambrai. 15 et 17 août 1838* (Cambrai, 1838). Three participants in the 1838 fête of intelligence, as depicted in the pageant's official program. "Our design, immense and varied in its unity, puts all eras and places at our disposal," proclaimed the organizers. The program accordingly introduced spectators, not to their own history, but to the various peoples they would encounter in the city's streets. Images depicted individuals rather than groups—an apt metaphor for a fête that portrayed achievement before territorial community. Courtesy of the Médiathèque Municipale de Cambrai, service d'histoire locale.

historiques.[3] In all instances, elites tightly orchestrated festivities whose rank-and-file had diverse social backgrounds. The topos of the Incas moreover had ancient paternalistic implications in French literary and historical discourse. Theirs was a communalist kingdom, stratified into three "perfectly distinct" ranks but free of private property and divergent opinions. Subjects received a plot of land from the state (to be returned on their death) and tilled "with great joy" the common fields whose produce went to the Inca dynasty, the cult of the Sun, and the needy. The Sun was "the father of these Kings" and the kings, in turn, were charitable protectors. Diderot's *Encyclopédie* described the Inca monarchy as "an immense family, in which the monarch was the father." The outcome was "mutual concord," a community that, until the European conquest, moved "in unison" and assembled for all-inclusive, community-building festivals.[4] Such local harmony, as we have seen, also underlay the *marches historiques.*

3. André Le Glay, *Fidèle Delcroix, sa vie et ses ouvrages* (Cambrai, 1844).

4. Garcilaso de la Vega, *Histoire des Yncas, rois du Pérou*, trans. J. Baudoin (Amsterdam, 1704), 85–87 and 407–13; Françoise de Graffigny, *Lettres d'une Péruvienne*, new ed., 2 vols. (Paris, 1752 [1747]), 1:29; Saint-Lambert, "Honneur," in Diderot and d'Alembert, *Encyclopédie*, 8:288; Alphonse de Beauchamp, *Histoire de la conquête et des révolutions du Pérou*, 2 vols. (Paris, 1808), 1: 33; Catherine-Joseph Girard de Propiac, *Beautés de l'histoire du Pérou* (Paris, 1824), 25; and Henri Lebrun, *Conquête du Pérou et histoire de Pizarre* (Tours, 1840), 13 and 17–18. See also

FIGURE 19. The *Société des Incas*' nocturnal pageant, in Jean-Baptiste Foucart, *Souvenirs de la terre natale* (Valenciennes, 1837). Set in Valenciennes's central square, this engraving illustrated a poem on the *Incas* by lawyer and pageant organizer Jean-Baptiste Foucart: "What almighty power has united Africa and Europe and Asia and the young America under the same flag?" The *marche des Incas* reaches its apex: a harmonious encounter of peoples and epochs under the benevolent gaze of the Inca monarch. At the bottom of the picture, donation collectors fraternize with well-to-do spectators. At once spontaneous and structured, this pageant, too, would yield social harmony. Courtesy of the Bibliothèque Municipale de Valenciennes.

Yet much clearly distinguished their respective rhetorics. Analytical precision thus requires that we distinguish between two kinds of historical pageants, each of which appealed to distinct geographical and cultural mindsets by the mid-1830s. One (the localist pageant) was concerned with local history and territorial affiliation; the other (the universalist pageant) revolved around progress and human solidarity. One turned inward and to its past, the other beyond the borders of its *pays*—or even of France and Europe—to worldwide fraternity and the future. One celebrated particu-

Jean Ehrard, "Les Lumières et la fête," *Annales historiques de la Révolution française* 47, no. 221 (July–September 1975): 372.

larity and difference, the other universality and commonality. Both affirmed social harmony and territorial identity in their practices: namely, collective projects that mobilized all social classes toward charitable ends. But while one affirmed this identity in its rhetoric as well, the other initially shunned this explicit identification. Behind this festive rift—to which we will return—we uncover a broader difficulty to delineate and assess the value of what I have called local difference. Benign and comforting as they were, local memories also proved problematic in their memorial dimension, exclusiveness, and origins in a specific land. What was, after all, the place of intrinsically local identifications in a modern nation-state?

LOCAL MEMORIES AND NATIONAL UNITY

Local memories were problematic, first and most predictably, as an excessive memorial investment in the locality. In this context, local difference entailed an all-encompassing attachment to a specific territory and its memories, threatening to redirect affection and loyalty away from the nation-state. By the mid nineteenth century, most French elites identified strongly, of course, with France. Interest in local memories—or other aspects of local life—could thus reflect confidence in the nation's strong foundations. "At a time when a general fusion brings all Frenchmen together," declared deputy Marie-Philippe-Aimé de Golbéry in 1838, "it is good that our provinces . . . look back to their antique individuality." But such statements remained infrequent until midcentury. In 1843, the Orléanist *Encyclopédie des gens du monde* expressed the hope that individuals with "relatively elevated mind[s]" would nowadays look beyond their native and even beloved commune. "Invincible attachment to the native land" betrayed the "ailment" of nostalgia, a neurotic, atavistic *"mal du pays."*[5] More significantly, many elites still deemed this national unity fragile. Despite its ancient roots, France had only vanquished its "thousand small nationalities" during the French Revolution. Pierre-René Auguis, a reformist liberal deputy, thus deemed the cult of local memories premature:

> This [provincial] asks [the CTH] to publish the chronicle of his department or province; this other one, retreating within narrower boundaries, wants us to publish the history of his arrondissement; yet another asks for the history of his canton, and, if we continue in this direction, everyone will want to

5. Parliamentary session of 6 June 1838, in J. Madival and E. Laurent, eds., *Archives parlementaires*, 121: 89–90; and S., "Pays," and L. S., "Incas," in *Encyclopédie des gens du monde*, 19:324 and 14:558. See also Philippe Martel, "Historiens du début du XIXe siècle," 62.

have the history of the commune to which he has the honor of belonging. All of this may happen one day; but I do not think the time has come.[6]

The antitaxation riots that mobilized individuals from diverse social stations in the summer of 1841 reinforced such apprehensions. This "revolt of the commune" displayed the depth of exclusionary local attachments, concluded Amiens's *Glaneur* and the *Courrier de la Sarthe*. "Half-a-century has not sufficed to carry out in the minds the revolution that the Constitutional Assembly undertook in the political arena." Paris's Orléanist *Journal des débats* likewise feared for the recent "unity of France."[7] While this unity remained secure that summer, the reaction of this liberal press reveals persisting qualms about local particularism in a young nation-state.

Within the field of local memories, these qualms underlay a series of disputes regarding the proper place of local difference in the nation. The most revealing one pitted fellow republicans Jules Michelet and Aristide Guilbert. Both men gravitated toward local history: Guilbert by editing the *Histoire des villes de France*, Michelet by relying on local historians for his *Histoire de France*. Traveling through France in 1831, Michelet wrote in his diary that, in Angers, concrete, local studies alone would enable "the Anjou [to] rise again." In Dijon, however, he uncovered "a spirit of the locality, *parlementaire* pride." Concern with this "spirit" suffused his 1833 *Tableau de la France*, the counter-clockwise tour of France he based on this journey. The *Tableau* introduced a succession of distinct provincial "geniuses," each of which possessed a distinctive character that it willingly contributed to French identity while remaining subordinate to Paris, the "center [that] knows itself and knows all the rest." Michelet, who began and ended the *Tableau* in the capital, believed that national unification entailed the elimination of "all divergent Frances," the "annihilation of [a] local spirit" that he equated with "internal dissidence." In the center—byproduct of an organic, natural centralization—the provinces recognized themselves "in a superior form."[8] His *History of France* likewise encountered "France's ancient diversity," but as a weakening force, ceding ground before national unity.[9] Guilbert denounced such views in 1848, arguing that the provinces played a central role in the formation of modern

6. Charles Cassou, "Pau," in Aristide Guilbert, ed., *Histoire des villes*, 1: 460; and Parliamentary session of 6 June 1838, in *Archives parlementaires*, 121: 92–93.

7. *Le Glaneur*, 31 July and 7 August 1841; *Le Courrier de la Sarthe*, [July?] 1841, quoted in Félix Ponteil, "Le ministre des finances Georges Humann et les émeutes antifiscales en 1841," *Revue historique* 179 (1937): 352; and *Le Journal des débats*, 21 July 1841.

8. Jules Michelet, *Journal, tome 1 (1828–1848)*, ed. Paul Viallaneix, 4th ed. (Paris, 1959), 77 and 99; idem, *Tableau de la France* (Brussels, 1995 [1833]), 133–35; and idem, *Le peuple*, 217. See also Paule Petitier, *Géographie de Michelet*, 59; and Roland Barthes, *Michelet par lui-même* (Paris, 1954 and 1988), 22.

9. Michelet, *Histoire de France* [1833], in his *Oeuvres complètes*, ed. Viallaneix, 21 vols. (Paris, 1971–82), 4:614.

France. "It is not Paris that absorbs the provinces," he explained, openly disagreeing with Michelet. "It is rather the provinces that appropriate Paris [and] renew its mind through repeated immigrations." The point of contention was not the putative autonomy of local territories and memories, but their conceptual boundaries.[10]

Other disputes revolved around a language of local identification that surfaced above all within traditionalist circles, typically in peripheral regions. Toulouse's *Gazette du Languedoc* predicated "Southern nationality" on "love of the *pays*" in 1841; pageant organizers from Cambrai likewise spoke of local "nationality" and "Flemish independence."[11] Rare as they were, such claims led other elites to insist that while "love of one's native hometown is a beautiful thing, . . . love of the *patrie* is even more beautiful." Cambrai's reformist liberals took aim at the town's Société de bienfaisance in 1839. How could it represent the 1540 entry into Cambrai of Charles V, this "irreconcilable enemy of France"? And why stage Francis I's 1529 entry, a dark moment for a king who was forced to confirm Spanish sovereignty over Flanders, Artois, and Tournaisis? This entry was a "local memory," granted, but "from the truly French, the truly national vantage point," it was an unfortunate choice.[12] In 1860, members of Châlons-sur-Marne's leading learned society praised the Comité flamand's erudition, but regretted its undue "veneration for the old debris of patois in each *contrée*."[13]

This tension explains why some elites sought to attenuate their own affection for local memories. In 1833, for instance, *littérateur* François Ragon began each of his historical *Précis* on ancient provinces by celebrating "this great French family, henceforth, we hope, indivisible." Three decades later, a contributor to the Parisian *Gazette littéraire, artistique et scientifique* distinguished the latter's calls for decentralization and "rapprochement" from the "isolation" of localism. The "idea of fracturing what is united, of localizing literature, of reconstituting as different forms Provencal art, Breton art, Flemish art," he assured readers, was not the *Gazette's* intention.[14] Such semantic acrobatics mirrored the apologetic rhetoric of elites who either downplayed their devotion to local dif-

10. Guilbert, Introduction to *Histoire des villes*, 1: ix–x. Guilbert had nonetheless asked Michelet in 1844 to "resurrect" a French city—any one he wished—in his collection. Michelet refused for personal reasons. See Michelet, *Correspondance générale*, ed. Louis Le Guillou, 11 vols. (Paris, 1994–2000), 4:339–40.

11. *La Gazette du Languedoc*, 1 March and 10 May 1841; and Delloye 38/100: Eugène Bouly, "Littérature locale. Programme de la fête communale. 15 août 1838" (n.p., 1838), 2.

12. *La Gazette littéraire, artistique et scientifique* 31 (3 December 1864): 307; *La Feuille de Cambrai*, 12 March 1839; and Delloye 39/13 and 14: Clippings from *La Feuille de Cambrai*, n.d. (March 1839).

13. *Mémoires de la Société d'agriculture, commerce, sciences et arts du département de la Marne* (1860): 39.

14. François Ragon, *Précis de l'histoire de Bourgogne et de Franche-Comté* (Paris, 1833), 3; and *La Gazette littéraire, artistique et scientifique* 24–25 (1 October 1864): 236 and 238.

ference or carefully situated their local memories within the nation. In 1833, the editor of the *Revue de Rouen* assured his readers that, despite his recent praise for Rouen's arts, commerce, and industry, "national glory is the first to deserve our wishes." Under the Second Republic, Cambrai's pageant organizers also emphasized that while their "love of the *pays*" celebrated a "practically sovereign old city," it never threatened national unity.[15]

The problem confronting such elites was not so much whether self-identifications as French and, say, Cambrésien or Flemish were inherently compatible or not. Nearly all concurred that their interest in the local past had no "pretensions to nationality." The problem, rather, was to integrate local and national identifications—and draw the benefits of both—without resorting to a threatening local vocabulary. These citizens inserted enough national referents in, for instance, their pageants (flags, inscriptions such as "Beloved France") to anchor their locality within the nation. They nonetheless struggled to, as they put it, "individualize" the local without "particularizing" it.[16] They struggled, in other words, to situate their locality within the nation while acknowledging its distinctiveness and thereby legitimating the connection with monuments, memories, and landscape that undergirded their authority and sense of self. This tension ultimately transcends the historical specificity of any town, *pays*, or province. It points toward spatial and political categories—diversity, difference, particularity—that, to paraphrase Claude Lévi-Strauss, were both good and bad to think with at this time.

THE TYRANNY OF LOCAL INTERESTS

Indeed, local difference also impeded the cult of local memories as abstract proximity: a concern with a local territory and its interests that might conflict with the public good. From this perspective, local memories could entail territorial self-sufficiency, "ideas of exclusion" that extolled a small domain alone, an egoism and particularism that could lapse into social fragmentation. "The local spirit shrinks and narrows the ideas," declared the editors of the *Revue des départemens de France* in 1828. In Douai, the Société d'agriculture, des sciences et des arts claimed to embrace "broad and useful ideas, no longer confined to narrow and local applications," while the newspaper *L'Indépendent* castigated local residents who followed the motto, "Douai and nothing but Douai." If the Institut

15. *Revue de Rouen* 1 (10 January–10 June 1833): 7; and *La Gazette de Cambrai*, 28 July and 20 August 1851.

16. These were the terms of a debate between two members of the Commission historique du Nord, regarding the relationship between Lille's patois and the French language. See *BCN* 4 (1851–53): 353–55; and Alcibiade Wilbert, *Notice sur l'origine, la constitution et les travaux de la Société d'émulation de Cambrai* (Cambrai, 1847), 43.

des provinces called for a general council of learned societies in 1847, it was to counter two perils: the yoke of Paris and the localism of provincial elites, "so invariably attached to their land."[17] A term captured this sentiment: the *esprit de clocher* ("spirit of the belfry," or parochialism). Ubiquitous within this discursive field, it carried positive connotations (as agent of local unification or antidote to rural depopulation) and, far more commonly, negative ones. As early as 1795, Constantin-François Volney had encouraged secondary schools to teach the *pays*'s history (easy to grasp and relevant to one's daily life)—but as the preamble to a comparative study. To restrict oneself to "one's *clocher*," to know only one's community yielded egoism and intolerance.[18] Decades later, some Parisian *littérateurs* praised provincial elites while lamenting their "ostracism and love of the *clocher*," their excessive "love of the city, of the province." *L'Illustration* reported on Valenciennes's 1851 pageants, but assured its readers that, as a "universal newspaper," it was "not devoted to a single interest, but served them all." Such sentiments were not limited to Paris. Although *Martin de Cambrai* concerned itself with local affairs, literature, and memories, its editor likewise professed to shun "pure literature *de clocher*" in 1862. The "affections" that the commune aroused become reprehensible, explained Valenciennes lawyer Louis Legrand at century's end, when "they give birth to what has been called *patriotisme de clocher*, . . . a narrow particularism that . . . restrict[s] the intellect and the horizon."[19]

Legrand accordingly vowed to eschew provincial egoism and "local interests" that could damage the public good.[20] In this respect, local difference evoked the era of privilege and social inequality that had preceded the French Revolution. Many liberals and republicans endorsed Condorcet's view of "particular patriotism" as a danger to "national patriotism" and "the public spirit." "Particular," in this sense, denoted both local and corporate sentiments. In 1834, the *Revue de Rouen* amalgamated the "spirit of locality" and the "spirit of coterie" into a common obstacle to provincial "regeneration." Eight years later, republican *littérateur* Auguste Billiard—a contributor to Guilbert's *Histoire des villes de France*—likewise condemned indivisible "interests of particular association and locality."[21]

17. Prospectus for *Revue des départemens de la France* (September 1828): 3; *MSD*, 1st ser., 6 (1835–36): 8; *L'Indépendant*, 25 August 1848; and AN F17 3026: Charles Richelet to Narcisse de Salvandy, 10 April 1847.

18. Constantin-François Volney, *Leçons d'histoire prononcées à l'Ecole normale* (Year III [1795]), repr. in Volney, *Oeuvres*, 3 vols., ed. Anne and Henry Deneys (Paris, 1989), 1:566–67, quotation on 566.

19. *La Célébrité* (27 August 1864): 249; *L'Illustration* 17, no. 428 (8 mai 1851): 294; *Martin de Cambrai*, 27 August 1862; and Louis Legrand, *L'idée de patrie* (Paris, 1897), 260 and 262 (I have inverted the order of this quotation).

20. Legrand, *De la division du département du Nord et de la création d'un département de l'Escaut (Avesnes, Cambrai, Valenciennes)* (Valenciennes, 1870), 8.

21. Marquis de Condorcet, "Essai sur la constitution et les fonctions des assemblées provinciales," in *Oeuvres de Condorcet*, ed. A. Condorcet O'Connor and François Arago, 12 vols. (Paris,

Some contemporaries furthermore denounced the literary dominion of "local influences" who stifled the exchange of ideas and prevented "independent" authors from flourishing.[22] Once again, the challenge for provincial elites was to cultivate local memories while avoiding "the spirit of egoism." Some provincials accordingly exonerated themselves in advance. Inaugurating Valenciennes's monument to Jean Froissart in 1856, the deputy mayor declared that, in celebrating this local son, "we are not following, rest assured, a purely local, a purely egoistic sentiment." Instead, they were undertaking a work of broad social utility.[23]

Similar misgivings surfaced in official circles—a theme I develop in greater depth in the next chapter. The *Journal officiel de l'instruction publique,* for one, contrasted a new regime that embraced publicity (the July Monarchy) with the obfuscation of its predecessors, but complained that, "out of carelessness or design," the country's thousands of communes were hoarding information on their resources and revenue.[24] Local knowledge, be it administrative or historical, had to be wrenched from the hands of provincials who stored it in secret places. Such accusations echoed seventeenth- and eighteenth-century recriminations against monasteries that selfishly concealed knowledge or against an unaccountable "bureaucracy," hidden from public view.[25] Piercing open local enclosures nonetheless acquired a new urgency as the pathway toward cumulative knowledge and a unified social body. "No more egotistical enterprises," declared the *Revue des sociétés savantes* in 1848. "No more hidden advances, no more personal discoveries."[26]

PLACE, WILL, AND HUMAN CIVILIZATION

Whether they evoked memorial attachment or devotion to particular interests, local memories have so far proven problematic as inherently *local* entities. On a third and final plane, the problem was broader yet: the shape and pertinence of territorial identity—be it local or national—in a modern era. The internal debates and equivocation that suffused the field

---

1847–49), 8:275; *Revue de Rouen* 3, no. 2 (10 July–10 December 1834): 179; and Auguste Billiard, "Canton" in Eugène Duclerc and Laurent-Antoine Pagnerre, eds., *Dictionnaire politique,* 184.

22. Prospectus for *Presse départementale* (Paris, May 1830), n.p.; and AN F17 3034: Proceedings of the *Société dunkerquoise,* 7 January 1855.

23. *RAN 8,* no. 3 (September 1856): 109.

24. *Journal officiel de l'instruction publique,* 7 March 1833.

25. Robert Morrissey, *L'empereur à la barbe fleurie: Charlemagne dans la mythologie et l'histoire de France* (Paris, 1997), 227; Condorcet, *Esquisse d'un tableau historique des progrès de l'esprit humain* (Paris, 1988 [1795]), notably 225 and 255; and Keith Michael Baker, "Science and Politics at the End of the Old Regime," in his *Inventing the French Revolution,* 161–62.

26. "General facts, . . . general principles, and . . . general interests" deserve greater attention, wrote Henri de Saint-Simon, than "particular facts, . . . secondary principles and . . . private interests." See his *Le nouveau christianisme* (Paris, 1825), 181; and *RSS* 1 (January 1848): 8–9.

of local memories display two intertwined tensions about self-definition in postrevolutionary France. The first pitted conflicting models of territorial identity—one rooted in will, the other in a historical sense of place—against one another. The second saw a universalist paradigm challenge territorial identity per se, whether will- or place-based.

TERRITORIAL IDENTITY   UNIVERSALISM
Patrie, Pays   Reason, Humanity

  / \

Voluntarist Model Organic Model
(will, consent, law) (sentiment, place)

In 1842, the republican *Dictionnaire politique* distinguished between two reigning definitions of the *patrie* in France. While both revolved around a territory (alternatively called *patrie* or *pays*), one "tells us that the *Patrie* is the land [*le sol*]" whereas the other claims that "the *Patrie* is the law." At issue was membership in a territorial community and, more precisely, the proper weight therein of "love of the native land [*du sol natal*]."[27] On the one hand, we find an organic, place-based model that suffused the field of local memories and appealed chiefly to traditionalists and conservative liberals. Following this model, individuals derived their identity from the geographical and historical community that, due to birth or sometimes residence, won their affection. A contributor to the *Revue de Rouen* captured this model best while explaining why, of all the *pays* in France, he preferred his own. "People have often asked what [the] *patrie* means . . . What is it, then?" he asked in this 1833 article. It sprang from "these mountain or coastal breezes, . . . these edifices, pride of one's town, these old churches, these dilapidated monasteries, whose every stone holds, engraved, the *pays*'s history" and awakened its memories. "Considered from the perspective of the land," explained a member of the Société royale académique de Savoie in 1837, "the *patrie* is . . . a painting of the soul, . . . alive with memories."[28] Local historical, linguistic, and natural circumstances shaped the social world. Traditions, ancestors and *illustrations*, cultural artifacts, the landscape and urban architecture: all of this created distinctive local differences and what Le Glay called "communit[ies] of interests and above all . . . of sentiments." They shaped the individual prior to all social or political interaction.[29]

27. Bernard Horéau, "Patrie," in Duclerc and Pagnerre, *Dictionnaire politique*, 693.
28. *Revue de Rouen* 1 (10 January–10 June 1833): 7–9; and *Mémoires de la Société royale académique de Savoie* 8 (1837): 297 and 300.
29. Georges Gusdorf, *Les sciences humaines et la pensée occidentale*, vol. 9: *Fondements du savoir romantique* (Paris, 1982), 402; and *Procès-verbal de la séance générale du 23 février 1842 de l'Association lilloise*, 7.

Proponents of a will-based model of identity (most of them republican, some liberal) questioned this exclusive "love for those places we have known." Granted, "we love the land of the *Patrie*," continued the *Dictionnaire politique*, but such love had its limitations. Of greater import was "the communion, the fraternity, the solidarity of all individuals," a "metaphysical unity" that hinged on "the will of the masses." Without necessarily effacing geography and history, this voluntarist model substituted free choice, law, and "love of the *patrie*" for the perceived determinism of place and past. "It is no longer the territory that is the *patrie*," explained the *Encyclopédie des gens du monde* in 1843, but "all those who think and feel as we do."[30] Michelet could not have said it better. He linked the organicism above to Cousin's "fatalism," the conviction that circumstances or an underlying plan, rather than human agents, determined the course of history. "The local spirit has vanished every day," Michelet famously declared. "The influence of the land, of climate, of race has yielded to social and political action. The fatefulness of places has been vanquished."[31]

This tension between organic and voluntarist models underlay the field of local memories. While the voluntarist model led some actors to reject local difference, it typically complicated the task of individuals who, for diverse reasons, resolved to investigate the local past. Consider BTH official Désiré Nisard, who, under the July Monarchy, wrote about the history of Nîmes, urged Guizot to launch a vast series of urban monographs, but also denounced romantic "local color" and excessive attachment to one's place of birth. Northern European literature is "not only more individual, but also more local" than its French counterpart, he explained in his 1844 *Histoire de la littérature française*. Northern Europeans "prefer . . . the *pays* to everything, and to the *pays* itself the place of birth." In France, on the other hand, "we do not love the *patrie* with this jealous love." France rejects "this narrow patriotism, born from the body's dependence upon the material *patrie*, . . . [that] restricts one's thoughts to the valley in which one is born." In France, the *patrie* is not exclusively "individual or local," Nisard continued. One loves it as the "dwelling place of reason, . . . the best *patrie* for man in general."[32] The cult of local memories promised much, but required vigilance before an exclusive attachment to the *pays*, be it local or national.

30. Horéau, "Patrie," 693; and Chevalier Artaud, "Patrie," *Encyclopédie des gens du monde*, 19:293–94.

31. Michelet, *Tableau de la France*, 139–40; idem, *Journal*, 1:101; and Viallaneix, *Michelet, les travaux et les jours, 1798–1874* (Paris, 1998), 121. This opposition has ancient roots in Western civilization. Patrick J. Geary identifies two "models of peoplehood" in Roman antiquity, one "based on descent, custom, and territory," the other on "law and adhesion." See his *The Myths of Nations: The Medieval Origins of Europe* (Princeton, N.J., 2002), 55.

32. Désiré Nisard, *Nîmes* (Paris, 1835); idem, *Histoire de la littérature française*, 1:21–25; and idem, *Souvenirs de voyages* (Paris, 1855), 12.

Nisard moreover endorsed the republican conception of the French *patrie* as—per Michelet—a "necessary initiation to the universal *patrie*." The better one understood the genius of the French *patrie*, the better one "work[ed] towards the harmony of the globe." Yet such arguments rang hollow for some contemporaries—liberals whose universalist view of human nature tolerated neither will- nor place-based models of territorial identity. For such individuals, identity stemmed, not from membership in a cultural and political community, but from the universal reason and benevolence that characterized humanity.[33] Equality and concord—rather than territorial difference and artificial borderlines—defined the modern era.

This "planetary utopia," as Armand Matellart fittingly calls it, had early antecedents, including the prelate Fénelon, who declared in 1715 that "one owes infinitely more to the human species, that is the *grande patrie*, than to the particular *patrie* in which one is born."[34] Such views, as we know, spread throughout the eighteenth century. In its entry "Cosmopolitan," Diderot's *Encyclopédie* endorsed the oft-cited claim that "I prefer my family to myself, my *patrie* to my family, and the human species to my *patrie*." (It attributed this statement to Montesquieu, who had proclaimed: "I am a man before being French." Most eighteenth-century dictionaries—and modern-day scholars after them—credit Fénelon.)[35] Like other *philosophes*, Mably likewise deemed "love of humanity" a higher "virtue" than "love of the *patrie*." But such language expanded beyond the reaches of literature and political philosophy. "Humankind forms but one family," asserted the *Affiches du Poitou* in 1774. "If the nations were to isolate themselves, the Provinces would soon follow suit, then the families, then the individuals: what becomes of man?"[36] Prevalent within certain Enlightenment circles, this universalism rested on several intertwined convictions and aspirations. First, came a conception of human unity and equality that originated in natural reason and natural right, crossed borders, and led *philosophes* and others to define themselves as cosmopolitan

33. Michelet, *Le peuple*, 219–20; and Sylvie Mesure and Alain Renaut, *Alter ego: les paradoxes de l'identité démocratique* (Paris, 1999), 92–93.

34. Armand Mattelart, *Histoire de l'utopie planétaire: de la cité prophétique à la société globale* (Paris, 1999), 73; and Fénelon, *Dialogues des morts* (1715), in his *Oeuvres*, ed. Jacques Le Brun, 2 vols. (Paris, 1983–97), 1:283 and 329.

35. "Cosmopolitain, ou Cosmopolite," in Diderot and d'Alembert, *Encyclopédie*, 4: 297, quoted in Michel Delon, "Les Lumières aujourd'hui: l'universel et le particulier," *Transactions of the Ninth International Congress on the Enlightenment*, 3 vols. (Oxford, 1996), 1:171; Montesquieu, *Mes pensées*, in his *Oeuvres complètes*, ed. Roger Caillois, 2 vols. (Paris, 1949–51), 1:981; and Henri Duranton, "Humanité," in Rolf Reichardt and Eberhard Schmitt, eds., *Handbuch politisch-sozialer Grundbegriffe in Frankreich 1680–1820*, 20 vols. (Munich, 1985–2000), 19/20:17.

36. Mably, *Entretiens de Phocion* (Amsterdam, 1767), quoted in Marcel Merle, *Pacifisme et internationalisme* (Paris, 1966), 108; and *Affiches du Poitou*, 17 March 1774, quoted in Jean Sgard, "Presse provinciale," 54.

"citizens of the universe." Second was the conviction that a humanitarian equation existed between such unity and universal solidarity and charity. Third was an economic internationalism, the conviction that history was progressing toward free international trade—and, for some, a mercantile Republic. Be it economic or social, commerce led to peace. Fourth was an aspiration to political internationalism, rooted in the belief that the peaceful association of nations—a civil society of nations, as it were— would likewise yield world peace.[37]

While universalism waned—or grew intertwined with patriotism—during the early nineteenth century, it soon resurfaced in diverse locales. In 1842, for instance, the Parisian *Revue de la province et de Paris* praised the president of a provincial learned society for broadening the topic of his annual address: "The more one moves away from the exclusive idea of self, of one's native city, of one's nation, of one's continent, the more one has brothers."[38] Doctrinal factors came into play: liberals harking back self-consciously to these Enlightenment currents; Saint-Simonians reorganizing society according to a scientific rationality and a religious creed that crossed borders and yielded universal beliefs; positivists unearthing social facts that transcended particular nations; socialists seeking solidarity within what Lamennais called "the universal family of humankind."[39] According to some, the disappearance of local and national differences typified the nineteenth century. A spate of technological, commercial, and political innovations—transnational trade and banking, new means of transport and communication (from railroads to telegraphs), the dissemination of political rights—heralded an integrated world economy and "the fraternity of modern peoples." This "immense phenomenon [is] bound to radically alter relations between states."[40] In one of his most popular songs, liberal songwriter Béranger glorified the "alliance of the [European] peoples," peacefully united under the rule of law. In 1839, at the scientific congress of Le Mans, liberal *littérateur* Marc-Antoine Jullien predicted that railroad lines would soon destroy "narrow local biases" by creating an "analogy in mores, customs, laws, and a kind of fusion or identity of sentiments, opinions, aspirations." He added: "No more of this

---

37. Marc Belissa, *Fraternité universelle*, 50–67; Thomas J. Schlereth, *The Cosmopolitan Ideal in Enlightenment Thought: Its Form and Function in the Ideas of Franklin, Hume, and Voltaire, 1694– 1790* (Notre Dame, 1977); and Paul Hazard, "Cosmopolite," in *Mélanges d'histoire littéraire générale et comparée offerts à Fernand Baldensperger*, 2 vols. (Paris, 1930), 1:356.

38. *Revue de la province et de Paris* 4 (October 1842): 66.

39. Mattelart, *Histoire de l'utopie*, 103–196, quotation on 196. See also Théodore Ruyssen, *Les sources doctrinales de l'internationalisme*, 3 vols. (Paris, 1954–61), vol. 3; and Lisa Moses Leff, "Jewish Solidarity in Nineteenth-Century France: The Evolution of a Concept," *The Journal of Modern History* 74, no. 1 (March 2002): 45–49.

40. Artaud, "Patrie," 294; and Saint-Simon, *Du système industriel* (Paris, 1820), 76.

narrow and local patriotism that deems . . . whoever was not born on this specific portion of the land a barbarian."[41]

PERU IN VALENCIENNES

To grasp the uneasy interplay between this "local patriotism" and universalism, we could listen to elites complain, as one did in Provins in 1839, that proponents of a "fusion of peoples" castigated the "patriotism" of local historians as exclusionary and adverse to modern philanthropy. Victor Derode blamed such ideas for a declining interest in the Société dunkerquoise's local history contests. "For some philosophers," he remarked, "patriotism is no longer a virtue . . . [but] an egoistic sentiment."[42] Nothing, however, better illustrates this tension's impact on the field of local memories than the emergence of two distinct historical festivities in the Nord.

Valenciennes's *fêtes des Incas* took place every year or other year between 1825 and 1840 and episodically afterward (1851, 1866, 1880, 1882). By midcentury, elites from Amiens to Bordeaux recognized the Société des Incas as France's "first Society of charitable Fêtes" and a model worth emulating.[43] The *Incas* furthermore encouraged neighboring towns and villages to stage their own universalist pageants, if necessary by lending them costumes and props. The small town of Le Cateau's 1840 "Triumphal March of the Four Parts of the World," depicting the "fraternal concord" between "the peoples of Europe, Asia, Africa, and America," thus expressed "Homage and gratitude to the Société des Incas."[44] Much clearly separated these spectacles from local historical pageants. Subscription lists reveal, for one, that the *Incas*'s donors made smaller contributions and spanned a broader professional gamut—from barbers and pastry cooks to lawyers, rather than elites alone.[45] Whereas conservative liberals and traditionalists dominated historical pageantry, moreover, the leading *Incas* were reformist liberals (along with a few republicans). They embraced Polish and Greek independence and staged their pageant as a

41. BNF Ye 49381: Béranger, "L'alliance des peuples" (Paris, 1832), n.p.; Jean Touchard, *La gloire de Béranger*, 2 vols. (Paris, 1968), 1:222–23; and *CS* 7, 2 vols. (Le Mans, 1839), 1:174–76.

42. Félix Bourquelot, *Histoire de Provins*, 7; and *MSDu* 9 (1864): 21. See also *Actes de l'Académie des sciences, belles-lettres et arts de Bordeaux* 20 (1858): 565.

43. Charles de Pelleport, *Historique des fêtes bordelaises*, 71; and, for instance, AMV 3 II 140: Mayor Amiens to president Société des Incas, 30 April 1857.

44. AMV 3 II 142: President Société de bienfaisance d'Anzin to president Société des Incas, 25 February 1858; and AMD 5 D 39: Poster advertising the *Marche triomphale des quatre parties du Monde*, 26 April 1840.

45. See the subscription lists in *Le Mémorial de la Scarpe*, 11 June 1840; and *L'Echo de la frontière*, 11 December 1850.

FIGURE 20. Publicizing the *Fête des Incas* in Valenciennes—and elsewhere.
L'Illustration, 8 May 1851. Courtesy of the General Research Division, The New
York Public Library, Astor, Lenox, and Tilden Foundations.

secular counterpart to Valenciennes's Corpus Christi procession and cult
of Notre-Dame du Saint-Cordon, profusely mocked by local anticleri-
cals.[46]

Why the Incas? To answer this question, we must situate these fêtes in
their thematic context: a topos of the benevolent Incas that had entered
the European imagination in the sixteenth century. The key figure in its
intellectual genealogy is Garcilaso de la Vega, the Spanish-Peruvian histo-

---

46. A moderate liberal Catholic, Delcroix likewise envisioned a state of law in "a democratic and religious Europe, brought back to faith by the Enlightenment and . . . in the true
name of the Gospels." See Jean-Baptiste Foucart, *Souvenirs de la terre natale* (Valenciennes,
1837), 8; Louis Trénard, "Aux origines," 419; and Delloye 38/102: Delcroix, manuscript notes,
n.d. (1839?), n.p.

FIGURE 21. Participants in the 1866 *Fête des Incas*, in *Fêtes populaires des Incas, 18 et 19 juin 1866. Souvenirs photographiques* (Valenciennes, 1867). On the left, *Inca* president Jean-Baptiste Meurice as Inca monarch Huáscar (1866). Meurice reprised a role he had played in earlier pageants. His pose—but not his aspirations—evokes that of stage actors. On the right, a participant in the float on Persia, Chaldea, Assyria, and Phoenicia. Courtesy of the Bibliothèque Municipale de Valenciennes.

rian whose *Royal Commentaries* (1609) were translated into French in 1633 and then went through six French editions, including one "at the expense of the government" in August 1830. His wistful portrait of the Incan Empire imprinted not only Europe's incipient utopian tradition, but also a stream of French literary, philosophical, and economic works during the following centuries. These ranged from Denis Vairasse d'Allais's *Histoire des Sévérambes* (1677) to Fénelon's *Aventures de Télémaque* (1699), Jean-Philippe Rameau's *Indes galantes* (1735) to Voltaire's *Essai sur les moeurs* (1756), Dom Pernety's *Dissertation sur l'Amérique et les Américains* (1770) to Girard de Propiac's *Beautés de l'histoire du Pérou* (1824).[47] None did more to popularize the Incas in France than *encyclopédiste* Jean-François Marmontel's *Les Incas, ou la destruction de l'Empire du Pérou* (1777). This paean to the precolonial Incas had yielded five translations, at least thirty edi-

47. John Renwick, "Marmontel, *Les Incas* et l'expansion de l'Europe," in Kees Meerhoff and Annie Jourdan, eds., *Mémorable Marmontel 1799–1999* (Amsterdam, 1999), 24–25; and Benjamin Keen, *The Aztec Image in Western Thought* (New Brunswick, 1971), 210–11, 254–55, and 267–68.

tions, wallpaper models, and several stage adaptations by 1850. "Everyone has read the touching history of the destruction of the Incas by Marmontel," declared a Parisian *littérateur* in 1840. Available in Valenciennes's reading rooms, the novel was reissued by the Société des ouvriers typographes du Nord in 1842.[48] In 1801, one Joseph de Rosny published *Le Péruvien à Paris*, a novel on French mores that, like Marmontel's, exalted the Incas's "paternal love." Excluded from Parisian literary coteries, Rosny settled in Valenciennes, where he befriended future members of the Société des Incas. The latter made use of his historical expertise and named their association after Marmontel. Such is the path from Peru and literary motifs to middling subprefectoral seats and festive display.[49]

Valenciennes's young liberals were drawn, not only to the Incas' paternalism and internal harmony, but to their politics and religion as well. Sixteenth-century pamphleteers such as Las Casas and Théodore de Bry had produced an enduring equation between the Incas and a pure and exemplary New World, oppressed by Catholic tyranny. Hierarchical as it was, the Inca kingdom rested on moderate rule and reasonable laws. It was a benevolent regime—an enlightened despotism even. In the eighteenth century, physiocrat François Quesnay praised the Incan monarchy, born "in the purest state of nature," for its economic system, "fair" constitution, and concern with the happiness of its subjects. Voltaire depicted the Incas as standard-bearers of natural religion, this direct encounter with the divine.[50] A century later, French anthropologists traveled to South America

48. L. S., "Incas," 564; *Catalogue par noms d'auteurs des principaux ouvrages en lecture chez J. Giard* (Valenciennes, 1845); *Société de bienfaisance des Incas. Souvenir de la marche qui a eu lieu à Valenciennes les dimanche et mardi 17 & 19 juin . . .* (Valenciennes, 1866), 4; and Jacqueline Lauret, "Une épopée en prose au XVIIe siècle: *Les Incas, ou la destruction de l'empire du Pérou*," in Ehrard, ed., *Jean-François Marmontel (1723–1799)* (Clermont-Ferrand, 1970), 228.

49. Joseph de Rosny, *Le Péruvien à Paris, ouvrage critique, historique et moral, contenant la relation du voyage d'un jeune Indien, fait en France au commencement du dix-neuvième siècle . . .*, 4 vols. (Paris, 1801), quotation on 1:17; Joseph Dubois, "De la région Nord/Pas-de-Calais au Japon: quatre générations d'hommes de lettres du nord de la France," *RN* 73, no. 289 (January–March 1991): 74–77; and Paul Lefrancq, "Les Incas de Marmontel et les Incas de Valenciennes: un roman éponyme d'une société philanthropique (1777–1826)," *102e Congrès des sociétés savantes* (Limoges, 1977), section of modern history, 1:117–34.

50. Having won its independence in 1824, Peru also symbolized resistance to despotism. See Jean David, "Voltaire et les Indiens d'Amérique," *Modern Language Quarterly* 9 (1948): 93–95; Gilbert Chinard, *L'Amérique et le rêve exotique dans la littérature française au XVIIe et au XVIIIe siècle* (Geneva, 1934), 386–89; and François Quesnay, "Analyse du gouvernement des Incas de Pérou," in *Éphémérides du citoyen ou Bibliothèque raisonnée des sciences morales et politiques* (January 1767), repr. in his *Oeuvres économiques et philosophiques, accompagnées des éloges et d'autres travaux biographiques sur Quesnay*, ed. Auguste Oncken (Frankfurt-upon-Main, 1888), 562. I am stressing but one strand—albeit a dominant one—in the Western representation of the Incas. Other thinkers (including Montesquieu, Humboldt, and Gobineau) denounced their superstition, collectivism, and despotic cult of "passive obedience." I thank John Shovlin for pointing me toward Quesnay's text.

to explain how an advanced civilization had emerged in the Andes.[51] The Société des Incas's kinship with Marmontel is still more revealing, for, in his anticlerical hands, the deistic Incas became first and foremost victims of priestly zealotry and "destructive fanaticism." Marmontel's interest in their cult of the sun reflects, according to one scholar, his freemason beliefs. So do the *Incas'* charity, use of symbols, evangelical ethic (operating beyond the confines of organized religion), and rhetoric of tolerance and fraternity.[52] More illuminating yet, the Incas symbolized "the universalization of peoples." Respecting their enemies as "their equals and brothers," they had created a multireligious, multilinguistic, and multi-ethnic empire, wrote playwright Leblanc de Guillet in 1763. The *Encyclopédie* likewise lauded the Incas' "humanity," a term denoting charity as well as universal fraternity. The Incas sought to "draw all nations towards their amiable mores." Their roads and canals prefigured the technological advances of modern "civilization": printing presses and railroads that broke down territorial boundaries. If these French liberals looked to South America, finally, it was also due to Simon Bolívar's efforts to create a confederation of New World nations in the early nineteenth century.[53]

Universalist pageants thus provided a symbolic means of self-definition that, for its sponsors, better suited modernity—this era of "fusion of peoples"—than exclusive recourse to local memories. Such views had detractors, however. In the eighteenth century already, critics had denounced aristocratic and commercial universalism as egoistic or else argued, like Rousseau, that love of the *patrie* alone was a civic virtue.[54] Now, the republican left castigated a "conception of a borderless *patrie*" that turned "love of the *pays* [into] a reprehensible egoism." This "humanitarian dream," added Michelet, "believes it is saving the individual by destroying the citizen, by . . . renouncing the *patrie*." On the far right, Joseph de Maistre denounced the elimination of territorial specificity. Written for all nations, universal and "abstract" constitutions applied to none. Each nation, by

51. Pascal Riviale, *Un siècle d'archéologie française au Pérou (1821–1914)* (Paris, 1996).

52. Valenciennes's lodges numbered several *Inca* members and helped finance their pageants. See Jean-François Marmontel, *Les Incas, ou la destruction du Pérou*, in his *Oeuvres complètes*, 19 vols. (Paris, 1819–20), 8:27 and 35; James M. Kaplan, "The Stockholm manuscript of Marmontel's *Les Incas*," *Studies on Voltaire and the Eighteenth Century* 249 (1987): 366; and Pierre-Yves Beaurepaire, *Franc-maçonnerie et cosmopolitisme au siècle des Lumières* (Paris, 1998). On the Société des Incas: AMV 3 II 2*: Master of the lodge *Saint-Jean* to Jean-Baptiste Meurice, 10 March 1836; and *Indicateur administratif, judiciaire et commercial de la ville de Valenciennes* (1852): 103.

53. David, "Voltaire et les Indiens," 91; Leblanc de Guillet, "Manco-Capac, premier Ynca du Pérou," repr. in Pierre Lepeintre, ed., *Suite du Répertoire du théâtre français . . .* (repr., Geneva, 1970 [1822]), 152; "Législateur," in Diderot and d'Alembert, *Encyclopédie*, 9: 359; and V. M., "Incas," *Dictionnaire politique*, 456.

54. [Delcroix?], *Sur le programme de la fête communale de Cambrai en 1838. Lettre à M.* *** (Cambrai, 1839), 23; and Belissa, *Fraternité universelle*, 52–55.

FIGURE 22. Float representing the discovery of print, in the 1851 *Fête des Incas*. The monument to Jean Froissart is in the backdrop. Source: Arthur Dinaux, *Description des fêtes populaires données à Valenciennes les 11, 12, 13 mai 1851 par la Société des Incas* (Lille, 1856). Courtesy of the Bibliothèque Municipale de Valenciennes.

virtue of its "population, mores, religion, geographical situation, political relations, riches," required its own.[55] In the Nord, universalist pageants came under a barrage from conservative liberals and traditionalists for evacuating, not national, but local sentiments. Critics concurred in the 1830s and 1840s that, by replacing local crusaders with ancient Greeks or Bedouins, Cambrai's fête of intelligence had deprived the historical pageant of its raison d'être: the assertion of local identity. A "procession of the *pays*'s celebrities would have been more appropriate." There was "nothing less local" than this fête, which could "be adapted to all [the] solemnities and all the cities in the world." It was as morally vacuous as the *marche des Incas*, this "jumble of savages and barbarians."[56]

In Cambrai, this tension produced a public debate on the contours of territorial identity. The fête of intelligence's organizers replied to their critics that

> as glorious, as interesting as the history of Cambrai may be, our city will surely not claim to constitute a complete, independent entity. Great many ties bind us to France . . . But many more ties bind us to humanity; we are not only from Cambrai, but also French, but also men.

55. Horéau, "Patrie," 694; Michelet, *Le peuple*, 246; and Joseph de Maistre, *Considérations sur la France* (Brussels, 1988 [1797]), 87.
56. Bouly, "Littérature locale," 1–2; Delloye 38/72 and 110: Clippings from *L'Emancipateur*, n.d. (1838–39); and *Revue cambrésienne* 1 (1835–1836): 165.

Localism, they said, produced "isolation, private interests" as well as "rivalries," that "arise from differences from country to country, nation to nation, province to province." The alternative, then, was to follow Fénelon and "prefer one's family to oneself, one's *patrie* to one's family, humankind to one's *patrie.*"[57] Far from subscribing to an inflexible universalism (tolerating no territorial attachment whatsoever), Fidèle Delcroix and his acolytes sought to integrate universalist aspirations with local identity. As a member of the Société d'émulation de Cambrai, Delcroix had after all helped inventory the Cambrésis's monuments in 1837—a critical enterprise, he said, during "a period of transition such as ours." He also included two floats on the local past in the fête of intelligence: one on medieval communes, the other on Cambrai's first printing press, savings bank, and other modern institutions. The fête thus "celebrate[d] the locality with dignity," explained Delcroix—who nevertheless felt compelled to rebuke "the private interest that causes us to descend from great things to petty [local] ones."[58]

Delcroix thus attempted to lodge local memories within a narrative of utility and universal concord. More than a quest for a much-maligned *juste milieu,* the fête of intelligence constituted a meditation on modern identity by liberals who struggled to conciliate their local roots and authority with ideals that defined one according to humanity rather than birth. They, too, hoped that a stronger sense of place would soothe a society that did not know itself. At the same time, they were sensitive to the implications of a rhetoric that could suggest isolation from humanity or the national will—a rhetoric that they could neither relinquish nor easily incorporate into their conceptual framework. Delcroix's resignation from the fête of intelligence's organizing committee, in 1839, hence reflected a deeper impasse. It also signaled the fête's demise.

The Société des Incas' universalist aspirations proved equally troublesome for some members. Local "historical celebrities" and episodes from the city's past slowly entered the program during the 1830s, revealingg fissures in the founding model. In 1840, the *Incas* staged a localist pageant in the afternoon—valorous local crusaders at the 1098 Battle of Antioch—and their universalist one at night. The latter now opened with a Valenciennes herald alongside Mexican scouts—clear evidence that, as contemporaries noted, the organizers were "making their fête historical and local."[59] By 1851, the increasingly conservative *Incas* were celebrating the nation, the locality, and humanity on successive days. First, a pageant "re-

57. [Delcroix?], *Sur le programme,* 4–6, 12–13, 15, and 23.
58. Idem, *Une promenade dans le Cambrésis* (Valenciennes, 1838), 4.
59. AMV 3 II 2*: Proceedings of the Société des Incas, 11 February 1835; *Mémorial de la Scarpe,* 1 March 1840; and AMD 5 D 41: [Jean-Baptiste?] Wallez, "Rapport fait à la commission administrative des fêtes historiques par son président dans la séance du 1er mai 1841."

FIGURE 23. Float representing the Incas, in the 1851 *Fête des Incas*. While the "Allegorical *marche* of the peoples" resembled previous Inca pageants, Columbus, Pizarro, and other conquistadors now surrounded these "Americans." Universalism had receded to the background. Source: Arthur Dinaux, *Description des fêtes populaires données à Valenciennes les 11, 12, 13 mai 1851 par la Société des Incas* (Lille, 1856). Courtesy of the Bibliothèque Municipale de Valenciennes.

calling the memorable epochs of French history"; second, a ceremony honoring Jean Froissart; third and finally, the "Allegorical *marche* of the peoples led by the genius of civilization toward universal concord." From a celebration of humanity, the latter had become one of French and European civilization, with floats on the origins of Christianity, the French Revolution, and Valenciennes's contribution to the progress of the human mind. The organizers had abrogated the "heterogeneous assemblage of groups that, however dazzling, are not made to be together." The peoples they retained, including Incas and "Negroes," now illustrated the "great discoveries" and colonial encounters of the fifteenth and nineteenth centuries (see figures 23 and 24).[60]

Commercial considerations and France's growing colonial designs certainly contributed to this evolution. They hardly explain, however, the discrepancy between this pageant's title and contents. It appears, rather, that the organizers grew disenchanted with an undiluted universalist credo that ill suited their investments in place and past. They, too, sought to integrate territorial self-definition with "the great family of humanity."

60. AMD 5 D 48: Public notice advertising the "allegorical *marche*" of Valenciennes, 26 March 1851; and AMV 3 II 3*: Henri Caffiaux to Société de Incas, 16? July 1850.

FIGURE 24. The float of local "celebrities"—last of twenty-three in the 1851 *Fête des Incas*—honored Valenciennes's accomplishments. An allegorical representation of the city towered above its "beloved children": knights, historians, artists, writers. In the back, flag-bearers celebrated the city's traditional industries, from lace to porcelain. The implication was clear: "civilization" had not bypassed Valenciennes. Source: Arthur Dinaux, *Description des fêtes populaires données à Valenciennes les 11, 12, 13 mai 1851 par la Société des Incas* (Lille, 1856). Courtesy of the Bibliothèque Municipale de Valenciennes.

Their decision to stage three distinct pageants may thus be seen as an attempt to conciliate these vocabularies—or, perhaps, to compartmentalize them. Either way, their progressive evacuation of universalism is but one indication that, as in Cambrai, this amalgamation proved elusive. What is more, local identification was also problematic in Valenciennes. In 1850, *Inca* president Jean-Baptiste Meurice declared predictably that "love of humanity" had to prevail over "all parochial and even national considerations" in the upcoming pageant. This did not prevent him from extolling "our celebrities from Valenciennes" and the *Incas'* forthcoming homage to "the *patrie*, this France, so great, so noble." The praise that he and other *Incas* thereafter lavished on Cambrai's localist pageant—as depiction of local history alone—further displays the incongruities of this historical spectacle.[61]

The question thus seems inescapable: why, beginning in the 1830s, did two distinct festive languages flourish in Valenciennes and Cambrai,

61. AMV 3 II 3*: Meurice, "Appel aux habitants de Valenciennes," in the proceedings of the Société des Incas, 16 April 1850; and Delloye 40/54: Bouly, "Notice anecdotique sur le programme de la fête de Cambrai composé par Eugène Bouly" (n.d. [1852?]).

neighboring towns with comparable social composition, economic pro-
files, and patterns of growth? We could conjecture that Valenciennes's
weaker religiosity prior to the Third Republic fueled a more ardent anticlerical discourse; or that Cambrai's status as first "emancipated" town in
France led its intellectual elites toward the urban past. No city in the Nord
had invoked its history with greater ardor in the eighteenth century
(though Valenciennes was not far behind).[62] Ultimately, local personalities and political affiliations tell us as much as structural or historical factors. At any rate, these distinctions faded before a shared ambivalence regarding the pertinence of territorial self-representation. Liberals such as
Théodore Jouffroy and Charles de Rémusat purported as early as the mid-
1820s to have integrated the new "spirit of civilization" with local traditions—provided the latter steered clear of exclusive patriotism.[63] Others,
as we have seen, found this reconciliation more arduous. While diverse investments wed them to their *pays*, the nefarious connotations of local difference complicated their public assertions of territorial identity.

ELUSIVE IDENTITIES

The French Revolution constitutes, with respect to local difference as
well, the backdrop of the field of local memories. Some revolutionaries, it
is true, found territorial identity less problematic as a principle than had
some Enlightenment-era philosophes. Be it in the 1790 Fête de la Fédération—with its international themes and national modulation—or their
designs for an unadulterated French language, rooted in a universal
grammar and the laws of nature, revolutionaries such as Henri Grégoire
managed to integrate patriotism and universalism. This synthesis suited
some during the nineteenth century, but not those elites who, like Delcroix, had reservations about territorial self-definition. Paradoxically,
elites from the Nord equated the revolutionary tradition with both the nation and "universal concord." While Cambrai's fête of intelligence reaffirmed "what the great drama of the Revolution has ordained," the city's
traditionalist elites presented their historical pageants as alternatives to
the "saturnalia [of] the insane revolution."[64] From this vantage point, the

---

62. Whereas Valenciennes had embraced Protestantism in the mid sixteenth century, the
archbishopric of Cambrai had been a doctrinal center for the Catholic Reformation. See Trénard, "Aux origines," 404–5; and Philippe Guignet, *Le pouvoir dans la ville*, 38–39 and 76–78.

63. Théodore Jouffroy, "De l'état actuel de l'humanité" [1826], in his *Mélanges
philosophiques*, 6th ed. (Paris, 1886), 99–100; and Jean-Jacques Goblot, *Jeune France libérale*, 342
and 366.

64. *L'Echo de Cambrai*, 28 August 1851; Delcroix, manuscript notes; and *Gazette de Cambrai*,
20 August 1851. To be fair, some eighteenth-century philosophes had likewise perceived affection for humanity and for the *patrie* as complementary: see David A. Bell, *Cult of the Nation*, 45.

split between localist and universalist fêtes revolved around the revolutionary legacy.

The organizers of both types of pageants moreover encountered a local difference that, as an intrinsically local (rather than merely territorial) entity, they could neither conjure away nor fully embrace. This ambivalence, too, evoked the Revolution. The words of Desmoulins or Sieyès against reprehensible local, and corporate, affiliations still resonated half-a-century later. During the Revolution, an older antipathy to private interests had combined with a new ideology of equality and uniformity to denounce all forms of particularism, buttress calls for publicity, and render private efforts and singularity increasingly suspect. Republican unity entailed uniform weights and measures—"free[ing] men from this difference ... that impedes all social transactions"—and the eradication of local affiliations, these obstacles to national unity and the creation of "universal man."[65] Particularistic ceremonies, like the one commemorating Valenciennes's liberation by the Virgin Mary in 1008, gave way before rational and ahistorical fêtes that depicted the fundamental unity of humanity.[66] Yet, the revolutionary yearning for homogeneity encountered a regional diversity of unexpected resilience. Frenchmen spoke different languages, engaged in a variety of rituals and cared deeply for their *pays*. While the Revolution may have made France aware of its preexisting unity, it also produced an enduring contradiction between national unity and a newfound, potentially threatening diversity.[67] Nineteenth-century portrayals of the Revolution—be they liberal, Saint-Simonian, or traditionalist—were in agreement: the latter had "sacrificed provincial individualities ... to the need for unity." Its "universal tendency toward the public spirit ... [had] proscribed what one called the *patriotisme de clocher.*"[68] In its dual yearning for unity and diversity, the cult of local memories thus begs to be situated within revolutionary political culture in its *durée longue*.

It also generated, as I have sought to show, a vibrant inquiry on place and identity. What are the ramifications of a discourse and practices that

65. Sarah Maza, "Luxury, Morality, and Social Change: Why There Was No Middle-Class Consciousness in Prerevolutionary France," *The Journal of Modern History* 69, no. 2 (June 1997): 228; Proceedings of the Convention, 25 September 1792, quoted in Denis Guedj, *La Révolution des savants* (Paris, 1988), 41; Mona Ozouf, "La Révolution française et la perception de l'espace national: fédérations, fédéralisme et stéréotypes régionaux," in her *L'école de la France* (Paris, 1984), 27; and idem, *Fête révolutionnaire*, esp. 322–23 and 468.

66. *Musée des familles* 1 (1834): 279.

67. Jacques Revel, "La région," in Pierre Nora, ed., *Lieux de mémoire*, 5: 864–75. See also Joan Wallach Scott, *Only Paradoxes to Offer: French Feminists and the Rights of Man* (Cambridge, Mass., 1996).

68. *La Revue des provinces* 3 (1 December 1834): 92; J. F. Schnakenburg, *Tableau synoptique et comparatif des idiomes populaires ou patois de la France* (Berlin, 1840), 8; and *La Dunkerquoise*, 16 January 1851.

identify the individual with a *pays*, that anchor public identity within local specificity? Intentionally or not, intellectual elites posed this question within this field, confronting its implications and weighing the appropriate grounds—birth, history, reason—on which to define modern individuals and citizens. Without exploring all such grounds (gender and the family, for one, were elided), they nonetheless manipulated multiple territorial referents while seeking to resolve it. This question clearly held particular urgency under the July Monarchy. In reclaiming the legacy of the French Revolution, the regime not only renewed interest in the origins of the nation and the bourgeois order, but also reactivated the question of national unity—with its internal ambiguities. What is more, liberalism flourished during these two decades. Most traditionalists could embrace local difference as the linchpin of their cultural and political identity; many republicans could as easily subsume it to the national *patrie*. Liberals, however, often found themselves caught between their affection for the local, their trepidation before local particularism, and for some, their universalist convictions.

The tensions above did not vanish in ensuing decades. As late as 1868, a member of the Société d'agriculture, sciences et arts de l'arrondissement de Valenciennes admonished a local poet for depicting their city as the "center of the world." Love of the *clocher*, this "narrow sentiment, no longer has a raison d'être in our century," he declared.[69] This said, local difference proved less problematic than in decades past. The passage of time—and such innovations as railroad lines and telegraphs—boosted confidence in the country's "indissoluble" unity and ability to withstand affirmations of local identity. At the same time, the progress of "civilization" threatened to corrupt, if not destroy, local communities and "originalities," the organic rootedness that underlay a peaceful and paternalistic social order. Preserving, or at least documenting, increasingly inoffensive local differences (be they historical or linguistic) grew all the more pressing under the Second Empire. So did, after the social and political turmoil of 1848, reaffirming the "chain of facts that link [people's] existence to . . . the generations that preceded them in the same place." Reviewing Guilbert's *Histoire des villes de France* in 1851, *littérateur* Charles Louandre thus passed over the author's radical politics. Instead, he praised the work for allaying the era's "moral sickness": its predilection for utopias. Centralization, he added, now posed a greater danger than "provincial" or "municipal spirit."[70] Elites of all political per-

---

69. *RAN* 22, no. 10 (October 1868): 315.

70. *L'Instituteur du Nord et du Pas-de-Calais* 14 (1851): 289–90; and Charles Louandre, "Histoire et statistique morales de la France," *RDM*, new period., 9 (January–March 1851): 546–564, citations on 555 and 563.

suasions exalted the local past as a conduit toward order, tradition, "the honor of the family, love of the hearth and the *pays*." Such sentiments were vanishing from Paris, this "abyss" without "memor[ies]," as the *Constitutionnel* put it. Yet they still nourished this "devotion to which France has owed its salvation."[71]

What is more, Napoleon III's military adventures in Crimea and Mexico, the escalating rivalry with Prussia, and France's growing colonial ambitions fueled a sometimes militaristic patriotism that could overshadow—without suppressing—localism and universalism alike. The Nord's pageant organizers thus began depicting events in national history (the Franks, for instance) or transmogrifying universalism into a paean to French civilization. Embracing this imperial revival of *la grande nation*, the *Incas* welcomed Napoleon III to Valenciennes in 1853 by arraying fifty live figures from French history on a triumphal arch.[72] A decade later, their pageants presented a national narrative alone. While "humanitarian ideas" continued to flourish, they hence proved increasingly compatible with the *patrie*. The *Encyclopédie du dix-neuvième siècle* could thus recognize a growing rapprochement between nations in 1852 without equating it—as had many encyclopedias a decade earlier—with the demise of national sentiments. This international fraternity weakened patriotism, not in "its noble aspects," but "in its vanity, its egoism, its oppressiveness" alone.[73] Still missing, however, were both a seamless integration of local diversity within the nation and a full synthesis of organic and voluntarist conceptions of territorial identity. The latter began taking shape in the 1850s. First came the *patrie terrestre*, a "*patrie* of the body" based on "love of the native land, the nourishing earth," but lacking a moral dimension. Then came its alter ego: the *patrie sociale*. Transcending "the narrow horizon that one takes in from the native hearth," the latter furnished common laws and principles.[74] But this synthesis imposed itself slowly. When it finally did, in the last third of the century, it was, again, as an interweaving of *petite* and *grande patries*—a conceptual resolution that owed much, as we have begun to see, to the inquiry undertaken in the field of local memories.

71. C. Brainne, J. Debarbouiller, and Ch.-F. Lapierre, *Les hommes illustres de l'Orléanais* (Orléans, 1852), v; and *Le Constitutionnel*, 6 September 1848.

72. *L'Illustration* 22, no. 553 (1 October 1853): 212–13.

73. This tension resurfaced at the turn of the century, pitting "internationalism," firmly anchored on the left, against an organic nationalism aligned with the New Right. See Stephen Kern, *The Culture of Time and Space 1880–1918* (Cambridge, Mass., 1983), 229–38; Mattelart, *Histoire de l'utopie*, 199–202; and A. C., "Patrie, patriotisme," *Encyclopédie du dix-neuvième siècle: répertoire universel des sciences, des lettres et des arts, avec la biographie de tous les hommes célèbres*, 28 vols. (Paris, 1836–59), 18:677.

74. A. C., "Patrie, patriotisme," 676.

SIX

Local Difference and the State

> It no longer suffices to be French [nowadays], one must remember
> that one is above all *Gascon, Picard,* or *Normand.* . . . [Yet] some of our
> most obscure villages possess charming churches that will never
> outshine cathedrals.
>
> EMILE EGGER, "Des dialectes et des patois,"
> *Revue de l'instruction publique* (15 July 1843)

LOCAL DIFFERENCE PROVED equally problematic in official circles during much of the century. Indeed, the Ministry of Public Instruction's devotion to local memories did not impress everyone in France. Aristide Guilbert applauded Thierry and Guizot in the mid-1840s for revitalizing historical science. But why had these eminent historians—architects of the ministry's intellectual policy—neglected "this multitude of details, incidents, episodes, traits, memories, traditions, legends that constitute the riches of local life"? He went on: "From a governmental point of view, and from a narrative one, everything has been reduced to a single center, a single authority." The central authorities and the new historical school rejected or reconfigured anything that did not fit within this "system"—including provincial cities, "completely absorbed, lost, in this ocean we call the history of France." Guilbert's vast *Histoire des villes de France* would thus serve several purposes: fill a glaring void, "call the government's attention" to local history, and critique a "political centralization" bequeathed by the Old Regime and French Revolution. It eventually expressed Guilbert's bitterness as well. "It would seem that an enterprise of such importance [as his *Histoire*] . . . could only be completed with the state's patronage and assistance," he wrote in 1848. But no subscription materialized.[1]

Guilbert was not, as we will see, the only contemporary to accuse the French state of sacrificing local memories—be it "particular histor[ies]" or "local idioms"—to its own legitimacy and national greatness. Minister-

---

1. Prospectus (1843) attached to the BNF copy of Aristide Guilbert, ed., *Histoire des villes,* 1, 3; and idem, "Introduction," *Histoire des villes,* 1: viii, xii–xiii, and xxiii.

ial officials had been forthright from the start, presenting the CTH as a "long-lasting institution in honor of France's origins, memories and glory." Like the Versailles gallery of historical paintings, it would reaffirm national and monarchical grandeur. It would also collect documents and popular songs because France lagged behind Germany and England in this eminently patriotic domain. Seeking to impose itself on the international scene, the Second Empire sought to establish the ancient supremacy of the French language. The "cult of the past," declared Minister Victor Duruy at the 1867 Congress of Learned Societies, ensured France's "indestructible grandeur."[2] National considerations prevailed, yet local memories carried far greater weight in such ventures, as we know, than Guilbert allowed. What he perceived as a mere dismissal of local traditions was but one facet of a complex amalgam of governmental forces, at once attracted to local memories and wary of the local difference lurking therein. As we move from official blueprints and investigative modalities to encounters between officials and elites, we further refine our portrait of a hesitant and conflicted intellectual state, cultivating local memories in some guises but not others. Like some of their contemporaries, officials and CTH members grappled with a local difference that, for fluctuating reasons, they could neither wholly endorse nor denounce.

A UNITARY DESIGN

Guilbert reproached officials for allowing "historical unity, . . . the unity of narration [and] facts," to govern their historical ventures. The yearning for unity within this field requires no further elaboration. Guilbert's tirade draws our attention, however, to the implications of this "single design" on the official cult of local memories. Some officials, such as the prefect of the Hérault, encouraged learned societies to spend less time "shak[ing] off the dust of communal charters" and instead "honor the memory of the men who have done the *pays* proud."[3] But they were not the norm. Until the early 1850s, ministerial officials and CTH members tolerated but seldom initiated, sponsored, or legitimated historical projects that extolled—or seemed to extol—local specificity. While their course of action was anything but straightforward, this much can be established about this first period: the ministry and CTH sought to anchor local memories within a united, national framework; they rejected local

2. François Guizot, report to Louis-Philippe, 27 November 1834, in Charmes, 22; Thomas Gaehtgens, *Versailles*, 63–64; Hippolyte Fortoul, report to Louis-Napoléon, 12 February 1856, in his *Réforme de l'enseignement*, 2: 1166; and *RSS*, 4th ser., 6 (2d sem. 1867): 10.
3. *Bulletin de la Société archéologique de Béziers* 3 (1839): 186 and 204.

initiatives that they deemed overly memorial; and they entered into isolated but public and revealing conflicts with provincial elites.

One of Guizot's first steps on behalf of provincial elites was to provide free exchange of periodical publications between learned societies. In 1843, for instance, Douai's Société d'agriculture, des sciences et des arts received periodicals from Nantes, Bordeaux, Perpignan, Toulon, Versailles, and Besançon. In addition to fulfilling scientific objectives, this procedure anchored these associations within a national network, nurturing an indispensable unity.[4] The CTH's intellectual ventures served similar purposes. The *Recueil des monuments de l'histoire du Tiers Etat* "does not only seek to make known . . . the interior regime of the cities of our ancient provinces," explained future CTH member Jean Yanovsky in 1841. Like other such collective projects, it also linked "the local histories with general history." In January 1848, its editor portrayed the new *Revue des sociétés savantes* as a meeting ground between isolated local ventures. Each locality would share "its moral revolutions, its political events" with the others. Each would contribute historical artifacts that "would be utterly surprised to form a complete whole" within the nation. Together, these localities would "reconstruct in their totality the monuments of which they were but partial samples."[5]

On a memorial plane, the parts clearly did not, and should not, exist in themselves. Guizot thus applauded the Société des antiquaires de Normandie's commitment to local history in 1837 and 1838, but as an "investigation on our national history." Like others, Guizot felt that French national unity was a recent accomplishment: only "today, and before our eyes, has it . . . achieved its definitive triumph." Without expecting centrifugal forces to split France, he and other officials looked askance at local sentiments that could weaken this fragile unity. Guizot thus reminded provincial elites to eschew "local patriotism, parochialism [*le patriotisme de localité, de clocher*]." Espouse "the idea of national unity," he told them. "Embrace all of France in [your] thoughts, affection, investigations," carry your zeal beyond purely "local investigations."[6] Poitiers's Société des antiquaires de l'Ouest grasped this ministerial concern all too well: its secretary assured Salvandy in 1837 that, while undertaking local studies, the association "does not forget that it works for the history of France."[7] Integrating *pays* and nation was not always as straightforward,

4. AN F17 3397: Decree of 30 March 1843; and Guizot, report to Louis-Philippe on the Ministry of Public Instruction's 1835 budget, 31 December 1833, in *Ministère de l'instruction publique. Budget des dépenses de l'exercice 1836* (Paris, 1835), 10.

5. *Le National,* 12 June 1841; and *RSS* 1 (January 1848): 8–9.

6. Guizot, speech in the public meeting of the Société des antiquaires de Normandie, 2 August 1837, in *Mémoires de la Société des antiquaires de Normandie* 11 (1837–39): xl–xli and xliii; and *Discours prononcé par M. Guizot,* 4.

7. AN F17 3041: Secretary Société des antiquaires de l'Ouest to Min. Pub. Instrc., 25 September 1837.

however. Ministerial subscriptions and treatment of local idioms both reveal an ambiguous state of affairs within official circles.

Some requests for governmental subscriptions met a happier fate than Guilbert's. In 1843, Eusèbe Girault de Saint-Fargeau persuaded the Ministry of the Interior to subscribe for one hundred copies of his *Histoire nationale et dictionnaire des communes de France*.[8] An author of geography, *statistique*, and travel books, Girault had powerful patrons, including a deputy and a *sous-secrétaire d'état*. More significantly, he submitted a work whose thematics and structure espoused the central government's unitary design. While such correspondence did not translate automatically into governmental aid, we should not dismiss its impact—conscious or not— on subscription patterns. In their prospectuses and correspondence with the ministry, Girault and his publisher presented their work as the "complement" of governmental undertakings: "a statistical, geographical, historical, industrial and commercial description of all French communes and more than 20,000 hamlets." This "general topography of places" resembled official *statistiques* and rested on the same referents as the CTH's collective ventures—description, dictionary, "public utility." Indeed, its final title—*Dictionnaire géographique, historique, industriel et commercial de toutes les communes de la France*—emphasized its status as dictionary. The work consisted of austere and near-identical entries on French communes: typically a few lines, several pages for important cities. Few touched on local history and celebrities. Girault included entries on all departments, but rarely discussed the ancient provinces. He also opted for an alphabetical plan—further diluting the specificity and traditions of French localities. This "monument to our *pays*" was clearly a national venture. Its organization, exhaustive accumulation, administrative portrait of France, and single authorial voice projected unity.[9]

Guilbert's *Histoire des villes de France* deviated from this model. This was a national venture, no doubt, but with cities and ancient provinces rather than departments as its main divisions. Departments had "no historical tradition"—a view shared by many contemporaries.[10] Embracing local difference, the project celebrated the "individuality" of each city, *pays*, and province, including "local traditions, legends, customs, mores," and patois. Guilbert promised his provincial collaborators to erect a "scientific, historical, artistic and literary monument . . . to the glory of your

8. The ministries of Public Instruction and of the Interior (which included the Division of Fines Arts) both subscribed to historical works during this period. See also AN F21 709: Decree of 27 June 1843.

9. Eusèbe Girault de Saint-Fargeau, prospectus for *Histoire nationale et dictionnaire géographique de toutes les communes de la France* (Paris, n.d. [late 1820s]), 1; AN F21 709: Girault and Firmin Didot frère to Min. Int., 22 October 1840; and Catherine Bertho-Lavenir, *Roue et le stylo*, 46.

10. Guilbert, Introduction to *Histoire des villes*, 1:xix; and, for instance, Eugène Dubarle, *Statisque du département de Seine-et-Marne*, vol. 7 of V.-A. Loriol, ed., *La France*, viii.

province." One contributor added that "although the history of Saint-Malo merges with the nation's, the *Malouins* still retain their character, their personality." While Girault's *Dictionnaire* featured a single author, Guilbert's *Histoire* was a multivocal work that enabled its 107 authors (many of them provincials) to present a singular point of view. Its emphasis on history over *statistique*, narrative over definition, and interpretation over factual description further distinguished it from Girault's work. In 1846, Guilbert urged a contributor to "analyze rather than recite" as he revised his article. Two years later, he castigated Girault for allowing "topographical or statistical description" to "smother or exclude" history in his *Dictionnaire*.[11]

This case study captures a broader trend in official subscriptions—at a time in which scholarly publishing still depended heavily on governmental assistance. Addressing the Chamber of Deputies, Guizot declared that 38 of the 128 works to which his ministry had subscribed in 1834 (29.7 percent) pertained to history, "nearly all to local history." While archival records are too fragmentary to fully confirm or refute this assertion, they nonetheless offer several lessons.[12] First, the ministries of the Interior and of Public Instruction indeed subscribed to more works of local history after 1830 than before. According to these records, the latter made up 4.7 percent of all subscriptions under the Restoration and 10.5 percent under the July Monarchy and Second Empire. In this domain as well, a rupture took place. Second, the number of subscriptions proved unimposing, be it in relative or absolute terms. For the years 1830–1850 alone, I can only confirm 59 subscriptions pertaining to local history. Seventeen (over a quarter) occurred between 1833 and 1835 alone. Partial as they are, these records thus suggest that Guizot's figures only hold true—if at all—for those early years. Third and more important, over half of these subscriptions consisted of archival guides, *statistiques*, source collections, topographical dictionaries, monumental descriptions, and the like. Of the 59 confirmed subscriptions, only 19—about one per year—were narratives of local history or studies of local idioms. The odd local publications that the Ministry of Public Instruction subsidized through direct indemnities (rather than subscriptions) also fit within its erudite and national framework. Such was the case, as its title indicates, of Aurélien de Courson's

11. Guilbert, Introduction to *Histoire des villes*, 1:xv; idem, "Résumé" on Poitou, *Histoire des villes*, 4: 438–39; idem, Circular letter to provincial elites, 15 March 1842, appended to vol. 1 of the BNF copy of ibid., 1–2; idem, Prospectus (1844?), appended to ibid., 3; Auguste Billiard, "Saint-Malo et Saint-Servan," in ibid., 1: 55; and Bibliothèque de l'Institut de France, Ms. 2277, pièce 1: Guilbert to Félicien de Saulcy, 9 October 1846.

12. This discussion focuses on book-length works alone, excluding the occasional—and poorly itemized—subscriptions to periodicals. It encompasses the Ministries of Public Instruction and of the Interior and rests on data in AN F17 2893–2899, 2905, and 13399–13401, and F21 708–709. See also Guizot, intervention in the session of 31 May 1836, in J. Madival and E. Laurent, eds., *Archives parlementaires*, 104: 483–84.

Recherches de documents relatifs à l'histoire de la Basse-Bretagne et au Tiers Etat.
Some petitioners accordingly assured the ministry that while their works
"pertain[ed] especially to certain localities," they also illuminated "general events."[13]

In the realm of subscriptions as in others, financial considerations curtailed ministerial largesse. "There are no funds," declared the ministry in
1840 as it turned down a subscription—endorsed by the CTH—for the *Mémoires et documents inédits pour servir à l'histoire de la Franche-Comté.* Beyond
these material limitations, this financial prudence displays now familiar
scientific priorities as well as a reticence to fund "communal life" and
works that, by definition, denoted individuality and local difference.
"Wealth is the condition for communal development," explained one
pamphleteer in 1844.[14] This was the root of the problem. Sociologists
Wendy Griswold and Fredrik Engelstad argue convincingly that governmental funding of provincial authors often promotes regional literature
and loyalties—especially in peripheral locales.[15] By making it easier to
earn a living through regional writing, this support broadens and
strengthens autonomous intellectual networks. By emancipating provincial authors from the market and the "institutional and cultural center," it
furthermore enables local elites to cultivate cultural or political, rather
than purely commercial, interests. It allows them to employ a regional
idiom with limited national appeal. While it does not necessarily create
local difference, it may end up emboldening it. The subscription patterns
above fit the designs of officials who, without framing the question in
these terms, grasped its possible implications in the provinces.

Governmental perceptions of local idioms—another conduit toward
local memories—amplify this portrait. In ministerial circles as elsewhere,
some contemporaries distinguished patois (this "corruption of the
mother-language") from dialects (stand-alone languages with fixed rules)
and "provincial languages" such as Basque. Patois also referred to the
speech of the "working-class and rural *peuple.*" Within the field of local
memories, however, many used "patois" and "dialect" interchangeably to
designate, simply, "the language of the *pays.*"[16] Breaking with the Old Re-

---

13. AN F17 3292: Dossier on Aurélien de Courson; and AN F17 13399: Adhelm Bernier to
Guizot, 4 May 1834.
14. AN F17 3291: Anon., "Note pour M. le Ministre," 15 April 1840, and Anon., *De l'importance des communes,* 11 and 37.
15. The word *regional* is anachronistic for this period, but, as defined by Griswold and Engelstad—"a common cultural identification with a particular place"—it constitutes an appropriate heuristic category. See Wendy Griswold and Fredrik Engelstad, "Does the Center Imagine the Periphery? State Support and Literary Regionalism in Norway and the United States,"
Comparative Social Research 17 (1998): 129–75.
16. "Patois," in Marie-Nicolas Bouillet et al., *Dictionnaire universel des sciences, des lettres et des
arts. 4e édition revue et corrigée* (Paris, 1859), 1230; and Louis Vermesse, *Vocabulaire du patois lillois*
(Lille, n.d. [1861?]), title page, iv, and xiv.

gime's tradition of linguistic tolerance, some French revolutionaries had sought to destroy these symbols of "superstition," clericalism, and internal fragmentation—obstacles to the unity of the secular republic and the creation of a perfect, universal language.[17] This impossible design was short-lived, as local idioms benefited from growing interest in not only national origins and local memories, but also rural traditions—at once pure and mysterious. In 1805, the Académie celtique's budding ethnologists included patois among those imperiled rural usages, those conduits toward Celtic origins that they deemed worth cataloguing.[18] Two years later, the Ministry of the Interior's Bureau de Statistique included questions on "dialects" in its questionnaires on France. Its "general work in French on . . . patois nomenclatures" would document popular usages and map the country's linguistic diversity—a social reality among others. Discontinued in 1812, the venture yielded several cartons of jumbled data and isolated publications.[19] Under the aegis of poet Charles Nodier, patois acquired a new importance in the 1830s and 1840s—first, as a conduit toward ancient French and, second, as "the innumerable roots through which the national language is tied to the native land and . . . receives its strength, its life, its color, its poetry." Many provincial elites likewise exalted patois, not only for their aesthetics and emotional valence (expressing the "soft affection found within families"), but also as popular vestiges of long-gone eras, evidence of the historical forces that had shaped their locality.[20] In 1843, the Société d'émulation de Cambrai thus offered two hundred francs to the best essay on the origins and singularity of "dialects or patois spoken in the Cambrésis."

Curiosity about this "interesting chapter in the history of popular mores" and the "origins of our language" surfaced only intermittently

17. Henry Peyre, *La royauté et les langues provinciales* (Paris, 1933), 14; Michel de Certeau, Dominique Julia, and Jacques Revel, *Une politique de la langue: la Révolution française et les patois* (Paris, 1975); Martyn Lyons, "Politics and Patois: The Linguistic Policy of the French Revolution," *Australian Journal of French Studies* 18 (1981): 264–82; and Pierre Encrevé, "La langue de la République," *Pouvoirs* 100 (2002): 123–36.

18. On the Académie celtique, see questions 37–39 of its 1805 questionnaire, repr. in Nicole Belmont, ed., *Aux sources de l'ethnologie française: l'Académie celtique* (Paris, 1995), 35; and Ozouf, "L'invention de l'ethnographie française: le questionnaire de l'Académie celtique," *Annales E.S.C.* 36, no. 2 (March–April 1981), repr. in her *L'école de la France* (Paris, 1984), 351–79.

19. *Extrait du rapport fait par M. Rouard, à l'Académie d'Aix, sur le Dictionnaire Provençal-Français, de M. le docteur Honnorat* (Aix, n. d.), 4; Isabelle Laboulais-Lesage, *Lectures et pratiques de l'espace: l'itinéraire de Coquebert de Montbret, savant et grand commis d'Etat (1755–1831)* (Paris, 1999), 411 and 422–24; Daniel Nordman, *Frontières de France: de l'espace au territoire, XVIe-XIXe siècle* (1998), 487–91; and Paul Bénichou, *Nerval et la chanson folklorique* (Paris, 1970), 50. Among the resulting publications: Jacques Joseph Champollion-Figeac, *Nouvelles recherches sur les patois ou idiomes vulgaires de la France, et en particulier sur ceux du département de l'Isère* (Paris, 1809).

20. J. F. Schnakenburg, *Tableau synoptique*, v; and Alexandre Ducourneau and Amans-Alexis Monteil, *Histoire nationale des départements de la France. Gironde* (Paris, [1844?]), 614.

within the Ministry of Public Instruction in the early 1830s. In 1845, Salvandy created a Commission des chants religieux et historiques de la
France to inventory "the popular songs of France from all provinces, all
languages, all patois." Yet, local idioms remained marginal within this official agenda during these years.[21] The Commission accomplished little;
CTH circulars referred to patois episodically; the ministry did not launch
collective projects around them. In 1841, Minister Abel-François Villemain asked a provincial correspondent to collect documents on "local or
general history," but to restrict himself, in this linguistic realm, to "the origins and various developments of the French language."[22] As intimated
earlier, the ministry subscribed to few works on patois—three by my
count, including Simon-Jude Honnorat's *Dictionnaire provençal-français*.
When Honnorat urged the ministry to invite Occitan-speaking communes to subscribe to his work, an official scribbled a revealing "hic"
(problem) in the margin of his letter.[23]

Indeed, not everyone agreed with Nodier that "the immeasurable influence of localities" should imprint this linguistic realm. Patois, as one
commentator noted in 1840, still "trace the . . . immutable boundaries of
provinces, cantons and communes, despite the conventional divisions
that politics could impose."[24] CTH member Jean-Jacques Ampère and
Désiré Nisard both granted local idioms a secondary status in their respective histories of the French language and French literature. "[Let us
find] what is general and dominant, before seeking what is particular and
exceptional," exhorted Ampère in 1841. According to Nisard, the
"human spirit" underlay both patois and French literature, but "it is less
complete, it appears in more or less defective forms" in the former.
François Génin, the CTH member and soon-to-be BTH official, articulated this unitary design with yet greater clarity. Without rejecting local idioms, he emphasized their subordinate position. "Even before modern
centralization," he explained, a tendency towards unity prevailed in
France. There had been a geographical center, "a French people and a
French language, to which the trouvère from Picardy or Burgundy . . .

21. Guizot to CTH correspondents, circular and instructions of 15 May 1835, in Charmes,
34–36; AN F17 13269: Proceedings of the CHAM, 26 April 1843; and Pengern, quoted in Francis Gourvil, *Théodore-Claude-Henri Hersart de la Villemarqué (1815–1895) et le 'Barzaz-Breiz'
(1839–1845–1867)* (Rennes, 1960), 303.
22. BMA ms. 440: Abel-François Villemain to François-César Louandre, 7 January 1841.
23. Historian René Merle claims that the ministry eventually endorsed Honnorat's request.
At any rate, the latter apparently provoked internal discussion. Also called langue d'Oc or
Provençal by contemporaries, Occitan is the collection of romance idioms spoken in southern
and southwestern France. See AN F17 2896: Simon-Jude Honnorat to Min. Pub. Instrc., n.d.
[January 1844]; and René Merle, "Le chemin d'Honnorat," *Amiras/Repères occitans* 13 (1986):
85–98.
24. Charles Nodier, "Comment les patois furent détruits en France," in his *Dissertations
philologiques et bibliographiques* (Paris, 1834–35), 4; and Schnakenburg, *Tableau synoptique*, v.

conformed himself." This still held true. "Before investigating dialects," he concluded, "let us pay attention to French. . . . The rest is secondary."[25]

It is common knowledge that the July Monarchy equated local idioms with priestly efforts to inculcate Catholic teachings and sought intermittently to exclude them from primary school classrooms. "Let us take drastic action against this ancient transmission of patois," declared one school inspector in 1837.[26] The more accommodating Salvandy decreed that schoolchildren should only use "local idioms" when indispensable. In the intellectual realm, however, the danger would also come from elites who recuperated these idioms to glorify local difference, a "freedom of distinctive life and individual originality for every part of France."[27] Emile Egger, a philologist who circulated in Thierry's circle, voiced this concern publicly in 1843. In France—this country "whose government, institutions, laws, even liberties tend toward centralization"—patois had for centuries been subsumed to "the cause of national unity." Nowadays, however, the "protests of provincial patriotism" contested the supremacy of French by glorifying patois and dialects. "Democracy, which advances everywhere in our world of progress, . . . is invading the peaceful domain of philology." As a result, "it no longer suffices to be French," he lamented. "One must remember that one is above all *Gascon, Picard*, or *Normand*."[28] Such anxieties imprinted the official cult of local memories, yielding both a rejection of local idioms as autonomous entities and their representation as mere "remains of the past," fossils bearing testament to the evolution of French. Imminent victims of "modern civilization and use of the general language," they were beautiful—not, as Michel de Certeau and others argued in a different context, because they were dead, but because their demise was imminent. If Thierry called for studies of patois, it was to trace the "degradation" of motley "primitive differences."[29] The inventory he contemplated would alleviate the convulsions of a dying body and reaffirm the unity of the rejuvenated nation.

---

25. Jean-Jacques Ampère, *Histoire de la formation de la langue française* (Paris, 1869 [1841]), 373; Désiré Nisard, *Histoire de la littérature française*, 1:23; and François Génin, *Variations du langage*, 270–71.

26. Paul Lorain, *Tableau de l'instruction primaire en France, etc.* (Paris, 1837), 29, quoted in Fabienne Reboul-Scherrer, *La vie quotidienne des premiers instituteurs, 1833–1882* (Paris, 1989), 28. See also the criticism in Mary Lafon, *Tableau historique et littéraire de la langue parlée dans le Midi de la France* (Paris, 1842), 8.

27. Salvandy to the rectors, circular of 25 October 1838, in *Circulaires et instructions*, 2: 680; and *La Revue des provinces* 4 (15 December 1834): 106.

28. Emile Egger, "Des dialectes et des patois," *Revue de l'instruction publique* 2, no. 16 (15 July 1843): 249–50.

29. *Lettres sur l'histoire de France*, in *Oeuvres d'Aug. Thierry*, 424; Guizot to correspondents, circular of 15 May 1835, in Charmes, 37; and Certeau with Julia and Revel, "La beauté du mort," in Certeau, *La culture au pluriel*, new ed., ed. Luce Giard (Paris, 1993), 45–72.

This unitary design narrowed the range of projects the ministry and CTH deemed acceptable and prevented them from developing a concerted policy toward local memories. It also produced revealing altercations with provincial elites. In 1841, one Claude-Charles Pierquin de Gembloux published a scathing, two hundred-page condemnation of a Ministry of Public Instruction that neglected patois and, more generally, local difference. Pierquin was a doctor, prolix author, and academic inspector in Bourges. "Vulgar idioms," he argued, had existed in France for centuries, bestowing French countless locutions and partaking in "the *patrie*'s true history." Like Nodier, Pierquin believed that patois still constituted a "lively and naked language, . . . the language of the *pays*, the language of the *patrie*." France, as he saw it, was a heterogeneous entity, deriving its strength from its diversity. "Each nation is always made up of several peoples, ethnologically speaking." The task at hand, for French citizens and officials, was to "popularize these primitive idioms," to cultivate this internal diversity through grammars, dictionaries, even a central academy of patois. Unfortunately, the CTH shirked this duty. Like the French revolutionaries, the July Monarchy perceived linguistic uniformity as "an essential condition of national unity, . . . the expression of a vigorous nationality." A committed Orleanist and veteran of the 1830 barricades, Pierquin was also a civil servant and dutiful CTH collaborator. One did not have to oppose the regime to lambaste its timidity before local difference.[30]

Pierquin's apology of local idioms included Occitan, which the CTH all but dismissed. "The committee," it told a supplicant from Carpentras in 1839, "must deal above all with the language of the North, which has contributed most to the formation of French."[31] This was an old debate, pitting partisans of northern and southern languages, but also of literary traditions (the trouvères of the North, the troubadours of the Midi). Pierquin accordingly commended learned societies from the Languedoc, including Toulouse's Académie des Jeux Floraux, for their devotion to Occitan. The Académie, too, was involved in a dispute with the CTH. Founded in 1323, the Académie des Jeux Floraux was and remains France's oldest learned society, a literary cenacle whose members "perfect themselves in the rules of criticism and taste." Its famed literary contests revolved initially around poetry (*amors*) and called on participants to fol-

30. Claude-Charles Pierquin de Gembloux, *Histoire littéraire, philologique et bibliographique des patois* (Paris, 1841), quotations on vi–vii, 2, and 6–8; and Guy Thuillier, "Les historiens locaux en Nivernais de 1815 à 1840," *101e Congrès des sociétés savantes*, section of modern history, 2 vols., (Lille, 1976), 2: 360–61.

31. AN F17 13268: Proceedings of the Committee on French language and literature, 6 March 1839.

low the 1340 *Las leys d'amors*, a compendium of precepts for a mystical and joyous poetry of the heart.[32] In 1839, the Académie resolved to celebrate the *Leys*'s quincentenary by publishing a bilingual edition in Occitan and French. Although it found support from local officials, it could secure neither a ministerial subscription nor a CTH subsidy for this project. The ministry insisted that it could only subscribe to published works—a loose regulation that did not cover subsidies.[33]

Philological considerations may have come into play. The literary worth of southern idioms was after all a contested issue among specialists, and the *Leys*'s editor, Adolphe-Félix Gatien-Arnoult, argued that the *langue d'Oc* had flourished long before the North's *langue d'Oïl*. CTH members did not, however, frame the question in such terms during their private meetings. Party politics may also have played a role. Toulouse's legitimist *Gazette du Languedoc* praised the Académie des Jeux Floraux for countering the *langue d'Oïl*'s "oppression" and helping the Languedoc "recover a more honorable existence." The local prefect and rector denounced Gatien-Arnoult, as a "radical" "party leader" who voiced "hatred of the authorities" in his philosophy courses and newspaper editorials.[34] A reformist liberal, Gatien-Arnoult, remained a disciple of Victor Cousin, however. His politics inspired little concern within the Ministry of Public Instruction.[35] More significant, the central authorities were reluctant to subsidize a "particular" undertaking, a learned society (from a city of notorious local pride) that refused to submit its publication to the CTH's judgment. "Published far from [the CTH], without its participation, . . . [the work] is utterly foreign to the committee," complained the latter. What is more, the *Leys d'amors* was infused with memorial sentiments. Gatien-Arnoult described it as "a thousand times more than an Académie française dictionary of its time." He spoke of a key moment "in our particular history," a celebration of "the city's and the *pays*'s literary honor." The *Gazette du Languedoc* and Toulouse's municipal council similarly praised the venture as a monument to "the *pays*'s glory, . . .

32. Regulations of the Académie des Jeux Floraux, in *Annuaire des sociétés savantes de la France et de l'étranger* (Paris, 1846), 551; François de Gélis, *Histoire critique des Jeux Floraux depuis leur origine jusqu'à leur transformation en académie (1323–1694)*, repr. (Geneva, 1981 [1912]); and Paul Cohen, "Courtly French, Learned Latin, and Peasant Patois: The Making of a National Language in Early Modern France," Ph.D. diss, Princeton University, 2001, esp. 583–85.

33. Adolphe-Félix Gatien-Arnoult, "Rapport fait à l'Académie des Jeux Floraux," in idem, ed., *Monumens de la littérature romane, publiés sous les auspices de l'Académie des Jeux Floraux*, 3 vols. (Toulouse, 1841–49), 1:vi; and AN F17 2810/1: Annotation in margin of letter from prefect Haute-Garonne to Min. Pub. Instrc., 17 March 1840.

34. Gatien-Arnoult had founded *L'Emancipation*, Toulouse's radical newspaper, in 1837. See AN F17 20802: Rector Toulouse to Min. Pub. Instrc., 23 December 1844; and prefect Haute-Garonne to Min. Pub. Instrc., 8 January 1845.

35. AN F17 20802: Min. Pub. Instrc. to prefect Haute-Garonne, 29 January 1845; and Gatien-Arnoult, *Cours de lectures philosophiques, ou Dissertations et fragments sur les principales questions de philosophie élémentaire* (Paris, 1838).

an *illustration* of Toulouse, our personal property and honor." Local difference, here as well, was the point of contention.[36]

We thus uncover an intellectual state that, under the July Monarchy, both cultivated and skirted local memories. Its misgivings display, on one level, contradictions between doctrine and imperatives of government. Some officials could espouse or tolerate local difference as individuals, but not as governmental agents. Salvandy, for one, proved receptive to such provincial rhetoric as a private citizen, yet, in an 1847 conflict with Arcisse de Caumont's circle, he argued that the term *province*, "applied to certain divisions of the territory, [is] irregular and today unconstitutional."[37] Whether couched in the language of the *pays* or the *province*, affirmations of local difference threatened the nation's unity of governance.

Internal diversity and particularity proved problematic, moreover, on doctrinal grounds. In these official circles, too, the cultural difficulty was to localize without particularizing—be it culturally (by feeding a memorial current) or socially (by encouraging devotion to local interests). Some liberals, it is true, found the question less troubling than others. In 1835, historian Prosper de Barante urged his CTH colleagues to include "all the historical memories, all the traditions" in their *Topographical Dictionary of the Communes of France*, this "nomenclature of places." Following some scholars, we could thus deepen the contrast between two liberal currents in this governmental arena: one (embodied by Thierry) sought to maintain "differences and a plurality of small nations"; another (embodied by Guizot) dissolved all social and territorial groups within a "unique body" and tolerated no departures from its unitary design.[38] All, true enough, endorsed diversity as a pillar of European civilization and a counterpoint to a stultifying uniformity. An emergent industrial and mass society threatened to efface cultural markers, social hierarchies, and the diversity of human talents. No liberal endorsed local diversity more wholeheartedly than Benjamin Constant. "Variety is organization," he posited in 1814. "The entire nation is nothing when one separates it from its constituent fractions." Constant accordingly granted "particular wills" a key role and a cautious autonomy in the public sphere. Yet Lucien

36. AN F17 13268: Proceedings of the Committee on French language and literature, 29 April 1840; Gatien-Arnoult, "Rapport," i-ii and v; idem, Report to the Académie des Jeux Floraux (1841), quoted in Armand Praviel, *Histoire anecdotique des Jeux Floraux* (Toulouse, 1923), 32; *Gazette du Languedoc*, 3 February 1840; and AN F17 2810/1: Proceedings of the municipal council of Toulouse, 30 December 1839.

37. ADN 1 T 245: Salvandy to prefects, circular of 4 January 1847.

38. Françoise Mélonio, "La culture comme héritage," in idem and Antoine de Baecque, *Lumières et liberté: les dix-huitième et dix-neuvième siècles*, vol. 3 of Jean-Pierre Rioux and Jean-François Sirinelli, eds., *Histoire culturelle de la France* (Paris, 1998), 256. See also AN F17 13268: Proceedings of the Committee on letters, philosophy, science, and arts, 14 June 1835.

Jaume rightly points out that Constant's brand of liberalism—with its emphasis on individual freedom, internal diversity, and local patriotism—remained marginal within the French liberal school.[39] The Doctrinaire current that dominated spoke of diversity and respected local needs, but sought above all to create a unified public space, strong enough to withstand the threats of corporations and what Guizot called "purely local interest[s]." Capturing this prevailing conviction in 1841, Finance Minister Jean-Georges Humann distinguished the "spirit of locality"—devoted to "private interests"—from a "spirit of nationality" that served "general interests." Little wonder, then, that the single critical quotation illustrating "local" in the 1873 *Grand Larousse* comes from Guizot. "Local tyranny is the worst of all."[40]

What is more, Thierry's own commitment to internal diversity was questionable. Granted, he applauded Mirabeau's affection for the "Provençal nation" and looked back fondly on an era in which provincial "nations . . . declared themselves joined, but not subjugated" in the "great common existence." He also praised the Middle Ages' new spirit of urban liberty and a "local patriotism that had its memories, its interest and its glory." Yet he quickly denounced the ensuing "sentiment of local patriotism," this tendency to wall oneself in and ignore the rest of the country. Here again, unity prevails. It dominates his historical narratives: the social, national, administrative unity of France, its "unity of territory," the unity of its "national spirit."[41] His unity may be "one in which particularity is subsumed, not suppressed" (L. Gossman), but it is nonetheless subordinated. Particularity constitutes a compound within a broader entity, deprived of value in-itself. It is relegated to the past, divorced from a present in which, as Jacques Neefs argued, bourgeois society apprehended itself as "one and indivisible."[42]

The outcome was an intellectual state that talked about internal diver-

39. François Guizot, *Histoire de la civilisation en Europe*, ed. Pierre Rosanvallon (Paris, 1985 [1828]), 77; Benjamin Constant, *De l'esprit de conquête et de l'usurpation dans leurs rapports avec la civilisation européenne*, ed. Ephraïm Harpax (Paris, 1986 [1814]), 122–23; 3; idem, *Principes de politique*, 101–2; and Lucien Jaume, *Individu effacé*, 85–86, 262, and 271.

40. Guizot to schoolteachers, circular of 28 June 1833, in *Circulaires et instructions*, 2:125; Jean-Georges Humann, intervention in the Chambre des Pairs, 22 April 1841, cited in Jean-Claude Caron, *L'été rouge: chronique de la révolte populaire en France* (Paris, 2002), 58; and "Local," in Pierre Larousse, *Grand dictionnaire universel du XIXe siècle*, 17 vols. (Paris, 1866–90?), 10:604.

41. Thierry, *Dix ans d'études historiques*, in *Oeuvres d'Aug, Thierry*, 625; idem, *Considérations sur l'histoire de France*, 3d ed., in *Oeuvres complètes de Augustin Thierry*, 10 vols. (Paris, 1846–56 [1834]), 7:164; and idem, *Lettres sur l'histoire de France*, in *Oeuvres d'Aug. Thierry*, 422.

42. Lionel Gossman, "Augustin Thierry and Liberal Historiography," in his *Between History and Literature* (Cambridge, Mass., 1990), 115; and Jacques Neefs, "Augustin Thierry: le moment de la 'véritable' histoire de France," *Romantisme* 28–29 (1980): 294 and 300–301. For a more sanguine view of Thierry's conception of particularity, see Marcel Gauchet, "Les *Lettres sur l'histoire de France* d'Augustin Thierry," in Pierre Nora, ed., *Lieux de mémoire*, 2:298–99.

sity and provincial "franchises," yet allowed its unitary design to prevail. The local memories it did extol—in statistical ventures or inquiries into national origins—existed through their symbiotic relationship with the nation. Its historical practices evoke those which Claudio Lomnitz-Alder has uncovered in contemporary Mexico: a state that, by publicly celebrating a local territory, defines it as its possession, "synchronize[s]" local and national histories, and thereby "silenc[es] the region's traditions and organizations."[43] At this point in time, the central French state could not cultivate these territories and their memories as anything other than amorphous, interchangeable components of a national matrix. Official localism was neutral not only because it was apolitical, but also because it revolved around in situ residence rather than personal, deeply felt attachments to a *pays*. The local belonged to an "abstract space" that, following Henri Lefebvre, "tends toward homogeneity, toward the elimination of existing differences."[44] Far from constituting a particular place, far from exhibiting the diversity advocated by Guilbert or Pierquin, the *pays* lost itself in a national continuum.

1848: TOWARD LOCAL DIFFERENCE

The period framed by the upheavals of 1848 and 1870 witnessed both radical changes and continuity in this domain. On the one hand, officials and CTH members cultivated local diversity, even memorial attachment to the *pays*, with growing ease. On the other hand, the persisting—albeit abated and altered—pregnancy of local difference in governmental circles still prevented these actors from fully developing their localist agenda. They granted this agenda an unprecedented amplitude while remaining cautious and tentative.

In 1852, the prefect of the Nord penned a favorable report on Lille's latest historical pageant, an orderly and charitable event that had attracted huge crowds. He noted the "religious patriotism" with which participants had represented the town's past, but, curiously, passed over the floats devoted to the counts of Flanders and the like. Instead, he drew attention to the depictions of Victory holding a French flag and Lille's incorporation into the "French community." The organizers' "passion for

43. Delloye 38/16: Louis-Philippe, speech of 8 January 1833 (Cambrai), repr. in clipping from unidentified local newspaper; and Claudio Lomnitz-Adler, *Exits From the Labyrinth: Culture and Ideology in the Mexican National Space* (Berkeley, 1992), 50–51.

44. Henri Lefebvre, *The Production of Space*, trans. Donald Nicholson-Smith (Oxford, 1991), 52. The same had been true of the Ministry of the Interior's statistical ventures between the Directory and First Empire. Unity, concluded Stuart Woolf, required uniformity and curtailed "local differences." See Woolf, "Statistics and the Modern State," *Comparative Studies in Society and History* 31, no. 3 (July 1989): 599; and Jean-Claude Perrot, "The Golden Age of Regional Statistics," in idem and Woolf, *State and Statistics in France, 1789–1815* (Chur, 1984), 54.

ancient legends, for local tradition" had not, he reassured the Minister of the Interior, "excluded the representation of great events in the general history of France."[45] His misgivings toward local memory mirrored those of the three entrepreneurs who, a year earlier, had drawn up plans for an eight-day fête in Paris. Their blueprint, which earned Louis-Napoléon's "approbation," celebrated industry, agriculture, and Western genius—but not the provinces. *L'Illustration* thus commended these men for emulating the festive societies of the Nord, but wondered why the latter were excluded. In Lille, *littérateurs* likewise called for a truly "French" fête, in which *sociétés de bienfaisance* represented French cities and "Bretons, Normands, Provençaux, Alsatians, Flemings, in a word the Frenchmen of all the provinces, arrived in their local costumes, ancient or modern."[46]

This plan fizzled, but such criticism was not lost on the regime's director of fine arts, Auguste Romieu. In June of 1852, while planning the Parisian festivities marking the new imperial holiday of 15 August, he asked the prefect of the Nord to help him stage "one of these great cavalcades that, for centuries, have been customary" in his region. Only two weeks after penning the ambivalent report above, the prefect thus invited pageant organizers from Lille, Valenciennes, and Cambrai to bring their spectacles to Paris.[47] This unprecedented request would grant local memories a national stage. But it came late, allowing a mere six weeks for preparations. Moreover, the contrast between this overture and the prefect's earlier report uncovers a play of conflicting forces in official circles. Unsurprisingly, the fête of 15 August 1852 featured a water tournament and a fireworks show—but no provincial pageants. Neighboring Belgium included provincial historical floats in its Independence Day pageants, but not Second Empire France.[48] The state's rapprochement toward local difference would be incremental.

45. AN F1c III Nord 12: Prefect Nord to Min. Int., 21 June 1852. On this pageant, see *Les fastes de Lille. Cortège-cavalcade organisé par souscription au profit des pauvres* (Lille, 1852).

46. Hector Horeau, Charles Place, and Désiré Ruggieri, *Projet de fêtes offertes à toutes les nations du globe, par souscription nationale, présenté à M. le président de la République, dans son audience du 6 mai* (Paris, 1851), citations on 1 and 15; *L'Illustration* 17, no. 431 (29 May 1851): 343–46; and *L'Artiste: revue hebdomadaire du Nord de la France* 2, no. 2 (15 June 1851): 13, and no. 13 (31 August 1851): 104.

47. ADN M 140/44: Auguste Romieu to prefect Nord, 30 June 1852, and prefect Nord to presidents Société des Fastes de Lille and Société des Incas, 8 July 1852.

48. I analyze local responses to this request in chapter 8. See AN F21 722: Program of the fête of 15 August 1852; *Le Moniteur universel*, 16 August 1852; Matthew N. Truesdell, *Spectacular Politics: Louis-Napoléon Bonaparte and the Fête Impériale* (New York, 1997), 35–45; and Louis Hymans, *XXVe anniversaire de l'inauguration du roi. Les fêtes de juillet: compte-rendu des solennités et cérémonies publiques célébrées à Bruxelles les 21, 22 et 23 juillet 1856* (Brussels, n.d. [1856?]), 98. I thank Tom Verschaffel for this reference. On nineteenth-century Belgian pageants, see his "Het verleden tot weinig herleid: de historische optocht als vorm van de romantische verbeelding," in Jo Tollebeek, Frank Ankersmit, and Wessel Krul, eds., *Romantiek en historische cultuur* (Groningen, 1996), 297–320.

That same year, newly appointed Minister of Public Instruction Hippolyte Fortoul launched a *Recueil des poésies populaires de la France*—a more ambitious version of Salvandy's Commission des chants. Under the direction of Ampère and the CTH, correspondents and other provincials began collecting those endangered popular poems and songs that captured "the precious origins of a literature" that honored France. The CTH "deems truly popular only those anonymous poems[,] born spontaneously among the masses," explained Ampère, "or else those that have an author, but which the *peuple* had made its own."[49] The ministry urged its provincial acolytes to locate and forward manuscripts, publications, and transcriptions of oral traditions, from "the national language as well as provincial idioms." Like Société dunkerquoise member Edmond de Coussemaker, it sought to preserve songs "in their traditional purity to preserve the seal of originality of each province."[50]

The *Recueil des poésies populaires* owed as much to the European interest in folklore as to Fortoul's own philological interests in "France's local idioms." In 1829, at the age of eighteen, Fortoul had presented a paper on the popular songs of Basses-Alpes. As a literature professor in Toulouse in the early 1840s, he joined the Académie des Jeux Floraux and grew enamored of the "diversities . . . one finds in the literature and history of the Provence and Languedoc." The Académie's publication of the *Leys d'amors* earned his unstinting praise. Ampère's trajectory is more revealing yet, for he now embraced local idioms he had belittled a decade earlier. The same was true of Génin, who declared in 1856 that "the French language still survives in the language of the *peuple* and provincial patois." The time had thus come to collect these "locutions and turns of phrases," spurned for so long, and to compile patois glossaries from Normandy or Lorraine.[51] The *Recueil des poésies populaires* ran into practical difficulties, but the ministry continued to investigate local idioms in the late 1850s and 1860s. The CTH now endorsed provincial dictionaries and geographies of patois, published patois bibliographies, and by the late 1860s awarded prizes for glossaries and studies "of our ancient provincial dialects." During those same years, a Committee for the Study of French Di-

49. AN F17 3245: Fortoul to primary school inspectors, circular of November 1853; Ampère, "Instructions relatives au Recueil des poésies populaires de la France, etc.," 13 August 1853, in *Réforme de l'enseignement*, vol. 1, part 2: 627; and Jacques Cheyronnaud, Introduction to *Instructions pour un Recueil général des poésies*, 20.

50. Fortoul to Louis-Napoléon, report of 13 September 1852, in Charmes, 153; and AN F17 3245: Edmond de Coussemaker to Ampère, 6 May 1853.

51. Though he had fallen victim to a political purge in 1852, Génin's evolution captures a trend in ministerial circles. See Fortoul, "Etude sur les troubadours," in his *Etudes d'archéologie et d'histoire*, 2 vols. (Paris, 1854), 2:12, 65, and 78; Louis-Napoléon, Decree of 13 September 1852, in Charmes, 154; and Génin, *Récréations philologiques*, 2 vols., 2d ed. (Paris, 1858 [1856]), 1:xv–xvii.

alects took form under the patronage of Louis-Lucien Bonaparte (first cousin of Napoleon III, linguistics enthusiast, and honorific member of the Comité flamand). By 1868, the CTH was paying one Hippolyte Caudéran, author of a *Dialecte bordelais*, a monthly allowance to "collect the necessary documents for the preparation of the various glossaries of the patois of France."[52]

Ministerial subscriptions to works of local history underwent a comparable but slower evolution. I uncovered seventy-five such subscriptions between 1851 and 1869.[53] This represented a notable though moderate 36 percent increase from the July Monarchy. The change was gradual, however: only seven of these subscriptions occurred during the 1850s. In relative terms, the percentage remained steady at around 10 percent or so of total subscriptions until 1865, when it jumped to 14.5 percent. More significantly, the proportion of historical narratives and works on local idioms jumped from 32 percent before 1851 to 51.3 percent under the Second Empire (61 percent between 1865 and 1869). This was the key transformation. "In recent years, the correspondents have been invited to send original documents and nothing else," observed Minister Gustave Rouland in 1858. From now on, however, the CTH will gladly accept "papers on questions of *local* history, philology or archaeology." Its public contests accordingly included questions on, for instance, the customary law of a particular commune or province. When addressing provincial elites, officials spoke with a new ease of "ancient provinces," local "franchises," and an "inviolable attachment to the native land and the cult of memories."[54] Inaugurating Nancy's *Palais des facultés* in 1862, Rouland called upon his audience to take inspiration from "the traditions that live upon this land of Lorraine, and which France, our common *patrie*, accepts and glorifies." Explained the *Revue des sociétés savantes*: "All these various elements, combined and modified, formed the France of 1789."[55] The intellectual state was beginning to answer the calls of Guilbert and Pierquin.

This evolution responded to several factors. In her recent study of the

52. *Bulletin du Comité de la langue, de l'histoire et des arts de la France* 2 (1853–55): 353–60; Rouland to correspondents, circular of 26 August 1858, in Charmes, 198; AN F17 2815: "Sujets des prix mis au concours des sociétés savantes," n.d.; AN F17 3291: Decree of 22 July 1868; and Jean-François Chanet, "Maîtres d'école et régionalisme en France sous la Troisième République," *Ethnologie française* 18 (1988): 253.

53. This paragraph is based on the sources cited in footnote 12. For the Second Empire, I have uncovered usable records regarding the Ministry of Public Instruction alone. The 1868 dossier is missing and the 1870 dossier rendered incomplete by war.

54. Rouland to correspondents, circular of 26 August 1858, in Charmes, 198 (italics in the original); and *RSS*, 2d ser., 3 (1st sem. 1860): 699.

55. Rouland, speech of 24 May 1862, in *Discours et réquisitoires de M. Rouland*, 2 vols. (Paris, 1863), 2:146–47; and *RSS*, 2d ser., no. 2 (2d sem. 1859): 622–23.

Ecole des Chartes, Lara Moore shows that the latter's new 1846 curriculum, which trained future archivists in historical analysis as well as paleography, produced a spate of local monographs a decade later. Archival collection was no longer the sole modus operandi: by 1854, the Minister of the Interior was inviting archivists to collect and classify local documents that "still contain the particular history of each of the provinces, localities, and families." Moore also argues convincingly that in order to seduce a wide political range of constituents, the Second Empire cultivated a variety of historical endeavors.[56] With respect to local difference, I would furthermore reemphasize the factors mentioned in the previous chapter: aspirations to social harmony in the wake of 1848; a growing preoccupation with endangered local particularities; and the conviction that France had grown "sufficiently strong" and united to recognize local cultures.[57] Such convictions, along with a renewed desire for surreptitious action, led officials to grant their cult of local memories a still broader dimension.

While apprehension of local difference weakened in these circles, it did not vanish. Concern shifted, however, toward peripheral regions and regional sentiments (although governmental anxiety about regional autonomy remained low throughout the century). In 1857, the *Revue des sociétés savantes* expressed misgivings about the resurgence of Languedocian poetry, this "effort of a local genius that fights to preserve and defend its own individuality and physiognomy." The "effort" in question was most probably the Félibrige, the association for the defense of Provençal language and poetry that conservative writer Frédéric Mistral had founded in 1854. Another contributor to the *Revue* castigated the old provincial estates and their contemporary "defenders," who regretted "this freedom of the provinces." Despite their growing tolerance for monographs, moreover, CTH members continued to value dictionaries as "the kind of local publication [that] deserves encouragement."[58] In one respect, these officials and CTH members continued, as in years past, to view local difference as both appealing and ominous. One of them praised the Comité flamand in 1855 for studying "particular language[s], . . . [an] important aspect of a province's history," but also urged its members to regret neither the primacy of French nor France's provincial "conquests." In another respect, a growing divide separated the majority that was coming to terms with local difference from the minority that was not. Around 1860,

56. Lara Jennifer Moore, "Restoring Order," 176–87 and 236–38; and *Revue archéologique* 10 (1853): 747, quoted in Ibid., 234.

57. *RSS*, 1st ser., no. 2 (1st sem. 1857): 257–58.

58. *RSS*, 1st ser., no. 3 (2d sem. 1857): 19–20; *RSS*, 2d ser., 2 (2d sem. 1859): 79–83; and AN F17 2905: Summaries of the reports of Henri de Longpérier on *Histoire du Velay* and *Dictionnaire historique du département de l'Aisne*, n.d. [1865].

the *Revue des sociétés savantes* could thus publish divergent articles in successive issues, one lauding "local patriotism," the other congratulating a learned society for transcending "narrow" local attachments.[59]

At this very time, Rouland's tripartite survey of France (geographical, archeological, and scientific) provoked an internal debate on this question—the first of its kind. The venture's departmental framework would yield eighty-six comparable volumes and a uniform portrait of the French territory and past. Some CTH members and officials questioned this format. Why, for one, produce countless, near-identical scientific descriptions of departments that lacked "special fauna, flora, mineralogical constitution[s]"? Why not undertake instead botanical or geological "descriptions of each province"—along with a "natural history of the entire country"?[60] Others pushed the point further. "Although France displays remarkable unity, from governmental as well as patriotic perspectives," wrote the dean of Nancy's Faculté des sciences, "this unity does not exist [within] the predominantly rural population as far as mores, habits, ethnological personality, natural aptitudes, etc. are concerned. The Lorrain does not resemble, in various respects, the Alsatian, the Francomtais, the Bourguignon." Beyond the opposition between administrative and natural divisions—an enduring debate among nineteenth-century geographers—internal diversity was the crux of the matter. The president of the Académie des sciences et lettres de Montpellier regretted, in fact, the ministry's disregard for internal "differences."[61]

Six CTH and BTH members urged Rouland to initiate a fourth collective venture: a "Tableau of the Internal Organization of France before 1789."[62] This project would "study the country's development in its most intimate and hidden elements," from topography to education and economic production. It would revolve around historical provinces rather than departments. This framework corresponded to the Old Regime's internal organization and brought out the "distinctive life and original character of each province." Provincial elites, added the authors, would no

---

59. *Bulletin des sociétés savantes* 2 (1854–55): 37–38; *RSS*, 2d ser., no. 3 (1st sem. 1860): 699; and *RSS*, 2d ser., no. 2 (2d sem. 1859): 23.

60. AN F17 3316: Proceedings of the Commission on the Scientific Dictionary, 15 November 1858; and AN F17 3042: Anon., memorandum to Min. Pub. Instrc., n.d. (1861?).

61. AN F17 3317: Dean of Faculté des sciences of Nancy to Min. Pub. Instrc., 21 June 1860; and AN F17 3316: President Académie des sciences et lettres de Montpellier to Min. Pub. Instrc., 22 August 1860. On the debates among geographers, see Numa Broc, "La pensée géographique en France au XIXe siècle: continuité ou rupture?" *Revue géographique des Pyrénées et du Sud-Ouest* 47, no. 3 (1976): 239.

62. The following discussion is based on AN F17 2823: Charles Jourdain et al. to Rouland, memorandum of 22 February 1859. I have identified five of the six signatories: Jourdain, then head of ministry's accounting division; Firmin Laferrière, a high-level ministerial official and ex-university inspector; Pierre Clément, an official in the Ministry of Finances; Victor Foucher, an important magistrate; and Hellenist Joseph Guigniaut.

doubt prefer provincial to departmental investigations, these "scattered aspects" of an abstract venture that was orchestrated in the capital. Was it not preferable to direct them toward "the *pays* they inhabit and whose memories they, better than anyone else, will be able to collect and coordinate with the zeal that sprang from the union of local patriotism and love of science?" Assurances that all monographs would follow the same blueprint proved insufficient. Rouland shelved their proposal and maintained a departmental grid, consonant with "the country's political and administrative state."[63] Local difference was winning converts, but most officials still found it easier to speak of vague local memories than to deepen the singularity—historical and other—of *pays* and provinces.

The evolution was nonetheless undeniable—and it intensified throughout the 1860s. Consider the ministry's response to two proposals for public contests. In 1851, Amiens's Société des antiquaires de Picardie had implored the ministry to at last recognize the diversity of French "provinces . . . with respect to memories or monuments." The best way of doing so was to create annual contests for provincial learned societies—but without imposing a uniform program that obscured each province's memories. The Société had thus asked the ministry "to abandon each [learned] society to its own decisions," allowing each one to "undertake the investigations that correspond best to the needs of the localities." Societies from Metz, Nîmes, and elsewhere—as well as the *Revue des deux mondes*—endorsed a project that would allay official scorn for the memories of "small localities." The ministry did not follow up on this request.[64] In 1865, however, it proved more receptive to a similar proposal from Montauban's Société des sciences et arts de Tarn-et-Garonne. Alarmed by the Parisian exodus of "intelligent and studious men," its president had long sought to grant learned societies "greater appeal [and] vigor." He accordingly urged Duruy to institute regional contests (in history, archaeology, and the like) that would serve this cause without "weaken[ing] . . . our great and precious national unity." Others in France were making similar proposals. Duruy established such contests in the eighteen rectoral academies in 1868, with learned society members as referees.[65] Despite their

63. Rouland to presidents of learned societies, circular of 1 June 1860, in Charmes, 207.
64. AN F17 3021: "Mémoire présenté à M. le Ministre de l'instruction publique au nom de toutes les sociétés savantes de la France départementale par la Société des antiquaires de Picardie. Demande d'un concours annuel," 1 September 1851; *Bulletin de la Société des antiquaires de Picardie* 4 (1850–52): 190–99; AN F17 3021: President Société d'histoire et d'archéologie de Chalon-sur-Saône to Min. Pub. Instr., n.d. [1851]; Charles Louandre, "Les études historiques et archéologiques en province depuis 1848. Les provinces du centre et du midi, dernière partie," *RDM*, new period, 12 (October-December 1851): 185; and Archives Municipales d'Amiens 2 R 2–1: Min. Pub. Instrc. to mayor Amiens, 7 November 1851.
65. *Recueil de la Société des sciences, belles-lettres et arts du Tarn-et-Garonne* (1867): 83; AN F17 3015/1: President Société des sciences, belles-lettres et arts du Tarn-et-Garonne to Min. Pub.

limitations—topics were devised in Paris—these contests betray a governmental overture. They marked the culmination of a twenty-year evolution,
an uneasy but steady integration of local difference within the official cult
of local memories.

"INFINITELY SMALL," INFINITELY MEDIOCRE

By the mid-1860s, cultural barriers against local difference had thus declined in intensity. While the *Revue des sociétés savantes* still reminded
provincials intermittently to "subordinate local sentiment to the sentiment of the common *patrie*," officials now invited provincials to cultivate
local memories outside the governmental framework. The CTH began ad-
vising learned societies to publish "in the *pays* to which [they] pertain"
those archaeological inventories and geographical dictionaries they could
not sponsor.[66] And yet, a surprisingly high number of officials and CTH
members still deemed local difference unpalatable. To understand why,
let us recall that positivistic science acquired a new dimension during the
1860s—an evolution that responded partly to the superiority of German
science and universities. This was a period of growing disaffection with
the shortcomings of French higher education and of initial reform under
Duruy: the beginnings of a transition toward academic practice. This
decade also saw the emergence of an incipient historical discipline—a
more thorough and critical historical scholarship—through the Ecole pra-
tique des hautes études (founded in 1868) and specialized journals such
as the *Revue des questions historiques* (founded in 1866). The Ecole des
chartes graduated ever-growing numbers of trained historians and
archivists, committed to rigorous scholarship. The creation in 1872 of the
Association française pour l'avancement des sciences further separated
amateurs from an increasingly professional and specialized scientific
arena.[67]

Scientific desiderata had, as we have seen, imprinted the BTH and
CTH from the start of our period. They grew more pressing, however,
under the Second Empire—all the more so during the 1860s—as the ministry took new steps to ensure greater rigor. In 1862, it created an Advi-
sory Committee for Literary and Scientific Subscriptions that gave CTH
members and intellectual figures such as historian Alfred Maury a greater

---

Instr., 18 June 1865; AN F17 3318: Anon., memorandum to Armand Dumesnil, 20 February
1866; and Victor Duruy, report to Louis-Napoléon on higher education, November 1866, in
Charmes, 233.

66. *RSS*, 4th ser., 10 (2d sem. 1869): 390–92; and AN F17 3309: Min. Pub. Instrc. to president Société archéologique de l'Orléanais, 27 April 1866.

67. William Keylor, *Academy and Community: The Foundation of the French Historical Profession*
(Cambridge, Mass., 1975), 20–35; and George Weisz, *Emergence of Modern Universities*.

say in governmental subscriptions.[68] The BTH and CTH began combing proofs of the *Revue des sociétés savantes* for "hardly serious" articles. They purged nonproductive, albeit influential, correspondents (72 out of 205 in 1863) and divided learned societies into three merit-based categories.[69] They also turned to university professors to impart "the direction most in keeping with the true interests of science" to other provincial elites. All of this reflected building disappointment with these amateurs. "It is certain that a great many [provincial] societies do not amount to much," an official wrote Duruy in 1866. Other officials scoffed at the Sorbonne congresses, these assemblies of "infinitely small" delegates whose papers, lacking "true value," no longer deserved publicity.[70]

In this new climate, localism came increasingly to denote mediocrity. Parisian *littérateurs* lambasted provincial societies with growing alacrity for their "research on insignificant points of history," a local inclination that was "the most serious cause of the[ir] sterility." Members of provincial learned societies even castigated colleagues for publishing overly detailed works on the smallest towns.[71] These works owed much to the state, of course, yet some officials and CTH members began questioning the value of such narrow studies. "This book ha[s] a purely local relevance, there is no reason to subscribe on state funds": such judgments multiplied. Histories of ancient provinces were, to some extent, immune from such criticism since they produced broader insights than local monographs. But not always. The *Légendes, curiosités et traditions de la Champagne et de la Brie*, for instance "may have held some appeal for the *pays*'s inhabitants," but it did "not carry a sufficiently general interest to justify a subscription."[72]

Some officials continued to encourage local erudition and even monographs, however mediocre, for a mixture of scientific and instrumental

68. AN F17 2905: Decree establishing the Comité consultatif pour les souscriptions littéraires et scientifiques, 7 January 1862.

69. Jean-Christophe Bourquin claims that, with respect to the ministry's missions, this rupture took place around 1882. I would argue that the ministry had begun moving in this direction two decades earlier. See Bourquin, "L'Etat et les voyageurs savants: légitimités individuelles et volontés politiques. Les missions du ministère de l'instruction publique (1840–1914)," Ph.D. diss, University of Paris I, 1993, 309. See also AN F17 3319: Proceedings of the commission of the *Revue des sociétés savantes*, 30 October 1858; and AN F17 2811: Anon., ministerial 'note', 16 January 1863.

70. Min. Pub. Instr. to rectors, circular of 29 March 1858, in Charmes, 189; AN F17 3254: Anon., "Note à M. le ministre," 27 December 1866; AN F17 3318: Anon., memorandum of 20 February 1866; and AN F17 3050: François-Louis Bellaguet to Duruy, memorandum of 22 June 1869.

71. *La Gazette littéraire, artistique et scientifique* 31 (3 December 1864): 307; *L'Echo des provinces* 1, no. 38 (8 October 1865): 4; and Léon de Maleville, *De la décentralisation de l'histoire et de l'abus des dissertations historiques* (Montauban, 1868).

72. AN F17 2890: Min. Pub. Instrc. to Abbé Dinet, 6 February 1862; and AN F17 2889/1: Anon., memorandum, June 1861.

purposes. Many CTH members, however, sought to rid the official cult of local memories of memorial attachment, "the description of local customs and the relation of local legends." This scientific current discredited those objects that, per Krzystof Pomian, "are without value for the historical attitude, even though memory has deemed them significant." In 1860, archivist Louis De Mas Latrie urged provincial correspondents to restrict themselves to "pure and simple description" in their archaeological inventories and eschew "descriptions of local customs and narrative on local legends." Two years later, numismatist Henri de Longpérier commented that, given the flood of pedestrian local histories, one could only endorse those rare monographs that rested on "the quotation of properly understood texts."[73] Local difference alarmed these men, not as a putative threat to national unity, but in its amateurism and as an affection for local memories that skewed the authors' priorities. The *Revue des sociétés savantes* hence expressed its perplexity before a 531-page *Histoire de la ville de Doullens* in 1866. "The prevailing deficiency of local histories," explained the reviewer, "is to broaden the topic instead of restricting it." The author had thus granted an inordinate "extension to what I would call the appetizers of history."[74] The author, to rephrase the objection, had allowed local memorial sentiments to overshadow scientific rigor.

THE *PETITE PATRIE* UNDER THE THIRD REPUBLIC

This chapter and the preceding one tell complementary stories. Local difference had lost much, but not all, of its cultural pregnancy by the end of our period. Like others, officials and CTH members believed that technological and communications advances were sealing France's geographical unification. The turmoil of 1848—followed by the political battles of 1851–52—led them as well to idealize with newfound zeal harmonious local communities as a counterweight to widening social divisions and political agitation. Affection for the *pays* and its memories could, if properly channeled, supply unmistakable social and political benefits. This draws us back to a *petite patrie* that was both an instrument of civic pedagogy and an explicitly memorial articulation of local and national identifications, of diversity-in-unity. While the concept's history remains to be written, it apparently emerged in the seventeenth century and surfaced episodically thereafter. Rousseau granted it a civic function in his *Emile* (1762). It is "through the *petite patrie*, which is the family, that the heart embraces the

73. Krzystof Pomian, "Conclusion de la journée du 6 janvier," in Jacques Le Goff, ed., *Patrimoine et passions*, 115; AN F17 3313: Louis De Mas Latrie, notes for a letter to secretary, Société académique des Hautes-Pyrénées, 15 May 1860; and AN F17 2983: Henri de Longpérier to Min. Pub. Instrc., report of 20 July 1862.

74. *RSS*, 4th ser., vol. 2 (2d sem. 1866): 127–28.

grande [patrie]," that one learns to love one's fellow citizens. This conception reappeared in early nineteenth-century political thought. The best school of civic virtue, argued liberal Sismondi in 1829, was "the narrow patrie [*patrie plus restreinte*]," or commune.[75] References multiplied in the field of local memories during the following decades. "Love of the French *patrie* and the local *patrie*" alone could "renew [French] literature without depriving it of its nationality," posited a participant in Lyons's 1841 scientific congress. For Amiens lawyer Hyacinthe Dusevel, the memories of one's birthplace—galvanized by historical understanding—buttressed a broader "love of the *patrie.*" In 1858, a member of the Société d'agriculture, sciences, arts et commerce du Puy defined the *petite patrie* as "one of those *patries* that one loves all the more when one knows it better." Addressing the Sorbonne congress of April 1870, Minister of Public Instruction Maurice Richard praised the assembled provincial elites as "a vibrant image of this free variety of tastes, sentiments, thoughts . . . that we must encourage more and more within the great national unity. . . . By attentively serving the *petite patrie,* you help strengthen the *grande.*"[76]

The *petite patrie* anchored, as we have seen, a series of concentric loyalties, a love of growing intensity that converged on the nation. Varied as they were, the thousands of *petites patries* that dotted France thus pointed toward the same direction; all enjoyed identical relationships with the nation. In chapter 3, I suggested several political and pedagogical reasons why left and right concurred in the last third of the century that attention to the nation's internal diversity, its abundance of complementary riches promised to regenerate France. Leading geographer Paul Vidal de la Blache contended in 1896 that French unity rested on its internal "active forces," a diversity that France, with her remarkable capacity for assimilation, could easily absorb.[77] The same could hold true on the cultural front, where the *petite patrie*'s benefits could offset eventual scientific shortcomings. The *petite patrie* model furthermore resolved the tensions that had

75. Jean-Jacques Rousseau, *Emile ou de l'éducation* (Paris, 1966 [1762]), 473; Norbert Dupont, "Les familles de *patrie, état, nation,*" in Sylvianne Rémi-Giraud and Pierre Rétat, eds., *Mots de la nation,* 174; and J. C. L. de Sismondi, untitled review article, in *Revue encyclopédique* 41 (January-March 1829): 644.

76. *CS* 9, 2 vols. (Lyons, 1841), 1:411–12; Hyacinthe Dusevel, *Histoire de la ville d'Amiens depuis les Gaulois jusqu'à nos jours,* 2d ed. (Amiens, 1848), vii; *Annales de la Société d'agriculture, sciences, arts et commerce du Puy* 21 (1857–58): 129; and *Discours prononcé par son excellence le Ministre de l'instruction publique à la réunion des sociétés savantes le 23 avril 1870* (Paris, 1870), 1 and 3.

77. Two leading articulations of the *petite patrie* had emerged by 1900: the version of Ferry and other mainstream Republicans and the physical determinism of "la terre et les morts," propounded by Maurice Barrès, the New Right, and others. What I have written so far above applies to both; what follows pertains essentially to the former. See Bertho-Lavenir, "Invention du monument," 25–26; and Paul Vidal de la Blache, *Annales de Géographie* (1896), quoted in Jean-Yves Guiomar, "*Le Tableau de la géographie de la France* de Vidal de la Blache," in Nora, ed., *Lieux de mémoire,* 3: 573.

surrounded local difference. It outlined a vertical relationship between France and its *pays* that made it possible to celebrate the latter's diversity and specificity within the nation. According to this model, all local elements retained their particularity, but as contributions to a broader entity that transcended them. This model integrated organic and voluntarist models of territorial identity, moreover, by conjugating place and memories with spontaneous memorial and civic participation at the local level. As such, it captured Ernest Renan's influential two-tiered conception of the nation. "Man is the slave of neither his race, his language, nor his religion, neither of the courses of rivers, nor of the mountain ranges," he declared in 1882, clearly distancing himself from the organic model. Instead, "two things, which strictly speaking are just one, constitute this soul, this spiritual principle"—the nation. "One is the common possession of a rich legacy of memories; the other is actual consent, the desire to live together."[78] A decade later, Renan lauded the *petite patrie* before an assembly of Félibrige members. "The bond that ties us to France, to humanity," he declared, "does not diminish the strength and tenderness of our individual and local sentiments." On the contrary, "consciousness of the parts" buttressed "consciousness of the whole."[79]

By attaching citizens to territorial communities (albeit open to outsiders), the *petite patrie* furthermore deflected the dangers of "individual pride [*amour-propre*]." Let us "transform the egoism that splits us apart," Cambrai's *Revue de l'Escaut* had proposed in 1859, "into this noble and generous sentiment that we call local patriotism."[80] By redirecting memorial sentiments that could lead one to "exalt local patriotism at the expense of national patriotism," this model furthermore alleviated the threat of cultural fragmentation. In an 1897 essay, *The Idea of the Patrie*, a member of the Société d'agriculture, sciences et arts de l'arrondissement de Valenciennes contrasted the *patriotisme de clocher*, which could prove "detrimental to national sentiments," with a *petite patrie* that granted national sentiments a "concrete form."[81] While its participants did not necessarily intend to do so, the field of local memories had helped fashion a working synthesis of local and national sentiments. Had he still been alive, Aristide Guilbert would no doubt have endorsed a delineation of place and past that neither exacerbated local difference nor reduced it to a single center.

78. Chanet, *Ecole républicaine*, 153; Ernest Renan, "What Is a Nation?" (1882), in Woolf, ed., *Nationalism in Europe, 1815 to the Present* (London, 1996), 57–59; and Anne-Marie Thiesse, *Création des identités*, 12 and 236. This analysis has benefited from my discussions with Anne-Marie Thiesse.

79. Sextius Michel, *La petite patrie* (Paris, 1894), 200, quoted in Martel, "Les gauches félibréennes," in *Cahiers Jean Jaurès* 152 (April–June 1999): 21.

80. *Revue de l'Escaut* 2, no. 80 (20 February 1859): 2.

81. *BUGN* 6 (1885): 91; and Louis Legrand, *Idée de patrie*, 262.

SEVEN

The Quandary of Local Initiative

Good citizens will understand that the cause of the state [*du pouvoir*] is nowadays the cause of society.

Prime Minister CASIMIR PÉRIER
to prefects, March 1831

L OCAL DIFFERENCE WAS not the sole conceptual difficulty in ministerial circles. In 1863, Louis Saint-Loup was a thirty-two-year-old mathematics teacher in Strasbourg, a "*professeur* with great prospects" who impressed his superiors with his keen intelligence and demanding teaching style. He was also a member of the Société des sciences, agriculture et arts du Bas-Rhin—but a disenchanted one, increasingly frustrated by the shortcomings of provincial learned societies. The pattern was unmistakable: publications that went unread, a failure to keep up with the latest advances, a tendency to "record painstaking investigations rather than making them known." Saint-Loup thus applauded Minister Gustave Rouland's call, that February, for greater "publicity" and exchanges between these societies. But this was not enough. Four months later, Saint-Loup sent the Ministry of Public Instruction a proposal for a complete overhaul of this associative domain. According to his plan, all provincial societies would join a loosely organized network under the ministry's aegis. Instead of publishing their own periodicals, they would contribute articles to the *Annales des sociétés savantes* (Annals of Learned Societies), a series of fifteen to twenty periodicals that would cover distinct disciplines, including history. Local commissions of intellectual elites would determine which articles deserved publication. This "new common organization" would ensure quality and publicity, Saint-Loup insisted, while respecting the societies' "independence."[1]

Three years elapsed without a reply. The proposal may have vanished in the mail, as one official later alleged, or it may have ended up in a

---

1. Saint-Loup retired as a university dean in 1901. See AN F17 3321: Louis Saint-Loup to Min. Pub. Instrc., June 1863; and AN F17 21686: Rector Strasbourg, reports on Saint-Loup, May and 10 June 1862.

drawer. In 1866, Saint-Loup sent the ministry another copy and, this time, the BTH paid attention—perhaps because the author now taught at the esteemed lycée Bonaparte in Paris. Officials annotated and summarized his plan, weighing its merits in several memoranda. While all praised its "excellent intentions," they also voiced reservations. One feared a deluge of "dismal productions" that would force the ministry to "quash, at our own risk, the judgment of local commissions." Others doubted that local elites would accept such ministerial oversight. Had Saint-Loup considered whether "his proposal had any chance of success with learned societies that want above all to be independent"? An official captured the crux of the matter: "We cannot think of centralizing everything, as Mr. Saint-Loup desires." The ministry had long sought, it is true, to "link these learned societies to one another." But it also "allows these bodies to maintain all of their initiative. Saint-Loup straightjackets them a little too much."[2] And so, for a mix of doctrinal and instrumental reasons, the ministry turned down the overzealous teacher.

This episode is but a footnote in the history of the French intellectual state, but an illuminating one. It draws a counterintuitive tableau: on the one hand, a provincial resident (albeit a civil servant) seeking greater administrative presence; on the other, officials of the Second Empire (albeit the liberal Empire) upholding the all-important initiative of provincial learned societies. These officials long debated this question before coming to a decision, however. They refused to "centraliz[e] everything" but could not deny a desire to centralize *something* in this intellectual realm. This is the topic of this chapter: the elusive boundary between the state and civil society in such official circles and its impact on the official cult of local memories.[3] Contemporaries used the locution "civil society" sparingly, but when they did—or when they spoke of society, civil association, and initiative—it was almost invariably in the context of an uneasy relationship with the state. An influential liberal credo taught, as we have seen, that the postrevolutionary order rested on two complementary forces: governmental direction and a free acting civil society, the good will of a growing "number of intermediaries" who would help govern and organize France. Like the officials who assessed Saint-Loup's proposal, Salvandy valued the indispensable "contribution" of resourceful individuals and learned societies, "free to accept or not" his invitation. Yet he also in-

2. AN F17 3021: Saint-Loup to Min. Pub. Instrc., 12 April and 21 May 1866; and AN F17 3321: Anon. memoranda to Victor Duruy on Saint-Loup's proposal, 2 June 1866 and n.d. [1866].
3. The state denotes here any form of governmental action or presence, be it ministerial, the CTH, or local. Civil society designates the sphere of voluntary action, association, and "private efforts" that is free from official tutelage.

structed the CTH to centralize this realm, "regularize" it, and make it "productive."[4]

Be it under the July Monarchy or Second Empire, French officials thus sought both to broaden the state's role and to uphold the necessary vigor of provincial elites. Certain questions captured this tension with particular acuity: ministerial subsidies to learned societies; prefectoral commissions of archaeology; and Arcisse de Caumont's circle, this independent network of associations and annual congresses. All encountered a self-same quandary—the quandary, we might call it, of local initiative.

FREE AND SPONTANEOUS ASSOCIATION

Most provincial learned societies were poor in the nineteenth century. Many battled near-constant—and sometimes fatal—debt. Presenting themselves as "paupers of science," they repeatedly wrote the ministry about their inability to fully investigate their "*pays*'s history." These self-serving claims typically preceded requests for a monetary "vote of approval," but internal records indicate that they were often true.[5] Officials knew as much and helped these associations in ways preceding regimes had not. Yet, ministerial subsidies to learned societies were insignificant at best until 1847 and small afterward (see table 1). Guizot and Salvandy both acknowledged providing but "small sums to help . . . local research," subsidies that were "quite insufficient when one considered the needs."[6] In 1857, BTH official Charles Jourdain insisted that subsidies to learned societies should be increased. And so they were, three years later, but timidly—all the more so if one recalls the growing number of such associations. Only 56 provincial learned societies received a ministerial subsidy in 1859; 124 did so in 1868.[7] In the Nord, fortunate recipients could expect a paltry average of two hundred francs per year—with no marked improvement between 1850 and 1870 (see table 2). This parsimony stymied the cult of local memories by curtailing provincial as well as governmental

4. Comte de Montalivet to Louis-Philippe, report of 5 November 1831, in *Circulaires et instructions*, 2: 46; and AN F17 13268: Proceedings of the Committee on chronicles, charters and inscriptions, 14 January 1838.

5. AN F17 3041: President Société des antiquaires de l'Ouest to Min. Pub. Instrc., 13 January 1849; and AN F17 3040: President Société littéraire et scientifique de Castres to Min. Pub. Instrc., 4 July 1860.

6. François Guizot, report on the 1837 budget, in *Ministère de l'instruction publique: budget des dépenses de l'exercice 1837* (Paris, 1836), 21; idem, *Mémoires*, 3: 162; and Narcisse de Salvandy, *Budget de l'exercice 1847. Rapport au roi* (Paris, n.d. [1846]), 87.

7. Charles Jourdain, *Budget*, 258; and AN F17 3022/1: Anon. memorandum, 1 August 1859, and Anon., "Sociétés savantes. Propositions pour des subventions. Résumé," 13 July 1868.

TABLE 1. Ministerial Subsidies to Learned Societies, 1837–1870 (in Francs)

	1837	1838	1839	1840	1841	1842	1843	1844	1845	1846	1847	1848	1849	1850	1851	1852	1853
Subsidies to learned societies	3,500	5,100	10,700	10,454	1,150	4,500	3,100	3,235	3,200	9,795	50,000	50,000	35,000	35,000	35,000	35,000	30,000
Sum distributed in the provinces											42,100			27,950			
Number of recipients							32			32	43	35		61			

	1854	1855	1856	1857	1858	1859	1860	1861	1862	1863	1864	1865	1866	1867	1868	1869	1870
Subsidies to learned societies	30,000	30,000	30,000	30,000	30,000	30,000	40,000	40,000	50,000	50,000	50,000	50,000	56,000	70,000	66,000	70,000	70,000
Sum distributed in the provinces			18,600			30,800	35,000					31,950	33,600	38,300	46,400	43,100	43,900
Number of recipients	52		52			75	89	86		92					124		

Methodology and Sources: No comprehensive list of subsidies has, to my knowledge, survived regarding this period. This incomplete table thus contains the information I collected in various archival and printed sources regarding the Ministry of Public Instruction.

Row 1: These figures cover both provincial and Parisian learned societies (excluding the Institut de France). Parisian societies were a distinct minority, ten at the most. Sources: annual Budget des dépenses de l'exercice 18xx and Compte définitif des dépenses de l'exercice 18xx pour les services de l'instruction publique; and Jourdain, Budget de l'instruction publique, 335.

Row 2: The difference between the budgeted allocation and the sum distributed to provincial societies went partly to Parisian societies, partly to such enterprises as the Revue des sociétés savantes. Source: AN F17 3022/1–2.

TABLE 2. Ministerial Subsidies to the Learned Societies of the Nord, 1847–1870 (in Francs)

Learned Society	1847	1848	1849	1850	1851	1852	1853	1854	1855	1856	1857	1858
Commission historique du Nord					300			300				
Société d'Emulation de Cambrai				300	300	300		200	200			300
Société d'agriculture . . . de Douai	600	600	400		500	400	300	300	200	300	300	
Société dunkerquoise . . .					Founded	200		200	200	200	200	
Comité flamand de France							Founded	200	200	200	200	
Société des sciences . . . de Lille		600	300	300	300				200	200	200	
Société d'agriculture . . . de Valenciennes			300	300	300	500		300	200	300	300	

(continued)

TABLE 2. (*continued*)

Learned Society	1859	1860	1861	1862	1863	1864	1865	1866	1867	1868	1869	1870
Commission historique du Nord				350	350	300			300	300	300	
Société d'émulation de Cambrai		400	300		350	300	350	350		300	300	300
Société d'agriculture . . . de Douai		300	400	350	350	300	300	350	350	400	400	400
Société dunkerquoise . . .		300	400	350				300	300	300	300	300
Comité flamand de France		200	300		300		300		300	300	300	
Société des sciences . . . de Lille	300	300	400	400	400	400	400	400	400	500	500	500
Société d'agriculture . . . de Valenciennes		300	400		300	300	350	300	350	300	300	300

Methodology and Sources: This table rests on ministerial records (AN F17 3022/1–2), correspondence, and the publications of learned societies. It does not purport to be complete and does not include subsidies from the Ministry of Agriculture, which several of these societies received. I confirmed these figures by cross-checking Parisian and provincial sources. Where I did not find any reference to a subsidy, I left a blank. In most cases, this means that the society received nothing that year from the Ministry of Public Instruction.

ventures. Around 1860, learned societies from Châlons-sur-Marne, Gap, and elsewhere informed the ministry that, without a larger subsidy, they could not contribute to its geographical dictionary of France.[8] No increase followed.

Financial restrictions came into play yet again. Some ministerial officials even questioned the urgency of historical ventures during an era of budgetary constraints. It is on this ground, after all, that deputies contested allocations for monuments and learned societies under the July Monarchy. There were other priorities. Agricultural societies and *comices*, in contrast, received more than 250,000 francs in 1840. Around this time, CTH member Jules Desnoyers claimed to understand that, in such a politically volatile period, the ministry would turn its attention to "far weightier issues than a work of historical erudition."[9] The ministry's fickle subsidies also call to mind an ancient tradition of selective patronage. The Bourbons had, after all, long kept French writers, artists, and scientists in check by granting them subsidies of varying sizes and unexpectedly naming new recipients while removing existing ones. Important enough to matter, yet small and unpredictable enough to prevent complacency, ministerial subsidies would foster dependence. Some provincials hence accused officials of intentionally sowing competition among them.[10]

More significant, this parsimony reflected doctrinal concern with local initiative. During the 1830s, liberal deputies argued that such subsidies would create a "hierarchy of civil servants" and a "passive" society. "One must not grow accustomed to getting everything done through the budget and the government," declared one Pelet (de la Lozère) in 1834. The state should allow "free institutions and private individuals" to "do something."[11] Such views emanated from the ministry as well. Traveling through England around 1850, Désiré Nisard wrote admiringly of the English youth's intimate knowledge of local history and *statistique*—a knowledge that owed little to the state. English communes and private cit-

8. See, for instance, AN F17 3302: President Société d'agriculture, commerce, sciences et arts du département de la Marne to Min. Pub. Instrc., 1 March 1860; and AN F17 3299: President Académie Flosalpine to Min. Pub. Instrc., 2 November 1861.

9. AN F10 1582: Tableau of agricultural subsidies in 1840, 17 March 1841; and AN F17 3293: Jules Desnoyers to Hippolyte Royer-Collard, 7 February 1836.

10. Julien Travers, *Des travaux collectifs que pourraient entreprendre les sociétés savantes des départements* (Caen, 1864), 11; Priscilla P. Clark and Terry Nichols Clark, "Patrons, Publishers, and Prizes: The Writer's Estate in France," in Joseph Ben-David and Terry Nichols Clark, eds., *Culture and Its Creators: Essays in Honor of Edward Shils* (Chicago, 1977), 202–3; and Mordechai Feingold, "Philanthropy, Pomp, and Patronage: Historical Reflections Upon the Endowment of Culture," *Daedalus* 116, no. 1 (winter 1987): 174–75.

11. Xavier de Sade and Privat-Joseph-Charamond Pelet (de la Lozère), interventions in the parliamentary session of 10 May 1834, in J. Madival and E. Laurent, eds., *Archives parlementaires*, 90: 153–54.

izens paid for the upkeep of local monuments, an expense for which "the state's budget does not allocate funds." In his memoirs, Nisard related that, back in France, some of his ministerial colleagues had likewise sought to limit subsidies. "The Ministry of Public Instruction is not a welfare office," an unnamed minister told him.[12] From this vantage point, the ministry's measly and fluctuating subsidies reveal a reticence to stifle "private efforts." The state should not overextend itself in the intellectual realm.

Such considerations curbed the official cult of local memories in other ways. The ministry's pledge to "multiply the centers of work and study throughout the Kingdom" excluded, for one, independent commissions of provincial elites, a departmental or regional echelon above learned societies.[13] In the late 1850s, several provincials argued forcefully that such "subcommittees" would benefit the ministry's geographical dictionary and archaeological inventory of France by collecting "documents and materials in each department" and scrutinizing local submissions. They would perfect a system in which "a single committee in the capital centralizes provincial investigations."[14] Yet, the BTH maintained its existing framework. The problem was not local difference (as with regional contests), but local initiative, embodied in provincial centers of authority that challenged the central state's preeminence. Yet had the ministry only sought to enhance its own authority, it would have done more for the archaeological and historical commissions that prefects were establishing in various departments. Two circulars from the Ministry of the Interior had, it is true, invited prefects to create commissions of antiquaries or architects in 1818 and 1831. Under the July Monarchy, CTH members also urged prefects to help "cover France with archaeological commissions."[15] This encouragement was limited, however, and such invitations haphazard. Ministerial officials neither established such agencies nor provided them with significant resources. They congratulated prefects intermittently for their zeal and left it at that. Unsurprisingly, fewer than twenty such commissions surfaced during our period.

---

12. Désiré Nisard, "Les classes moyennes en Angleterre et la bourgeoisie en France" (1849) and "Un voyage dans le Nottinghamshire" (1850), in his *Etudes de critique littéraire*, 223–24 and 256–57; and idem, *Souvenirs et notes biographiques*, 2 vols. (Paris, 1888), 1: 350.

13. Narcisse de Salvandy to Louis-Philippe, report of 31 December 1838, in *Budget général des dépenses pour l'exercice 1840*, 59.

14. AN F17 3302: President Société historique et archéologique de Langres to Min. Pub. Instrc., n.d. (November 1858); AN F17 3304/1: Georges Martin to Secretary Société littéraire de Lyon (letter transmitted to Min. Pub. Instrc.), 3 September 1859; and *AIP* 13 (1861): 250.

15. Min. Int. to prefects, circular of 16 November 1831, in *Notes circulaires et rapports sur le service de la conservation des monuments historiques* (Paris, 1862), 13; AN F17 13268: Proceedings of the CHAM, 22 May 1838; AN F17 13269: Proceedings of the CHAM, 27 January 1841; and *Bulletin du CHAM* 1, no. 1 (1840): 99.

The Commission historique du Nord is a case in point. In 1835, Douai magistrate and historian Eugène Tailliar wrote Guizot that, in the Nord, a departmental commission would best serve his *Recueil des monuments de l'histoire du Tiers-Etat*. The seven-member agency he envisaged (staffed by civil servants) would secure the cooperation of learned societies and forward its findings to the prefect and ministry. Guizot replied, but without addressing his proposal. The latter only came to fruition in 1839, through the efforts of Prefect Gabriel de Saint-Aignan and prefectoral secretary Antoine de Contencin. They enlisted local elites, secured the Ministry of the Interior's approval, and assured Paris that "far from obstructing" ministerial ventures, the Commission historique would prove an invaluable partner.[16] Apparently convinced, ministerial officials praised an agency that would inspire respect for monuments and historical study. The Commission's exchanges with Paris remained infrequent, however. Contencin sent the CTH reports on its activities, but secured little "moral" or financial encouragement in return. The Commission's financial situation—perpetually "weak, irregular, hence insufficient"—forced it to rely on its printer's credit to publish its *Bulletin*.[17] Whereas the ministry handed the Nord's five leading learned societies an average of two hundred francs per year between 1847 and 1870, it only awarded the Commission an average of 104 francs (see table 2). Officials may have expected the department's *Conseil général* to step in (which it did, intermittently). Yet, the ministry clearly refused to award the agency a special status. In 1859, Commission president André Le Glay wrote Rouland that the Nord's learned societies had begun work on the geographical dictionary. All of "these partial investigations will have to be linked and coordinated to form a whole that pertains to the entire department." This task, he insisted, befell the Commission.[18] The ministry thought otherwise.

It did so, partly, out of aversion to what Guizot called "collective administrations": these "expressions of the locality, the local spirit" rather than the "unitary administration." The ministry also sought, here again, to check administrative presence in this intellectual realm. For one, provincial elites could view this as a confiscation of authority, or even favoritism. The rector of Douai and Rouland agreed that Le Glay's proposal would "offend . . . [the] unfortunate susceptibilities" of other learned soci-

---

16. AN F17 2886/1: Eugène Tailliar to Min. Pub. Instr., 19 January 1835, and François Guizot to Tailliar, 5 February 1835; *BCN* 1 (1843): 1–4 and 10; ADN 1 T 248/1: Antoine de Contencin, "Projet d'institution et d'organisation d'un comité historique départemental," report to the prefect, n.d. [Summer 1839]; and MAP 80/2/1: Gabriel de Saint-Aignan to Min. Int., 17 July 1839.

17. MAP Nord 1827: Contencin to Min. Int., 11 August 1840; *BCN* 11 (1871): 17; and AN F17 2847: Contencin to president CHAM, April 1843.

18. AN F17 3303: André Le Glay to Min. Pub. Instr., 4 November 1859.

eties.[19] Some officials furthermore resisted a measure that would infringe on the prerogatives of civil society. Such doctrinal considerations had led the July Monarchy to shun agricultural commissions, a "kind of public administration, [an] official hierarchy of . . . committees." Governmental intervention should not obstruct the "zeal and emulation" of "free, voluntary, and nonadministrative" associations.[20] Such views endured. In 1866, one official rejected Saint-Loup's plan because it would turn provincial societies into "departmental commissions under the direction of the Parisian committee." Likewise with Le Glay's "delicate" proposal: the ministry resisted "influenc[ing] the determination of societies by intervening in their mutual relations." Rouland thus wrote Le Glay and his colleagues that "administrative intervention in these matters could have some drawbacks. The action of [learned] societies must be free and completely spontaneous."[21]

Did this hold true for Arcisse de Caumont's circle as well? This self-styled "estates general of departmental academies and societies" set itself up, after all, as counterpart to the ministry—or, at best, as dubious collaborator.[22] Many officials and CTH members distrusted its politics and claims to authority. The latter were not lost on Adolphe-Napoléon Didron, the inspector general of monuments. "No one will outdo or get ahead of the ministry" with respect to national archaeology, he wrote in a private report of 1834. Salvandy informed Caumont in 1847 that he could not tolerate the Institut des provinces' efforts to affiliate provincial learned societies, "this attempt at isolated action." It is "the fact of the association itself that I cannot and will not authorize," he told a prosecutor a month later.[23] Such wariness led officials to request increased surveillance of Caumont's circle, accuse it of breaching the law on illegal associations, reject its requests for recognition and subsidies, and take steps (under Rouland) to anchor it within a governmental framework.[24] And yet

---

19. Ministerial officials may also have perceived such prefectoral ventures as a challenge to their own preeminence. See AN 42 AP 289: Guizot, manuscript notes on the salaries of prefects, n.d.; and ADN 1 T 246/3: Correspondence between rector Douai and Min. Pub. Instr., 24–25 November 1859.

20. ADN M 508/1: Min. Commerce and public works to prefects, circular of 15 November 1833, and Min. Agriculture and commerce to prefects, circular of 22 February 1840.

21. AN F17 3321: Marginal annotation in letter from Saint-Loup to Min. Pub. Instrc., 21 May 1866; AN F17 3303: Desnoyers, report on the learned societies of the Nord and the Geographical Dictionary of France, n.d. [late 1860/early 1861]; and AN F17 3303: Rouland to Le Glay, 21 January 1860.

22. *CS* 17 (Nancy, 1851), 265.

23. AN 42 AP 21: Adolphe-Napoléon Didron, "Ce que doit être et ce que doit faire l'archéologue," November 1834; AD Calvados F 4513: Salvandy to Caumont, 7 January 1847; and AN F17 3026: idem to Public prosecutor of Orléans, 8 February 1847.

24. For representative responses to Caumont's circle, see AN F17 3090/1: Min. Pub. Instr. to prefect Moselle, 25 February 1837; AD Calvados F 4513: Salvandy to prefects, circular of 4 January 1847; AN F17 3021: Min. Pub. Instr. to Min. Justice, 23 February 1852; and ADN 1 N 72: Proceedings of the *Conseil général* of the Nord, 24 August 1858.

enmity alone did not prevail. Under the July Monarchy, several officials (including Guizot) commended the circle for providing learned societies with "direction, unity, and mutual relations." Under the Second Empire, CTH members listened to reports on the Institut des provinces' activities and published accounts of its meetings in the *Revue des sociétés savantes*.[25] Officials hesitated once again to impinge on a realm of civil society. They did so in part for tactical reasons. In 1846, Salvandy named Caumont ministerial delegate to the provincial learned societies, but asked him to remain discreet. "I would object to any administrative . . . intervention in their work," he warned Caumont. "Bodies upon which governmental action can only be officious would take umbrage at an inspection that indicates authority, control, government." In another respect, officials valued a network that embodied local initiative and "fostered a vigorous activity within the minds."[26]

Tentative before this network, the French state neither suppressed it nor co-opted it nor legitimated its claims to authority or full independence. Problematic as symbols of local initiative and administrative encroachment, provincial commissions provoked a similar ambivalence. Subsidies to learned societies, finally, reveal an increasingly present and yet hesitant state. In all instances, officials encountered a political and civic problem: the state's contours and proper attributes, its relationship with intellectual associations and civil society, the allocation of responsibility. In 1863, now in retirement, Guizot conceded that when Caumont had presented him with plans for an Institut des provinces thirty years earlier, "I welcomed them, I must have welcomed them favorably. But perhaps I did not do enough." Guizot timidly concurred with his critics that the ministry had failed to exploit this source of "free and spontaneous information."[27] For close to four decades, the question of local initiative had stymied the official cult of local memories.

LINES OF FRACTURE

How should we explain this quandary? In one respect, distinct doctrinal and instrumental currents yielded contrasting courses of action. Nisard, for one, oversaw the BTH and increased the ministry's presence within this field while expressing a doctrinal commitment to local initiative. This

---

25. *Journal officiel de l'instruction publique*, 14 July 1833; AN F17 17181: Guizot to Caumont, 11 August 1834; and AN F17 3319: Proceedings of the commission of the *Revue des sociétés savantes*, 24 April 1858.

26. AD Calvados F 4513: Salvandy to Caumont, 28 August 1846; and AN F17 3090/1: Anon. report to Guizot, 11 June 1836.

27. Guizot, speech to the Institut des provinces, 21 March 1863, *AIP* 16 (1864): 271; and Armand René Du Chatellier, *Du mouvement des études*, 22.

commitment melded with instrumental consideration of "touchy" provincials who, as some officials saw it, feared a state that would "direct them, supervise their investigations, and deprive them of the[ir] freedom."[28] As we have seen, however, this instrumental current also led central and local officials to increase official presence in civil society. It sufficed "not to *appear* to impose a direction to the learned societies." Some officials in fact held that, to secure "effective patronage and serious direction" (both political and scientific), the ministry should grant provincial learned societies larger subsidies. The intellectual state was clearly torn between "direction," in its myriad forms, and local initiative. After reminding his rectors that the state should not intervene in the "scientific" realm, Minister Jules Simon nonetheless asked them in September 1870 to keep watch over provincial elites. This "mission," he added, "can only succeed if it is not official, otherwise we would be flouting the principles we have set down."[29] Doctrinal conviction and the imperatives of governance thus bifurcated the governmental agenda.

In another respect, this quandary reflected discord between governmental actors, whose common interest in local memories did not yield consensus on how to cultivate them. Geography separated some actors. In this realm as in others, local officials were often—though not always—more pragmatic than their Parisian counterparts. Prefects and subprefects frequently endorsed provincial requests for subsidies. The same held true of Caumont's circle: whereas ministerial officials perceived a vast network, local officials typically monitored an isolated meeting, whose contributions to local society could outweigh its claims to authority. Adrien-Etienne de Gasparin—a high-level official in the Ministry of the Interior—thus denounced Douai's 1835 scientific congress as a "nonauthorized association," but officials from the Nord emphasized its "moderation" and "urbanity of forms and language." No wonder that Gasparin berated the "local authorities" for granting scientific congresses too much "initiative."[30] In other situations, the divide separated BTH officials from CTH members and other Parisian acolytes. The BTH showed greater concern for governmental authority—a predictable contrast that, without being invariable, yielded distinct priorities and modes of interaction with provincial elites. In 1866, for instance, the ministry asked a teacher from the lycée Saint-Louis, to report on the British Association for the Advance-

28. AN F17 3015/2: Anon. memoranda, n.d. [1862? and 1866].

29. AN F17 3318: Anon., "Composition d'un numéro de la *Revue*," n.d. [1857?] (my italics); AN F17 17130: Anon. memorandum to Min. Pub. Instr., n.d. (1857?); and Jules Simon to rectors, circular of December 1870, in Charmes, 247.

30. AN BB 18 1233: Adrien-Etienne de Gasparin to Min. Justice, 20 August 1835, and General prosecutor of Douai to Gasparin, 9 and 15 September 1835; AN F17 3090/1: Prefect Nord to Gasparin, 6 September 1835, and Gasparin to Guizot, 29 August 1835.

ment of Science, but ignored his recommendation: a comparable French association, under the ministry's aegis, with provincial meetings and elected officers.[31] Reluctant to increase administrative visibility, abandon the center, and yield a parcel of its authority, the ministry remained loyal to its Sorbonne congresses.

In yet other situations, a political divide cut across the BTH-CTH boundary. The question was not whether the state should intervene or not, but how best to do so. Whereas ministers such as Salvandy embraced a more controlling, hands-on approach (on issues ranging from the CTH to libraries), Guizot, Cousin, and others placed a greater premium on local "organizing and regulating centers," independent yet linked to the state.[32] They, too, sought to govern closely, but from below. Desnoyers hence congratulated Guizot in 1834 for turning to local elites for the *Recueil des monuments du Tiers Etat.* Guizot and Ludovic Vitet (the first inspector general of historical monuments) adopted a similar approach to protect the patrimony. Vitet's successor (Prosper Mérimée) accrued, in contrast, the responsibilities of ministerial agents.[33] Officials likewise espoused different styles of governance. Saint-Aignan, as we will recall, had presented the Commission historique du Nord as a discreet means of governmental action. Some officials expressed reservations about this political approach. In 1835, the prosecutor of Angers wrote a lukewarm report about Saint-Aignan, then prefect of the Sarthe. Saint-Aignan sought, he said, "to draw the minds closer together through an, as it were, unnoticed *politique.*" Deeming this approach "insufficient and hence ineffective," the prosecutor recommended instead "a moderate and firm *politique* that states clearly its principles, . . . encloses the parties in a circle that isolates them, and breaks down resistance."[34] Beyond the strategic disagreement between two conservative liberals, this report displays a deep-seated tension regarding a liberal state's attributes and authority.

THE FATE OF PARTIAL STUDIES

Local initiative, the other variable in this equation, was left unsaid here, but this was not always so. On a final plane, this quandary shows how difficult it could be to conceptualize the synthesis of state and civil society —

31. AN F17 3254: Henry Montucci, "Rapport sur l'Association britannique," 1 December 1866.

32. Pierre Rosanvallon, *Moment Guizot,* 234. See also Jean-François Foucaud, *La bibliothèque royale sous la Monarchie de Juillet* (Paris, 1978), 21 and 134.

33. Patrice Vermeren, *Victor Cousin,* 163; AN F17 2833: Desnoyers to Guizot, 22 September 1834; and Bernard Huchet, "Arcisse de Caumont," 1: 155–56.

34. AN F1b I 173/1: General prosecutor of Angers to Min. Justice, 7 January 1835.

or, as Guizot put it, to "constitute the government through the action of society and society through the action of government."[35] This was first and foremost a Doctrinaire quandary, articulated most eloquently under the July Monarchy—but it also involved other conservative liberals and endured throughout this period. For reasons that will become clear, a young BTH employee will guide us through this conceptual maze.

Born in 1810, Raymond Thomassy grew up in Montpellier, where he helped found a Société archéologique and penned articles on "the *pays*'s . . . traditions" and archaeology. Like so many provincials, he moved to Paris in his early twenties. He entered the Ecole des chartes, the training ground for archivists and librarians, and taught history at the prestigious collège Henri IV. A man of broad interests, Thomassy joined the Société de l'histoire de France and Société de géographie de Paris, wrote for numerous periodicals, and published books on such topics as Christine of Pisan and Louisiana geology. In 1836, the BTH hired him to assist Augustin Thierry with the *Recueil des monuments du Tiers Etat*. Thomassy thus joined a team of young men who earned between 100 and 150 francs a month to comb the Bibliothèque royale's manuscript collection for pertinent documents. A ministerial "employee" until 1843, Thomassy not only dug for documents in Paris, but also undertook "missions" in provincial libraries and shared his archaeological findings with the CTH.[36] Recommended by the likes of philosopher Jouffroy and historian Ballanche, Thomassy hence traveled within Orleanist circles.[37]

In 1837, he secured a private audience with Salvandy to convey his views on the ministry's historical investigations.[38] While there is no record of this conversation, Thomassy expressed these views in a rich "Bill on the Organization of Investigations into National History and Archaeology." This manuscript consists of a seven-article legislative bill and a four-page justification. We know little about it beyond the fact that Thomassy presented it to the Conférence Molé in 1839, a few months after joining this association. Founded in 1832, the Conférence was one of numerous debating societies in which, since the Restoration, young Parisian elites "practiced the art of speech" and examined "questions of legislation, ad-

35. *Archives philosophiques, politiques et littéraires* 2, no. 6 (December 1817), 184, quoted in Rosanvallon, *Moment Guizot*, 42; and Lucien Jaume, *Individu effacé*, 16.

36. Thomassy left Thierry's team for Champollion-Figeac's in 1837. See *Mémoires de la Société archéologique de Montpellier* 1 (1835–40): 80; AN F17 3265: Augustin Thierry to Hippolyte Royer-Collard, 19 June 1836; AN F17 3297: Decree of 18 August 1838; BNF ms. NAF 6359: *Commission des monuments de l'histoire du Tiers Etat*, 1836–42; and AN F17 2809: Jacques Joseph Champollion-Figeac to Min. Pub. Instrc., 7 August 1837. I am grateful to Lara Moore for her points of information on Thomassy.

37. AN F17 3283: Pierre-Simon Ballanche to Min. Pub. Instrc., 8 January 1834, and Théodore Jouffroy, marginal note in Raymond Thomassy to Min. Pub. Instrc., 8 May 1841.

38. AN F17 3266: Thomassy to Salvandy, 14 April 1837.

ministration, political economy and general politics." It met weekly, in a room that contained "desks as in the Chamber [of Deputies], a committee, a gallery." Members presented and discussed mock bills on topics ranging from prostitution to decentralization and—most popular of all—freedom of association. Nearly half were civil servants. These debating societies became a key training ground for young men with political aspirations—for future leaders—under the July Monarchy. Of the Conférence Molé's 265 members between 1844 and 1846, 8 became ministers and 59 deputies (half of them serving under two or more regimes). When Thomassy presented his bill, the Conférence Molé was thus a way station of the Orleanist establishment.[39]

We know one more thing about his document: it ended up in the Ministry of Public Instruction's archives. We may thus presume that it circulated in ministerial circles—although its trajectory and reception remain elusive. In all likelihood, Thomassy presented it to the BTH, perhaps even to the minister. All of this allows us to view the bill, albeit cautiously, as a microcosm of political questions and conceptual tensions that confronted the conservative liberals who held power in France.

Thomassy addressed three issues, all of them familiar by now. In ascending complexity, they were: ministerial funding of provincial learned societies; the organization of historical and archaeological investigations in a "new society"; and the quandary of local initiative.[40] He began with the "state of division and imperfection" of French historical and archaeological studies, "one of the most active agents of our social superiority." A reorganization was in order. For Thomassy, this meant both governmental direction and increased subsidies to provincial learned societies. The French Revolution had severed the ancient partnership between the crown and Benedictine communities in this domain. Two forces had emerged in the postrevolutionary vacuum: a multitude of learned societies ("academies") that assembled "spontaneously" to "collect all the materials of national history and archaeology"; and a liberal state that sought to "illustrate all of the nation's manuscript or monumental annals." "The state" undertook some historical investigations, "local academies" pursued others, and joint investigations were conducted "in common by these same academies and the state." Renewal entailed an extension of these

---

39. Much of this information is derived from Anne Martin-Fugier, "La formation des élites: les 'conférences' sous la Restauration et la Monarchie de Juillet," *Revue d'histoire moderne et contemporaire* 36 (April–June 1989): 211–244. See also Ximénès Doudan, *Mélanges et lettres* (Paris, 1876), quoted in Fugier, "La formation des élites," 211; Maurice Barrès, *Les déracinés* (Paris, 1986 [1897]), 243; *Conférence Molé. Projets de lois et rapports* (Paris, 1849), 14; and Philip Nord, *The Republican Moment: Struggles for Democracy in Nineteenth-Century France* (Cambridge, Mass., 1995), 122–24.

40. This discussion rests on AN F17 3254: Thomassy, "Projet de loi pour l'organisation des travaux d'histoire et d'archéologie nationale," n.d. [1839].

joint ventures, the necessary unification of forces that "must . . . complete one another."

This historical and sociological reading clearly owed much to the Doctrinaire views examined in preceding chapters. The state's new responsibilities paralleled the emancipation of civil society. French society rested on "simultaneous facts of two quite different orders: some proceeding from the government [*du pouvoir*], others from society; the first shining forth from the center on the entire kingdom; the second converging at once from all points of the territory on the central seat." The state's task was to unify "partial studies" while tapping the talents of "modern associations of free workers" who had to remain "voluntary recruits." This synthesis, Thomassy understood all too well, would prove tricky. "The general difficulties of the problem," he wrote, "reside in the means of freely associating the workmen and the architects, the local academies and the central authorities. . . . If the latter's intervention is essential to good order and the unity of views, freedom of participation is no less necessary." This quandary encompassed the question of subsidies. Necessary as they were to sustain and unify this realm, they should not degenerate into a stultifying patronage—"the great pitfall of any alliance with the authorities," as Thomassy put it. "A protection that would humiliate *esprit de corps* and dampen local life in order to better contain it would only generate disastrous and deadly lethargy," he continued. Subsidies were problematic as a threat to "free intellectual investigations"—or local initiative. The problem, for Thomassy, was civic rather than memorial.

His bill offered a solution. The ministry would subsidize learned societies according to their *pays*'s historical riches. In addition, "the funds awarded to the common investigations of the [CTH] . . . and local academies [would] belong equally to the academies and the committee [CTH]." Provincial elites would thus share responsibility for this budgetary line. This system, Thomassy explained, both "activate[d] and regularize[d]" local initiative "without infringing upon its freedom." Indeed, this synthesis of "order and freedom" was admirably suited to a modern, liberal society.

LOCALIZING THE MEANS OF GOVERNMENT

Meticulously crafted as it was, this document yielded neither new policies nor new funding patterns. The ministry maintained near-complete control over those investigations it undertook with provincial societies. This tension, in fact, surfaced in Thomassy's bill. Thomassy was committed to local initiative but also believed that it would wilt without "governmental regularization." The bill's driving idea was to "localize the means of government," adapting them to local situations while preserving the state's "freedom [and] . . . influence." One article specified that learned societies would only receive subsidies to complete unfinished investigations or undertake new ones whose program and "mode of publication" conformed to the CTH's stipulations. Torn between the two forces that underlay the liberal body politic, Thomassy tapped into the central predicament of an era that, in the words of King Louis-Philippe, had to conciliate public order and "freedom without license."[41]

This quandary underlay the official cult of local memories—all the more so under the July Monarchy. Their adherence to a broadly defined liberalism led Guizot, Salvandy, and even the young Rouland to praise provincial learned societies as "bodies that govern themselves," "free associations . . . [to which] one ought to entrust the hopes of the country." Within certain limits, said Guizot, this network of free-acting *capacités* "develops, acts, subsists on its own." As Minister of the Interior in 1830, Guizot had written a prefect that "what this country needs most of all is that independent opinions and influences appear in all places." In this way alone would France escape "centralization of the minds."[42] Decentralization, as intimated earlier, was a leitmotiv in his discourse. "The empire of form and habits suffocates me," wrote Guizot at the same epoch. The decentralization of "intelligence" was equally pressing. "The present administration has consistently sought to transfer knowledge and life from the center to the extremities," declared Salvandy. Provincial learned societies were "the natural instruments of this design." The rhetoric of decentralization also enabled Orleanists to differentiate themselves from the First Empire, their inescapable horizon. While Napoleon had accomplished great things at home—from a stronger state to a secular university—he had also produced "a nation of exhausted spectators who had lost the habit of intervening in their own fate." What he had achieved "through despotism," said Salvandy, "we must do through freedom, through discussion, through the work of the minds."[43]

Had their commitment to intellectual decentralization been steadfast, would officials have deemed it necessary to incessantly defend themselves? "This is no centralization of activities and power," Guizot assured the presidents of learned societies in 1834. "I have no intention of infringing on [your] freedom." The CTH "seeks solely to facilitate and ex-

41. Thomassy, *De la colonisation militaire de l'Algérie* (Paris, 1840), 16; and Louis-Philippe, undated apothegm, in Eugène Paignon, ed., *Code des rois*, 74–75.

42. *Revue de Rouen* 4, no. 1 (1st semester 1836): 133; Guizot to Louis-Philippe, report of 31 December 1833, in *Ministère de l'instruction publique: budget des dépenses de l'exercice 1836* (Paris, 1835), 10; and idem to Amédée Thierry, 14 September 1830, quoted in Guizot, *Mémoires*, 2: 57.

43. Guizot to prefect Tarn-et-Garonne, 16 October 1830, repr. in his *Mémoires*, 2: 57; Salvandy to Louis-Philippe, report of 31 December 1838, op. cit., 41; idem, *Budget de l'exercice 1847*, 24–25; Guizot, *Mémoires*, 1: 24–25; and Salvandy, *Vingt mois*, 608. See also Jaume, "Aux origines du libéralisme en France," *Esprit* 243 (1998): 44.

tend [your] studies," echoed Salvandy in 1839.[44] Such claims reflected, to be sure, a reluctance to asphyxiate civil society, but they also responded to the new investigative modalities surveyed in chapter 4. Officials could hardly deny that, while their ventures meant to strengthen local initiative, they also increased—willfully or not—official presence. "We could not allow the [CTH's] intentions to go astray," Gasparin explained in 1838, "nor abandon them to the individual whims of all those who would like to undertake a historical work on monuments." Provincial learned societies lacked the "powerful and fertile unity that the Convention sought to establish everywhere in France," commented the *Revue de l'instruction publique* in 1845. It thus fell on the state to imprint, in Salvandy's words, the "common direction" through which, in this domain as in others, "the provinces bind themselves to the central government."[45]

Guizot's shaky distinction between a political realm, in which "direct [governmental] action" was necessary, and an "intellectual" one, in which the central authorities had to use influence to "freely assemble" elites, fails to mask the ministry's acute and unremitting preoccupation with the center throughout these decades.[46] The CTH was a "central society" and the *Revue des sociétés savantes* "the center where everything ends up, the seat from which everything shines forth."[47] Norms, directives, documents, descriptions of monuments and artifacts: everything indeed emanated from or converged toward this institutional center. The acme of reason, this center grasped the needs of postrevolutionary society and would hence govern it. Decentralization thus denoted neither a check on governmental power nor a devolution of responsibility, but a careful extension of such reason and governance. Much as officials spoke of local initiative, their doctrinal attachment to the state's unity of governance prevented any significant transfer of authority. In his *History of European Civilization*, Guizot had after all presented the emancipation of medieval communes as an important event, but subordinated these oligarchic and unstable entities to the monarchy. Thierry granted the communes a greater historical importance than did Guizot, but he, too, saw "the application of administrative centrality to historical investigations [as] . . . a law of the nineteenth century."[48] The destiny of France accordingly hinged

44. Guizot to presidents of learned societies, circular of 23 July 1834, in Charmes, 9; and Salvandy to correspondents, 1 March 1839, in Charmes, 92.

45. Gasparin, report on the CHAM's activities in 1838, in *Budget général des dépenses pour l'exercice 1840*, 330; *Revue de l'instruction publique* 4, no. 73 (15 June 1845): 736–37; and Salvandy to Louis-Philippe, report of 31 December 1838, op. cit., 59.

46. Guizot, *Mémoires*, 3:16–17.

47. AN F17 3254: "Note à M. le ministre. Comité des travaux historiques et *Revue des Sociétés Savantes*. Aperçu de quelques améliorations," 27 December 1866.

48. Guizot, *Histoire de la civilisation en Europe*, 170–89; and Thierry, *Considérations sur l'histoire de France*, in *Oeuvres complètes de Augustin Thierry*, 7: 175.

first and foremost on a new type of social governance, which necessarily took precedence over "all legitimate interests, all conscientious opinions." Salvandy lauded the autonomy of provincial learned societies, but also "likened" their members to "functionaries." His inability to define these associations—as either independent entities or official corollaries—points toward a deeper conceptual confusion. We can only follow Sudhir Hazareesingh, therefore, when he emphasizes the intellectual incoherence of a liberal school that perceived local elites as both indispensable civic actors and governmental subordinates. The result was a "schizophrenic position on the role of the administration" and civil society, a fundamental inability to delineate—and draw the boundary between—these two indispensable realms.[49]

What is more, the notion of civil society, or *societas civilis*, remained deeply ambiguous at this time. Until the mid eighteenth century, contemporaries often referred interchangeably to "civil society" and "state" as, per political theorist John Keane, a "political association that places its members under the influence of its laws and thereby ensures peaceful order and good government." The two terms diverged after 1750, as some of Europe's best minds gravitated toward, and refined, the concept of civil society. Their formulations—of a commercial arena or a political one, harmonious or not, self-standing or dependent—varied markedly, however. As a term and a concept, civil society thus failed to acquire a fixed meaning.[50] By the early nineteenth century, four main conceptions had emerged, according to Keane. If the quandary of local initiative stymied this intellectual state, it is also because some of these conceptions coexisted uneasily in these governmental circles.

The first conception, personified by Thomas Paine, rested on a positive view of humanity. Equal, natural rights-bearing individuals were inherently predisposed towards harmonious social relations. Civil society thus constituted a free and potentially self-regulating sphere of private law, ontologically anterior to the state. Advanced civil societies accordingly had little use for the latter. With its democratic implications and minimal conception of the state (whose duties far outweighed its rights), this strand was all but absent from these governmental circles.[51] Of greater appeal therein was a second conception, articulated by Bernard de Mandeville

---

49. ADN M 137/37: Montalivet to prefects, circular of 23 September 1836; Decision of the Minister of Finance on the exchange of publications between learned societies, 3 March 1847, in Charmes, 108–9; and Sudhir Hazareesingh, *From Subject to Citizen*, 167 and 218.

50. John Keane, "Despotism and Democracy: The Origins and Development of the Distinction Between Civil Society and the State 1750–1850," in idem, ed., *Civil Society and the State: New European Perspectives* (London, 1988), 35 and 37; and François Rangeon, "Société civile: histoire d'un mot," in Jacques Chevallier et al., *La société civile* (Paris, 1986), 9–32.

51. Keane, "Despotism and Democracy," 44–49, quotation on 45.

and, yet more explicitly, Adam Ferguson in his 1767 *Essay on the History of Civil Society*. Civil society constituted a free play of interests and passions, tending toward individual self-gratification. If left unchecked, however, the latter could overcome public spirit. To counter this despotic peril, Ferguson advocated a network of citizens' associations. Civil societies, moreover, frequently required strong but restrained states: ideally, a constitutional monarchy (tied to an electoral college of male property owners). Its laws, centralized bureaucracy, and military would ensure tranquility and protect the economic and cultural spheres.[52] We recognize here several strands of the French intellectual state's discourse: the initiative of elites; necessary, but limited and protective, state intervention; and the civic function of voluntary association.

A third conception, personified by Alexis de Tocqueville, granted a yet more central function to these local associations. The nineteenth century, as he saw it, witnessed the emergence of two alarming political forces: a leveling democracy, which tended to dismiss minority opinions, and a new form of centralized, regulatory state power. Both threatened to suffocate civil society and turn citizens into subjects. Tocqueville recommended a stricter separation of powers and a rich network of juries and voluntary associations, including literary and scientific societies. This was the heart of civil society: associations that cultivated essential "local freedoms," taught citizens about their rights and obligations, and enabled them to fulfill the latter.[53] Here, too, we recognize familiar strands: antibureaucratism; decentralization; intellectual sociability; and local initiative ensconced in associations whose relationship to the state was more inimical than Ferguson would have had it.

A fourth and final conception of civil society, personified by Hegel, was in many respects antithetical to the preceding. Human beings sought first and foremost to satisfy private interests—with potentially disastrous effects. Where Tocqueville saw local initiative, Hegel perceived egoism and endemic conflict. Where Tocqueville saw autonomous voluntary associations that buttressed civic sentiments, Hegel perceived corporate particularism. Civil society was the indispensable repository of regional, professional, and judiciary institutions, but, left to its own devices, it grew restless and fragmented. Incapable of governing itself, civil society hence called for a centralized and bureaucratic state. Such a state alone could replace private interests by a universal interest it both defined and defended. Civil society was thus *aufgehoben* within the state: at once "preserved and overcome as a necessary but subordinate aspect" of a broader political entity.[54]

52. Ibid., 39–44.
53. Ibid., 55–62, quotations on 58 and 61.
54. Ibid., 50–55, quotations on 51 and 53. See also François Chatelet, *Hegel* (Paris, 1968), 140–42; and Jean-François Kervégan, "De la démocratie à la représentation: à propos de la politique hégelienne," *Philosophie* 13 (1986): 47–48 and 67.

The introduction of Hegel's ideas into nineteenth-century France proved slow and uneven. His *Philosophy of Right*, in which he sketched these political ideas, was summarized in French in 1869 and translated in 1940. This said, his ideas on law and politics began crossing the Rhine under the Restoration. While many in France rejected his pantheism and perceived despotism, others proved at least partially receptive. Louis-Philippe, Guizot, and Jean-Jacques Ampère all subscribed to the first volume of Hegel's collected works in 1832. Cousin, as is well known, met Hegel around 1817, corresponded with him for many years, and introduced him to leading liberals (including Thierry) during his 1827 visit to Paris.[55] Without presenting himself as a Hegelian disciple, Cousin incorporated strands of his philosophy into his eclectic doctrine. For critic Michaël Werner, Hegelianism became "in some respects the official philosophy of the July Monarchy."[56] However that may be, this intellectual state evoked the Hegelian model in its distrust of an independent (and immature) civil society; its conviction that the state alone could unify particularistic forces; and its desire to synthesize the state and civil society.[57] These officials did not endow the state with as wide-ranging attributes, or civil society with as meager responsibilities and guarantees as did Hegel. Neither, for that matter, were they willing to adopt a Tocquevillian vision, in which voluntary associations counterbalanced, or even eclipsed, the state. Drawing selectively from these various conceptual wells, they produced an unstable composite. While attachment to local initiative and voluntary association limited official action, concern with unfettered passions and confidence in the state's unifying powers gave it a new extension. From this perspective, the official cult of local memories ran into the daunting, if not impossible, task of integrating incompatible conceptual designs.

The quandary of local initiative did not vanish from these governmental circles under the Second Empire. Much naturally separated the latter from the July Monarchy on this civic plane. The regime introduced uni-

---

55. Michael Kelly, *Hegel in France* (Birmingham, 1992), 3–24; Michel Espagne and Michaël Werner, eds., *Lettres d'Allemagne: Victor Cousin et les Hégeliens* (Tusson, 1990); Paul Rowe, *A Mirror on the Rhine? The Nouvelle Revue Germanique, Strasbourg 1829–1837* (Oxford, 2000), 310; and Alice Gérard, "Le grand homme et la conception de l'histoire au XIXe siècle," *Romantisme* 100 (1998): 34.

56. Dominique Janicaud, "Victor Cousin et Ravaisson, lecteurs de Hegel et Schelling," *Les études philosophiques* (October–December 1984): 451–52; and Werner, "A propos de la réception de Hegel et de Schelling en France pendant les années 1840: contribution à une histoire sociale des transferts inter-culturels," in Jean Moes and Jean-Marie Valentin, eds., *De Lessing à Heine: un siècle de relations littéraires et intellectuelles entre la France et l'Allemagne* (Paris, 1985), 283.

57. Cousin: the state has "the interest of humanity" at stake and may hence receive "the formidable right of using force in order to do good to men." Pierre Rosanvallon likewise argues that Guizot's political sociology is closer to Hegel's than Adam Smith's. See Cousin, *Lectures on the True, the Beautiful and the Good*, trans. O. W. Wight (New York, 1890), 317–19; and Rosanvallon, *Moment Guizot*, 50.

versal male suffrage, but limited civic participation to technical, and often local, affairs while increasing governmental prerogatives. It also tended to prize loyalty over qualifications among its agents. While many prefects had been appointed under the July Monarchy, the regime broadened their authority as direct representatives of a strong administration.[58] The Ministry of Public Instruction similarly asked rectors to oversee learned societies and took other steps to watch over provincial elites. Yet the Second Empire also encouraged nonpolitical local associations and displayed growing sympathy with administrative decentralization.[59] Ministerial officials, their provincial underlings, and CTH members—including some who had survived regime changes—espoused the "freedom" and "initiative" of provincial elites in private settings (the Saint-Loup episode), circulars, and public ceremonies. The rector of Clermont-Ferrand did so (before the local Académie) in March 1858 and so did the prince Napoléon, in a speech that garnered considerable attention four months later. "What we must fear," he declared at the exhibition of Limoges, "is the absorption of individual forces by the collective power, the substitution of government for citizens . . . the weakening of personal initiative under . . . excessive administrative centralization."[60]

Rouland and other officials made similar claims in the late 1850s and 1860s—out of doctrinal conviction, to boost administrative efficiency, to placate provincial elites, and in response to an increasingly vocal opposition. They were at least as attached to governmental unity and the intellectual center's authority, however, as their July Monarchy predecessors. Rouland explained privately in 1861 that the CTH would first and foremost "centralize" the investigations of provincial elites. Five years later, officials were still searching for means of "making the departments yet more open to governmental intervention in their investigations." By the same token, the very status of provincial learned societies still eluded definition. While some officials labeled them "private institutions," others argued in the mid-1860s that these associations did not simply "answer to [themselves]." The "sole admissible definition" was accordingly "society, 'an aggregate of persons who take an interest in literary and scientific works, with the authorization of the superior authority, necessarily repre-

58. Theodore Zeldin, *The Political System of Napoleon III* (London, 1958), 158–59; and Roger Price, *The French Second Empire: An Anatomy of Political Power* (Cambridge, 2001), 85.

59. On this "fundamental ambivalence in Bonapartism," see Zeldin, *A History of French Passions, 1848–1945*, 2 vols. (Oxford, 1993 [1973]), 1:510 and 537–38. For an insightful portrait of Bonapartism, emphasizing its theoretical foundations and contradictions, see Hazareesingh, *From Subject to Citizen*, chap. 2.

60. *Annales scientifiques, littéraires et industrielles de l'Auvergne* 31 (1858): 193; and Prince Napoléon, speech of 12 July 1858, *Le Moniteur universel*, 15 July 1858. See also Duruy to rectors, circular of 14 December 1868, in Charmes, 234.

61. AN F17 3318: Rouland to Minister of State, 8 March 1861; "Note à M. le ministre," 27 December 1866; and AN F17 3021: Anon., memorandum to Duruy, 3 November 1865. See also

sented by the department of Public Instruction.'"[61] The parallel with Salvandy's own contradictions is striking. Whereas the Second Empire found local memories less problematic in their memorial dimension than did the July Monarchy, both regimes deemed them equally so in their civic dimension. In this intellectual realm, the boundary between state and civil society proved as elusive for one regime as for the next.

"THE GREAT PROBLEM OF MODERN SOCIETIES"

In a well-known passage of his memoirs (1863), Guizot declared that "the great problem of modern societies is the governing of the minds [*le gouvernement des esprits*]." One could emphasize the concluding words and the central state's efforts to tap underlying social forces, establish new alliances with civil society, and secure new forms of surreptitious authority. This chapter has drawn us, in contrast, toward the "problem" of a modern state that, for nearly four decades, struggled to demarcate its appropriate presence within this intellectual realm and to offer a coherent definition of civil society.[62] It struggled due to conflicting aspirations, internal divisions, and the conceptual contradictions of a conservative liberalism that held sway under the July Monarchy and persisted under the Second Empire. *Gouvernement des esprits* can after all mean both governing *by* the minds and *of* the minds. This intellectual state, then, was neither intent on accumulating all initiative nor committed to endowing these elites with authority. Instead of an elusive middle path, archival and published traces of this state's activities mark a zigzagging trajectory between a wholly directive approach and transfers of initiative and authority. The official cult of local memories clearly qualifies the received picture of an unabashedly centralizing intellectual state, seeking to "codify, censure, or officialize cultural activity."[63]

Instead, it confirms and amplifies recent portrayals of an internally conflicted and "blurred" French state. A parallel may be drawn with the charitable realm, on which the July Monarchy also tightened its hold. Schools for the deaf and dumb, hitherto self-regulating, fell under a single controlling agency in the 1830s. But material shortcomings and internal tensions impeded, in this realm as well, "unity of supervision." Appointed sole source of arbitration and regulation by the French Revolution but kept in

---

Hazareesingh and Vincent Wright, "Le Second Empire," in Louis Fougère, Jean-Pierre Machelon, and François Monnier, eds., *Communes et le pouvoir*, 325–26.

62. Guizot wrote this in 1860, as an unsympathetic observer of the Second Empire. We may also read this remark, therefore, as a critique of a regime that governed far too closely. See Guizot, *Mémoires*, 3: 16.

63. David L. Looseley, *Politics of Fun*, 12. For similar views, see Jean-Michel Leniaud, *L'utopie française: essai sur le patrimoine* (Paris, 1992), 121; and Kevin D. Murphy, *Memory and Modernity: Viollet-le-Duc at Vézelay* (University Park, Pa., 2000), 44 and 50.

check by liberal doctrine, this state and its proper sphere of action eluded definition in the nineteenth century. Broad governmental intervention was at once indispensable and disavowed.[64] In this intellectual realm, this tension manifested itself as policy reversals and contradictions: tentative overtures to provincial elites and sudden reassertions of official authority, new forms of governmental intervention and efforts to restrict administrative visibility. Officials turned to the nation's "enlightened" citizens, yet proved reluctant to create these "interpreter[s] of general reason" whom, under the July Monarchy at least, they purportedly sought out. The French Revolution had bequeathed France two kinds of "minds," Guizot wrote a correspondent in 1836. Some were "free but unsettled," others "modest but cowardly and narrow." He pledged "war" on the first and "disdain[ed]" the second, but did not propose an intermediate model.[65] Instead, we uncover claims to "regularize emulation" and contradictory, but equally justifiable, criticism of a state that was both omnipresent and overly timid.

The quandary of local initiative further impeded the official cult of local memories—by limiting governmental funding, by spurning innovative schemes such as Saint-Loup's, and by squandering the potential contributions of provincial elites. Once again, however, this narrative also lends itself to a more sanguine reading. In cultivating local memories, officials and their acolytes both posed and grappled with the era's "most pressing" question: the "substitution of individual initiative for the administration's universal action."[66] They posed the question of local citizenship: initiative, authority, and on another plane, unity in a modern nation-state. Thomassy's bill is but the most cogent expression of a prolonged effort to articulate a liberal compound of local initiative and governmental oversight. On this plane as well, the contours of postrevolutionary France constituted the horizon of the field of local memories.

This field's legacy to the Third Republic is cloudier on this civic plane than on the memorial one. In April 1870—a time of crisis for the Empire and, soon, the nation—the Ministry of Public Instruction entrusted provincial intellectual elites with an openly political responsibility. This was a first. Addressing the Sorbonne congress of learned societies, Minister Maurice Richard instructed delegates to tell their "provinces" that they had witnessed a "profound institutional revolution" in Paris. By doing so and urging the population to vote in upcoming elections, he explained,

64. Minard, *Fortune du colbertisme*, 369–72; and Gasparin, *Rapport au roi sur les hôpitaux, les hospices et les services de bienfaisance* (Paris, 1837), 91, quoted in François Buton, "Bureaucratisation et délimitation des frontières de l'Etat. Les interventions administratives sur l'éducation des sourds-muets au XIXe siècle," *Genèses* 28 (September 1997): 18.

65. Publisher's annotation in Guizot, *Mémoires*, 3:1; and Guizot to Madame de Gasparin (1836), cited in Louis Girard, *Les libéraux français 1814–1875* (Paris, 1985), 131–32.

66. Victor Modeste, *Du paupérisme en France*, 531.

they would "crown the patriotic mission [they] carry out with such perseverance through [their] daily toil." He added: "In a turbulent society such as ours, . . . your role is to instill love for your provinces, restore individual sentiments, [and] keep alive the spirit of the native home." Only in the 1880s, however, did Jules Ferry and others come to see provincial elites as true acolytes, the nation's local pedagogues, rather than as subordinates. The *petite patrie* model still bolstered the state's authority over a united country, but it now rested on a bottom-up rather than top-down dynamic. This dynamic reflected the rise of republican municipalism, a doctrine that we encountered in Montargis and elsewhere. Within municipal institutions, citizens would debate political issues and contribute to the nation's political life.[67] Without fully resolving the quandary of local initiative,[68] this model nonetheless attenuated it. It sprang, moreover, from a conceptual ground that contemporaries had been clearing for decades. They had done so through pamphlets and treatises—but also in less predictable venues. These included the blueprints, debates, and reversals that, in the field of local memories, surrounded the state's tenuous overtures to provincial minds.

67. *Discours prononcé par son excellence le Ministre de l'instruction publique à la réunion des sociétés savantes le 23 avril 1870* (Paris, 1870), 4; *RSS*, 6th ser., no. 3 (1876): 214; François Furet, preface to idem, ed., *Jules Ferry*, 10; and Hazareesingh, "Société d'Instruction Républicaine," 297–98.

68. See Marie-Claude Genet-Delacroix, *Art et état sous la IIIe République: le système des Beaux-Arts, 1870–1940* (Paris, 1992), esp. 12.

EIGHT

Sur les Lieux
PROVINCIAL ELITES BEFORE THE STATE

In drawing attention to the provincial estates [of the Cambrésis] . . . ,
[we] have sought to fulfill one of the needs of our epoch[:] . . . to harmonize local franchises with the freedom of action required by the
central authorities.

EMILE DE BEAUMONT,
Public meeting of
the Société d'émulation
de Cambrai, 17 August 1841

TWO INTELLECTUAL STATES have surfaced in this book: the
first ambitious and increasingly visible, the second conflicted and tentative. For most provincial elites, the news
from Paris—be it in the 1830s or 1860s—pertained to the former: an
unprecedented governmental interest in local history, monuments, topography, and the like. This official cult of local memories captured, for
better or for worse, the "statocentric" character of postrevolutionary
France—a legalistic nation-state that, per historian Alain Cottereau, entrusted general interests to official specialists, directed the citizenry
toward the "particular interests of 'civil society,'" and asserted the supremacy of national, uniform laws over local deliberations. While this governmental action has been a key strand in this narrative, so has the new
civic and memorial resonance of local memories—seen by many provincial elites as a personal possession, a foundation of their identity and authority. Without mobilizing the entire population, the cult of local memories contributed to the "public spirit"—the collective action, rational
debate, mediation, and "capacity for initiative"—that, according to Cottereau, constituted the underside of postrevolutionary statocentrism.[1]

Our inquiry would thus remain incomplete if we did not return one

1. Alain Cottereau, " 'Esprit public et capacité de juger': la stabilisation d'un espace public
en France aux lendemains de la Révolution," *Raisons pratiques* 3 (1992): 258–59, 264–65, and
268.

last time to the provinces to examine, in situ, the relationship between local elites and this state. We have already caught glimpses of elites following ministerial circulars or prefectoral suggestions. We have overheard others denouncing the state's reservations before local difference and initiative. We have not, however, asked how local elites responded to this governmental presence. How—regardless of official expectations—did the official cult of local memories unfold? This provincial vista has much to tell us about this state's reach, about local expressions of identity and citizenship within an official framework, and more broadly yet, about the negotiations that surround local memories in a modern nation-state. Without limiting ourselves to the Nord, we will nonetheless spend much time there in the pages that follow. Atypical as it is, this department displays the entire gamut of provincial responses to the official cult of local memories. We will also pay special attention to learned societies—the state's primary interlocutors within this field—and their participation in the geographical dictionary and archaeological inventory of France between 1858 and 1867. Dossiers from nearly all departments have survived, providing a unique window into the cooperation, refutation, and rerouting that, in this field, both fed and stymied the integration of state and civil society.

COMPLIANCE—AND MORE

Let us first examine this relationship in the terms set by contemporaries—as either endorsement or rejection of governmental ventures. A first, and most prevalent, strand of evidence depicts receptive provincial elites. Without necessarily emulating prerevolutionary academies and defining themselves as servants of the sovereign, they proved willing and sometimes eager to cultivate local memories within an official framework.[2]

For many elites, devotion to local memories expressed a concordance of views with the regime in power. "What everyone requests today in Cambrai, and what would be avidly sought out in all the cities of northern France," declared Cambrai lawyer Alcibiade Wilbert in 1836, "is a history of our province . . . following the blueprint of M. Guizot." Wilbert endorsed, not only Guizot's historical science, but Orleanist doctrine and government as well. The Société de bienfaisance de Cambrai—whose pageant programs Wilbert helped compose—deemed its "noble" depictions of local history most timely in the 1830s, "now that each citizen may aspire to the glory of ruling the country, either in the civil or judiciary adminis-

---

2. On Old Regime academies and service to the monarchy, see Daniel Roche, *Siècle des Lumières*, 1:148–49 and 390; and Jean Cousin, *L'académie des sciences, belles-lettres et arts de Besançon: deux cents ans de vie comtoise (1752–1952)* (Besançon, 1954), 88.

tration or on the legislative benches." Welcoming Louis-Philippe to Cambrai in 1833, André Le Glay likewise underscored the Société d'émulation de Cambrai's devotion to the local past. "By unearthing the old memories of the land we inhabit," he declared, "we recompose the history of this land in which, during the Middle Ages, our ancestors first uttered the cry of emancipation." Nothing, for Le Glay, better captured the Société's kinship with the July Monarchy than its municipal history.[3] In Besançon, the president of the Académie des sciences, belles-lettres et arts explained to Salvandy in 1838 that time constraints alone had caused him to neglect the historical study of the *pays* that Guizot and Thierry had requested. Local studies held similar connotations under the Second Empire. Angers's Société académique de Maine-et-Loire and Draguignan's Société d'études scientifiques et archéologiques both linked their local "works of departmental archaeology" to the ministry's "impetus" around 1860.[4] Be it under the July Monarchy or Second Empire, the cult of local studies enabled elites to position themselves within a broadly defined official sphere.

It also led them to celebrate regimes that galvanized "intelligence." Elites did so privately, in flattering letters to ministers who, as Le Glay wrote Fortoul in 1855, directed "the minds towards sound studies."[5] More significantly, they praised the regime publicly. As a young magistrate in Normandy in 1835, Rouland had endorsed Guizot's "energetic call" for local historical studies. What a "generous idea," Rouland wrote in the *Revue de Rouen*, "to call upon the learned societies to disseminate . . . the most serious teachings of experience and knowledge." From Angoulême to Saint-Brieuc, learned society presidents publicly applauded the ministry's dedication to local memories and intellectual pursuits.[6] Did such praise for the "mission" the ministry had "set aside for provincial societies" yield compliance with its requests? Assessing the latter poses methodological problems, for various criteria can be used—with different results. Ministerial appraisals are one starting point. Guizot declared with satisfaction that many provincial learned societies "began a lively correspondence with my de-

---

3. *Revue cambrésienne* 1 (1835–1836): 68; Delloye 26/27: *Société de bienfaisance* (Cambrai, n.d. [1839?]), 2; and Delloye 38/16: André Le Glay, speech of 8 January 1833, repr. in clipping from untitled local newspaper, n.d. [1833?].

4. AN F17 3291: President Académie des sciences, belles-lettres et arts de Besançon to Min. Pub. Instr., 23 October 1838; AN F17 3318: Secretary Société académique de Maine-et-Loire to secretary CTH, 6 April 1858; and AN F17 3315: President Société d'études scientifiques et archéologiques de la ville de Draguignan to Min. Pub. Instrc., 28 July 1860.

5. AN 246 AP 19: Le Glay to Hippolyte Fortoul, 24 February 1855. See also AN F17 3318: President Société libre d'émulation, du commerce et de l'industrie de la Seine-Inférieure to Min. Pub. Instrc., 27 April 1858.

6. *Revue de Rouen* 3, no. 1 (1st sem. 1835): 263; *Bulletin de la Société archéologique et historique de la Charente* 1 (1845): 179; and *Annales de la Société archéologique et historique des Côtes-du-Nord* 4 (1846): 10.

partment" in the 1830s. In 1856, an official likewise noted that more than 750 pieces had come in for the *Recueil des poésies populaires*.[7] Officials and CTH members were on the whole downcast, however. They regretted that more provincial elites had not contributed to the *Recueil des monuments inédits du Tiers Etat* or forwarded complete runs of their periodical publications.[8] CTH member Adolphe Granier de Cassagnac wrote Guizot as early as 1835 that out of "negligence, half-heartedness, or some other cause," many correspondents were slow to answer the CTH's circulars. Most of his colleagues attributed this response to the "despondency" of provincials who lacked time, training, and resources.[9]

They might have been less disappointed had they not harbored such vast ambitions. In 1869, for instance, 668 provincials traveled to Paris for the Sorbonne congress—less than the 1,500 the ministry expected, but a respectable number nonetheless. Officials expressed once again disappointment. But what about the hundreds of provincial manuscripts and documents that hopeful provincials forwarded to the CTH? What about the countless learned societies who asked the ministry to appoint correspondents from their ranks or cautiously heeded its warnings about Arcisse de Caumont's circle?[10] The Société des antiquaires de Normandie thus wrote Salvandy in 1847 that it understood his concern all too well to "compromise itself" with the Institut des provinces, this "*unauthorized* society." Provincials with sufficient leisure time, means, guidance, and intellectual ability tended to respond favorably to ministerial overtures—albeit with varying degrees of alacrity, ability, and commitment. If learned societies refused to participate in the CTH's collective ventures, it was often because of practical impediments, such as difficult travel conditions. The ministry's geographical dictionary, archaeological inventory, and scientific description of France had elicited 282 positive responses by 1863, including most of the largest learned societies. The ministry soon shelved the scientific description, but the first two projects tell an instructive tale. Contributions and promises came in from seventy-three of eighty-eight provincial departments for the inventory, sixty-nine for the dictionary.

7. AN F17 3319: President Société archéologique de Sens to Min. Pub. Instrc., 9 April 1858; Guizot, *Mémoires*, 3: 162; and AN F17 3245: Anon., "Note relative au Recueil des poésies populaires," 25 August 1856.

8. Augustin Thierry, report to Louis-Philippe, 6 May 1838, in Charmes, 79; Robert-Henri Bautier, "Recueil des Monuments," 98; and AN F17 3019: Vincent, report to Fortoul, 13 May 1853.

9. AN 42 AP 21: Adolphe Granier de Cassagnac, "Recherches historiques. Rapport à Monsieur le ministre de l'instruction publique," 13 May 1835; and AN F17 13268: Proceedings of the Committee on chronicles, charters and inscriptions, 12 June 1837.

10. AN F17 3050: Manuscript register on the Sorbonne congresses, entries of 23 January and 18–19 March 1869; and, for instance, AN F17 3311: President Société d'archéologie lorraine to Min. Pub. Instrc., 24 July 1861, and AN F17 3318: Secretary Académie du Gard to Min. Pub. Instrc., 6 June 1858.

Only five departments contributed to neither project. Rates of participation were lowest in the Jura, the Landes, and other underpopulated departments with few cities and weak intellectual networks.[11]

Many elites in fact furthered the state's agenda through diverse initiatives. The geographical dictionary and archaeological inventory are, again, most revealing. In Besançon, Le Mans, and dozens of other cities, learned societies formed special commissions to collect data and write the works. In Tarbes, Agen, and elsewhere, they drafted archaeological questionnaires and samples for schoolteachers and other potential collaborators.[12] Other learned societies reprinted the ministry's instructions in their periodicals and requested additional copies for nonresident members. Chambéry's Académie impériale des sciences, belles-lettres et arts de la Savoie opened a public contest for the best archaeological inventory of a local arrondissement. The Académie "could not have done more," explained its members, "to fulfill the Ministry of Public Instruction's wishes."[13] These elites thus became (at least partial) governmental operatives: they cultivated local memories within an administrative framework, according to administrative guidelines. They complied out of doctrinal conviction and allegiance to the regime in power; because merit had long denoted service to the state; to ingratiate themselves with the authorities; and to secure rewards. If Le Glay and the Société d'émulation de Cambrai lauded the city's glorious history while welcoming Louis-Philippe, it was also as a preamble to requesting royal "protect[ion]" of local agriculture against foreign imports (a pending bill threatened to remove tariffs on colonial and foreign sugar).[14] Five years later, Cambrai's subprefect wrote his prefect that the Société's investigations on local monuments deserved a financial reward. Autun's Société éduenne sent the ministry its *Essai historique sur l'abbaye de Saint Martin d'Autun* in 1848 because local publications were in "favor" in governmental circles and a suitable recompense would presumably follow. In 1860, a member of Tours's Société d'agriculture, sciences, arts et belles-lettres du département d'Indre-et-Loire reminded an official of his promise to consider his son for an administrative position. To show his loyalty and buttress his case, he enclosed "a few his-

11. These tabulations rest on a thorough analysis of twenty-one cartons in the Archives Nationales (F17 3298–3317). I do not count the departments in which, having failed to secure the collaboration of elites, officials enlisted the departmental archivist. See also AN F17 3026: President Société des antiquaires de Normandie to Narcisse de Salvandy, 9 February 1847.

12. See, inter alia, AN F17 3300: Secretary Académie des sciences, belles-lettres et arts de Besançon to Min. Pub. Instrc., 29 October 1861; and AN F17 3310: President Société d'agriculture, sciences et arts d'Agen, circular letter of 20 March 1860.

13. AN F17 3313: Brochure published by the Académie impériale des sciences, belles-lettres et arts de Savoie, n.d. [1862].

14. On this theme, see also Jean-Pierre Chaline, *Les bourgeois de Rouen: une élite urbaine au XIXe siècle* (Paris, 1982), 352.

torical notes on cities and communes in my department." The ministry, he added for emphasis, "has requested such works."[15]

Equally alluring were the symbolic rewards—the public recognition and authority—that governmental affiliation invariably conferred within the *pays*. It was not "financial subsidies" alone that the Société des sciences et lettres de Loir-et-Cher and Société dunkerquoise sought from the ministry in the early 1850s, but "official approval, . . . visible in broad daylight," "some honorific encouragement."[16] Louis Debaecker claimed to have founded his Société de l'histoire et des beaux-arts de la Flandre maritime de France in 1856 to obtain the "recognition [of] the superior authorities" in a small town (Bergues) where "one fears being taken for a *savant*." A few years earlier, he had applied for the post of corresponding inspector of monuments. According to Dunkirk's subprefect, he did so because he lacked "consistency" in his town and "want[ed] to be something." The post of CTH correspondent was equally prestigious: appointments commonly landed on the front pages of provincial newspapers. In the Nord, about half of the men who secured this title during our period had lobbied for it. Debaecker first requested the title in 1843, offering to send the CTH "some old charters on our ancient communal institutions or our local history."[17] Seven years elapsed before the CTH accepted his candidacy—but his persistence reflects the enduring allure of such governmental imprimatur. One could not underestimate the "value that the slightest encouragement from above acquires for provincial savants," explained the rector of Douai in 1859.[18]

The numerous civil servants who peopled this field constitute, finally, a particular case. "Now in Flanders, tomorrow in Alsace" as one engineer put it, these "mobile" men moved from one posting to the next to further their career. On settling in a new town, many joined the local learned society—in part to occupy their idle hours and develop a social circle—and embraced its localist agenda.[19] Learned societies thus formed an associative network in which civil servants circulated freely, taking up in one as-

15. ADN 1 T 253: Subprefect Cambrai to prefect Nord, 23 February 1838; AN F17 3037: President Société éduenne to Min. Pub. Instrc., 23 November 1848; and AN F17 3309: Baron Papion du Chateau to Min. Pub. Instrc., 2 November 1860.

16. AN F17 3031: President Société des sciences et lettres de Loir-et-Cher to Min. Pub. Instrc., 15 June 1852; and *MSDu* 1 (1853): 13.

17. ADN 1 T 246/1: Proceedings of the Société de l'histoire et des beaux-arts de la Flandre Maritime de France, 26 January 1856; ADN 2 T 767: Louis Debaecker to rector Douai, 22 March 1856; ADN 1 T 252/2: Subprefect Dunkirk to prefect Nord, 8 January 1850; and AN F17 2838: Debaecker to Min. Pub. Instr., 29 July 1843.

18. AN F17 3321: Rector Douai to Min. Pub. Instrc., 8 July 1859.

19. As Jean-Pierre Chaline points out, these educated men also had considerable leisure time and few other cultural outlets. See Michelet, *Le peuple*, 126; *MSV* 1 (1833): 29; and Chaline, *Sociabilité et érudition*, 109–10. See also Maurice Agulhon, *Le cercle dans la France bourgeoise: 1810–1848. Etude d'une mutation de sociabilité* (Paris, 1977), 40.

sociation and in one town where they had left off in another. François Balson, a prefectoral bureaucrat who joined the Commission historique du Nord in 1849, had previously presided over a learned society in Montpellier; Narcisse Delye, a judge who presided over the Société dunkerquoise in the late 1850s, fulfilled identical functions in the Société académique de l'arrondissement de Boulogne-sur-Mer after his transfer in 1863. For these men, the cult of local memories was also a quasi-professional obligation, a means of publicly embracing one's successive postings, penetrating local society, and demonstrating one's zeal. It was still directed at ministers and other high officials, but this time as hierarchical superiors.

DEFENDING OUR HOME

A second, far less harmonious strand of evidence depicts the field of local memories as a battleground between inimical forces. Some elites contested or rejected the state's designs over local memories from the early 1830s on—either in opposition to the regime or, much more commonly, to preserve local autonomy. Because they often leave considerable paper trails, conflicts may lead the unsuspecting observer to draw a bleaker picture than warranted. Suggestive as it is, the evidence below thus calls for a cautious analysis. Contestation did not drown out concord within this field, but it was vocal enough to curtail the official cult of local memories.

Parisian and provincial *littérateurs* denounced, as we have seen, the central government's evacuation of local difference. This was but one ground of public criticism, voiced on the left and the right. From 1834 on, reformist liberal deputies accused Guizot and Salvandy of trying to depoliticize young French men (especially republicans) through collective ventures that threatened "independence of thought." Some provincials likewise depicted a cynical state, whose interest in local memories reflected above all instrumental motives. "It is probable that amidst these parchments half eaten away by worms," wrote Victor Derode in the *Revue du Nord* in 1835, "these ardent minds who now insist so strongly on writing about freedom, justice, etc. and whose subversive pretensions disturb our government's economy . . . [will] cool down."[20] During the following decades, critics continued to question the Ministry of Public Instruction's predilection for anodyne antiquarian pursuits, its unease before "[galvanizing] discussion." The geographical dictionary, they pointed out, confined provincial elites to local erudition rather than "the life and movement of our era."[21] Some provincials also denounced the ministry's

20. Odilon Barrot and Alexandre Glais-Bizoin, interventions in the parliamentary sessions of 10 May 1834 and 6 June 1838, in J. Madival and E. Laurent, eds., *Archives parlementaires*, 90: 157–62 and 121: 90; and *RN*, 1st ser., 4 (June 1835): 155.

21. *CS* 26, 2 vols. (Limoges, 1862), 2: 150; Julien Travers, *Des travaux collectifs*, esp. 3–7; and Armand René Du Chatellier, *Du mouvement des études*, 59–60.

yearning for control. In 1840, the legitimist *Gazette du Languedoc* lambasted the Académie du Gard for accepting a ministerial subsidy that enslaved it to the authorities. Two decades later, the president of the Société archéologique de l'Orléanais castigated the Ministry of Public Instruction for asking provincial societies to simply collect materials that others would put in order. In doing so, it forgot that "the sentiment of their individuality" drove such associations. Under the Second Empire, Caumont's circle similarly accused the ministry of "confiscat[ing] the ideas and endeavors of academic societies" to consolidate its "monopoly."[22]

Such sentiments explain why some elites responded tardily to ministerial circulars or, in the early 1860s, steered clear of Sorbonne congresses that would "absorb, and, up to a point, annihilate" what *la province* had accomplished.[23] Disputes with the ministry sometimes ensued. One, in 1841, revolved around the "ownership" of local historical documents. It pitted Amiens's Société des antiquaires de Picardie against a commission of apprentice archivists—students from the Ecole des chartes whom Thierry had instructed to locate materials on the history of the Third Estate. According to Amiens's mayor, the Société had welcomed this "scientific" endeavor, but objected when a commission member returned to Paris with several volumes of local documents. The said member sent the volumes back, but months later and with the inscription "requiescat in pace." According to the commission, the Société des antiquaires had sought to close local archives to the ministry's "foreign hand." These provincials had refused to sanction an official venture, to contribute "on the native soil [to] the great compendium being executed in Paris" by the CTH. "They want to maintain a monopoly over the history of Picardy: that is what they call defending their home [*foyer*], keeping their patrimony, upholding their rights and independence."[24]

Earlier that year, the Société's president had indeed invited the local population to "defend . . . our home; . . . preserve our local history as our patrimony; uphold our rights and our independence." He further glorified local memories a few months later: "Our traditions, our monuments are a dear patrimony to whoever still believes in the *patrie*'s glory."[25] Although BTH officials and Thierry eventually smoothed the matter over, this incident unveils an underlying tension between governmental over-

22. *Gazette du Languedoc*, 22 September 1840; AN F17 3301: President Société archéologique de l'Orléanais to Min. Pub. Instrc., 7 March 1859; and *AIP* 19 (1867): 275. See also *Le Temps*, 12 March 1863, quoted in S. Reinach, "La commission de topographie et le Dictionnaire archéologique de la Gaule," *Revue archéologique*, 5th ser., 2 (July-December 1915): 213.

23. AN F17 3043: Academic Inspector of the Yonne to secretary BTH, 1 October 1861.

24. AN F17 2810/1: Mayor Amiens to Min. Pub. Instr., 27 June 1841; and *Le National*, 12 June 1841.

25. *Bulletin de la Société des antiquaires de Picardie* 1 (1841–43): 24; *Journal de la Somme*, 30 July 1841; and Thierry, *Recueil des monuments inédits de l'histoire du Tiers Etat* (Paris, 1850), 1:cclxxii.

sight and local difference and initiative—what one ministerial acolyte termed the objections of "local ambitions and parochialism [*patriotisme de clocher*]."[26]

Such "ambition" could lead elites to rebuff the central authorities yet more bluntly. We will recall from chapter 6 that, in June 1852, Napoleon III's director of fine arts asked the Nord's three largest festive societies to stage their pageants during the Parisian fête of 15 August. All three declined. The Société des Incas claimed to need more time to plan such an event. Lille's Société des lits en fer replied that its participation would compromise "the interests of our fellow citizens." It would diminish the association's income and hurt local commerce and Lille's poor. More significantly, it would erode the "prestige" of a spectacle meant to advance "local charity and interests." Lille's "heroine Jeanne Maillote would pale before the memory of the dauntless Maid of Orléans" and Parisian spectators might ridicule the town's folkloric figures. In Cambrai, finally, Eugène Bouly turned down the supposedly "magnificent" offers made to his Société des fêtes historiques because such Parisian festivities had "nothing in common with our history."[27] Such was the heart of the matter: authority over local place and past. These pageant organizers were not necessarily opposed to the central government. The Incas after all staged a pageant to welcome the emperor to Valenciennes a year later. They nevertheless sought to collaborate on their own terms, outside what one of them called a "cold, . . . stilted, and, in a word, *official*" framework.[28]

In 1854, the Société nivernaise des arts, lettres et sciences likewise refused to contribute to the prefect's departmental history, commune by commune. Yet, relatively few elites openly contested or spurned the authorities. Those who did tended to be political adversaries of the regime in an era in which "slaves crawl under the governmental rod" (Bouly); or single-minded *littérateurs*, who cultivated the memories of their place of birth in regions that were peripheral (such as Languedoc or Flanders) or had a rich past (such as Normandy).[29] They frequently belonged to Caumont's circle—or, at the very least, attended nearby congresses—and nei-

26. *Bibliothèque de l'Ecole des chartes* 2 (1840–41): 501–2. Contrast *Panthéon de la jeune France* 10 (15 December 1841): 192–95.

27. The prefect of the Nord apparently wrote to the first two societies alone. According to his biographer, Bouly received his offer directly from Paris. See ADN M 140/44: Correspondance between prefect Nord and Jules Scrive (president Société des lits en fer) and Jean-Baptiste Meurice (president Société des Incas), July 1852; as well as Victor Delattre, "M. Eugène Bouly," 84.

28. *L'Illustration* 22, no. 553 (1 October 1853): 212–13; and Jean-Baptiste Foucart to the editor of *L'Illustration*, 14 May 1851, in *Fêtes historiques* (Valenciennes, n.d. [1866]), 6. Italics in the original.

29. Guy Thuillier, "Les historiens locaux en Nivernais de 1840 à 1860," *102e Congrès des sociétés savantes*, section of modern history, 2 vols. (Limoges, 1977), 2:326; and Delloye 38/100: Eugène Bouly, "Littérature locale. Programme de la fête communale. 15 août 1838" (n.p., 1838), 7.

ther needed nor expected material or symbolic rewards from the state. What is more, they usually expressed their aversion or frustration through direct communications, pamphlets, or the press. Rarely did they do so in the public meetings or publications of learned societies. These associations were on the whole too cautious, conservative, and dependent on the ministry to hazard such explicit slights. Whatever misgivings they entertained about the official cult of local memories they sought to voice discreetly.

TO ABET AND OVERSEE

Cooperation and resistance: it is in such terms, as I said, that contemporaries—and many scholars after them—have understood the relationship between the authorities and these provincial elites.[30] The notion of pure cultural or political resistance masks, however, the inherent ambivalence of such cultural practices. The cult of local memories constituted, as elites understood all too well, a powerful instrument of historical validation and territorial demarcation, a means of fending off external designs over one's *pays*. Yet, as historian William Sewell aptly reminds us, even as they criticize official designs, subordinate social groups must acknowledge the centrality of those "systems of meaning . . . recognized as dominant." Sewell thus speaks of a "dialectical dance" in which such groups define themselves in relationship to dominant forces, whose hold they seek to escape or loosen.[31] On a more concrete plane, this binary analysis has skirted this field's porosity and inherent indeterminacy. Elites frequently held several positions within the field: at once local *littérateurs*, contributors to Parisian publications, and quasi-administrative agents (as CTH correspondents, for instance). Circulating from one arena, one site to another, they modulated their comportment and adapted their public selves to their audiences and interlocutors. No relationship was exclusive, no association impervious to circumstantial imperatives. Elites could accordingly depart from, or even criticize, the ministry's agenda without shunning its framework. The Société des antiquaires de Picardie's objections did not prevent its members from applauding Thierry's *Recueil* or participating in the CTH's historical and archaeological ventures under the July

30. See, for instance, Françoise Bercé, "Arcisse de Caumont et les sociétés savantes," in Pierre Nora, ed., *Lieux de Mémoire*, 3:533–67; and Françoise Mélonio, "La culture comme héritage," in idem and Antoine de Baecque, *Lumières et liberté: les dix-huitième et dix-neuvième siècles*, vol. 3 of Jean-Pierre Rioux and Jean-François Sirinelli, eds., *Histoire culturelle de la France*, 230–31.

31. William H. Sewell, Jr., "The Concept(s) of Culture," in Victoria E. Bonnell and Lynn Hunt, eds., *Beyond the Cultural Turn: New Directions in the Study of Society and Culture* (Berkeley, 1999), 56–57.

Monarchy.[32] Fifteen years apart, the Société des sciences et lettres de Loir-et-Cher and the Société des sciences, agriculture et arts du département du Bas-Rhin both endorsed the ministry's interest in local memories, but urged Salvandy and Rouland to spare the independent "spirit of association" from the "centralizing system that is spreading everywhere."[33] Learned, benevolent, and festive societies belonged to a network of bourgeois sociability that, in France as elsewhere, expressed new social and political aspirations within the established order.[34]

Between this field and colonial situations yet another parallel begs to be drawn (see chapter 4). In one as in the other, we find heterogeneous and unequal forces that sought to forge working relationships. To succeed, actors frequently engaged in fluctuating, sometimes contradictory patterns of behavior. In colonial South Africa, anthropologists John and Jean Comaroff tell us, colonized subjects "sometimes subvert[ed] imperial ambitions, sometimes appropriat[ed] them to their own purposes, sometimes abet[ted] them, sometimes accomodat[ed] to them." The same was true of French intellectual elites, many of whom sought to plot an optimal location vis-à-vis the state: sufficiently distant to bolster their autonomy and authority, sufficiently close to prove themselves worthy acolytes, partake in governmental aura, and bolster their influence over neighboring residents.[35] The Comaroffs argue persuasively that, in British South Africa, the colonizing process resembled a "many-layered conversation," through which the colonized seized elements of the colonizers' culture and rendered them meaningful according to their own cultural logic. The religious practices of the South African Barolong boo Ratshidi—a mix of Christian and local elements—both conformed to a dominant culture and subverted it. The same was true of the Bangla novels that, in late nineteenth-century India, incorporated prenovelistic forms into a European genre, fusing affiliation and differentiation. Without constituting "the site of an absolute cultural resis-

---

32. *Bulletin de la Société des antiquaires de Picardie* 1 (1841–43): 24; AN F17 13269: Proceedings of the CHAM, 6 December 1840; and *Le Glaneur*, 10 July 1841. In her study of official *statistiques* and provincial elites under the First Empire, Marie-Noëlle Bourguet also points to an interplay of collaboration with the state and what she aptly calls a struggle over the legitimate "mastery of the conditions of perception of local reality." See Bourguet, *Déchiffrer la France*, esp. 200–205.

33. AN F17 3026: President Société des sciences et lettres de Loir-et-Cher to Salvandy, 27 January 1847; and *Nouveaux mémoires de la Société des sciences, agriculture et arts du département du Bas-Rhin* 2 (1862): 23 and 351.

34. Françoise Thelamon, ed., *Sociabilité, pouvoirs et société: actes du colloque de Rouen, 24–26 novembre 1983* (Rouen, 1987), esp. 218.

35. John L. Comaroff and Jean Comaroff, *Of Revelation and Revolution* 2: *The Dialectics of Modernity on a South African Frontier* (Chicago, 1997), 215. See also Jacques Revel, "L'histoire au ras du sol," in Giovanni Levi, *Le pouvoir au village: histoire d'un exorciste dans le Piémont du XVIIe siècle*, trans. Monique Aymard (Paris, 1989), xxv-xxvi.

tance," these cultural practices and artifacts nonetheless reconfigured the relationship between the protagonists.[36]

French intellectual elites participated of course in the dominant culture. Yet colonial ethnography invites us, first, to examine the manifold layers, the subtle interplays that unfurled within the field of local memories and, second, to apprehend local memories as negotiations with forces such as the state. Like the *littérateur* from Dijon who embraced *"provincialist* emancipation" yet still paid the Académie française "homage" in 1837, elites could play on several registers to integrate their multiple positions.[37] They amalgamated strands of official and nonofficial parlance in a public discourse that they directed toward diverse audiences. Pointing to their intimate knowledge of "local, archaeological, or historical particularities," some of them presented themselves as the state's privileged interlocutors, capable of providing unmatched "free and spontaneous information" (see chapter 2). In doing so, they furthered ministerial objectives, to be sure, but also buttressed their authority to delineate place and past. Calling for intellectual decentralization was one way of reorienting French society toward provincial *capacités*. Associating with Caumont's circle was another. Most of the elites who joined the latter sought, not to confront the state, but to secure "moral force" and propound resolutions with "important authority." Alcibiade Wilbert's doctrinal affinities with the ministry did not stop him from coordinating Cambrai's 1858 archaeological congress (founded by Caumont) and inviting Caumont to use his home as a resting and meeting place.[38]

The stake of this negotiation was not only local authority, but also the enduring specificity and memorial dimension of local history and topography. While their devotion to the local past often owed much to official endorsements, many provincial learned societies were unwilling, or unable, to sacrifice memorial narratives before austere, descriptive erudition. No wonder, then, that such negotiations surfaced most frequently,

36. John and Jean Comaroff, *Revelation and Revolution*, 2:xvi, 28, 100, and 116–17; Jean Comaroff, *Body of Power, Spirit of Resistance: The Culture and History of a South African People* (Chicago, 1985), 195, 218–19, and 263; and Ranajit Guha, *Dominance Without Hegemony*, 180. See also Alain Babadzan, "Tradition et histoire: quelques problèmes de méthode," *Cahiers ORSTROM*, série sciences humaines 21, no. 1 (1985): 115–22; and William F. Hanks, "Authenticity and Ambivalence in the Text: A Colonial Maya Case," *American Ethnologist* 13, no. 4 (November 1986): 721–44.

37. The *littérateur* in question, Jules Pautet, had founded the *Revue de la Côte-d'Or et de l'ancienne Bourgogne* and belonged to several learned societies in Dijon. See Archives de l' Académie française 5 B 16: Pautet to Abel Villemain, 3 January 1837, italics in the original.

38. AN F17 3299: Printed circular of the Société d'émulation des sciences, arts et belles-lettres de l'Allier, 23 August 1859; Du Chatellier, *Du mouvement des études*, 22–23; and AD Calvados F 4520: Wilbert to Arcisse de Caumont, 20 June 1858.

again, in provinces endowed with rich pasts. We will recall that, in answer to official requests for a monumental inventory of their arrondissement, Wilbert and the Société d'émulation de Cambrai created a research commission on the ancient monuments of the Cambrésis in 1838. Although they promised to disregard Cambrai's ancient "usages and ways of life," the resulting work addressed thorny questions of local history and described the usages of local medieval towns and estates. Its title said it all: *Report on the History, the State of Preservation and the Character of the Ancient Monuments of the Arrondissement of Cambrai.* Twenty years later, the Société d'émulation agreed to send the Ministry of Public Instruction documents on ancient Gaul, but reminded the rector that it had previously considered "the interesting question" that the emperor now addressed. Wilbert then sought to orient the investigation toward historical questions of local importance, such as the counts of Hainaut's "encroachments on the Cambrésis."[39] The prospectus for Henri Duthilloeul's *Lille et Douai à la fin du XIIe siècle* told a similar story in 1849. Its author, a Douai librarian, followed the ministry's erudite directives, but also investigated the habits, mores, customs, and topography of what he called "*our* Flanders."[40] These elites sought to integrate a memorial, identity-centered logic, which favored local singularity, with a governmental logic that, for political and scientific reasons, favored enumeration, uniformity, and abstraction.[41] In doing so, they reaffirmed their local identity and carved a niche for local difference within this official field. Intentionally or not, they diluted the intellectual state's designs while participating in its ventures.

Le Glay illustrates and deepens this point. As a doctor and amateur librarian, he launched ventures that, from pageants to historical tableaus, originated in a personal attachment to his *pays* and its past. He penned memorial narratives of local history, spoke of decentralization and local "independent existence," and sat on the executive committee of the Institut des provinces' inaugural congress. As a CTH correspondent and departmental archivist, however, he cultivated local memories within a governmental arena. We have seen how, in this capacity, he followed official circulars, participated in the ministry's collective ventures, and penned questionnaires and reports whose terseness and dry erudition conformed not only to scientific but also to administrative imperatives. No wonder that his su-

---

39. *Rapport sur l'histoire, l'état de conservation et le caractère des anciens monumens de l'arrondissement de Cambrai*, esp. the foreword by Wilbert, repr. in *MEC* 17 (1841), 2 vols., 2: iv-xxxv; and ADN 2 T 767: Wilbert to rector Douai, 7 May 1858.

40. AN F17 2851/2: Henri Duthilloeul, prospectus for *Lille et Douai à la fin du XIIe siècle* (Douai, n.d. [sent to the Ministry on 12 April 1849]).

41. See Henri Lefebvre, *Production of Space*, 383 and 386.

periors praised Le Glay as "a conscientious and zealous functionary."[42] All of this places him among these most "acculturated" elites who are commonly at the forefront of local cultural movements.[43] Integrating one's personal agenda and official priorities could, however, require creative language games. Before delivering a series of conferences on the history of northern France (under the auspices of the Association lilloise), Le Glay assured Salvandy in 1838 that he would "abet and oversee the studious activities of this land [*contrée*]." His ambiguous, if not oxymoronic, choice of words ("abet and oversee") exemplifies this elite's tenuous relationship with the central government. Three years later, Le Glay opposed Victor Derode's recommendation that the Commission historique du Nord study a local hamlet's "mores, language and character." Administrative duty, Le Glay explained, must take precedence over "philological geography."[44] Like many of his fellow elites, Le Glay operated at the juncture of the governmental and civil realms, harmonizing as best as he could civic duties, political interests, and the personal prospects afforded by local memories.

It is in this context that we should apprehend the Nord's contribution to the geographical dictionary and archaeological inventory of France. The department's intellectual elites did not dither upon receiving the first circulars in the fall of 1858. A year later, Le Glay assured the minister that learned societies in six of the department's seven arrondissements had begun work. The Société dunkerquoise (which now numbered BTH officials François-Louis Bellaguet and Jacques Servaux among its honorary members) appointed special commissions and began collecting data at once. The Comité flamand likewise sent the ministry a first report after three months of labor. Even the small Société archéologique d'Avesnes forwarded a pertinent monograph by its vice-president.[45] Despite this initial enthusiasm, the Nord was one of thirty-five departments whose elites had promised, but not sent, a complete archaeological inventory of the department by 1860. Submissions trickled in during the following decade: one on Cambrai, a larger one encompassing three arrondissements around Dunkirk, a *Statistique archéologique* by the Commission historique

---

42. ADN M 121/30: Unsigned report requesting the *Croix d'officier de la Légion d'honneur* for Le Glay, n.d. [1862].

43. Marshall Sahlins, "Goodbye to Tristes Tropes: Ethnography in the Context of Modern World History," *The Journal of Modern History* 65, no. 1 (March 1993): 1–25.

44. AN F17 3034: Le Glay to Min. Pub. Instr., 5 May 1838 (my italics); and *BCN* 1 (1843): 82–83.

45. AN F17 3303: Le Glay to Min. Pub. Instr., 5 November 1859; ASD 1857–59: Proceedings of the Société dunkerquoise's Topography commission, 25 March and 16 July 1859; *BCF* 1 (1857–59): 434; AN F17 3303: Edmond de Coussemacker to Min. Pub. Instr., 9 September and 18 December 1859; and AN F17 3303: President Société archéologique d'Avesnes to Min. Pub. Instr., 22 December 1859.

du Nord. The geographical dictionary elicited a larger number of contributions, but no acceptable work on the entire department.[46]

This was partly because, eager as they were to help the ministry, the Nord's intellectual elites failed to band in a departmental network, follow directives to the letter, renounce authority over local memories, and forsake local difference in a venture that, as we have seen, excised "any literary research" and "the history, even abridged, of the localities."[47] In 1859, the CTH asked Le Glay, Debaecker, and Dunkirk's Edmond de Coussemaker to integrate their respective contributions into a single departmental dictionary. Le Glay and de Coussemaker eventually accepted "this request for fusion," but never saw it through. Jules Desnoyers, the longtime CTH member, attributed this failure to a "rivalry" between learned societies.[48] He understood that, in this region as in others, urban pride and competition would impede ministerial ventures.

So would, yet more significantly, memorial investments in local memories. Paradoxically enough, it was the Société d'agriculture, sciences et arts de l'arrondissement de Valenciennes—upon which the official cult of local memories had had such a pronounced effect from the 1840s on—that first expressed this ambivalence. The Société's leaders endorsed this ministerial venture as early as December 1858. Its president and secretary urged their colleagues to participate, out of duty toward the government and their own past, in a project that would transcend the "scope of their locality." While several did so, the two men wrote Rouland three months later that, much as they applauded his geographical dictionary of France, its framework left much to be desired. "France's layout has not always been what it is today," they explained. "The various *pays* that comprise France were subject to other powers or constituted separate states and hence have a history that is in some sense special." Why, then, did the ministry send identical questions to all French localities? Echoing some of the critics we encountered in previous chapters, they asked for "complete latitude" in the choice of topics, "to the extent, naturally, that they pertain exclusively to local history," the preamble to a complete "general history."[49] Desnoyers deemed this request "completely foreign to the committee's activities." By May 1859, the Société had nonetheless completed a topographical glossary of its arrondissement—coordinated by Louis Cel-

46. F17 3305: Tableaus of provincial submissions to the archeological inventory of France, 17 November 1860, 27 June 1862, and June 1868.

47. Anatole Chabouillet, *Répertoire archéologique de la France. Programme*, 2–3.

48. AN F17 3303: Jules Desnoyers to Rouland, report on the learned societies of the Nord and the geographical dictionary of France, n.d. [end 1860 or early 1861].

49. *RAN* 10, nos. 5 and 6 (November–December 1858): 98 and 119; *RAN* 10, nos. 7 and 8 (January–February 1859): 187; and AN F17 3303: President and Secretary Société d'agriculture, sciences et arts de l'arrondissement de Valenciennes to Min. Pub. Instr., 29 March 1859.

lier, its archivist and a newspaper editor. The ministry had asked for "nomenclatures," succinct definitions of ancient place names. Cellier's glossary, in contrast, included longer entries on local towns, abbeys, and the like—with special consideration of their origins and history. The Société still claimed to "respect the [CTH's] intentions" and would, in fact, continue to collaborate with the ministry. But it conceded that its work departed from the latter's "arid" specimen, "stripped of all historical or archeological elements." The ministry rejected its contribution. The Société thus voted unanimously to print the glossary "in extenso" and at its own expense, thereby placing its stamp on the delineation of its *pays*.[50]

This pattern repeated itself in neighboring towns. Douai's Société d'agriculture, des sciences et des arts informed Rouland in December 1858 that it had penned a "research program for the preparation of a geographical dictionary of France"—following ministerial directives. This was only true of its second part: a bibliography of relevant works. The first part, a detailed blueprint for the study of "*our* ancient cities and communities," outlined a five-tier investigation:

1. The province, canton, archdeaconry, and deaconry to which the ancient cities and communities belonged.
2. Their "origins (Celtic, Roman, Barbaric [Saxon or other], Merovingian, Austrasian, feudal, ecclesiastical, secular, or regular)."
3. Their geographical situation and the "nature of their land."
4. Their population, including the "classes" and professions of local residents.
5. The "memories pertaining to each locality," including memorable historical events, secular or religious assemblies, local celebrities, and "aspect[s] of life."

Beginning as it did with territorial circumscriptions, this program respected the administrative tenor of ministerial directives. But its interest in local origins and the quasi-personal history of local residents clearly transcended the ministerial agenda. Its first-person references capture a memorial investment for which Desnoyers, once again, found no place in this governmental venture.[51]

In Lille, the Commission historique du Nord seized upon Rouland's cir-

---

50. Desnoyers, report to Rouland, op. cit.; Louis Cellier, *Glossaire topographique de l'arrondissement de Valenciennes* (Valenciennes, 1859); *RAN* 10, nos. 10 and 11 (April–May 1859): 274–75; and AN F17 3303: President Société d'agriculture, sciences et arts de l'arrondissement de Valenciennes to Min. Pub. Instr., 25 December 1860.

51. AN F17 3303: Secretary Société d'agriculture, des sciences et des arts centrale du département du Nord, "Programme de recherches pour la préparation d'un dictionnaire géographique de la France," 14 December 1858; AN F17 3303: idem to Min. Pub. Instr., 24 December 1858; *MSD*, 2d ser., vol. 5 (1858–59): 26–27; and Desnoyers, report to Rouland, op. cit. My italics.

culars to jump-start its own monumental and archaeological *statistique*, a project begun in 1843 but never completed. The Commission thus sent its resident and corresponding members a programmatic circular that incorporated several ministerial instructions. It also insisted, however, that this "old project . . . must not be confused with [the ministry's] archaeological inventory." The outcome was a *Statistique archéologique du département du Nord* that included indications on each commune's "origins and history." The ministry rejected it—predictably—as overly historical and the Commission published the work later that year.[52] In Cambrai, finally, the Société d'émulation began work on the geographical dictionary in 1858, studying local towns and place names that "have remained famous in the memory of the populations." But some members voiced early "observations and objections" (unfortunately lost) to the ministerial framework. One member later asked the ministry whether the Société could include historical celebrities, prerevolutionary industry, and etymologies in its dictionary. The answer was no. Later that year, the Société sent the ministry its "Geographical Dictionary of the Arrondissement of Cambrai and the Part of This Arrondissement That Was Included in the Old Cambrésis." Rich in local data, the latter did "not correspond at all to [our] program," commented one official. The Société accordingly turned this 91-page manuscript into a 371-page descriptive work on its *pays*, which it published in 1862.[53]

The pattern is unmistakable: provincial elites who sought to assert their descriptive authority and slip in their own—inherently memorial—criteria into an official venture. Without categorically rejecting the ministry's uniform blueprints, they displayed a greater flexibility than Parisian officials. Fusing erudition and narrative, descriptive nomenclature and analysis, grids and an abundance of local detail, they attempted to redirect these official investigative modalities toward personal memories and narrative history. They turned their geographical dictionaries and archaeological inventories into "syncretic formations" (A. Babadzan) whose representations of place and past would satisfy local and, if possible, official audiences.[54]

52. *BCN* 5 (1853–60): 209–11 and 238; *BCN* 8 (1865): 14; *RSS*, 3d ser., no. 2 (2d sem. 1863): 527–28; AN F17 3034: President Commission historique du Nord to Min. Pub. Instr., 30 December 1866; *Statistique archéologique du département du Nord*, 2 vols. (Lille, 1867), 1:v; and *RSS*, 4th ser., 6 (2d sem. 1867): 53.

53. *MEC* 25, 2 vols. (1859–62), 1: 21 and 26, and 2: 25; AN F17 3303: Charles-Aimé Lefebvre to Min. Pub. instr., n.d. [May 1859?], and Min. Pub. Instr. to Lefebvre, 7 June 1859; and AN F17 3303: Marginal annotation in letter from Min. Pub. Instr. to President Société d'émulation de Cambrai, 22 December 1859. See also *Dictionnaire topographique de l'arrondissement de Cambrai. Géologie, archéologie, histoire*, in *MEC* 27, 2 vols. (1862), vol. 2.

54. Babadzan, "Tradition et histoire," 120. See also Odile Parsis-Barubé, *Représentations du Moyen âge*, 1:146–51.

The ministry proved vigilant and returned many submissions. Archaeological inventories from Dijon, Rouen, and the Haute-Saône contained too many "historical digressions, discussions of origins." In Toulouse, a manuscript on the Haute-Garonne contained unneeded indications "on the *pays*'s first inhabitants and ancient topographical divisions."[55] The CTH told a member of the Société des sciences naturelles et archéologiques de la Creuse to "eliminate all that is purely narrative or historical discussion." In 1860, it likewise urged a correspondent from Albi to "eliminate completely the historical part on cities or monuments" and restrict himself to "description and factual observations."[56] Some elites accepted these recommendations. Others, as we have seen, published their dictionary or inventory on their own. To do so was not necessarily to turn one's back on the state. Eager to maintain their ties with the ministry, elites from Lille, Valenciennes, and elsewhere forwarded copies of published dictionaries that, while diverging from the CTH's "nomenclature[s]," were "written at [its] behest."[57] These publications, too, could denote both autonomy and governmental affiliation.

The ministry thus informed two learned societies—from Châlons-sur-Marne and Bordeaux—that their initial submissions to the geographical dictionary contained superfluous "details on mores and habits" as well as "historical, archaeological, and even biographical entries" that did not belong in this venture. The Société d'agriculture, commerce, sciences et arts du département de la Marne accordingly published a *Study of the Communes of the Department of the Marne to Serve the Geographical, Historical and Archeological Dictionary of France* in 1861. While its title clearly evoked the governmental framework, the work included "all that pertained to each *pays*'s history." The Société deemed it essential to collect historical data on local villages and, hence, "preserve the memory of . . . [local] public actions."[58] As for the Commission des monuments historiques de la Gironde, it lauded the ministerial venture while expressing its attachment

55. AN F17 3308: Anon. CTH member, report on Paul Foisset, "Répertoire archéologique des arrondissements de Beaune, Dijon et Saumur," n.d. [1861?]; AN F17 3314: Chabouillet, report on abbé Cochet, "Répertoire archéologique de la Seine-Inférieure," n.d. [1861]; AN F17 3313: Anon. CTH member, report on abbé Gatin, "Notes pour le Répertoire archéologique du département de la Haute-Saône," n.d. [1860?]; and AN F17 3308: Ferdinand de Guilhermy, report on the "Répertoire archéologique de Haute-Garonne," n.d. (1862?).

56. AN F17 3308: Min. Pub. Instrc. to Antoine Fillioux, 12 December 1862; and AN F17 3315: Min. Pub. Instrc. to Hippolyte Crozes, 27 May 1860.

57. AN F17 3303: Adolphe-Martial Bruyelle to Min. Pub. Instrc., 26 July 1861.

58. AN F17 3302: Min. Pub. Instrc. to President Société d'agriculture, commerce, sciences et arts du département de la Marne, 16 April 1860; and "Notice sur les communes du département de la Marne pour servir au Dictionnaire géographique, historique et archéologique de la France," in *Mémoires de la Société d'agriculture, commerce, sciences et arts du département de la Marne* (1861), 2:6–7.

to local memories. "While these persisting and vigorous traces of a past that did not lack glory" contributed little to *statistique*, explained its president in 1865, "they hold a much greater interest for local history." The Commission ultimately produced two versions of its dictionary: one "following the official program" and another, "undertaken from the Girondin perspective alone." With its statistical entries and historical articles on Aquitaine, the Gironde department, and *pays* (such as the Blayais), the latter amalgamated ministerial desiderata with "love of the native land."[59]

THE INTERSTICES OF OFFICIAL LOCALISM

This range of responses and interactions captures the relationship between provincial elites and the state in all its complexity. The dominant model was, as I said, one of provincial compliance—or, at least, acceptance of a new administrative framework. Victor Derode's concern about the Ministry of Public Instruction's instrumental uses of "parchments" did not prevent him from contributing to the geographical dictionary of France, this "vast and magnificent" endeavor.[60] This chapter thus displays the reach and publicity of newfangled governmental ventures and procedures. The French intellectual state co-opted provincial demands and "live forces," maintaining thousands of intellectual elites within its loose orbit. Seen from the provinces, the central authorities deepened their presence in this intellectual field, turning their brand of benign local erudition into a permanent fixture of the French landscape.

At the same time, the official cult of local memories provided provincial elites with new opportunities for self-affirmation and civic participation. At once hegemonic and counterhegemonic, it was both a new instrument of governmental affiliation and a new platform from which to reroute, if not contest, such forces. As such, it draws us back to the inherent indeterminacy of a field traversed by forces of autonomy and heteronomy, of dependence on and distance from the state.[61] The negotiation favored by Le Glay and others captures, better than any other response, this play between antinomic forces. Manipulating multiple identities and affil-

59. AN F17 3301: E.-J.-B. Rathery, memorandum of 23 July 1861; AN F17 3301: President Commission des monuments historiques de la Gironde to Min. Pub. Instrc., 22 June 1865; *Compte-rendu des travaux de la Commission des monuments et documents historiques et des bâtiments civils du département de la Gironde pendant les exercices de 1862 à 1864* (Bordeaux, 1865), 34–42; and De Lacologne, preface to J. Reclus, *Dictionnaire géographique et historique de la Gironde rédigé sous les auspices de la Commission des monuments historiques du département* (Bordeaux, 1865), 4.

60. *MSDu* 7 (1861): 18.

61. Alain Viala, *Naissance de l'écrivain: sociologie de la littérature à l'âge classique* (Paris, 1985), esp. 50 and 176. On this flux and ambivalence in nineteenth-century France, see Terdiman, *Discourse/Counter-Discourse*, 52–59.

iations, these elites alternatively—sometimes concurrently—followed, anticipated, and subverted the central state's political and scientific agenda. That some of them proved more adept at such negotiation than others is important—most notably, to gauge the state's presence within this field. But, with respect to provincial cultural politics, these protracted *attempts* to conjugate official and nonofficial logics are in themselves significant, regardless of the outcome.

The Nord, as I said at the outset of this book, is not representative of all French departments. Elites from neighboring Picardy and Artois, for instance, tended to associate medieval urban liberties with, respectively, municipal uprisings (Thierry's thesis) and aristocratic liberties. In the Nord, by contrast, elites such as Wilbert produced "synthetic" tableaus that emphasized ancient urban liberties but stopped short of castigating the aristocracy. Some regions and departments were clearly more inclined to synthesis or negotiation than others.[62] As we have seen, however, the latter surfaced in various parts of France, both peripheral and not. The syncretic dictionaries and inventories of Douai, Guéret, or Albi encapsulate the dual legacy of an official cult of local memories that both strengthened the nation-state and yielded new spaces of difference and authority. Such negotiation—along with scarcer contestation—nuances yet again portraits of a modern state that extended its hold over civil society, be it as embodiment of the nation or component of a disciplinary structure.[63] These depictions neglect or underestimate the multiple, sometimes hidden operations that mitigated such forces. Actors put social practices to multiple uses, participating in official schemes while redirecting them from within.[64] Historian Michel de Certeau's discussion of post-Renaissance maps and personal "itineraries" (or narratives) is most pertinent here. In contradistinction to the map—a synchronic tableau or "totalizing stage"—the narrative inscribes space with individual experiences and trajectories. It "creates a field that authorizes dangerous and contingent social actions" and weakens the map's stability.

62. Odile Parsis-Barubé, from whom I derive this comparative tableau, suggests three explanatory factors. First, history: insurrections took place in medieval Picardy but not Artois, for instance. Second, geography: the Nord's elites were open to Belgian arguments about ancient Flemish municipal liberties. Third, social composition: Artois had a high proportion of nobles. See Parsis-Barubé, *Représentations du Moyen âge*, 2:752–802.

63. Cf. Pierre Rosanvallon, *Etat en France*, 116; Jean-Christophe Bourquin, "L'Etat et les voyageurs savants"; and, among others works by Michel Foucault, *Discipline and Punish*.

64. Among other critiques, see Jann Matlock, *Scenes of Seduction: Prostitution, Hysteria, and Reading Difference in Nineteenth-Century France* (New York, 1994), 12–13; and Ben Highmore, "Unmanageable Materials: Visualization and Typology at the Pitt Rivers Museum," paper presented at the Nineteeth Annual Conference of the Nineteenth Century Studies Association, Philadelphia, 19 March 1999.

Subversive as it may be, however, the narrative is flexible enough to accommodate an established order.[65] Certeau's framework helps us understand the behavior of provincial elites who responded to ministerial circulars while stubbornly incorporating historical narratives into dictionaries and inventories.

65. Michel de Certeau, *The Practice of Everyday Life*, trans. Steven Randall (Berkeley, 1984), 121, 125, and 130. See also Levi, *Pouvoir au village*, 12–13.

The Return to the Local

BUILT ON PREEXISTING institutions, practices, and, to a degree, aspirations, the field of local memories came into its own after 1830. The July Monarchy brought liberalism to power, reactivated revolutionary memories, called for collective histories of the nation, kindled civic and literary ambitions, inspired rejection and disappointment, and reminded France, as Hugo put it in 1831, that it lay between "the ruins of a society that no longer exists and the outline of a society that does not yet exist."[1] Other designs—from science to philanthropy—converged during these decades to deepen the resonance of local memories, link them to a renewed sense of place, and equate the latter with local and national recomposition. Wedded to erudition and what they defined as science, some contemporaries refused to cultivate local memories in any other form. Others were more flexible. In the early 1840s, Douai's pageant organizers established their scientific credentials by publishing footnoted articles on Philip the Good's 1437 entry, which they would now reenact. This did not prevent them, however, from selling historical banners or borrowing elements from other fifteenth-century pageants to amplify Philip's "glory" and hence serve cultural, economic, and political ends.[2] Despite its shortcomings, the cult of local memories thus reveals new commercial and political practices, pedagogical models, civic and ideological designs, modes of governmental action, and weavings of diverse territorial identities. At once private and public, political and apolitical, local and embedded in national, if not universal, frameworks, it captured and promised to allay the indeterminacy of a postrevolutionary era.

By displaying the vigor of provincial political culture, moreover, the cult of local memories illuminates the all-pervading politicization of nineteenth-century France. Its appeal across the political spectrum shows that

---

1. Hugo, "Préface" to *Les feuilles d'automne* (1831), in *Oeuvres poétiques*, ed. P. Albouy (Paris, 1964), 3 vols., 1:712.

2. *Mémorial de la Scarpe*, 29 August 1840 and 30 July 1842; and H. Pilate-Prévost, *Notice sur Philippe-le-Bon, duc de Bourgogne et Comte de Flandre, considérée sous les rapports des faits généraux de l'histoire, et principalement des actes particuliers qui intéressent la ville de Douai . . .* (Douai, n.d. [1840]), 15.

the left did not reject all forms of local culture or identification based on the land and past. Scholars of the nineteenth century often emphasize the political nature of French territorial identity, founded on law and voluntary membership in the nation. The cult of local memories qualifies this portrayal: be it on the left or the right, this territorial identity could also hinge on place.[3]

If this field constituted a laboratory, it is also because its protagonists confronted the quandaries of local difference and initiative. The latter generated misgivings and debates that stymied the cult of local memories, but they also provoked a vast inquiry on the delineation of self and community, the integration of governmental oversight and private initiative in a modern era. Such questions and their multiple referents (local, national, universal) chart the winding itinerary that, in this field, led to modern territorial identity. While art historian Roland Schaer contrasts "identity encyclopedism" with Enlightenment universalism in his study of nineteenth-century provincial museums, some elites clearly sought to reconcile such languages.[4] In this domain, French identity was neither produced in the center nor generated—or appropriated—in the provinces, but articulated at the juncture of Paris and the provinces, of state and civil society. Some contemporaries elaborated satisfying memorial and civic models; others produced more fragile articulations. We have encountered individuals who anchored territorial identity in place and past while, in other circumstances, defining human beings according to will or membership in a universal humanity. We have encountered others who committed themselves to intellectual decentralization, yet espoused greater governmental intervention in civil society. These were chiefly, though not exclusively, liberal tensions. Beyond its internal varieties, the liberal school that dominated much of nineteenth-century France linked modern citizenship to local initiative. In its aversion to fragmentation and corporatism, however, it struggled to conceptualize the local and upraised the state as emblem and guarantor of national unity.[5] It sought to create a postrevolutionary settlement while grappling with questions—cultural diversity, the role of the state, the reach of politics—that the French Revolution had left unresolved. This incongruous marriage of conceptual reflection and tentativeness constitutes this field's fundamental paradox.

By uncovering such reflection in middling provincial towns, this study feeds a growing historiographical turn, which apprehends French politics

---

3. Other such revisions include Anne-Marie Thiesse, *Création des identités*, 171; and Caroline Ford, *Creating the Nation*, 10. Cf. Rogers Brubaker, *Citizenship and Nationhood in France and Germany* (Cambridge, Mass., 1992).

4. Roland Schaer, "Des encyclopédies superposées," in Chantal Georgel, ed., *Jeunesse des musées*, esp. 50–51.

5. On these contradictions, see Sudhir Hazareesingh, *From Subject to Citizen*, esp. 207–209.

and culture at ground level and shuns an exclusively top-down (and Paris-centered) perspective.[6] The French state has nonetheless played a central role in this story. Indeed, the cult of local memories amplifies one dimension of Alexis de Tocqueville's classic argument: the emergence and consolidation, across the revolutionary divide, of a "vast central power" that extended its political and administrative hold over society. The investigative modalities we have uncovered take their place in an "all-powerful bureaucracy [that] not only took charge of affairs of state but controlled men's private lives." Officials did seek to extend their hold over "public matters"—at the expense of intermediary powers and, more specifically, "free association."[7] The pull of internal unity, administrative order, and scientific rationality led ministerial officials to situate local difference within abstract and uniform national grids. Such procedures characterize modern states, which, per James C. Scott, neglect "local ecology," the particular circumstances and needs of localities, in their quest for utility and rationality.[8]

At the same time, this study tempers Tocqueville. "Independent life" did not vanish before cultural and political centralization.[9] In this realm, the authorities had neither the intention nor the means to suppress all initiative or voluntary association in the provinces. Moreover, we have seen how much the cult of local memories owed to French ministers and officials, both Parisian and provincial. Rigid dichotomies between a state that stifled and provincial elites who tenaciously upheld local memories are clearly untenable. Utter aversion to local memories—or even difference—did not alone guide this state's action. Jurist André-Hubert Mesnard voiced the prevailing view of the nineteenth-century state three decades ago: "The liberal state, which inherited its administrative structures from the Revolution and Empire, from a Jacobinism of the left and the right, has neither recognized nor encouraged partial cultures." More recent scholars have likewise spoken of the nineteenth century's "internal homogenization," a straightforward desire to eliminate localism.[10]

6. See, for example, Ruth Harris, *Lourdes;* Christine Guionnet, *L'apprentissage de la politique moderne: les élections municipales sous la monarchie de Juillet* (Paris, 1997); and Gilles Laferté, "La production d'identités territoriales à usage commercial dans l'entre-deux-guerres en Bourgogne," *Cahiers d'économie et sociologie rurales* 62 (2002), 65–95.

7. Alexis de Tocqueville, *L'ancien régime et la Révolution*, ed. J.-P. Mayer (Paris, 1967 [1856]), 45, 66, and 136.

8. James C. Scott, *Seeing Like a State: How Certain Schemes to Improve the Human Condition Have Failed* (New Haven, 1998), 22–23 and 46–47. On the modern nation-state's ambivalence toward localism, see also Arjun Appadurai, *Modernity at Large: Cultural Dimensions of Globalization* (Minneapolis, 1996), 190–91.

9. Tocqueville, *Ancien régime*, 148.

10. André-Hubert Mesnard, *Action culturelle*, 146; Yves Lequin, "La France, une et indivisible?", in Lequin, ed., *Histoire des Français, XIXe-XXe siècles*, 3 vols. (Paris, 1984), 1:91; and Thierry Gasnier, "Le local: une et indivisible," in Pierre Nora, ed., *Lieux de mémoire*, 6: 475. On

This was not the case—but neither did French officials embrace the local without reservations. They gravitated toward and kept a distance from local memories—struggling on both conceptual and instrumental planes to define communities and arenas of authority. Their misgivings about local difference, local authority, and excessive administrative presence hampered their action and frustrated provincial elites. The official cult of local memories nonetheless yielded important results, some of them unintended. Many officials knew well what kind of localism they wanted to see sprout in the provinces: erudite, apolitical, and anchored in the nation. But none could control the uses and semantic proliferation of this inherently ambiguous local idiom. Without necessarily endorsing pedagogical, civic, or memorial investments in local memories, they indirectly fueled them by validating a broadly defined localism. This field thus displays yet another paradox: a modern state that simultaneously curbed and galvanized local difference; a state that, like its colonial alter ego, produced "new constraints and new sites for creative self-expression."[11] Local loyalties—commonly seen as antithetical to the forces of modernization—found sustenance within these very forces.

In this respect, the French field of local memories contributes to a growing transnational study of the local and its relationship with the modern nation and nation-state.[12] Recent scholarship on Germany, for example, has demonstrated the growing resonance of *Heimat*, a flexible term that, like *pays*, denotes both a local place (and community) and a national one. There are striking similarities with France. Voluntary associations of provincial elites (most of them urban, liberal professionals and bureaucrats) began to delineate their *Heimat*'s geographical, ethnological, and historical specificity in the 1820s. Their ostensibly apolitical representations reaffirmed the region's cultural and political individuality at a time of growing homogeneity and social transformation. They granted meaning to a world in flux, sustained claims to local leadership, and bolstered bourgeois hegemony by depicting a local reconciliation that excluded contestatory voices. They also sustained commercial ventures (selling the locality), promoted local activism and civic consciousness, and eventually fostered pedagogical programs that rooted the ab-

---

the "Jacobin" character of the nineteenth-century French State, see also Philippe Vigier, "Diffusion d'une langue nationale et résistance des patois, en France, au XIXe siècle," *Romantisme* 25–26 (1979): 196.

11. John L. Comaroff and Jean Comaroff, *Of Revelation and Revolution*, 2:217.

12. See, for instance, Antonio Pasinato, ed., *Heimat: identità regionali nel processo storico* (Rome, 2000); Roberto Maria Dainotto, *Place in Literature: Regions, Cultures, Communities* (Ithaca, 2000); and Fredrik Engelstad, Grete Brochmann, Ragnvald Kalleberg et al., eds., "Regional Cultures," special issue of *Comparative Social Research* 17 (1998).

stract Fatherland in the tangible, affective *Heimat*. The result was a conception of Germany and national identity that rested on internal diversity. Nostalgia and reaction did not prevent this localism from participating in nation building and modernization. The imperatives of German unification meant, however, that *Heimat* resonated most loudly after 1871. In France, this was true of the *petite patrie*, but not of the cult of local memories in itself. While some German states directed elites and associations toward benign local studies, only in France did the authorities cultivate local memories with such resolve—and on a national scale— throughout the century.[13] Only in France were local memories inherently embroiled with questions of centralization and decentralization. And only in France did the cult of local memories originate in, and respond as clearly to, the French Revolution. Inescapable horizon of its imaginary and pedagogy, of its political aspirations and territorial nostalgia,[14] the Revolution also bequeathed nineteenth-century France an antinomy between national unity and particularistic local traditions. This antinomy helps explain why, unlike its German counterpart, the French local proved at once appealing and problematic during most of the nineteenth century.

Alongside the French Revolution, a second horizon hangs over this book: the present era. Historians comment on their own era at their own peril, yet they do not write in a vacuum. While I did not embark on this project to elucidate contemporary phenomena, I could not ignore the convergence between my research and the current "return to the local," as some call it, in France.[15] Present since the 1970s, spreading during the 1980s, the interest in the local past has grown inescapable over the past decade. In 1998, the *Gazette des communes* published a dossier entitled "Why Municipalities Are Searching For Their History." "Local municipalities have lately begun excavating their past and commemorating," noted the lead article. *Le Monde* concurred: "Local history is . . . increasingly revisited." The daily has not only reported on this "reappropriation of local

13. This composite tableau rests on Stephen L. Harp, *Learning to Be Loyal: Primary Schooling as Nation Building in Alsace and Lorraine, 1850–1940* (DeKalb, Ill., 1998), 114–24; Alon Confino, *The Nation As Local Metaphor: Württemberg, Imperial Germany, and National Memory, 1871–1918* (Chapel Hill, N.C., 1997); Suzanne L. Marchand, *Down from Olympus: Archaeology and Philhellenism in Germany, 1750–1970* (Princeton, N.J. 1996), 165–66; Charlotte Tacke, "Nation in the Region," 691–703; Celia Applegate, *A Nation of Provincials: The German Idea of Heimat* (Berkeley, 1990); and Katharine D. Kennedy, "Regionalism and Nationalism in South German History Lessons, 1871–1914," *German Studies Review* 1 (1989): 11–33. The following book appeared too late for consideration: Jennifer Jenkins, *Provincial Modernity: Local Culture and Liberal Politics in Fin-de-Siècle Hamburg* (Ithaca, 2003).
14. On the latter: Jacques Revel, "La région," in Nora, ed., *Lieux de mémoire*, 5:878–79.
15. Albert Mabileau, "Variations sur le local," in idem, ed., *A la recherche du 'local'*, 21.

memory," but also fueled it through a special series on those French *pays* that, "anchored in History, have maintained . . . a strong identity."[16]

This is above all a rhetorical revisiting, the celebration of preexisting places and memories, rather than a vast social transformation. Local identification had not, after all, vanished in the course of the twentieth century. Yet such identification has grown increasingly vocal and visible.[17] Evidence is plentiful: the innumerable commemorations of local figures and events; the return to "traditional music" or archery; the creation of a periodical entitled *Histoire locale* (Local History) in 1997. Be it in Ancenis (1999) or Montbrisson (2001), small and middling towns are staging public gatherings to bolster and grasp a "'reappropriation' of History at the local level." By 2002, a Fédération française des fêtes et spectacles historiques was sponsoring eighty-three historical pageants throughout France (with clusters in Brittany, the Nord-Picardie region, Provence, and the Languedoc). Mennetou-sur-Cher's "medieval festival," Castillon-la-Bataille's "reconstitution" of the eponymous 1453 battle: French towns and villages "valorize with historical rigor the local patrimony in its diversity," explains the Fédération.[18] Indeed, these spectacles betray a wider fascination with heritage: a yearning for the "thickness of time" of preindustrial eras and an unmediated encounter with one's past. For Pierre Nora, such yearnings characterize a desolate modern society, bereft of the warm traditions of ancient communities, seeking new forms of sacrality, new attachments to the past through artificial and undiscriminating patrimonial practices. "The most modest vestige, the humblest testimony" becomes "memorable."[19]

Most pertinent to our inquiry is this phenomenon's inherently local dimension, what anthropologist Joël Candau calls a multiplication of "local, particular memories and identities." This is what caught the attention of the Mission du Patrimoine Ethnologique, an offshoot of the French Ministry of Culture. In 1995, its annual grant competition revolved around the "Contemporary Production, Producers and Stakes of Local History." The Mission asked applicants to study the "field of local history's" actors,

16. Jean-Marc Binot, "Pourquoi les collectivités partent à la recherche de leur histoire," *La Gazette des communes* 1462 (13 July 1998): 18–25, quotation on 18; *Le Monde*, 30 October 1998, 17 July 2001, and 30 January 2002; and Jean-Louis Andreani, preface to *Les pays d'ici: 15 terroirs de France* (La Tour d'Aigues, 2002), 7. See also Nora, "L'ère de la commémoration," in his *Lieux de mémoire*, 7:986–87.

17. Henri Mendras, *La seconde Révolution française, 1965–1984*, 2d ed. (Paris, 1994), 251. I am grateful to Susan Carol Rogers for pushing me on this point.

18. *Le Monde*, 11 July 2002; http://www.fffsh.com; and Deontological charter of the Fédération française des fêtes et spectacles historiques, quoted in Laferté, "Le spectacle historique de Meaux (1982–2000): l'invention locale d'un modèle national," *Genèses* 40 (September 2000): 95. See also Marie Percot, ed., *Histoire locale. Rencontres d'Ancenis* (Nantes, 2000).

19. Marc Abélès, "Le local à la recherche du temps perdu," *Dialectiques* 30 (1980): 41; Nora, "Entre mémoire et histoire: la problématique des lieux," in his *Lieux de mémoire*, 1:xvii-xviii and xxvi; and David Lowenthal, *Past is a Foreign Country*.

institutions, "techniques" and ritual practices, values, and relationships to space and time.[20] From this vantage point, the recovery of local memories is intertwined with the current proliferation of voluntary associations and the enthusiasm for patois and regional languages. Musical groups, radio stations, adult classes, theatrical productions: evidence abounds here as well.[21] For many commentators, this historical and linguistic localism marks a rupture in France's history. "A new passion has seemingly taken hold of the French," posited *Le Monde* in 1998, before citing anthropologist Isac Chiva on the novelty of this "return to the local, to the past."[22]

This phenomenon is indeed unprecedented in its sheer size and sociological diversity. Elites long controlled the past, but today individuals from various social backgrounds purport to defend the memory of their group of membership. "People—and not only erudites—now want to reappropriate the history of their region and city," asserted Lille's deputy mayor in 2001. Middling elites are joined by other social actors, including students, retirees, vacation home owners, union activists, and second-generation immigrants. Eager to lure outside investors and visitors, local officials and councils cultivate the local past with growing alacrity and the help of learned residents, advertisers, and other "mediators." Women are also playing a greater role in this public arena than in the nineteenth century. These actors accordingly outline different kinds of memories—those of seasonal workers or local detention camps, for instance.[23] Nostalgia for rural authenticity and purity has furthermore intensified. Decades after the mass postwar rural exodus, the countryside has grown sufficiently foreign to most French men and women—urban dwellers that they are—to foster seductive images and touristic pilgrimages.[24]

Equally new is the geopolitical context. On the one hand, France's integration into the European Union and the advent of a global web of information, technology, markets, and capital are, as elsewhere, deepening the

20. Joël Candau, *Mémoire et identité*, 198; and "Appel d'offres 1996: production, producteurs et enjeux contemporains de l'histoire locale," n.d. I thank Lise Morellet-Treullé, librarian at the Mission du Patrimoine Ethnologique, for providing me a copy of this document.

21. *The New York Times*, 17 October 1999; and *Le Monde*, 21 July 1999 and 23 July 2001. On voluntary associations, see Mendras, *La France que je vois* (Paris, 2002), 49.

22. *Le Monde*, 30 October 1998.

23. Candau, *Mémoire et identité*, 189; Serge Reneau, "L'Etat et le patrimoine en France de la Révolution à nos jours," *Trames* 2 (1997): 12; and Benoît de l'Estoile, "Le goût du passé. Erudition locale et appropriation du territoire," *Terrain* 37 (September 2001): 125. Regarding Lille, see *Le Monde*, 10 September 2001. On the memories of new groups and institutions, see "Ce qui reste de la mine dans la région stéphanoise: la mine faite objet, la mine faite sujet," in Alban Bensa and Fabre, eds., *Histoire à soi*, 252; and *Cicatrices. 3 camps français. Pithiviers, Jargeau, Beaune-la-Rolande* (Pithiviers, 1999).

24. See *Le Monde*'s editorial on "The New Rurality," 11 August 2001; Susan Carol Rogers, "Which Heritage? Nature, Culture, and Identity in French Rural Tourism," *French Historical Studies* 25, no. 3 (summer 2002): 475–503; and Françoise Bercé, "Arcisse de Caumont et les sociétés savantes," in Nora, ed., *Lieux de mémoire*, 3:534. Jean-Didier Urbain complicates our understanding of such rural enthusiasm in his *Paradis verts: désirs de campagne et passions résidentielles* (Paris, 2002).

resonance of endangered territorial differences. As actual localities grow—
or seem to grow—increasingly indistinct, argue anthropologists Akhil
Gupta and James Ferguson, "ideas of culturally and ethnically distinct places
become perhaps even more salient."[25] On the other hand, postcolonial immigration has altered the French landscape over the past half-century. The
1980s and 1990s were marked by debates on immigration law and the electoral success of the extreme right. The National Front party has accordingly
recuperated Maurice Barrès's cult of "the land and the dead" to root national identity in ostensibly pure local traditions. The party's slogan is un-
ambiguous: "For France, the regional struggle." The "soul of our provinces"
will protect France from the corruptive spirit of May 1968 and foreign elements. In the cities it governs, the Front stages traditional jousts, celebrates
local historical celebrities, replaces Senegalese by regional crafts in open-air
markets, and purges libraries to, as one inspector reported, "accentuate national and regional roots [and] reject cosmopolitanism and globalization."[26] France's other extreme-right party, the Mouvement National
Républicain, has likewise embraced local traditions, "provincial identities,"
and "regional languages" within a unified nation. Adversaries of the extreme right have resolved to fight it in this domain as others. We must "wrest
the idea of regional cultural identity from the National Front," declared
one socialist official from southern France.[27]

Novel as it is, this phenomenon bears a striking resemblance to the
mid-nineteenth-century cult of local memories. Now as then, this mix of
recent and distant memories attracts diverse political schools and augurs
personal, even emotional relationships with the past and other local en-
thusiasts. It promises to assuage the malaise of vanishing distance and
boundaries: physical and social transformations that elude understanding
and control.[28] Yesterday's culprits were, in brief, the French and industrial
revolutions, the railroad, and the press; today's are high-speed trains

25. José Bové and François Dufour, *Le monde n'est pas une marchandise: des paysans contre la
malbouffe* (Paris, 2000), 201; and Akhil Gupta and James Ferguson, "Beyond 'Culture': Space,
Identity, and the Politics of Difference," *Cultural Anthropology* 7, no. 1 (February 1992): 10.

26. Electoral program of the Front National (2002), "De la culture," http://www.front-
national.com; *Le Monde*, 10 January and 28 August 1997, and 22 February 2001; and Denis Pal-
lier, "Mission d'inspection de la Bibliothèque municipale d'Orange" (1996), http://www.
ladocumentationfrançaise.fr/brp/notices/974039200.shtml. See also Christian Bromberger,
"Ethnologie, patrimoine, identités: y a-t-il une spécificité française?" in Fabre, ed., *Europe entre
cultures et nations*, 12.

27. See the Mouvement National Républicain's 2002 program, http://programmepoli-
tique.free.fr/mnr_2002_12.htm; *Libération*, 28 December 2002; and *Le Monde des livres*, 16 October 1998.

28. Sylvie Sagnes, "De l'archive à l'histoire: aller-retour," in Bensa and Fabre, eds., *Histoire
à soi*, 72–3; and Marie-Hélène Guyonnet, "Chercheurs de patrimoine en Haute-Provence: une
passion et ses enjeux," in Bromberger, ed., *Passions ordinaires: football, jardinage, généalogie, concours de dictée . . .* (Paris, 1998), 149–54. See also Gustaf Sobin, *Luminous Debris: Reflecting on Vestige in Provence and Languedoc* (Berkeley, 1999), 17 and 20.

(which turn Tours or Lille into Parisian suburbs), the internet, immigration, and as I said, supranational economic and political forces.[29] Present-day historical spectacles make the same promises as their forebearers. Medieval scenes abound because, once again, they evoke the lost coherence and conviviality of small communities, a natural and authentic life-style revolving around seasonal changes and immemorial attachment to one's *pays*.[30] Like nineteenth-century pageants, today's "heritage productions" and theme parks hinge on claims of authentic mimesis and active participation to create a self-contained "imagined world," which neither divides nor excludes.[31] Responding to growing uniformization, they sell and commodify "spaces of nostalgia" (M. Roux) that permit a tactile encounter with the past and a recovery of the self at the margins of modern civilization. These local spectacles, too, are apolitical and transformative. Organizers promise to "engage in neither politics nor polemics." In addition to their costumes and accessories, participants in Le Puy du Fou's historical spectacle retain the spirit of a quasi-"familial" community to which they have humbly subordinated themselves.[32]

A united, harmonious locality that accommodates all residents: such is, here again, the cult of local memories' end-point. The latter feeds a broader yearning for community—visible, not only in the provinces, but also in literary and cinematographic depictions of neighborhoods and the everyday. From their respective vantage points, Cédric Klapisch's film, *Chacun cherche son chat* (1996), and Philippe Delerm's phenomenally successful vignettes on daily, local "pleasures" betray the same mix of neighborliness, conviviality, and solidarity.[33] Le Kremlin-Bicêtre, a town of twenty thousand inhabitants near Paris, celebrated its 1996 centennial by commissioning a monograph on its past and staging historical pageants. "The city suffers from numerous social and urban fractures," explained

29. On the particular challenge which globalization poses to France, see Philip H. Gordon and Sophie Meunier, *The French Challenge: Adapting to Globalization* (Washington D.C., 2001). On memory as a response to globalization in contemporary France, see Benjamin Stora, "La mémoire retrouvée de la guerre d'Algérie?", *Le Monde*, 18 March 2002.

30. Christian Amalvi, *Le goût du Moyen Age* (Paris, 1996), 261; and *Le Monde*, 1 June 2001. On contemporary nostalgia and yearning for the past, see Isac Chiva, "Ethnologie, patrimoine, écomusée," in Marc Augé, ed., *Territoires de la mémoire: les collections du patrimoine ethnologique dans les écomusées* (Thonon-les-Bains, 1992), 13.

31. Barbara Kirshenblatt-Gimblett, *Destination Culture: Tourism, Museums, and Heritage* (Berkeley, 1998), esp. 7, 72, and 194–95; Patricia A. Morton, *Hybrid Modernities: Architecture and Representation at the 1931 Colonial Exposition, Paris* (Cambridge, Mass., 2000), 316; and Richard Handler and Eric Gable, *The New History in an Old Museum: Creating the Past at Colonial Williamsburg* (Durham, N.C., 1997), 70–71.

32. Michel Roux, *Géographie et complexité: les espaces de la nostalgie* (Paris, 1999), 255; Garcia, *Bicentenaire*, 194 and 283; and Jean-Clément Martin and Charles Suaud, *Le Puy du Fou, en Vendée: l'histoire mise en scène* (Paris, 1996), 147 and 160–62.

33. By 2002, Delerm had sold close to one million copies of his *La première gorgée de bière et autres plaisirs minuscules* (1997).

one local official. "The commemoration could ... [help] reunify the commune." We clearly recognize the nineteenth century's memorial investments. Le Kremlin-Bicêtre's monograph is subtitled *The Identity of a City.* Mulhouse's municipality resolved to teach its residents their own history "in order to make them proud of belonging to a common patrimony."[34] The sociologists and ethnologists who have studied these spectacles or the current vogue for genealogy uncover a recurring desire to anchor an identity—imperiled or not—within a tangible, historical locality.[35] Maryvonne de Saint Pulgent, then national *directeur du patrimoine,* agreed in 1996: "The patrimony contributes directly to the constitution or preservation of local identity." When the Observatoire Interrégional du Politique asked French men and women how they perceived their region in 1998, the leading answer was "a place of history and culture"—clear evidence of memorial sentiments.[36]

Much else is familiar here, including the social trajectories of provincials who parlay knowledge of the local past into local credibility, social relations, and public recognition (such as seats on charitable boards).[37] We also recognize the civic dimension of ventures that seek to engage disenchanted and alienated citizens and hence regenerate the body politic from the ground up. Knowledge of local history would "integrat[e]" newly arrived residents, explained the mayor of Le Kremlin-Bicêtre. It would make them "full" citizens, capable of "determining their collective future." In Meaux (Marne region), sociologist Sylvie Rouxel found that local residents derive both social identity and a sense of citizenship from the city's historical spectacle. Participation in such collective ventures helps create "full social agents."[38] As in the nineteenth century, today's cult of local memories feeds a broader recovery of the local as a space in which citizens may experiment with new forms of political sociability and

---

34. Binot, "Pourquoi les collectivités," 20; Madeleine Leveau-Fernandez, *Histoire du Kremlin-Bicêtre: l'identité d'une ville* (Le Kremlin-Bicêtre, 1997); and Isabelle Frimet, "Mulhouse célèbre les valeurs de la République," *La Gazette des communes* 1462 (13 July 1998): 24.

35. Françoise Lautman, "Fête traditionnelle et identité locale: rêve? ... ou recherche d'équilibre politique?" *Terrain* 5 (October 1985): 29–36; Laferté, "Spectacle historique," 98–99; and Garcia, *Bicentenaire,* 306–307. On genealogy: Tiphaine Barthelemy and Marie-Claude Pingaud, eds., *La généalogie entre science et passion* (Paris, 1997).

36. Maryvonne de Saint Pulgent, quoted in *La politique culturelle des régions* (Laval, 1996), 61; and Observatoire Interrégional du Politique (OIP) and *Conseils régionaux,* "Enquête 1998. Le baromètre du fait régional. L'action régionale: images et attentes," 55 and 71. This document is available at the OIP, 71, boulevard Raspail, 75007 Paris. I am grateful to Martine Jounaud for allowing me to consult it.

37. Stéphane Baciocchi et al., "La carrière d'un historien local entre entreprise touristique, érudition et patrimoine," in Bensa and Fabre., eds., *Histoire à soi,* 119–33.

38. Jean-Luc Laurent, "Postface" to Leveau-Fernandez, *Kremlin-Bicêtre,* 156; and Sylvie Rouxel, *Quand la mémoire d'une ville se met en scène ... Etude sur la fonction sociale des spectacles historiques: l'exemple de Meaux* (Paris, 1995), 23.

decision-making, new relationships to territory and community.[39] A 1999 poll shows that 70 percent of French men and women support the creation of *pays*: administrative entities made up of "historical territories that have always had a social, economic, or cultural cohesion." Feeding and drawing on this desire for a "democracy of proximity," politicians from left and right have endorsed the *pays* as an indispensable space of "voluntary service," "mediation," and negotiation with the state. Established by a conservative government in 1995, recast by the left in 1999, the *pays* have imposed themselves as "pertinent perimeters" for grass-roots social and economic ventures; 280 such *pays* existed by October 2001, date of the first "National Conference of *Pays*."[40] The French state is once more a key protagonist in this story. Whether taking the lead or responding to external pressures, it has sustained and legitimated interest in the local through diverse initiatives, including the creation of a Direction du Patrimoine within the Ministry of Culture in 1980.[41] Once again, the local's indeterminacy is ideally suited to an era of transition, in which the role of the state and the configuration of France's territory and identity are unsettled or contested.[42]

As in the mid nineteenth century, moreover, this localism must surmount economic constraints and political debates.[43] It is also problematic in its local dimension. Echoing some of his nineteenth-century counterparts, the mayor of La-Roche-sur-Yon assured that his municipality sought to bolster a local "sense of belonging" without encouraging a nefarious "withdrawal into oneself." Concurred an official from the Midi: "We must defend the individual's right to a cultural identity without lapsing into disdain for the other."[44] Indeed, the debates and misgivings that suffused the nineteenth-century cult of local memories prefigure the tension between

39. Alain Faure, "Penser local pour agir global?," *Le Monde*, 17 July 2002; Pascal Perrineau, "Un néo-localisme," *Le Monde des débats* 23 (March 2001): 6–7; and Jean-François Chanet, "Terroirs et pays: mort et transfiguration," *Vingtième siècle* 69 (January-March 2001): 61 and 70. On the explosion of micropolitics in France, see *La Pensée de midi* 7 (spring 2002), issue entitled "La politique a-t-elle encore un sens?"

40. Sondage IFOP—La présidence du Sénat (April 1999), *Le Journal des pays* 5 (July 1999): 4; Michel Kostal, editorial, *Journal des pays*, 5 (July 1999): 1; and *Le Monde*, 8–9 April and 10 October 2001.

41. On its impact, see Fabre, "L'ethnologie devant le monument historique," in idem, ed., *Domestiquer l'histoire: ethnologie des monuments historiques* (Paris, 2000), 2–3.

42. Nicole Mathieu, "Les riches heures de la notion de pays," *Autrement* 47 (February 1983): 27–28; and Faure, "Vers une République régionale?," *Pouvoirs locaux* 26, no. 3 (September 1995): 23.

43. Hélène Clastres and Solange Pinton, "Les maçons de la Creuse: la mémoire et le mythe," in Bensa and Fabre, eds., *Histoire à soi*, 110–11; and Rogers, "Which Heritage?" On these economic constraints, see the debates surrounding Mulhouse's architectural patrimony: *Le Monde*, 20 September 2002.

44. Martin and Suaud, *Puy du Fou*, 228; *Le Monde*, 30 October 1998; and *Le Monde des livres*, 16 October 1998.

universal and territorial thought that ethnologist Marc Augé associates
with modernity. Republican France is finding it especially difficult to resolve this question and find a place for internal diversity within the nation.[45] With respect to the local, the Third Republic's *petite patrie* model
long offered a satisfactory solution. Over the past two decades, the rise of
neoliberalism, the reform of the welfare state, and the inroads of multi-
culturalism have turned local singularity into a safe value. "The locality tri-
umphs"—often but not always as a conduit toward the nation.[46] Globalization and European unification further test the republican model by
challenging the nation's primacy. In his rich study of the 1989 bicenten-
nial of the French Revolution, Patrick Garcia shows that while the universalism of the ballyhooed Parisian parade would have made Fénelon
proud, provincial commemorations tended to celebrate inherently local
memories and communities. Countless communes turned revolutionary
history into a synecdoche for a broader local past. As a historical horizon
and a mode of voluntary association, the local proved more concrete than
abstract universal referents and more tangible than an increasingly distant nation, incapable perhaps of unifying the social body. The severity of
this decline remains unclear. When polled, French men and women after
all profess a deep attachment to France.[47] In France as elsewhere, moreover, the attacks of 11 September 2001 have arguably bolstered (provi-
sionally or not) the standing of the nation-state.

Garcia's work nonetheless suggests that, for many, the local's relationship with the nation is far from straightforward today.[48] Tensions permeate
all expressions of local "cultural diversity," be they historical or linguistic.
To cite but one example, socialist and conservative governments have endorsed, for more than two decades, a "right to difference" and "the diversity of cultural identities." Starting with François Mitterrand's 1981 platform, they have purported to encourage "the promotion of regional
identities" and languages. Indeed, more than 300,000 French pupils now
study the latter in public schools. But, after many debates and reversals,
France refused in 1999 to ratify the European Charter on Regional and Minority Languages, a document that affirms the citizenry's inalienable right
to use nonofficial languages in private life and certain domains of public

45. Marc Augé, *Non-Places: Introduction to an Anthropology of Supermodernity*, trans. John
Howe (London, 1995). On these debates in contemporary France, see Sylvie Mesure and Alain
Renaut, *Alter ego: les paradoxes de l'identité démocratique* (Paris, 1999).

46. Alain Bourdin, *La question locale* (Paris, 2000), 10; and Michel Wieviorka, "La France à
l'écoute," *Le Monde des débats* 24 (April 2001): 23–25.

47. Garcia, *Bicentenaire*, 304–307; and Claude Dargent, "Identités régionales et aspirations
politiques: l'exemple de la France d'aujourd'hui," *Revue française de science politique* 51, no. 5
(October 2001): 790–93.

48. On the "crisis of national sentiment," see also Fabre, introduction to idem, ed., *Europe
entre cultures et nations*, 3.

life. The charter, as many commentators remarked, was politically innocuous and limited to, at minimum, those thirty-five articles (out of ninety-four) the French government deemed acceptable. But France must remain one and indivisible, ruled the Conseil constitutionnel.[49]

Local memories, regional languages: the same tensions and fractures traverse the public discourse on the local. The same is true of Corsica, this "concentrate of French passions" about citizenship and territorial identity. Few issues proved more contentious in the late 1990s and early 2000s than its administrative status. Lionel Jospin's socialist government cautiously expanded Corsican autonomy in certain social, economic, and even linguistic domains, but the Conseil constitutionnel partially censored the law as unconstitutional in 2002. Noting this law's "timidity" within Europe, a French editorialist regretted that "official France still fears the regions." Another described Corsica as a "laboratory of experimentation about a certain modernity": the citizen's relationship to the state and the individual's relationship to geographical "entities" and his or her "roots."[50] In a 1999 poll, exactly 50 percent of respondents endorsed ratification of the Charter on Regional and Minority Languages; 31 percent opposed it.[51] Dismayed by the current "withdrawal into local memories" and languages, one camp thus rejects an "infatuation with [things] local and individual," "divided patrimonial claims," a "territorial integrism" that will erode national sovereignty and "balkanize" a hitherto unified and egalitarian France. "The rise of identity-centered cultures can only lead to cultural ghettoes," explains one intellectual.[52] A less alarmist camp applauds, in contrast, the return to the local as a democratic boon

49. Catherine Trautmann, "Toutes les autres langues de la France," *Le Journal du dimanche*, 27 June 1999; François Mitterand, quoted in Henri Giordan, *Démocratie culturelle et droit à la différence* (Paris, 1982), 7; and Jack Lang, quoted in *Le Monde*, 26 April 2001. On the teaching of regional languages in public schools, see Dominique Schnapper, "Making Citizens in an Increasingly Complex Society: Jacobinism Revisited," in Hazareesingh, ed., *The Jacobin Legacy in Modern France* (Oxford, 2002), 208. On France and the Charter on Regional and Minority Languages, see Paul Cohen, "Of Linguistic Jacobinism and Cultural Balkanization: Contemporary French Linguistic Politics in Historical Context," *French Politics, Culture, and Society* 18, no. 2 (summer 2000): 21–48; and Christos Clairis et al., eds., *Langues et cultures régionales de France: état des lieux, enseignement, politiques* (Paris, 2000).

50. In July 2002, conservative premier Jean-Pierre Raffarin reaffirmed the island's "right to experimentation," but as a form of decentralization to which all regions could accede. See Alain Duhamel, "La peur des régions," *Libération*, 27 January 2002; and Jacques Follorou, "La Corse, concentré des passions françaises," *Le Monde*, 6 December 2001.

51. Poll CSA Opinion—*Dernières nouvelles d'Alsace*, cited in Bruno Etienne, Giordan, and Robert Lafont, *Le temps du pluriel: la France dans l'Europe multiculturelle* (La Tour-d'Aigues, 1999), 63.

52. Jean-Michel Leniaud, *Utopie française*, 30–35, quotation on 35. See also Martin and Suaud, *Puy du Fou*, 11; Jean-Pierre Rioux, "La mémoire collective," in idem and Jean-François Sirinelli, eds., *Pour une histoire culturelle* (Paris, 1997), 347–48; idem, "Le temps présent du patrimoine," in Jean-Yves Andrieux, ed., *Patrimoine et société* (Rennes, 1998), 315; and Patrick Viveret, "Discours sur les passions," in *Passion et décloisonnement* (Limoges, 1992), 20.

that embodies the "movement" and "adaptation" of all great nations. In political terms, it constitutes "a different and freely chosen form of collective association," or "participatory democracy," that broadens the French civic sphere. In cultural terms, it lessens the hold of "large organizing memories," outlines hybrid identities that fuse the local and the national, and points toward true pluralism.[53]

As in the nineteenth century, these are doctrinal (and, to an extent, generational) lines of fracture that transcend traditional party cleavages. As in the nineteenth century, furthermore, contemporaries are turning to the local to address key questions: the delineation of territorial identities and community; the state's contours and relationship with civil society; and the articulation between the various planes of French society.[54] In 1999, in the midst of Franco-French debates on the Charter on Regional and Minority Languages, a reader from Grenoble wrote the daily *Libéra-tion* that France stood before a three-pronged fork. It could choose a particularistic "communitarianism," in which "particular identities" become autonomous. It could embrace an abstract universalism that rejects all "difference" from the public sphere. Or it could recognize these differences and thereby "change in order to remain itself." Far from being "marginal," he concluded, "the question of cultural diversity is decisive at the dawn of the twenty-first century."[55] The nineteenth-century's cult of local memories cannot tell us how this will unfold. It calls, no doubt, for vigilance toward historical practices that, in times of crisis, feed nostalgia and sanction both exclusion and hierarchy under the guise of identity and harmony.[56] But if the parallel above continues to hold, the return to the local also promises—like any good laboratory—to foster reflection and, possibly, new cultural and civic configurations of *pays* and nation.

53. Garcia, *Bicentenaire*, 303; Jean-Marie Colombani, *Les infortunes de la République* (Paris, 2000), 173; Candau, *Mémoire et identité*, 199; Chanet, "Terroirs et pays," 73; and Duhamel, "L'île et la République," *Libération*, 18 May 2001.

54. Bourdin, *Question locale*, 18–20.

55. Jacques Renard, letter to the editor, *Libération*, 5 July 1999.

56. See the reactionary and sometimes racist editorials in *Histoire locale*, notably 4 (spring 1998): 3, and 5 (summer 1998): 3. On the perils of the local, see also Thiesse, *Ils apprenaient la France*, 121; and Matthew Lazen, "Living-Dead Culture: The Ecomusée d'Alsace and the Local Heritage in Postmodern France," *French Cultural Studies* 13, no. 38 (June 2002): 125–44.

Selected Bibliography

MANUSCRIPT DOCUMENTS

Archives Nationales, Paris (CARAN)

Private Archives (AP). Papers of François Guizot, Narcisse de Salvandy, and Gustave Rouland: 42 AP 21, 212, 241, 289; 152 AP 2–3, 12, 21; 246 AP 16, 18–19.

Ministry of Justice (BB). Official reports: BB18 1233, 1395/a–c; BB30 377.

Ministry of the Interior (F1). General administration: F1a 36–49, 62; F1b I 157/31, 158/41, 173/1, 176/13; F1c I 161, III Nord 12.

Police (F7). Prefectoral reports: F7 6770–71.

Agriculture (F10): F10 1582.

Public Instruction (F17)

   Division of science and letters (Bureau and Comité des Travaux Historiques, correspondents, subscriptions, etc.): F17 2765, 2809–12, 2815, 2823, 2826, 2831–34, 2893–99, 2905–6, 3015/1–2, 3019–20, 3042–56, 3090/1, 3245–46, 3254, 3265–66, 3283, 3288, 3291–3321, 3334, 4334, 13268–69, 13272, 13399–401, 17130.

   Provincial learned societies: F17 1097, 3021–41, 17181.

   Personnel dossiers: F17 2838, 2847, 2851/2, 2865, 2886/1, 20128, 20594, 20802, 20822, 21686, 21723.

Fine Arts (F21). Subscriptions, statues: F21 708–9, 721–22, 4387–89.

Bibliothèque Nationale de France (manuscripts), Paris.

Freemasonry lodges, correspondence, *Monuments de l'histoire du Tiers État:* FM² 498; NAF ms. 6359, 11144–45, 15674, 24209.

Institut de France, Paris

Archives. Proceedings and correspondence of the academies: 2 B 8; 5 B 16; 2 D 2; 4 D 4–5; E 81–82, 350; 5 E 26–27.

Library. Correspondence: Ms. 2277, 2656.

Médiathèque de l'Architecture et du Patrimoine, Paris.

Historical monuments: 80/1/17, 80/1/56–57, 80/2/1, Nord 1827.

Archives Départementales du Calvados, Caen.

Arcisse de Caumont, museums: F 4513, 4520, 6040; T 2345.

Archives Départementales du Loiret, Orléans.

Historical monuments: 10 T 2.

Archives Départementales du Nord, Lille

Learned societies, monuments, intellectual life: 15 J 8–11, 29; 149 J 106; 1 T
217/5, 222, 241–54; 2 T 763–67; 3 T 129, 509, 853.
General administration/Police: M 6/8, 6/17, 121/30, 137/37–49, 137/61, 140/5,
140/44, 161/21, 216/1–5, 508/1, 510/8.
Proceedings of the *Conseil Général* of the Nord, charity, subprefectures: 1 N; X
24/9; 2 Z 101; 5 Z 401, 1183; 7 Z 140.

Archives Municipales d'Amiens

Proceedings of the Municipal Council of Amiens, Société des Antiquaires de Picardie: 1 D 1–31; 2 R 2–1.

Archives Municipales de Douai

Public festivals and ceremonies, charity: 5 D 38–39; 2 Q 8, 15, 21.

Archives Municipales de Dunkerque

Police, charity, public festivals, learned societies: 1 J 47–50; 2 J 81; 2 Q 5, 8; 2 R
15–17.
Archives of the Société dunkerquoise pour l'encouragement des sciences, des lettres et des arts (separate series, cartons numbered by year, 1851–84).

Archives Municipales de Montargis

Town hall, proceedings of the Municipal Council of Montargis: M A 13.

Archives Municipales de Valenciennes

Proceedings of the Municipal Council of Valenciennes, festivals, Société des
Incas: 1 D; 3 T 194; 3 II 2*-4*, 9*, 42, 45, 55, 139–42, 150.

Bibliothèque Municipale d'Abbeville

Papers of local historians, museums: ms. 324, 440, 487, 491.

Bibliothèque Municipale de Lille

Associations: Fonds Humbert XLI/263 and 267, XLII/274; Fonds Mahieu B/3.

Médiathèque Municipale de Cambrai

Festivals and local historians: Fonds Delloye 27, 36–42, 133–36.
Victor Delattre, "M. Eugène Bouly de Lesdain, historien de Cambrai. Sa vie—ses
travaux" (1885): ms. 1439.

PUBLISHED PRIMARY SOURCES

The State and the Comité des Travaux Historiques

Annuaire des sociétés savantes de la France et de l'étranger. Paris: V. Masson, 1846.
Annual budgets of the Ministry of Public Instruction. Usually titled *Budget des
dépenses de l'exercice [year]; Rapport au roi sur le budget du Ministère de l'instruction
publique pour l'exercice [year];* or *Compte définitif des dépenses de l'exercice [year].*
*Archives parlementaires de 1787 à 1860: recueil complet des débats législatifs et politiques
des chambres françaises. Seconde série: 1800 à 1860.* J. Madival and E. Laurent,
eds., 127 vols. Paris: Paul Dupont, 1862–1913.

Chabouillet, Anatole. *Répertoire archéologique de la France. Programme lu et adopté dans la séance du 17 janvier 1859.* Paris: Imprimerie nationale, 1859.

Champollion-Figeac, Jacques-Joseph, ed. *Documents historiques inédits tirés des collections manuscrites de la Bibliothèque Royale et des archives ou des bibliothèques des départements.* 4 vols. Paris: Fimin Didot frères, 1841–48.

Charmes, Xavier. *Le Comité des travaux historiques et scientifiques (histoire et documents).* 3 vols. Paris: Imprimerie nationale, 1886.

Cheyronnaud, Jacques, ed. *Instructions pour un Recueil général des poésies populaires de la France (1852–1857).* Paris: CTHS, 1997.

Circulaires et instructions officielles relatives à l'instruction publique. 12 vols. Paris: Jules Delalain, 1863–1900.

Discours, allocutions et réponses de S.M. Louis-Philippe, roi des Français . . . 16 vols. Paris: Veuve Argasse, 1833–47.

Discours et réquisitoires de M. Rouland. 2 vols. Paris: Imprimerie impériale, 1863.

Extraits des procès-verbaux des séances du Comité historique des monuments écrits, depuis son origine jusqu'à la réorganisation du 5 septembre 1848. Paris: Imprimerie nationale, 1850.

Fortoul, Hippolyte. *Réforme de l'enseignement, ou Recueil des décrets, arrêtés, circulaires, instructions et notes ministérielles concernant les modifications apportées à l'instruction publique depuis le 2 décembre 1851 jusqu'au 31 décembre 1853.* 2 vols. Paris: Paul Dupont, 1854–56.

[Guizot, François.] *Rapports au roi et pièces.* Paris: Imprimerie royale, 1835.

Jourdain, Charles. *Le budget de l'instruction publique et des établissements scientifiques et littéraires depuis la fondation de l'Université impériale jusqu'à nos jours.* Paris: Hachette, 1857.

Louis-Philippe. *Code des rois, pensées et opinions d'un prince souverain sur les affaires de l'état.* Edited by Eugène Paignon. Paris: Cotillon, 1848.

Notes circulaires et rapports sur le service de la conservation des monuments historiques. Paris: Imprimerie impériale, 1862.

Rapports au ministre. Paris: Imprimerie royale, 1839.

Robiquet, Paul, ed., *Discours et opinions de Jules Ferry.* 7 vols. Paris: Armand Colin et Cie, 1893–98.

Newspapers and Periodicals: *Bulletin archéologique publié par le Comité historique des arts et monuments; Bulletin des sociétés savantes; Bulletin du Comité de la langue; de l'histoire et des arts de la France; Bulletin du Comité historique des monuments écrits de l'histoire de France. Histoire—sciences—lettres; Journal officiel de l'instruction publique; Journal officiel de la République française; Le Moniteur universel; Revue des sociétés savantes de la France et de l'étranger; Revue des sociétés savantes (des départements).*

Newspapers and Periodical Publications

Parisian Newspapers: *Le Charivari; Le Constitutionnel; Journal des départements et des colonies; Le National; La Presse.*

Parisian Periodical Publications: *Album des provinces; Bibliothèque de l'Ecole des chartes; Conférence Molé, projets de lois et rapports; Courrier de l'Europe; La Décentralisation littéraire et scientifique; L'Echo des Provinces; France départementale; La France littéraire; La Gazette littéraire, artistique et scientifique; L'Illustration; Journal de l'Institut historique; Le Magasin pittoresque; Le Musée des familles; Le Panorama; La*

Province et Paris (becomes *Panthéon de la jeune France*); *Revue archéologique; Revue des deux mondes; Revue générale de l'impôt; Revue de l'instruction publique; Revue pédagogique; Revue de la province; Revue des provinces; Revue provinciale; Vieille France et jeune France.*

Prospectuses for: *L'Association; Les Communes de France; L'Echo de la province; L'Intermédiaire; Le Manifeste des provinces; La Méduse; Presse départementale; Revue des départemens de la France.*

Provincial Newspapers: *L'Autorité* (Dunkirk); *Le Courrier du Nord* (Valenciennes); *La Dunkerquoise; L'Echo de Cambrai; L'Echo de la frontière* (Valenciennes); *L'Echo du Nord* (Lille); *L'Emancipateur* (Cambrai); *La Feuille de Cambrai; La Feuille de Douai; La Gazette constitutionnelle de l'arrondissement de Cambrai; La Gazette de Flandre et d'Artois* (Lille); *La Gazette du Languedoc* (Toulouse); *La Gazette de Picardie* (Amiens); *Le Glaneur* (Amiens); *L'Impartial du Nord* (Valenciennes); *L'Indépendant* (Douai); *Le Journal de Dunkerque; Le Journal de Lille; Le Journal de la Somme* (Amiens); *Le Libéral du Nord* (Douai); *Le Loing* (Montargis); *Le Mémorial de la Scarpe* (Douai); *L'Orléanais* (Orléans).

Provincial Periodical Publications: *Album de Valenciennes; Annales des Basses-Alpes* (Digne); *Annuaire de l'Institut des provinces et des congrès scientifiques; Archives historiques et littéraires du Nord de la France et du Midi de la Belgique* (Valenciennes); *L'Artiste, revue hebdomadaire du Nord de la France* (Lille); *Bulletin scientifique; historique et littéraire du département du Nord et des pays voisins* (Lille); *Congrès scientifique de France; La Flandre illustrée* (Lille); *L'Instituteur du Nord et du Pas-de-Calais* (Douai); *Journal central des académies et des sociétés savantes* (Valenciennes); *Martin de Cambrai; Revue cambrésienne; Revue d'Alsace* (Strasbourg); *Revue de l'Escaut* (Cambrai); *Revue de Rouen; La Revue du mois littéraire et artistique* (Lille); *Revue du Nord (de la France)* (Lille); *Souvenirs de la Flandre wallonne* (Douai); *La Vedette cambrésienne.*

Almanacs and *annuaires* of Cambrai; Douai; Dunkirk; Lille; Valenciennes; and the Nord.

Learned Societies

Achmet d'Héricourt. *Annuaire des sociétés savantes de la France et de l'étranger.* 2 vols. Paris: Paul Durand, 1863–64.

Annales du/de la: Comité flamand de France (Dunkirk); Société académique de Nantes et du département de la Loire-Inferieure; Société d'agriculture, sciences, arts et commerce du Puy; Société archéologique et historique des Côtes-du-Nord (Saint-Brieuc).

Annales scientifiques, littéraires et industrielles de l'Auvergne (becomes *Mémoires de l'Académie des sciences, belles-lettres et arts de Clermont-Ferrand*).

Association lilloise. Ouverture des conférences hebdomadaires de 1844. Lille: Vanackere fils, 1844.

Association lilloise pour l'encouragement des lettres et des arts dans le département du Nord. Séance d'installation. 17 décembre 1836. Lille: Vanackere fils, 1836.

Bulletin du/de la: Comité flamand de France (Dunkirk); Commission historique du département du Nord (Lille); Société des antiquaires de Picardie (Amiens); Société archéologique, scientifique et littéraire de Béziers; Société archéologique et historique de la Charente (Angoulême); Société dunkerquoise pour l'encouragement des sciences, des lettres et des arts (becomes *Mémoires*); Société d'études scientifiques et archéologiques de la ville de Draguignan; Société des sciences, belles-lettres et arts du département du Var (Toulon); Société des sciences historiques et naturelles de l'Yonne (Auxerre); Union géographique du Nord de la France (Douai).

Galerie historique valenciennoise. Catalogue. Valenciennes: B. Henry, 1858.

Lasteyrie, Robert de, Eugène Lefevre-Pontalis, then A. Didier. *Bibliographie générale des travaux historiques et archéologiques publiés par les sociétés savantes de la France, dressée sous les auspices du Ministère de l'Instruction Publique.* 6 vols. Paris: Imprimerie nationale, 1888–1918.

Lefèvre-Pontalis, Eugène. *Bibliographie des sociétés savantes de la France.* Paris: Imprimerie nationale, 1887.

Mémoires de la/de l': Académie des sciences, arts et belles-lettres de Caen; Académie des sciences, arts et belles-lettres de Dijon; Société académique de Savoie (Chambéry); Société d'agriculture, des sciences, arts et belles-lettres du département de l'Aube (Troyes); Société d'agriculture, des sciences et des arts centrale du département du Nord séant à Douai; Société d'agriculture, des sciences et des arts de l'arrondissement de Valenciennes (becomes *Revue agricole, industrielle et litteraire du Nord*); Société d'agriculture, sciences, arts et belles-lettres de Bayeux; Société des antiquaires de Normandie (Caen); Société d'émulation d'Abbeville; Société d'émulation de Cambrai; Société de l'histoire et des beaux-arts de la Flandre maritime de France (Bergues); Société des lettres, sciences et arts de l'Aveyron (Rodez); Société des sciences, agriculture et arts du département du Bas-Rhin (Strasbourg); Société des sciences, de l'agriculture et des arts de Lille.

Mémoires et documents inédits pour servir à l'histoire de la Franche-Comté publiés par l'Académie de Besançon. Vols. 1–4. Besançon: L. Saine-Agathe, 1838–69.

Mémoires historiques sur l'arrondissement de Valenciennes publiés par la Société d'agriculture, des sciences et des arts de l'arrondissement de Valenciennes.

Procès-verbal de la séance générale du 23 février 1842 de l'Association lilloise. Lille: L. Danel, 1842.

Recueil de l'Académie des Jeux Floraux (Toulouse).

Séances publiques de la/de l': Académie des sciences, belles-lettres et arts de Bordeaux (becomes *Actes*); Société d'agriculture, commerce, sciences et arts du département de la Marne (Châlons-sur-Marne) [becomes *Mémoires*].

Sociétés littéraires de la France, par provinces et par départements. Paris: Crapelet, 1840.

Historical Pageants

Programs for the processions and pageants of Cambrai since 1724 may be found in the Médiathèque Municipale de Cambrai (Fonds Delloye) and the Bibliothèque Nationale de France (Li 31). I only cite a few of them below.

Blaze, Elzéar. *Fête triomphale des Incas à Valenciennes le 29 mars 1840.* Valenciennes: Prignet, 1840.

Bonnard. *Récit historique et détaillé de l'entrée de Jean-sans-Peur en la ville de Douai, en l'an 1405 fait d'après les documents les plus avérés.* Douai: Bonnard-Obez, n.d. [1861].

Brassart, Félix. *Fêtes communales de Douai depuis les temps les plus reculés jusqu'à nos jours.* Douai: L. Crépin, 1876.

La cavalcade du Cateau au profit des pauvres. Notice sur les fêtes du dimanche 27 et du lundi 28 juin 1869. Le Cateau: Jules Lempereur, 1869.

Cellier, Louis. *Société des Incas de Valenciennes fondée en 1820. 40e anniversaire. Fêtes populaires des 17, 18 et 19 juin 1866.* Valenciennes: L. Henry, 1867.

Clément née Hémery, Albertine. *Histoire des fêtes civiles et religieuses, usages anciens et modernes du département du Nord.* 2d rev. ed. Cambrai: J. Chanson, 1836 [1834].

Decottignies, Charles. *Les fastes de Lille. Faits historiques racontés en chanson patoise.* Lille: Alcan Levy, 1863.

[Delcroix, Fidèle]. *Programme de la marche triomphale des chars, cavalcades, etc. à la fête communale de Cambrai. 15 et 17 août 1838.* Cambrai: J. Chanson, 1838.

———. *Sur le programme de la fête communale de Cambrai en 1838. Lettre à M.***.* Cambrai: Hurez, 1839.

Les fastes de Lille. Cortège cavalcade (14 juin 1863). Lille: Horemans, 1863.

Les fastes de Lille. Grande cavalcade organisée par souscription au profit des pauvres. Lille: L. Danel, 1851.

Fête communale de Cambrai. Cambrai: J. Chanson, 1838.

Fête du Moyen Age sous Philippe-le-Bon, représentée pour la première fois à Douai, le 14 juillet 1839, par les soins de la Société de bienfaisance. Douai: V. Adam, n.d. [1839].

Fête extraordinaire qui aura lieu à Dunkerque le 29 mars 1840 en faveur des veuves et enfants des marins péris en 1839. Dunkirk: Drouillard, n.d. [1840].

Fêtes d'Aups à l'occasion de la Saint-Pancrace. Bravade et entrée historique de Charles, comte d'Anjou et de Provence. Aix: Illy, 1857.

Fêtes de charité de la ville d'Angers. Juin 1853. Angers: Cosionier et Lachèse, 1853.

Fêtes populaires des Incas, 18 et 19 juin 1866. Souvenirs photographiques. Valenciennes: Louis Henry, 1867.

Foucart, Jean-Baptiste. *Fêtes historiques.* Valenciennes: Louis Henry, n.d. [1866].

Gayant ou le géant de Douai, suivi du programme de la fête de 1840. Douai: F. Robaut, 1840.

Grande fête de charité donnée à Bourg au profit des pauvres de la ville. Cavalcade historique et promenade en char. Bourg: Milliet-Bottier, n.d. [1863].

Horeau, Hector et al. *Projet de fêtes offertes à toutes les nations du globe, par souscription nationale, présenté à M. le président de la République, dans son audience du 6 mai.* Paris: Plon frères, 1851.

Le Glay, André. *Programme des faits historiques représentés par la marche des chars et phaétons, à la fête communale de Cambrai, le 15 et le 18 août 1833.* Cambrai: Hurez, 1833.

———. *Notice sur les principales fêtes et cérémonies publiques qui ont eu lieu à Cambrai depuis le XIe siècle jusqu'à nos jours.* 2d ed. Cambrai: S. Berthoud, n.d. [1827].

Legougeux, Louis. *Souvenirs lillois. Relation des fêtes qui furent célébrées à Lille les 12, 13, 14 et 15 juin 1825 à l'occasion du sacre de S. M. le roi Charles X et du rétablissement de la fête et de la procession de Lille.* Lille: Leleu, 1902.

Méhédin, Léon. *Projet de fêtes publiques à Paris.* Paris: L. Bailly, Divry et Cie, 1852.

Merlet, Kergestain Lucien. *Cavalcade historique représentant l'entrée du roi Henri IV dans la ville de Chartres, lorsqu'il vint s'y faire sacrer Roi de France.* Chartres: Garnier, 1860.

Notice historique sur Philippe-le-Bon, contenant le programme détaillé de la troisième fête, avec addition de nouvelles notes, la proclamation, l'itinéraire, l'amour du pays, pièce inédite de Mme Desbordes-Valmore. Douai: A. Obez, 1842.

Notice sur la cavalcade de Flers. Flers: Paul Martin, n.d. [1857].

Pelleport, Charles de. *Historique des fêtes bordelaises.* Bordeaux: Mme Crugy, 1858.

Pilate-Prévost, H. *Notice sur Philippe-le-Bon, duc de Bourgogne et Comte de Flandre, considérée sous les rapports des faits généraux de l'histoire, et principalement des actes particuliers qui intéressent la ville de Douai . . .* Douai: F. Robaut, n.d. [1840].

Portelette, Constant. *Les fastes de Lille et les invalides du travail.* Lille: L. Quarré, 1858.

Précis de ce qui s'est passé à Cambrai, en l'année 1529, à l'occasion de la Paix des Dames, et représenté aujourd'hui par la Société de bienfaisance. Cambrai: Lesne-Daloin, 1837.

Programme de la fête donnée à l'hippodrome. Tournoi et carrousel. Marseille: Arnaud et Cie, n.d. [1858].

Programme des fêtes qui seront célébrées à l'occasion du sacre de sa majesté Charles X et de l'anniversaire de la procession de Lille instituée en 1269, par Marguerite de Constantinople, comtesse de Flandres. Lille: L. Jacqué, 1825.

Programme officiel et détaillé des fêtes de charité données à Toulouse les 26, 27, 28, 29, 30 mai 1866. Toulouse: L. Hébrail, 1866.

Quertinier, J. *La fête des Incas en 1851 ou les agréments de Valenciennes, chansonnette comique en patois du pays.* Valenciennes: A. Prignet, n.d.

Société de bienfaisance. 5e solennité historique. Programme général de la fête historique des 8, 9 et 10 juillet 1861. Douai: L. Crépin, 1861.

Société de bienfaisance. Programme de la fête et du cortège historiques, réunis au programme de la fête communale. Douai: Crépeaux, n.d. [1849].

Société de bienfaisance dite des Incas. Programme de la marche qui aura lieu à Valenciennes les 17, 18 et 19 juin 1866. 3rd ed. Valenciennes: E. Prignet, 1866.

Société des fêtes de charité de Rochefort-sur-Mer 16–17–18 août 1862. Rochefort-sur-Mer: Ch. Thèze, n.d. [1862].

Société des Incas. Fêtes populaires à Valenciennes et programme de la marche allégorique des peuples conduits par le génie de la civilisation à la concorde universelle. Valenciennes: A. Prignet, 1850.

Société des Incas de Valenciennes. Règlement. Valenciennes: E. Prignet, 1850.

Statuts de la Société de bienfaisance de la ville de Douai. Douai: V. Adam, 1839.

Tournois et fête équestre de 1850. Notice historique sur la cérémonie du mariage du roi Louis XII et de la reine Anne. Nantes: Bourgine, Masseaux et Comp., n.d. [1850].

Ville de Comines. Programme détaillé du cortège-cavalcade augmenté d'une notice historique pour servir d'explication aux différentes scènes représentées au Cortège. Lille: E. Reboux, 1853.

"Ville de Dunkerque. Fêtes des 2, 3 et 4 septembre 1860." Dunkirk: Lorenzo, n.d. [1860].

Ville de Rambouillet. Fête de bienfaisance. Lundi de Pâques 17 avril 1865. Cavalcade historique organisée par les habitants, etc. Rambouillet: Raynal, n.d. [1865].

Books

Ampère, Jean-Jacques. *Histoire de la formation de la langue française.* Paris: Didier et Cie, 1869 [1841].

Anon. *De l'importance des communes et des départements, et de la nécessité d'accroître les ressources communales et départementales.* Tulle: P. Detournelle, 1844.

Association française pour l'avancement des sciences. Lille, 1874. Compte-rendu de la 3e session. Paris, 1875.

Augustin-Thierry, A. *Augustin Thierry (1795–1856), d'après sa correspondance et ses papiers de famille.* Paris: Plon-Nourrit, 1922.

Barrès, Maurice. *Les déracinés.* Paris: UGE, 1986.

Berthoud, Samuel-Henry. *La France historique, industrielle et pittoresque de la jeunesse.* 2 vols. Paris: Astoin, 1835–36.

——. *Chroniques et traditions surnaturelles de la Flandre.* 3 vols. Paris: Werdet, 1831–34.

Bertrand, Raymond de. *Notice historique sur la sous-préfecture de Dunkerque.* Dunkirk: B. Kien, 1863.

Bost, Alexandre-Armand. *Traité de l'organisation et des attributions des corps municipaux d'après la législation et la jurisprudence actuelles.* 2d ed. 2 vols. Paris: Chez l'auteur, 1840.

Bouchet, Emile. *Histoire populaire de Dunkerque.* Dunkirk: J. Liénard, 1871.

Bouillier, Francisque. *L'Institut et les académies de province.* Paris: Hachette, 1879.

Boulanger, Emile. *Fleurs et jalons: poésies et souvenirs historiques.* Paris: Paul Masgana, 1858.

Bouly (de Lesdain), Eugène. *Histoire de la municipalité de Cambrai depuis 1789 jusqu'à nos jours.* 2 vols. Cambrai: P. Lévêque, 1851–52.

——. *Histoire de Cambrai et du Cambrésis.* 2 vols. Cambrai: Hattu, 1842.

——. *Lettres sur Cambrai.* Cambrai: J. Chanson, 1835.

Bourquelot, Félix. *Histoire de Provins.* Provins: Lebeau, 1839.

Boyer de Sainte-Suzanne, Charles. *L'administration sous l'ancien régime. Les intendants de la généralité d'Amiens (Artois et Picardie).* Paris: P. Dupont, 1865.

——. *La vérité sur la décentralisation.* Amiens: T. Jeunet, 1861.

Brassart, Félix. *Notice historique et statistique sur Dechy, village du canton sud de Douai.* Douai: Adam d'Aubers, 1844.

Brun-Lavainne, Elie. *Mémoire sur les institutions communales de la France et de la Flandre au Moyen Age.* Lille: V. Vanackere, 1857.

——. *Mes souvenirs.* Lille: Lefebvre-Ducrocq, 1855.

Bruneel, Henri. *Epaves littéraires.* Lille: L. Danel, 1850.

——. *Histoire populaire de Lille.* New ed. Steenvoorde: Foyer culturel de l'Houtland, 1991 [1848].

Bruyelle, Adolphe. *Notes historiques sur les communes de l'arrondissement de Cambrai.* Cambrai: n.p., 1841–49.

Buret, Eugène. *De la misère des classes laborieuses en Angleterre et en France,* 2 vols. Paris: Paulin, 1840.

Camescasse, Valentine de. *Souvenirs de Madame de Camescasse. Douai au 19e siècle, salons parlementaires sous la IIIe République.* 3rd ed. Paris: Plon-Nourrit et Cie, 1924.

Capelle, Louis-François. *Vie du cardinal P. Giraud, archevêque de Cambrai.* Lille: L. Lefort, 1852.

Cellier, Louis. *Glossaire topographique de l'arrondissement de Valenciennes.* Valenciennes: B. Henry, 1859.

Chon, François. *Promenades lilloises.* Lille: L. Danel, 1888.

——. *Impressions et souvenirs, 1812–72.* Lille: L. Danel, n.d. [1872?].

Clément, Pierre. *Histoire de la Flandre, depuis l'invasion romaine jusqu'au XIXe siècle.* Lille: Baly, 1836.

Congrès archéologique et historique. Séances générales tenues à Dunkerque, au Mans et à Cherbourg en 1860. Paris: Derache, 1861.

——. *Séances générales tenues à Perigueux et à Cambrai en 1858.* Paris: Derache, 1859.

——. *Séances générales tenues à Lille, en 1845, par la Société française pour la conservation des monuments historiques.* Caen: A. Hardel, 1846.

Congrès des délégués des sociétés savantes des départements, sous la direction de l'Institut des provinces. Bulletin. Paris, 1850–51.

Constant, Benjamin. *Principes de politique.* Paris: Guillaumin, 1872 [1815].

——. *De l'esprit de conquête et de l'usurpation dans leurs rapports avec la civilisation européenne.* Edited by Ephraïm Harpax. Paris: Flammarion, 1986 [1814].

Cormenin, Louis-Marie de. *Entretiens de village.* 6th ed. Paris: Pagnerre, 1846 [1845].

——. *Notice biographique des illustrations de Montargis.* Montargis: Fortin, 1844.

Courmaceul, Victor de. *Etude statistique sur l'arrondissement de Valenciennes et considérations sur son état ancien et moderne et sur ses progrès au XIXe siècle.* Dunkirk: B. Kien, 1860.

Cousin, Victor. *Lectures on the True, the Beautiful, and the Good.* Translated by O. W. Wight. New York: D. Appleton, 1890.

——. *Fragments philosophiques.* 3rd ed. Paris: Ladrange, 1838 [1826].

Coussemaker, Edmond de. *Chants populaires des flamands de France.* Ghent: F. and E. Gyselynck, 1856.

Debaecker, Louis. *Recherches historiques sur la ville de Bergues en Flandre.* Bruges: Vandecasteele-Werbrouck, 1849.

Delcroix, Fidèle. *Une promenade dans le Cambrésis.* Valenciennes: A. Prignet, 1838.

Deligne, Jules. *Eloge de Jeanne de Constantinople, comtesse de Flandre et Hainaut.* Lille: Vanackere, 1844.

Dénoix des Vergnes, Fanny. *Çà et là: études historiques.* Paris: Collignon, 1865.

——. *Beauvais.* Paris: Le Doyen, 1858.

Département du Nord. Inauguration du nouvel hôtel des archives. Lille: Vanackere, 1845.

Derode, Victor. *Le livre de la cité.* Lille: Lefebvre-Ducrocq, 1862.

——. *Histoire religieuse de la Flandre maritime, et en particulier de la ville de Dunkerque.* Paris: Didron, 1856.

Diderot, Denis, and Jean Le Rond d'Alembert, eds. *L'Encyclopédie, ou dictionnaire raisonné des sciences, des arts et des métiers.* 35 vols. Repr. Stuttgart-Bad Cannstatt: Frommann, 1966 [1751–80].

Dinaux, Arthur. *Louis-Philippe à Valenciennes ou les trois séjours, par un garde national à cheval.* Valenciennes: A. Prignet, 1833.

Donnet, Ferdinand. *Instructions, mandements, lettres et discours de Mgr l'archevêque de*

Bordeaux, sur les principaux objets de la sollicitude pastorale de 1837 à 1850. Bordeaux: Henry Faye, 1850.

Dubois, Auguste. *Essai sur l'histoire municipale de la ville de Valenciennes.* Valenciennes: A. Prignet, 1840.

Dubois-Druelle, M. *Douai pittoresque, ou description des monumens et objets d'antiquité que renferment cette ville et son arrondissement . . .* Douai: Adam d'Aubers, 1845.

Du Chatellier, Armand-René. *Du mouvement des études littéraires et scientifiques en province (histoire des congrès).* Paris: Dumoulin, 1865.

Duclerc, Eugène, and Laurent-Antoine Pagnerre. *Dictionnaire politique: encyclopédie du langage et de la science politiques.* Paris: Pagnerre, 1842.

Ducourneau, Alexandre and Amans-Alexis Monteil. *La France ou histoire nationale des départements par une Société d'hommes de lettres et d'élèves de l'Ecole des Chartes.* Paris: Maulde et Renou, 1844.

Dufey (de l'Yonne), P.-J.-S. *Histoire des communes de France et législation municipale, depuis la fin du XIe siècle jusqu'à nos jours.* Paris: Goeury, 1828.

Du Mesnil, Armand. *Souvenirs de lectures. Histoire et morale.* Paris: Hachette, 1894.

Durant, Etienne. *Les tablettes d'un bourgeois de Lille.* Lille: Leleux, 1874.

Durieux, Achille. *Un village de l'ancien Cambrésis, fonts baptismaux et pierre tumulaire.* Cambrai: Simon, 1869.

Duthilloeul, Hippolyte. *Douai ancien et nouveau, ou historique des rues, des places de cette ville et de ses alentours.* Douai: Foucart, 1860.

———. *Petites histoires des pays de Flandre et d'Artois.* 2 vols. Douai: Foucart, 1835 and 1858.

Encyclopédie des gens du monde, répertoire universel des sciences, des lettres et des arts. 22 vols. Paris: Treuttel et Würtz, 1833–1844.

Fons, baron de Mélicocq. *Privilèges et franchises de quelques-unes des villes de la Flandre, de l'Artois, de la Picardie et du Valois.* Paris: Noyon, 1832.

Fortoul, Hippolyte. *Etudes d'archéologie et d'histoire.* 2 vols. Paris: Firmin Didot, 1854.

Foucart, Jean-Baptiste. *Souvenirs de la terre natale.* Valenciennes: A. Prignet, 1837.

Franck, Adolphe, ed. *Dictionnaire des sciences philosophiques.* 2nd ed. Paris: Hachette, 1875 [1844–45].

Gatien-Arnoult, Adolphe-Felix, ed. *Monumens de la littérature romane, publiés sous les auspices de l'Académie des Jeux Floraux.* 3 vols. Toulouse: J-B Paya, 1841–49.

Génin, François. *Récréations philologiques, ou recueil de notes pour servir à l'histoire des mots de la langue française.* 2 vols. 2nd ed. Paris: Chamerot, 1858 [1856].

———. *Des variations du langage français depuis le XIIe siècle, ou recherche des principes qui devraient régler l'orthographe et la prononciation.* Paris: Firmin Didot, 1845.

Gérando, Gustave de. *Des récréations populaires considérées comme un des moyens les plus efficaces de détourner les ouvriers des cabarets.* Paris: Adrien Le Clere, 1857.

Gérando, Joseph-Marie de. *De la bienfaisance publique.* 4 vols. Paris: J. Renouard, 1839.

Giraud, Pierre. *Instructions et mandements de Mgr l'évêque de Rodez, transféré à l'Archevêché de Cambrai, sur les principaux objets de la sollicitude pastorale.* 2 vols. Lille: L. Lefort, 1842.

Girault de Saint Fargeau, Eusèbe. *Dictionnaire géographique, historique, industriel et commercial de toutes les communes de la France et de plus de 20,000 hameaux en dépendant.* 3 vols. Paris: Firmin Didot, 1844–46.

Girod, Edouard. *Esquisse historique, légendaire et descriptive de la ville de Pontarlier.* Pontarlier: J.-C. Thomas, 1857.

Godde de Liancourt. *De la confédération des corps savants.* Paris: L. Vassal, 1841.

Groult, Edmond. *La France des musées cantonaux en 1891.* Lisieux: Maurice Lefebvre, n.d. [1893?].

——. *Les oeuvres patriotiques cantonales.* Caen: Le Blanc-Hardel, 1883.

——. *Fêtes nationales et patriotiques: projet présenté à M. le Ministre de l'Instruction publique, le 23 juin 1879.* Caen: F. Le Blanc-Hardel, n.d. [1879?].

——. *Lettre à messieurs les délégués des sociétés savantes à la Sorbonne.* Paris: Claude Motteroz, 1877.

Guilbert, Aristide, ed. *Histoire des villes de France, avec une introduction générale pour chaque province.* 6 vols. Paris: Furne, 1844–48.

Guizot, François. *Histoire parlementaire de France: recueil complet des discours prononcés dans les chambres de 1819 à 1848 par M. Guizot.* 5 vols. Paris: Michel Lévy frères, 1863–64.

——. *Mémoires pour servir à l'histoire de mon temps.* 8 vols. Paris: Michel Lévy frères, 1858–67.

——. *Discours prononcé par M. Guizot, directeur de la Société des Antiquaires de Normandie, ancien ministre de l'Instruction publique, dans la séance du 27 août 1838.* Caen: A. Hardel, 1840.

——. *Histoire de la civilisation en Europe.* Edited by Pierre Rosanvallon. Paris: Hachette, 1985 [1828].

——. "Encyclopédie" and "abrégé." *Encyclopédie progressive, ou collection de traités sur l'histoire, l'état actuel et les progrès des connaissances humaines.* Paris: Bureau de l'Encyclopédie progressive, 1826.

Kuntz de Rouvaire. *La profession littéraire au XIXe siècle.* Paris: Société française fondée pour l'émancipation des provinces, 1862.

Landsvriend, H. *Bouchard d'Avesnes.* Paris: Magen and Comon, 1841.

Laplane, E. de. *Essai sur l'histoire municipale de la ville de Sisteron.* Paris: Paulin, 1840.

Lebeau, Isidore. *Recueil de notices et articles divers sur l'histoire de la contrée formant l'arrondissement d'Avesnes, . . .* Avesnes: Michaux ainé, 1859.

——. *Précis de l'histoire d'Avesnes.* Avesnes: C. Viroux, 1836.

Lecocq, H. and J.-B. Bouillet. *Plan d'association entre les principales académies départementales.* Clermont-Ferrand: Perol, 1838.

Lefebvre, Charles-Aimé. *Spécimen d'un abrégé de l'histoire de Cambrai et du Cambrésis destiné à servir de livre de lecture dans les établissements d'instruction.* Cambrai: L. Carion, 1864.

Lefils, Florentin. *Géographie historique et populaire des communes de l'arrondissement d'Abbeville.* Abbeville: J. Gamain, 1868.

Le Glay, André. *Mémoire sur les bibliothèques publiques et les principales bibliothèques particulières du département du Nord.* Lille: L. Danel, 1841.

——. *Analectes historiques, ou documents inédits pour l'histoire des faits, des moeurs et de la littérature.* Paris: Téchener, 1838.

——. *Nouveau programme d'études historiques et archéologiques sur le département du Nord.* Lille: Vanackere fils et Téchener, 1836.

——. *Chronique d'Arras et de Cambrai, par Baldéric, chantre de Térouane au XIe siècle.* Cambrai: Lesne-Daloin, 1834.

———. *Mélanges historiques et littéraires.* Cambrai: Lesne-Daloin, 1834.

Le Glay, Edward. *Histoire de Jeanne de Constantinople, comtesse de Flandre et de Hainaut.* Lille: Vanackere, 1841.

Legrand, Louis. *L'idée de patrie.* Paris: Hachette, 1897.

———. *De la division du département du Nord et de la création d'un département de l'Escaut (Avesnes, Cambrai, Valenciennes).* Valenciennes: Georges Giard, 1870.

Legrand, Pierre. *Dictionnaire du patois de Lille.* 2nd ed. Lille: Vanackere, 1856 [1853].

———. *Le bourgeois de Lille.* Lille: Beghin, 1851.

Lemonnier, Henry. *L'enseignement de l'histoire dans les écoles primaires.* Paris: Imprimerie nationale, 1889.

Leroux, Pierre, and Jean Reynaud, eds. *Encyclopédie nouvelle, ou dictionnaire philosophique, scientifique, littéraire et industriel offrant le tableau des connaissances humaines au dix-neuvième siècle.* 6 vols. Paris: Charles Gosselin, 1836–42.

Loriol V.-A., ed. *La France. Description géographique, statistique et topographique universelle, etc.* 7 vols. Paris: Verdière, 1834–36.

Marchangy, Louis de. *Tristan le voyageur, ou la France au XIVe siècle.* 6 vols. Paris: F. M. Maurice, 1825.

Marissal, L.-E. *Recherches pour servir à l'histoire de la ville de Roubaix, de 1400 à nos jours.* Roubaix: Beghin, 1844.

Marmontel, Jean-François. *Les Incas, ou la destruction du Pérou.* In Marmontel, *Oeuvres complètes.* 19 vols. Paris: Verdière, 1819–20. Vol. 8.

Maurice, Etienne. *Décentralisation et décentralisateurs.* Paris: Librairie nouvelle, 1859.

Michelet, Jules. *Le peuple.* Edited by Paul Viallaneix. Paris: GF-Flammarion, 1974 [1846].

———. *Le tableau de la France.* Brussels: Complexe, 1995 [1833].

Modeste, Victor. *Du paupérisme en France: Etat actuel—Causes—Remèdes possibles.* Paris: Guillaumin et Cie, 1858.

Morand, François. *Lettres à Augustin Thierry et autres documents relatifs à un projet de Constitution des Archives communales, proposée en 1838 et années suivantes.* Paris: J-B. Dumoulin, 1877.

Nietzsche, Friedrich. *On the Advantage and Disadvantage of History for Life.* Translated by Peter Preuss. Indianapolis: Hackett, 1980 [1874].

Nisard, Désiré. *Nouvelles études d'histoire et de littérature.* Paris: Michel Lévy frères, 1864.

———. *Etudes de critique littéraire.* Paris: Michel Lévy frères, 1858.

———. *Histoire de la littérature française.* 4 vols. Paris: Firmin Didot frères, 1844–1861.

———. *Précis de l'histoire de la littérature française depuis ses premiers monumens jusqu'à nos jours.* Paris: Mme veuve Maire-Nyon, 1841.

Nodier, Charles. *Dissertations philologiques et bibliographiques.* Paris: Techener, 1834–35.

Oeuvres dunkerquoises. 4 vols. Dunkirk: C. Drouillard, 1853 and B. Kien, 1857–59.

Pétiaux, Casimir. *Monument à Jehan Froissart, chroniqueur et historien au XIVe siècle.* Valenciennes: B. Henry, 1858.

Piérart, Z. *Recherches historiques sur Maubeuge, son canton et les communes limitrophes, avec des notes . . .* Maubeuge: E. Levecque, 1851.

Pierquin de Gembloux, Claude-Charles. *Histoire littéraire, philologique et bibliographique des patois, et de l'utilité de leur étude.* Paris: A. Aubry, 1841, repr. 1858.

———. *Notices historiques, archéologiques et philologiques sur Bourges et le département du Cher.* Bourges: Just Bernard, 1840.

Piers, H. *Histoire de la ville de Bergues-Saint-Winoc. Notices historiques sur Hondschoote, Wormhoudt, Gravelines, Mardick, Bourbourg, Watten, etc.* Saint-Omer: Vanelslandt, 1833.

Quiquet, P.-F. *Géographie politique, statistique, industrielle et commerciale du département du Nord.* Dunkirk: chez l'auteur, 1853.

Ragon, François, and Fabre d'Olivet. *Précis de l'histoire de Flandre, d'Artois et de Picardie.* Paris: Hachette, 1834.

Raudot, Claude-Marie. *La décentralisation.* 2 vols. Paris: C. Douniol, 1858–61.

Reclus, J. *Dictionnaire géographique et historique de la Gironde rédigé sous les auspices de la Commission des monuments historiques du département.* Bordeaux: Eugène Bisei, 1865.

Reybaud, Louis. *Jérôme Paturot à la recherche d'une position sociale.* Paris: J.-J. Dubochet, Le Chevalier et Cie, 1846 [1843].

Richard de Radonvilliers, Jean-Baptiste. *Enrichissement de la langue française: dictionnaire de mots nouveaux.* 2nd ed. Paris: Léautey, 1845.

Richelet, Charles. *Le budget et la centralisation.* Paris: Garnier frères, 1850.

Rozoir, Charles du. *Relation historique, pittoresque et statistique du voyage de S. M. Charles X dans le département du Nord.* Paris: A. Belin, 1827.

Salvandy, Narcisse de. *Vingt mois, ou la Révolution et le parti révolutionnaire.* New ed. Paris: Victor Masson, 1849 [1832].

Schnakenburg, J. F. *Tableau synoptique et comparatif des idiomes populaires ou patois de la France.* Berlin: A. Foerstner, 1840.

Souvenirs à l'usage des habitants de Douai, ou notes pour faire suite à l'ouvrage de M. Plouvain sur l'histoire de cette ville, depuis le 1er janvier 1822 jusqu'au 30 novembre 1842. Douai: D. Ceret-Carpentier, 1843.

Statistique archéologique du département du Nord. 2 vols. Lille and Paris: Quarré and Durand, 1867.

Tailliar, Eugène. *Notice sur l'origine et la formation des villages du Nord de la France.* Douai: V. Wartelle, 1862.

———. *De l'affranchissement des communes dans le Nord de la France, et des avantages qui en sont résultés.* Cambrai: Lesne-Daloin, 1837.

Thévenot, Arsène. *De la décentralisation intellectuelle et des progrès des arts, des sciences et des lettres en province.* Paris: Dentu, 1864.

Thierry, Augustin. *Recueil des monuments inédits de l'histoire du Tiers Etat.* Paris: Firmin Didot, 1850.

———. *Considérations sur l'histoire de France.* 3rd ed. In *Oeuvres complètes de Augustin Thierry.* 10 vols. Paris: Furne et Cie, 1846–53. Vol. 7.

———. *Oeuvres d'Aug. Thierry.* Brussels: J. Jamar, 1839.

Travers, Julien. *Des travaux collectifs que pourraient entreprendre les sociétés savantes des départements.* Caen: A. Hardel, 1864.

Van Hende, Edouard. *Histoire de Lille de 620 à 1804, avec annotations et tables.* Lille: L. Danel, 1874.

Vermesse, Louis. *Vocabulaire du patois lillois.* Lille: A. Béhague, n.d. [1861?].

Vitet, Ludovic. *Histoire des anciennes villes de France: recherches sur leurs origines, sur leurs monumens, sur le rôle qu'elles ont joué dans les annales de nos provinces. 1e série. Haute-Normandie. Dieppe.* Paris: Alexandre Mesionier, 1833.

Vivien, Auguste. *Etudes administratives.* 2 vols. Paris: Guillaumin et Cie, 1852.

Wickham, Georges. *Les musées cantonaux.* Paris: Librairie de l'Echo de la Sorbonne, 1879.

Wilbert, Alcibiade. *Formation et administration des villages.* Arras: A. Brissy, 1854.

——. *Des anciennes coutumes du Nord de la France et de leur influence sur la première organisation communale de ces contrées.* Lille: L. Danel, 1846.

SECONDARY SOURCES

Books and Articles

Actes du colloque François Guizot (Paris, 22–25 octobre 1974). Paris: Société de l'Histoire du Protestantisme Français, 1976.

Agulhon, Maurice. *Histoire vagabonde.* 3 vols. Paris: Gallimard, 1988.

——. *Le cercle dans la France bourgeoise 1810–1848. Etude d'une mutation de sociabilité.* Paris: Armand Colin, 1977.

Amalvi, Christian. *Le goût du Moyen âge.* Paris: Plon, 1996.

Antoine, Marie-Elisabeth. "Un service pionnier au XIXe siècle: le Bureau des travaux historiques." *Bulletin de la section d'histoire moderne et contemporaine du CTH* 10 (1977): 11–37.

Appadurai, Arjun. *Modernity at Large: Cultural Dimensions of Globalization.* Minneapolis: University of Minnesota Press, 1996.

Applegate, Celia. "A Europe of Regions: Reflections on the Historiography of Sub-National Places in Modern Times." *American Historical Review* 104, no. 4 (October 1999): 1157–82.

——. *A Nation of Provincials: The German Idea of Heimat.* Berkeley: University of California Press, 1990.

Augé, Marc. *Non-Places: Introduction to an Anthropology of Supermodernity.* Translated by John Howe. London: Verso, 1995.

Babadzan, Alain. "Tradition et histoire: quelques problèmes de méthode." *Cahiers ORSTROM,* série sciences humaines 21, no. 1 (1985): 115–23.

Baker, Keith Michael. *Inventing the French Revolution: Essays on French Political Culture in the Eighteenth Century.* Cambridge: Cambridge University Press, 1990.

Bakhtin, Mikhaïl [Medvedev, P. N.]. *The Formal Method in Literary Scholarship: A Critical Introduction to Sociological Poetics.* Translated by Albert J. Wehrle. Baltimore: The Johns Hopkins University Press, 1978 [1928].

Barret-Kriegel, Blandine. *L'histoire à l'âge classique.* 4 vols. Paris: PUF, 1988.

Bautier, Robert-Henri. "Le Comité des travaux historiques et scientifiques: passé et présent." *Actes du 115e congrès national des sociétés savantes,* 2: 381–96. Paris: Editions du CTHS, 1991.

——. "Le Recueil des Monuments de l'histoire du Tiers-Etat et l'utilisation des matériaux réunis par Augustin Thierry." *Annuaire-Bulletin de la Société de l'histoire de France* (1944): 89–118.

Baycroft, Timothy. "Changing Identities in the Franco-Belgian Borderland in the Nineteenth and Twentieth Centuries." *French History* 13, no. 4 (December 1999): 417–38.

Belissa, Marc. *Fraternité universelle et intérêt national (1713–1795): les cosmopolitiques du droit des gens.* Paris: Kimé, 1998.

Bell, David A. *The Cult of the Nation in France: Inventing Nationalism, 1680–1800.* Cambridge, Mass.: Harvard University Press, 2001.

Ben-Amos, Avner. *Funerals, Politics, and Memory in Modern France, 1789–1996.* Oxford: Oxford University Press, 2000.

Benjamin, Walter. *Ecrits français.* Edited by Jean-Maurice Monnoyer. Paris: Gallimard, 1991.

———. *Reflections.* Edited by Peter Demetz. Translated by Edmund Jephcott. New York: Shocken, 1978.

Bennett, Tony. *The Birth of the Museum: History, Theory, Politics.* London: Routledge, 1995.

Bensa, Alban, and Daniel Fabre, eds. *Une histoire à soi: figurations du passé et localités.* Paris: Editions de la MSH, 2001.

Bercé, Françoise. *Les premiers travaux de la commission des monuments historiques, 1837–1848.* Paris: A. et J. Picard, 1979.

Bernard, Claudie. *Le passé recomposé: le roman historique français du dix-neuvième siècle.* Paris: Hachette, 1996.

Bernard-Griffiths, Simone, et al. *Révolution française et "vandalisme révolutionnaire."* Paris: Universitas, 1992.

Bertho-Lavenir, Catherine. *La roue et le stylo: comment nous sommes devenus touristes.* Paris: Odile Jacob, 1999.

———. "L'invention du monument historique." *Quarante-huit/Quatorze* 4 (1992): 15–28.

———. "L'invention de la Bretagne: genèse sociale d'un stéréotype." *Actes de la recherche en sciences sociales* 35 (1980): 45–62.

Bidart, Pierre, ed. *Régions, nations, états: composition et recomposition de l'espace national.* Paris: Publisud, 1991.

Birnbaum, Pierre. *La France imaginée: déclin des rêves unitaires?* Paris: Fayard, 1998.

Blanckaert, Claude, ed. *Le terrain des sciences humaines: instructions et enquêtes (XVIIIe–XXe siècles).* Paris: L'Harmattan, 1996.

Blowen, Sarah, Marion Demossier, and Jeanine Picard, eds. *Recollections of France: Memories, Identities and Heritage in Contemporary France.* New York: Berghahn Books, 2000.

Boiral, Pierre, and Jean-Pierre Brouat. "L'émergence de l'idéologie localiste." *Sociologie du Sud-Est* 41–44 (July 1984–June 1985): 35–50.

Bodnar, John. *Remaking America: Public Memory, Commemoration, and Patriotism in the Twentieth Century.* Princeton, N.J.: Princeton University Press, 1992.

Bosquet, Pierre, et al. *Histoire de l'administration de l'enseignement en France, 1789–1981.* Geneva: Droz, 1981.

Bourdieu, Pierre. *The Field of Cultural Production: Essays on Art and Literature.*

Edited and translated by Randal Johnson. New York: Columbia University Press, 1993.

——. "L'identité et la représentation: éléments pour une réflexion critique sur l'idée de région." *Actes de la recherche en sciences sociales* 35 (1980): 63–72.

Bourdin, Alain. *La question locale.* Paris: PUF, 2000.

Bourguet, Marie-Noëlle. *Déchiffrer la France: la statistique départementale à l'époque napoléonienne.* Paris: Editions des Archives contemporaines, 1988.

—— et al., eds. *L'invention scientifique de la Méditerranée: Egypte, Morée, Algérie.* Paris: Editions de l'EHESS, 1998.

Brelot, Claude-Isabelle. *La noblesse réinventée: nobles de Franche-Comté de 1814 à 1870.* 2 vols. Paris: Les Belles Lettres, 1992.

—— et al. "La Franche-Comté à la recherche de son histoire (1800–1914)." Special issue of *Cahiers d'études comtoises* 31. Paris: Les Belles Lettres, 1982.

Burdeau, François. *Liberté, libertés locales chéries.* Paris: Cujas, 1983.

Burguière, André, and Jacques Revel, eds. *Histoire de la France.* 4 vols. Paris: Seuil, 1989.

Cabanes, Robert. "Les associations créatrices de la localité." In Odile Benoît-Guilbot et al., *L'esprit des lieux: localités et changement social en France,* 209–31. Paris: CNRS, 1986.

Cabantous, Alain, ed. *Histoire de Dunkerque.* Toulouse: Privat, 1983.

Candau, Joël. *Mémoire et identité.* Paris: PUF, 1998.

Carbonell, Charles-Olivier. *Histoire et historiens: une mutation idéologique des historiens français: 1865–1885.* Toulouse, Privat, 1976.

Carrière, Victor. *Introduction aux études d'histoire ecclésiastique locale.* 3 vols. Paris: Letouzey et Ané, 1934–40.

Carter, Erica, James Donald, and Judith Squires, eds. *Space and Place: Theories of Identity and Location.* London: Lawrence and Wishart, 1993.

Certeau, Michel de. *La culture au pluriel.* Edited by Luce Giard. New ed. Paris: Christian Bourgeois, 1993.

——. *The Practice of Everyday Life.* Translated by Steven Randall. Berkeley: University of California Press, 1984.

Chaline, Jean-Pierre. *Sociabilité et érudition: les sociétés savantes en France: XIXe-XXe siècles.* Paris: Editions du CTHS, 1995.

Chanet, Jean-François. "Terroirs et pays: mort et transfiguration." *Vingtième siècle* 69 (January-March 2001): 61–77.

——. *L'école républicaine et les petites patries.* Paris: Aubier, 1996.

Charle, Christophe. "Région et conscience régionale en France: questions à propos d'un colloque." *Actes de la recherche en sciences sociales* 35 (1980): 37–43.

Chartier, Roger. "Les deux France: histoire d'une géographie." *Cahiers d'histoire* 23 (1978): 393–415.

Cohen, William. "Symbols of Power: Statues in Nineteenth-Century Provincial France." *Comparative Studies in Society and History* 31, no. 3 (July 1989): 491–513.

Cohn, Bernard S. *Colonialism and its Forms of Knowledge: The British in India.* Princeton, N.J.: Princeton University Press, 1996.

Collingham, H. A. C. *The July Monarchy: A Political History of France 1830–1848.* London: Longman, 1988.

Colloque interdisciplinaire sur les sociétés savantes. Actes du 100e congrès national des sociétés savantes. Paris: Bibliothèque nationale, 1976.

Comaroff, Jean, and John L. Comaroff. *Of Revelation and Revolution.* 2 vols. Chicago: University of Chicago Press, 1991–97.

Confino, Alon. *The Nation as Local Metaphor: Württemberg, Imperial Germany, and National Memory, 1871–1918.* Chapel Hill, N.C.: University of North Carolina Press, 1997.

Coornaert, Emile. *La Flandre francaise de langue flamande.* Paris: Les éditions ouvrières, 1970.

Corbin, Alain. *Le monde retrouvé de Louis-François Pinagot: sur les traces d'un inconnu 1798–1876.* Paris: Flammarion, 1998.

———. *Les cloches de la terre: paysage sonore et culture sensible dans les campagnes au XIXe siècle.* Paris: Albin Michel, 1994.

———, Noëlle Gérôme, and Danielle Tartakowsky, eds. *Les usages politiques des fêtes aux XIXe-XXe siècles.* Paris: Publications de la Sorbonne, 1994.

Cottereau, Alain. "Esprit public et capacité de juger: la stabilisation d'un espace public en France aux lendemains de la Révolution." *Raisons pratiques* 3 (1992): 239–73.

De l'Estoile, Benoît. "Le goût du passé. Erudition locale et appropriation du territoire." *Terrain* 37 (September 2001): 123–38.

Den Boer, Pim. *History as a Profession: The Study of History in France, 1818–1914.* Translated by Arnold J. Pomerans. Princeton, N.J.: Princeton University Press, 1998.

Deyon, Pierre. *Paris et ses provinces: le défi de la décentralisation, 1770–1992.* Paris: Armand Colin, 1992.

Dhombres, Jean, and Nicole Dhombres. *Naissance d'un nouveau pouvoir: sciences et savants en France 1793–1824.* Paris: Payot, 1989.

Dion, Marie-Pierre. "La Société des Incas: du carnaval à la philanthrophie." *Valentiana* 7 (June 1991): 53–60.

Dolan, Claire. "L'identité urbaine et les histoires locales publiées du XVIe au XVIIIe siècle en France." *Canadian Journal of History/Annales canadiennes d'histoire* 27 (August 1992): 277–93.

Dondin-Payre, Monique. *La commission d'exploration scientifique de l'Algérie. Une héritière méconnue de la commission d'Egypte.* Abbeville: F. Paillart, 1994.

Dubois, Vincent, with Philippe Poirrier, eds. *Politiques locales et enjeux culturels: les clochers d'une querelle, XIXe-XXe siècles.* Paris: La documentation française, 1998.

Dumont, Louis. *Essays on Individualism: Modern Ideology in Anthropological Perspective.* Chicago: University of Chicago Press, 1986.

Dutacq, François. *Gustave Rouland, ministre de l'instruction publique, 1856–1863.* Tulle: Mazeyrie, 1910.

Fabre, Daniel, ed. *Domestiquer l'histoire: ethnologie des monuments historiques.* Paris: Editions de la MSH, 2000.

———, ed. *L'Europe entre cultures et nations.* Paris: Editions de la MSH, 1996.

Ferguson, Priscilla Parkhurst. *Paris as Revolution: Writing the Nineteenth-Century City.* Berkeley: University of California Press, 1997.

Ford, Caroline. *Creating the Nation in Provincial France: Religion and Political Identity in Brittany.* Princeton, N.J.: Princeton University Press, 1993.

——. "Which Nation? Language, Identity and Republican Politics in Post-Revolutionary France." *History of European Ideas* 17, no. 1 (1993): 31–46.

Foucault, Michel. *Discipline and Punish: The Birth of the Prison.* 2nd American ed. Translated by Alan Sheridan. New York: Random House, 1995.

——. "Prison Talk." In *Power/Knowledge: Selected Interviews and Other Writings, 1972–1977.* Edited by Colin Gordon, 37–54. New York: Pantheon, 1980.

Fougère, Louis, Jean-Pierre Machelon, and François Monnier, eds. *Les communes et le pouvoir de 1789 à nos jours.* Paris: PUF, 2002.

Fox, Robert. "Science, the University, and the State in Nineteenth-Century France." In *Professions and the French State, 1700–1900.* Edited by Gerald L. Geison, 66–145. Philadelphia: University of Pennsylvania Press, 1984.

——. "The Savant Confronts His Peers: Scientific Societies in France, 1815–1914." In *The Organization of Science and Technology in France 1808–1914.* Edited by Fox and George Weisz, 241–82. Cambridge and Paris: Cambridge University Press and Editions de la MSH, 1980.

——. "Learning, Politics, and Polite Culture in Provincial France: The Sociétés Savantes in the Nineteenth Century." *Historical Reflections/Réflexions historiques* 7 (summer-fall 1980): 543–64.

François, Etienne, ed. *Sociabilité et société bourgeoise en France, en Allemagne et en Suisse, 1750–1850.* Paris: Recherche sur les Civilisations, 1987.

Furet, François, ed. *Patrimoine, temps, espace: patrimoine en place, patrimoine déplacé.* Paris: Fayard and Editions du Patrimoine, 1997.

——, ed. *Jules Ferry, fondateur de la république.* Paris: Editions de l'EHESS, 1985.

Gaehtgens, Thomas W. *Versailles: de la résidence royale au musée historique: la galerie des batailles dans le musée historique de Louis-Philippe.* Paris: Albin Michel, 1984.

Garcia, Patrick. *Le bicentenaire de la Révolution française: pratiques sociales d'une commémoration.* Paris: CNRS, 2000.

George, Jocelyne. *Paris Province: de la Révolution à la mondialisation.* Paris: Fayard, 1998.

Georgel, Chantal. "L'Etat et 'ses' musées de province ou comment 'concilier la liberté d'initiative des villes et les devoirs de l'Etat.'" *Le mouvement social* 60 (September-July 1992): 65–77.

——, ed. *La jeunesse des musées: les musées de France au XIXe siècle.* Paris: Editions de la réunion des musées nationaux, 1994.

Gérard, Alice. "Le grand homme et la conception de l'histoire au XIXe siècle." *Romantisme* 100 (1998): 31–48.

Gerson, Stéphane. "La représentation historique du pays, entre l'état et la société civile." *Romantisme* 110 (4th quarter 2000): 39–49.

——. "Town, Nation, or Humanity? Festive Delineations of Place and Past in Northern France, 1825–1865." *The Journal of Modern History* 72, no. 3 (September 2000): 628–82.

——. "Parisian Littérateurs, Provincial Journeys and the Construction of National Unity in Post-Revolutionary France." *Past and Present* 151 (May 1996): 141–73.

Gildea, Robert. *The Past in French History.* New Haven: Yale University Press, 1994.

——. *Education in Provincial France, 1800–1914: A Study of Three Departments.* Oxford: Clarendon Press, 1983.

Gillis, John R., ed. *Commemorations: The Politics of National Identity.* Princeton, N.J.: Princeton University Press, 1994.

Goblot, Jean-Jacques. *La Jeune France libérale: "Le Globe" et son groupe littéraire, 1824–1830.* Paris: Plon, 1995.

Goldstein, Jan. "Mutations of the Self in Old Regime and Post-Revolutionary France: From Ame to *Moi* to *le Moi.*" In *Biographies of Scientific Objects: A Historical Ontology.* Edited by Lorraine Daston, 86–116. Chicago: University of Chicago Press, 2000.

Gossman, Lionel. *Between History and Literature.* Cambridge, Mass.: Harvard University Press, 1990.

Gras, Christian, and Georges Livet, eds. *Régions et régionalisme en France: du XVIIIe siècle à nos jours.* Paris: PUF, 1977.

Griswold, Wendy, and Fredrik Engelstad. "Does the Center Imagine the Periphery? State Support and Literary Regionalism in Norway and the United States." *Comparative Social Research* 17 (1998): 129–75.

Guha, Ranajit. *Dominance without Hegemony: History and Power in Colonial India.* Cambridge, Mass.: Harvard University Press, 1997.

Guignet, Philippe. *Le pouvoir dans la ville au XVIIIe siècle: pratiques politiques, notabilité et éthique sociale de part et d'autre de la frontière franco-belge.* Paris: Editions de l'EHESS, 1990.

Guillemin, Alain. "Aristocrates, propriétaires et diplômés: la lutte pour le pouvoir local dans le département de la Manche, 1830–1875." *Actes de la recherche en sciences sociales* 42 (April 1982): 33–60.

Guillet, François. *Naissance de la Normandie: genèse et épanouissement d'une image régionale en France, 1750–1850.* Caen: Annales de Normandie, 2000.

Guiomar, Jean-Yves. *La nation entre l'histoire et la raison.* Paris: La Découverte, 1990.

——. *Le Bretonisme: les historiens bretons au XIXe siècle.* Mayenne: Société d'histoire et d'archéologie de Bretagne, 1987.

Gupta, Akhil, and James Ferguson. "Beyond 'Culture': Space, Identity, and the Politics of Difference." *Cultural Anthropology* 7, no. 1 (February 1992): 6–23.

Habermas, Jürgen. *The Structural Transformation of the Public Sphere.* Translated by Thomas Burger with Frederick Lawrence. Cambridge, Mass.: MIT Press, 1989 [1962].

Hanks, William F. "Discourse Genres in a Theory of Practice." *American Ethnologist* 14, no. 4 (1987): 668–92.

——. "Authenticity and Ambivalence in the Text: A Colonial Maya Case." *American Ethnologist* 13, no. 4 (1986): 721–44.

Harris, Ruth. *Lourdes: Body and Spirit in the Secular Age.* New York: Penguin, 1999.

Harrison, Carol E. *The Bourgeois Citizen in Nineteenth-Century France: Gender, Sociability, and the Uses of Emulation.* Oxford: Oxford University Press, 1999.

Haupt, Heinz-Gerhard, Michael G. Müller, and Stuart Woolf, eds. *Regional and National Identities in Europe in the XIXth and XXth Centuries.* The Hague: Kluwer Law International, 1998.

Hazareesingh, Sudhir. "The Société d'Instruction Républicaine and the Propagation of Civic Republicanism in Provincial and Rural France, 1870–1877." *The Journal of Modern History* 71, no. 2 (June 1999): 271–307.

———. *From Subject to Citizen: The Second Empire and the Emergence of Modern French Democracy.* Princeton, N.J.: Princeton University Press, 1998.

Hutton, Patrick H. *History as an Art of Memory.* Hanover, N.H.: University Press of New England, 1993.

Jaume, Lucien. *L'individu effacé, ou le paradoxe du libéralisme français.* Paris: Fayard, 1997.

Kale, Steven D. *Legitimism and the Reconstruction of French Society, 1852–1883.* Baton Rouge: Louisiana State University Press, 1992.

Keane, John. *Civil Society and the State: New European Perspectives.* London: Verso, 1988.

Keen, Benjamin. *The Aztec Image in Western Thought.* New Brunswick, N.J.: Rutgers University Press, 1971.

Keylor, William. *Academy and Community: The Foundation of the French Historical Profession.* Cambridge, Mass.: Harvard University Press, 1975.

Kirshenblatt-Gimblett, Barbara. *Destination Culture: Tourism, Museums, and Heritage.* Berkeley: University of California Press, 1998.

Knibiehler, Yvonne. *Naissance des sciences humaines: Mignet et l'histoire philosophique au XIXe siècle.* Paris: Flammarion, 1973.

Koshar, Rudy, ed. *Histories of Leisure.* Oxford: Berg, 2002.

Kroen, Sheryl. *Politics and Theater: The Crisis of Legitimacy in Restoration France.* Berkeley: University of California Press, 2000.

Laboulais-Lesage, Isabelle. *Lectures et pratiques de l'espace: l'itinéraire de Coquebert de Montbret, savant et grand commis d'Etat (1755–1831).* Paris: Champion, 1999.

Lacroix, Pierre. "Prêtres érudits du Jura aux XIXe et XXe siècles." *Revue d'histoire de l'église de France* 71 (1985): 47–63.

Lalouette, Jacqueline. "L'éducation populaire au canton. Edmond Groult et les musées cantonaux." *Jean Jaurès cahiers trimestriels* 152 (April-June 1999): 91–104.

Lebovics, Herman. *True France: The Wars over Cultural Identity, 1900–1945.* Ithaca, N.Y.: Cornell University Press, 1992.

Lefebvre, Henri. *The Production of Space.* Translated by Donald Nicholson-Smith. Oxford: Blackwell, 1991.

Lefrancq, Paul. "Les Incas de Marmontel et les Incas de Valenciennes: un roman éponyme d'une société philanthropique (1777–1826)." *102e congrès des sociétés savantes* 1: 117–34. Limoges, 1977. Section of modern history.

Le Goff, Jacques, ed. *Patrimoine et passions identitaires. Actes des Entretiens du Patrimoine.* Paris: Fayard and Editions du Patrimoine, 1998.

Leniaud, Jean-Michel. *L'utopie française: essai sur le patrimoine.* Paris: Mengès, 1992.

Les catholiques libéraux au XIXe siècle. Grenoble: Presses Universitaires de Grenoble, 1974.

Levine, Philippa. *The Amateur and the Professional: Antiquarians, Historians, and Archaeologists in Victorian England, 1838–1886.* Cambridge: Cambridge University Press, 1986.

Lomnitz-Adler, Claudio. *Exits from the Labyrinth: Culture and Ideology in the Mexican National Space.* Berkeley: University of California Press, 1992.

Looseley, David L. *The Politics of Fun: Cultural Policy and Debate in Contemporary France.* Oxford: Berg Publishers, 1995.

Lowenthal, David. *The Past Is a Foreign Country*. Cambridge: Cambridge University Press 1985.

Mabileau, Albert. *A la recherche du "local."* Paris: L'Harmattan, 1993.

Maguet, Frédéric, and Anne Tricaud, eds. *Parler provinces: des images, des costumes*. Paris: Réunion des musées nationaux, 1994.

Manent, Pierre. *Histoire intellectuelle du libéralisme: dix leçons*. Paris: Calmann-Lévy, 1987.

Martel, Philippe. "Les historiens du début du XIXe siècle et le Moyen Age occitan: Midi éclairé, Midi martyr ou Midi pittoresque." *Romantisme* 35 (1982): 49–71.

Martin, Jean-Clément. *La Vendée de la mémoire, 1800–1980*. Paris: Seuil, 1989.

—— and Charles Suaud. *Le Puy du Fou, en Vendée: l'histoire mise en scène*. Paris: L'Harmattan, 1996.

Martin-Fugier, Anne. "La formation des élites: les 'conférences' sous la Restauration et la monarchie de Juillet." *Revue d'histoire moderne et contemporaine* 36 (April-June 1989): 211–244.

Mathieu, D., et al. "La Franche-Comté à la recherche de son territoire. Eléments de géographie historique de l'espace comtois." Special issue of *Annales littéraires de l'Université de Besançon* 309 (1985).

Mattelart, Armand. *Histoire de l'utopie planétaire: de la cité prophétique à la société globale*. Paris: La Découverte, 1999.

Mesnard, André-Hubert. *L'action culturelle des pouvoirs publics*. Paris: Librairie Générale de Droit et de Jurisprudence, 1969.

Mélonio, Françoise, and Antoine de Baecque. *Lumières et liberté: les dix-huitième et dix-neuvième siècles*. Vol. 3. *Histoire culturelle de la France* . Edited by Jean-Pierre Rioux and Jean-François Sirinelli. 4 vols. Paris: Seuil, 1998.

Minard, Philippe. *La fortune du colbertisme: état et industrie dans la France des Lumières*. Paris: Fayard, 1998.

Nisbet, Robert A. *The Sociological Tradition*. 2nd ed. New Brunswick: Transaction, 1993.

Nora, Pierre, ed. *Les lieux de mémoire*. 7 vols. Paris: Gallimard, 1984–92.

Nord, Philip. *The Republican Moment: Struggles for Democracy in Nineteenth-Century France*. Cambridge, Mass.: Harvard University Press, 1995.

Nordman, Daniel. *Frontières de France: de l'espace au territoire, XVIe-XIXe siècle*. Paris: Gallimard, 1998.

——. *Profils du Maghreb: frontières, figures et territoires (XVIIIe-XXe siècle)*. Rabat: Publications de la Faculté des lettres de Rabat, 1996.

Oulebsir, Nabila. "La découverte des monuments de l'Algérie: les missions d'Amable Ravoisié et d'Edmond Duthoit (1840–1880)." *Revue du monde musulman et de la Méditerranée* 73/74 (1994): 57–74.

Ozouf, Mona. *L'école de la France*. Paris: Gallimard, 1984.

——. *La fête révolutionnaire, 1789–1799*. Paris: Gallimard, 1976.

Ozouf-Marignier, Marie-Vic. "Centralisation et lien social: le débat de la première moitié du XIXe siècle en France." In *Per un Atlante storico del Mezzogiorno e della Sicilia in età moderna*. Edited by Enrico Iachello and Biagio Salvemini, 75–91. Naples: Liguori Editore, 1998.

——. *La formation des départements: la représentation du territoire français à la fin du XVIIIe siècle*. Paris: Editions de l'EHESS, 1989.

Parsis-Barubé, Odile. *Les représentations du Moyen âge au XIXe siècle dans les anciens Pays-Bas français et leurs confins picards. Essai d'historiographie comparée.* 2 vols. Villeneuve d'Ascq: Presses Universitaires du Septentrion, 1999.

Petitier, Paule. *La géographie de Michelet: territoire et modèles naturels dans les premières oeuvres de Michelet.* Paris: L'Harmattan, 1997.

Picon, Antoine, and Jean-Paul Robert. *Un atlas parisien: le dessus des cartes.* Paris: Picard, 1999.

Pierrard, Pierre. *Les diocèses de Cambrai et de Lille.* Paris: Beauchene, 1978.

——. *La vie ouvrière à Lille sous le Second Empire.* Paris: Bloud & Gay, 1965.

Planhol, Xavier de, with Paul Claval. *Géographie historique de la France.* Paris: Fayard, 1988.

Platelle, Henri, ed. *Histoire de Valenciennes.* Lille: Presses Universitaires de Lille, 1982.

Poinsignon, Jean-Claude. "Famille éclatée recherche galerie d'ancêtres. Intérêt des collections artistiques de la Société d'agriculture, sciences et arts de Valenciennes." *Valentiana* 13 (June 1994): 65–74.

Poole, Deborah. *Vision, Race, and Modernity: A Visual Economy of the Andean Image World.* Princeton, N.J.: Princeton University Press, 1997.

Poulot, Dominique. *Musée nation patrimoine 1789–1815.* Paris: Gallimard, 1997.

——. "The Birth of Heritage: 'Le Moment Guizot.'" *Oxford Art Journal* 11, no. 2 (1988): 40–56.

Rabinow, Paul. *French Modern: Norms and Forms of the Social Environment.* Cambridge: MIT Press, 1989.

Raphael, Paul, and Maurice Gontard. *Hippolyte Fortoul, 1851–1856: un ministre de l'instruction publique sous l'Empire autoritaire.* Paris: PUF, 1975.

Rearick, Charles. "Festivals in Modern France: The Experience of the Third Republic." *Journal of Contemporary History* 12 (1977): 435–60.

Rémi-Giraud, Sylvianne, and Pierre Rétat, eds. *Les mots de la nation.* Lyons: Presses Universitaires de Lyon, 1996.

Riemenschneider, Rainer. "Décentralisation et régionalisme au milieu du XIXe siècle." *Romantisme* 35 (1982): 115–33.

Rioux, Jean-Pierre, and Jean-François Sirinelli, eds. *Histoire culturelle de la France.* 4 vols. Paris: Seuil, 1998.

Roche, Daniel. *Les républicains des lettres: gens de culture et Lumières au XVIIIe siècle.* Paris: Fayard, 1988.

——. *Le siècle des Lumières en province: académies et académiciens provinciaux, 1680–1789.* 2 vols. Paris: Editions de l'EHESS, 1978.

Roldán, Darío. *Charles de Rémusat: certitudes et impasses du libéralisme doctrinaire.* Paris: L'Harmattan, 1999.

Rosanvallon, Pierre. *L'Etat en France de 1789 à nos jours.* Paris: Seuil, 1990.

——. *Le moment Guizot.* Paris: Gallimard, 1985.

Rouche, Michel, ed. *Histoire de Douai.* Dunkerque: Westhoek, 1985.

Rouxel, Sylvie. *Quand la mémoire d'une ville se met en scène . . . Etude sur la fonction sociale des spectacles historiques: l'exemple de Meaux.* Paris: La documentation française, 1995.

Saunier, Pierre-Yves. *L'esprit lyonnais, XIXe–XXe siècle: genèse d'une représentation sociale.* Paris: CNRS, 1995.

Schnapp, Alain. *La conquête du passé. Aux origines de l'archéologie.* Paris: Editions Carré, 1993.

Schweitz, Daniel. *Histoire des identités de pays en Touraine, XVIe-XXe siècles.* Paris: L'Harmattan, 2001.

Scott, James C. *Seeing Like a State: How Certain Schemes to Improve the Human Condition Have Failed.* New Haven: Yale University Press, 1998.

Sfez, Lucien, ed. *L'objet local.* Paris: UGE, 1977.

Sherman, Daniel J. *Worthy Monuments: Art Museums and the Politics of Culture in Nineteenth-Century France.* Cambridge, Mass.: Harvard University Press, 1989.

Sire, Marie-Anne. *La France du patrimoine: les choix de la mémoire.* Paris: Gallimard, 1996.

Sirinelli, Jean-François, ed. *Histoire des droites en France.* 3 vols. Paris: Gallimard, 1992.

Smith, Bonnie. *The Gender of History: Men, Women, and Historical Practice.* Cambridge, Mass.: Harvard University Press, 1998.

——. *Ladies of the Leisure Class: The Bourgeoises of Northern France in the Nineteenth Century.* Princeton, N.J.: Princeton University Press, 1981.

Tacke, Charlotte. "The Nation in the Region. National Movements in Germany and France in the 19th Century." In *Nationalism in Europe: Past and Present.* Edited by Justo G. Beramendi, Ramón Máiz, and Xosé M. Núñez, 691–703. Santiago de Compostela: Universidade de Santiago de Compostela, 1994.

Terdiman, Richard. *Present Past: Modernity and the Memory Crisis.* Ithaca, N.Y.: Cornell University Press, 1993.

Thiesse, Anne-Marie. *La création des identités nationales. Europe, XVIIIe-XXe siècle.* Paris: Seuil, 1999.

——. *Ils apprenaient la France: l'exaltation des régions dans le discours patriotique.* Paris: Editions de la MSH, 1997.

——. *Ecrire la France: le mouvement littéraire régionaliste de langue française entre la Belle Epoque et la Libération.* Paris: PUF, 1991.

Tierny, Gonzague. *Les sociétés savantes du département de la Somme de 1870 à 1914.* Paris: Editions du CTHS, 1987.

Tocqueville, Alexis de. *The Old Regime and the French Revolution.* Translated by Stuart Gilbert. New York: Doubleday, 1955 [1856].

Tollebeek, Jo. "L'historiographie en tant qu'élément culturel dans la France du dix-neuvième siècle. Une étude historiographique exploratoire." *Storia della Storiografica* 26 (1994): 59–81.

Trénard, Louis, *Salvandy en son temps, 1795–1856.* Lille: Publications de la Faculté des lettres et sciences humaines de l'Université de Lille, 1968.

——. "Aux origines de la déchristianisation: le diocèse de Cambrai de 1830 à 1848." *Revue du Nord* 47 (1965): 399–459.

——, ed. *Histoire de Lille.* 3 vols. Toulouse: Privat, n.d.-1991.

——, ed. *Histoire de Cambrai.* Lille: Presses Universitaires de Lille, 1982.

——, ed. *Histoire des Pays-Bas Français: Flandre, Artois, Hainaut, Boulonnais, Cambrésis.* Toulouse: Privat, 1972.

Tudesq, André-Jean. *Les grands notables en France (1840–1849): étude historique d'une psychologie sociale.* 2 vols. Paris: PUF, 1964.

Turner, Victor. *The Ritual Process: Structure and Anti-Structure.* Chicago: Aldine, 1969.

Vermeren, Patrice. *Victor Cousin: le jeu de la philosophie et de l'état.* Paris: L'Harmattan, 1995.

Vigier, Philippe. "Diffusion d'une langue nationale et résistance des patois, en France, au XIXe siècle." *Romantisme* 25–26 (1979): 191–208.

Waquet, Françoise. *Les fêtes royales sous la Restauration ou l'Ancien Régime retrouvé.* Geneva: Droz, 1981.

Weber, Eugen. *Peasants into Frenchmen: The Modernization of Rural France, 1870–1914.* Stanford: Stanford University Press, 1976.

Weisz, George. *The Emergence of Modern Universities in France, 1863–1914.* Princeton, N.J.: Princeton University Press, 1983.

White, Hayden. "The Value of Narrativity in the Representation of Reality." In *On Narrative.* Edited by W. J. T. Mitchell, 1–23. Chicago: University of Chicago Press, 1981.

Yaeger, Patricia, ed. *The Geography of Identity.* Ann Arbor: University of Michigan Press, 1996.

Theses

Barksdale, Dudley C. "Liberal Politics and Nascent Social Science in France: The Academy of Moral and Political Sciences, 1803–1852." Ph.D. diss., University of North Carolina–Chapel Hill, 1986.

Bernard, Claude. "L'enseignement de l'histoire, en France, au XIXe siècle (selon les ministres de l'instruction publique)." Doctoral thesis, University of Paris VIII, 1976.

Bourquin, Jean-Christophe. "L'Etat et les voyageurs savants: légitimités individuelles et volontés politiques. Les missions du ministère de l'instruction publique (1840–1914)." Doctoral thesis, University of Paris I, 1993.

Chanet, Jean-François. "L'école républicaine et les petites patries: enseignement primaire et sentiment d'appartenance sous la Troisième République (1879–1940)." Doctoral thesis, University of Paris I, 1994.

Huchet, Bernard. "Arcisse de Caumont (1801–1873)." Thesis, Ecole Nationale des Chartes, 1984.

Lange, Pascal. "Le Comité flamand de 1853 à 1914." Masters thesis, University of Lille III, 1971.

Le Pottier, Jean. "Histoire et érudition: recherches et documents sur l'histoire et le rôle de l'érudition médiévale dans l'historiographie française du XIXe siècle." Thesis, Ecole Nationale des Chartes, 1979.

Ménager, Bernard. "La vie politique dans le département du Nord de 1851 à 1877." Doctoral thesis, University of Paris IV, 1979.

Moore, Lara Jennifer. "Restoring Order: The Ecole des Chartes and the Organization of Archives and Libraries in France, 1820–1870." Ph.D. diss., Stanford University, 2001.

Index